MAX EASTMAN

MAX EASTMAN

A LIFE

Christoph Irmscher

Yale UNIVERSITY PRESS   *New Haven and London*

Published with assistance from the foundation established
in memory of Calvin Chapin of the Class of 1788,
Yale College.

Frontispiece: Max Eastman in 1918. Author's collection.

Yale University Press books may be purchased in quantity
for educational, business, or promotional use. For
information, please e-mail sales.press@yale.edu (U.S. office)
or sales@yaleup.co.uk (U.K. office).

Set in Scala type by IDS Infotech Ltd., Chandigarh, India.
Printed in the United States of America.

Library of Congress Control Number: 2016954486
ISBN 978-0-300-22256-2 (hardcover : alk. paper)

A catalogue record for this book is available from the British
Library.

This paper meets the requirements of ANSI/NISO
Z39.48-1992 (Permanence of Paper).

10 9 8 7 6 5 4 3 2 1

For Julia and Nick

Contents

MAX EASTMAN

Introduction • Faun with a Typewriter

Max Eastman was, for quite some time, one of the most widely known American writers both at home and abroad. He was admired and loved, loathed and lambasted. Joseph Stalin called him a "gangster of the pen," a characterization quite at odds with the man even casual acquaintances found irresistibly charming in person. Once a well-known radical, the Prince of Greenwich Village, he later in life became an advocate for anti-left causes and a frequent contributor on the payroll of *Reader's Digest*. With his handsome, perennially tanned face, topped by a shock of prematurely white hair and hazel eyes that some described as golden, he looked less like a political pundit than an actor of some distinction, a man more intent on looking good than on being good (fig. 1).[1]

When he was well into his eighties, a teenage Carly Simon, the daughter of the cofounder of Simon and Schuster and soon to become famous in her own right, thought Max was the most beautiful man she had ever met.[2] Patrician in bearing and looks, he had a voice to match his face: tremulous, neither too high nor too low, a voice that would invariably pronounce "literature" as "litetyoor" and "poetry" as "poitree," and "Marxism" as "Maaksism."

Max didn't fit the part of the stereotypical writer. With him, there were no frayed shirt collars, no cracked or bent reading glasses, no scuffed shoes, no two-day stubble. In a casual portrait taken in Hawaii in 1965, a sweater-clad Max appears hunched over his small typewriter, index fingers hovering over the keys, a clear devotee of the hunt-and-peck method (fig. 2).[3] His head slightly cocked, he stares directly at us, a languid faun, pressed into benevolence by old age. "I am not a hard worker," he claimed in an interview, "but a regular one," a statement that deliberately downplays his extraordinary productivity.[4]

Figure 1. Max Eastman, 1950s. EMIIA1.

Figure 2. Max Eastman, ca. 1965. EMII.

Over the course of five decades Max published more than a dozen books of political and cultural analysis, two doorstop-sized volumes of autobiography, four books of translations, five collections of poetry, one novel, and an untold number of essays in magazines and newspapers. He coproduced the first talking documentary about the downfall of the tsar, *Tsar to Lenin,* released in 1937. And he lectured everywhere in the United States from Fargo, North Dakota, to Houston, Texas, on topics ranging from "the enjoyment of poetry" to "the changing attitude toward sex in modern literature." For a few months in 1938 he acted as the host of a radio show called *Word Game,* popular with listeners interested in unusual words, grammar, and pronunciation problems.

Max was loved by many women, and he loved many of them in return, not infrequently at the same time. Women enjoyed looking at him, and they evoked his beauty in lyrical prose, in letters to him, in poems, and in stories. Max was not immune to such praise. He proudly reported that John Barrymore, the most prominent member of a dynasty of good-looking actors, had once overheard someone ask which one of the two, Barrymore or Eastman, "was the better-looking and loved the most women," a question, he said, that "puts me in a very high class."[5] One of Max's many lovers, the brilliant painter, critic, and writer Charmion von Wiegand, dedicated a story to him, "Arrows of the Sun," which was at least in part a tribute to the sheer beauty of a man named Jude (Max's alias in the story). Charmion's narrator, Esther, dwells on Max's body as if it were a work of art: "His face was turned away from her but she could see his strong, clear profile—the high forehead with the waving mass of white hair, the well-defined imperious nose, the sensuous delicate lips and the strong shaped chin—a face in which the bones were very firm and ample, but the expression gentle, tender, self-indulgent. How beautiful he seemed!" Jude / Max moves through Charmion's story as if his sole purpose in life were to enjoy himself, a realization that leaves Esther frustrated with unfulfilled desire.[6] "I have the gift of leisure and of life," Max had rhymed in an unpublished poem likely written when he was in his early thirties. "I stand unbaffled as Old Buddha stands / Or move slow-footed o'er the battle-sands." Languid, soft, slow-footed, unsurprised by life, and relishing its opportunities, Max gave women the sense that being with him would be the pinnacle of their lives. When he died, *Time* magazine referred to him as a "lusty lion of the left."[7]

But such leisureliness was a pose. In the photograph taken in Hawaii, the stack of airmail envelopes on Max's right, behind the unlit cigarillo, also reminds us that he was one of the best-connected political writers of the first half of the twentieth century. Max knew everybody, and everybody knew him. And he wrote to everybody—long letters, brimming with detail and, as he got older and the political situation in the United States and the world more worrisome, bristling with irritation. And everybody wrote to him. Once you had met Max, he was hard to forget. Six feet tall or maybe even a bit taller, an incorrigible worshiper of the sun's warmth, he took pride in his tanned skin, the subject of many a line in his letters to friends and lovers. On more than one occasion, when he was younger and his hair still black, people mistook him for a Mexican. A persistent rumor had it that he was Jewish.[8] And while he was not athletic (and his weight became a small worry once he had passed middle age), he played tennis and, later, badminton with graceful abandon and remained fit well into his seventies. Ted Daniel, the son of the Eastmans' housekeeper Eula, remembers how he was trying to keep up with the seventy-something-year-old Max as the latter was surveying the boundaries of his extensive property on Martha's Vineyard and how he kept saying to him in his sing-songy voice, "You can do it, Ted. You can do it."[9]

Max certainly showed that one "can do it." His literary archive, still largely unprocessed, comprises over eighty boxes of letters, drafts, journals, and newspaper clippings. Two years before his death, writing to a doctoral student interested in his work, Max said that "it would require a revolution, or a military invasion for someone to go through all my files and shelvesful of documents and papers."[10] Max wrote constantly and saved most everything he wrote, even scribbled-on envelopes and random "while-you-were-out" notes. He collected women at an even faster rate, and after he had parted ways with them he would keep their letters, photographs, and the poems he had written about them or they had written about him. "Don't you know," he wrote to his secretary and on-again, off-again lover Florence Norton, a few weeks after his seventy-third birthday, "I preserve in separate files and packages every shred of paper that bears a sentiment about every girl I ever loved even if she's dead and gone, and that they are piled up in my attic in such quantities that the fire insurance company has warned me of the danger if my house catches fire?"[11] Max was a King Bluebeard of the erotic archive, though the dead bodies hidden in Max's apartment were love notes.

Not surprisingly, Max made quite a few enemies. Even some of his friends were appalled by his unabashed taste for the finer things in life—good food and extensive travel, summer homes on Martha's Vineyard and later on Barbados, his tennis court, the private secretary paid out of *Reader's Digest* funds. His previous biographer, William O'Neill, declared his affection for Max, only to accuse him later of selfishness and to admit that his book had "frequently made note of Eastman's failings."[12] But there was no sharper critic of Max than Max himself. In a draft poem from his 1915 sketchbook, titled "Myself," Max compared himself to water, which "takes the shape it touches / And the color it beholds." Since he was infinitely variable, like water, people would find in him what they wanted to see: "All creatures play in it, / And love and love themselves / In its too yielding sympathy."[13]

At one time or another in his long life Max would self-identify as a philosopher, poet, psychologist, novelist, and editor. The son of two progressive Congregationalist ministers and the grandson of another minister, he studied with John Dewey at Columbia University in New York and promptly rejected the religious roots of his youth in favor of science, or at least a faith in the ability of science to predict and produce outcomes that would lead to the betterment of society. Radicalized by his brilliant activist sister Crystal Eastman and his first wife, the feminist Ida Rauh, he abandoned his academic career, supported women's suffrage, became a socialist, and threw himself into editing the magazine the *Masses,* one of the period's most important outlets for radical writing and art. Crystal was instrumental in the creation of New York State's first Workers' Compensation Law, helped write the 1923 Equal Rights Amendment, and cofounded the Civil Liberties Bureau, which grew into the American Civil Liberties Union. After the *Masses* was shut down by the authorities Max and Crystal jointly edited the *Liberator,* where they published some of the most visible writers and artists of the day.

A prolonged stay in Soviet Russia in the 1920s planted the seeds of Max's close relationship with Lenin's heir apparent, Leon Trotsky, whom he continued to defend as he became disenchanted with party communism. In the final decades of his life he embraced an idiosyncratic form of antistatism and became an advocate of free-market economy. Even then, however, Max resisted all attempts to label him, especially by his new right-wing friends. He died in Barbados in 1969, still holding on to his dream of a "sweetly reasonable world," a phrase from Max's only novel, *Venture* (1927).[14]

Max Eastman's life didn't follow neat narrative lines. An opponent of marriage as an institution, he married three times but cheerfully continued his extramarital pursuits, a habit his tolerant second wife, Eliena, referred to as "seizures." Jean-Paul Sartre's and Simone de Beauvoir's term for their more extreme erotic investments was "contingent love affairs."[15] But Max's many affairs had nothing of the manipulative intensity of Sartre's liaisons with young admirers; in fact, Max's longest-lasting relationship was with a woman only a bit younger than he was, the actress and singer Rosalinde Fuller (and Crystal Eastman's sister-in-law). Yet there's no doubt Max's domestic arrangements disconcerted even some of his friends. When Max left his first wife, Ida, he relinquished all parental rights to his son, Daniel. Unpublished letters show that he stayed in touch with Daniel and later tried to help him find work, but the fact remains that Max's son did grow up without a father; we know he did not have a happy life. Similarly, after Max's beloved sister Crystal succumbed to nephritis in 1928, Max's primary concern was to divest himself of any custodial involvement in her orphaned children's lives. In the political arena Max's renunciation of the socialist politics that had dominated most of the first half of his life in favor of some fuzzy libertarian-atheist advocacy of free-market economy left many of his former friends angry. It also gave Max a sense of being hounded by Stalin's henchmen, strengthening his desire to lecture his fellow countrymen and -women about their uninformed tolerance of communist infiltration.

The 1950s were probably the darkest period of Max's life. While his former leftist friends could not forgive him for his apparent warmongering and betrayal of their cause, his newfound allies on the Right had a hard time forgetting his past as a Bolshevik. "A lot of people are still angry with Max," a well-known labor historian told me abruptly when I first spoke to him about my plans to write a new biography of Max. And this, for better or worse, has become the image associated with Max—that of a libidinous turncoat, someone who exchanged the radical views of his youth for the more comforting falsehoods of right-wing punditry. Max certainly wasn't the only writer in recent memory to have undergone a conversion from Left to Right. Contemporaries such as the journalist James Burnham and the writer Arthur Koestler come to mind, as does, more recently, the pundit and professional atheist Christopher Hitchens. But if Koestler sought refuge in parapsychology and alternative modes of consciousness and Hitchens shouted his boozy support for military intervention in Iraq over the Washington rooftops, the contours of the supposedly new Max were less distinct.

He was a writer, first and foremost, and he hated any form of dependency. Apart from his first tentative years as an instructor at Columbia University he never held an academic appointment or, for that matter, worked at any other job that would have required him to interrupt, for significant periods of time, his writing or public speaking. His only consistent income came in later years, when *Reader's Digest* made him a roving editor, a misleading designation in that Max had little influence on editorial decisions. But even as he was trying to conform to the expectations of his *Digest* editors, the unabridged, unedited Max demanded to be let out.

The major work of the last three decades of Max's life was his autobiography, published in two volumes in 1947 and 1966, as *Enjoyment of Living* and *Love and Revolution*. Here Max speaks to us unrestrainedly, unashamedly, with an iconoclastic boldness that reminded some reviewers of Rousseau and others—since so much of his retrospective revelations concerned his sheer irrepressible sexual desires—of that Midwestern Professor of Desire Alfred Kinsey. To his friend, the writer Edmund Wilson, Max meant multiple things: he was the irritable professor whose class we cannot afford to miss as well as the wild poet dancing through the summer rain, his mind "flicker[ing] electrically with bright perception." In his prose he was a superb stylist, a master of the short, crisp, pithy declarative sentence. And his poems, though he preferred traditional forms, sparkle with latent erotic energy, with a pagan delight in the pleasures of nature and the human body flashing up behind his recherché rhymes and conventional images.[16]

Eastman was not an Eastmanian, his friend Daniel Aaron observed after I had shown him a first draft of this book.[17] And this hits the nail right on the head. Max Eastman spent the first half of his life trying to fit himself into larger frameworks: Christianity (provided, somewhat unorthodoxly, by his mother); feminism (promoted even more unconventionally by his sister); and then socialism (advocated by his uncompromising first wife). When each ideology appeared to fit Max into prescribed patterns of institutional behavior— of the church, the party, or any other organization—he balked. Max spent the second half of his life looking for an ideological home while trying to defend himself against those who seemed to know exactly what he was thinking and where he belonged.

It doesn't cheapen the aims of this biography or the ambitions of its subject to describe what follows as a story largely about sex and communism. Max, who struggled with repression throughout his adolescence and early adulthood, forever afterward held sacred people's right to do with their bodies what they please. And he felt passionately about communism even after he had rejected it in disgust over Stalin's betrayal of the world revolutionary movement.[18] We often think of the history of American progressivism as a history of failures, as a series of promises not kept, hopes betrayed, strikes broken, and unions busted. And yet, as Michael Kazin has suggested, the United

States is a better and fairer country today because of the battles fought by the courageous men and women of the past.[19] For many years, Max, perhaps the most glamorous among the revolutionaries, was at the forefront of these fights. He campaigned for women's rights when other men wouldn't, exposed the fallacies of American nationalism even as American troops were being sent to the battlefields of Europe, and practiced an enlightened approach to sexual mores long before Kinsey provided the scientific evidence that heterosexual marriage was not the gold standard of sexual pleasure. When it came to reproductive rights, Max never changed his views and never yielded an inch to his critics.

"A poet lives—that is the primary thing," declares Jo Hancock, the aptly named, chronically indecisive protagonist of *Venture*.[20] Life mattered to Max, which meant he lived it as if every minute of it mattered, and I have striven to write this book as if every page, indeed every word of it, matters. To Max, there was unbearable pathos and heartbreak in each moment of joy, he once said, in a note found among his papers in which he also tried to explain why he often cried for no apparent reason.[21] Max also believed in candor, and he paid a high price for it. I have made this book a candid one, too, since I am convinced that Max wouldn't have wanted it any other way, and I have at times allowed myself to become swept up in the momentum of all he thought and did. But what has stayed with me through it all is the memory of an afternoon spent in the apartment of Max's widow, Yvette Eastman, who was then one hundred years old. Still beautiful and showing that sparkle in her eyes that had captivated generations of men, Yvette was having trouble figuring out exactly where she was—a confusion to which anyone of her age is fully entitled. Nevertheless, she graciously signed her own book, *Dearest Wilding*, a sprightly memoir of her relationship with Theodore Dreiser, who had preceded Max as her lover. When I told Yvette about my interest in Max, she steadied herself and said, very distinctly, although the words no longer came easily to her: "Max . . . was a very special person." Her cat Sgubi, sitting right next to her on a small side table, an infinitely dignified, appropriately large-sized reincarnation of the many cats Max had loved so much, seemed to agree, carefully watching the hand I had extended toward him, warning me not to come too close.

1 • The Devil at Park Church

Max Forrester Eastman was born in Canandaigua, New York, on January 4, 1883—the result of a mistake, as he later asserted, almost proudly, right at the beginning of the first volume of his autobiography: "If my mother had known what I know," wrote Max, a lifelong supporter of women's reproductive rights, "I would never have been born." But his mother, Annis, welcomed him into her life nevertheless. He was, she told Max later, "the lovingest baby I ever saw—and the prettiest."[1]

Annis Ford, from Peoria, Illinois, who then still went by her quaint middle name, Bertha, was the daughter of George W. Ford, a gunsmith and raging alcoholic, whose temper problems overshadowed her childhood and that of her four sisters. She escaped her abusive parent and dreary Peoria, with its "muddy stream of water," to study at Oberlin College.[2] Later on, during a period of despair, of which there were many in her life, she would say she was made from the mud of the Mississippi Valley: "I can never rise higher than my source."[3] Annis had wanted to be a teacher. But that changed when she met Samuel Elijah Eastman, a Civil War veteran of old New England stock. Handsome, lean, with a finely chiseled face, Sam seemed reassuringly devout. But he also had an independent streak that was powerfully appealing. His hardscrabble youth—his father had eked out a living as a minister in rural Lawrence County, New York, in charge of a congregation that never scraped together more than a few hundred dollars a year to pay him—had taught him early on to rely on what nature could provide. By the age of thirteen Samuel had planted a quarter of an acre near his home with peas and potatoes, which he sold in the nearby village of Ogdensburg. Money remained scarce in the Eastman family, though not for lack of industry. Max enjoyed telling the story that Sam once asked their remote relative, George Eastman of Eastman Kodak fame, to support a seminary of which he was a trustee and got turned down.[4]

When Annis Ford's and Sam Eastman's paths crossed, Sam was getting ready to attend seminary in Andover, Massachusetts. Annis quit Oberlin and began teaching school in Erie, Pennsylvania. They stayed in touch through frequent letters: pages and pages of laments about their being separated from each other, along with religious sentiments and reminders to each other to be steadfast in their faith. Annis and Sam were no ordinary couple. The usual gender roles seemed inverted in their relationship: while Annis was outgoing and extroverted, Sam, who had returned from the war with a withered lung, appeared withdrawn and uncomfortable around strangers. But when it came to expressing his love for Annis, Sam became quite the poet, resorting to odd organic metaphors that made him sound like a pious version of Whitman: "*I know you love me & you know I love you and we are in each other's lives* with separation impossible. All the *fibers of our being are intergrown*. The rootlets are all woven together into a perfect whole without the least defect." Sam imagined moonlit nights when he would kiss Annis "until every nerve in my lips was atremble with the rapture of holy love." But the emphasis in that scene was on holiness, not happiness. Unabashed about her rather more concrete desire for intimacy, Annis responded to Sam's fantasies by describing one of her own: falling asleep in his arms with his head resting on her breasts. She would wake up—and he would be gone: "*O Love, you did not stay.*" If Annis's love was holy, it was physical, too. In the same letter she made Sam promise never to leave her alone, ever.[5]

Briefly at least, Annis and Sam discussed plans to relocate to the West Coast and start a church there, maybe in Santa Barbara, a prospect that frightened Sam more than it did his bride: "There would be few luxuries, even few conveniences. . . . Would it not be better to stop somewhere nearer friends for the first few years?" And so Annis followed Samuel, after they got married in Peoria on August 28, 1875, to his first ministerial appointment in Swampscott, Massachusetts, and then to subsequent postings in Newport, Kentucky, and Marlboro, Massachusetts, and, finally, to an old village in Ontario County, New York—"lazy, leaf-abounding village" Canandaigua, as Max affectionately remembered it.[6] Annis bore Sam four children: Morgan Stehley Eastman, born in Swampscott in 1877; Anstice Ford Eastman, born in Newport in 1878; and then Crystal Catherine and Max Forrester Eastman, born two years apart from each other in 1881 and 1883, Crystal in Marlboro and Max in Canandaigua. At least initially, Annis embraced her role as the minister's wife: "It's

beautiful to have such opportunities of helping people and helping the minister," she wrote to a friend back in Peoria. Her new life was exciting, and she
vowed to "build a stairway of love right over" all the unfamiliar obstacles of
housekeeping and escape by it when necessary.[7] When their new servant
drank, an uncomfortable reminder of her father's lack of self-control, she
went right ahead and founded a local temperance society: "This is a reform
much needed here as in every other place. . . . Do you realize how the world
would be lifted up if universal temperance reigned?" The picture of her everyday life she painted for the benefit of her Peoria friend was as cheerful as she
could make it. On any given day, while Sam worked on his sermons in his
study, Annis was contentedly moving through the rooms of her light-filled
home taking care of her plants: "I have a heliotrope and geranium in bloom
and a happy little pink oxalis. Wish you could see them. Our house is flooded
with sunshine all day so my plants do well."[8]

No amount of domestic care, however, could prevent the disaster that soon
befell her family. On July 25, 1884, the seven-year-old Morgan, the oldest Eastman child, succumbed to scarlet fever, an event that cast a permanent shadow
over the lives of Annis and Sam and their surviving children. Crystal was infected, too, but survived the illness, though she remained in precarious health
for the rest of her short life. Sam and Annis struggled on, through "hard
storms" and "rough seas," hoping for that Indian summer of their lives when
"the air is pure and sweet and golden." But that time never came. In the Eastman family, money was perennially tight. Modeling a practice that would later
on become very familiar to her son, Annis was an expert at staggering pay-
ments, buying meat and milk first before taking care of coal and the dentist. "I
wish I could be delivered from thinking about the pecuniary side of things."[9]
As Sam's condition worsened (often he would come home ashen-faced, weak,
barely able to move), Annis accepted a job as a teacher at the Granger Place
School in Canandaigua, keeping Anstice with her, and sent Max and Crystal
off to join their invalid father on his farm in the country. Having assisted Sam
with his sermons, she began preaching herself, first at a small church in
Brockton, near Ithaca, with such apparent success that she was ordained a
fully vested minister in 1889. She took over a parish in West Bloomfield, thirteen miles west of Canandaigua. They got, Annis's youngest son said later,
"more brains and eloquence for their money than they could have in a man."[10]

Max was eleven when the Reverend Thomas Beecher, a half brother of the
famous Henry Ward Beecher, invited the Eastmans to join him as assistant

ministers at his progressive Park Church in Elmira, New York, about seventy miles south of Canandaigua. Reverend Beecher, a skillful cricket player as well as a man of science, was a different kind of preacher. He liked beer and base-ball, target shooting, and carpentry. Working hard to shed the Calvinist influ-ence of his father, Lyman, he had created a church that was more a community center than a house of worship, one equipped with billiard tables, a free public library, a dance hall, and a children's "Romp Room." The members of the Langdon family, living across the street from the church, were among Beech-er's most generous supporters, and when Mark Twain, who had married Olivia Langdon in 1868, visited Elmira, young Max Eastman found him free of any hauteur. Julia Beecher, Olivia Langdon's Sunday school teacher, a granddaughter of the stern lexicographer Noah Webster, was the creator of the "Beecher baby doll," an idea that had occurred to her as she was mending an old stocking. Close to a thousand rag dolls she produced, with all profits going to the Park Church. The "indiscriminate fury" she brought to her daily tasks made her a natural enemy of "mid-Victorian" junk of all kinds. Max would remember her as a moral as well as an aesthetic rebel: sitting next to her mother, she would read out loud, "with an expression of grim and yet joyful determination in her gentle features," Whitman's scandalous celebration of homosexual love, the Calamus poems from *Leaves of Grass*.[11]

While Annis officially shared her Elmira appointment with Sam, the lat-ter's subdued temperament increasingly sidelined him. As a minister, Max's father never fit conventional expectations, but for different reasons than An-nis. Adult company made him nervous, but he was a great favorite with the children of the Park Church. Years later Marion S. Bryan of Elmira remem-bered how Reverend Eastman would join them in the church's romp room and entice them to a game in which blindfolded kids would take a stick to a bag filled with candy hanging from a chandelier in the middle of the room (a "piñata," in current party parlance). They would hit the bag until a shower of hard candy rained down on them: "The children all seemed to know what was expected of them for they shouted and sprang forth after the glittering frag-ments. How your father enjoyed this. He would stand back and his face would beam all over and he would laugh and laugh."[12]

Reverend Beecher died on March 14, 1900. To Annis's tear-filled eyes, na-ture acknowledged his death by covering Elmira with a blanket of pure white snow, as if it "rejoiced at the passing of a great soul." The congregation elected Mr. and Mrs. Eastman to succeed him as co-ministers. From the beginning Annis saw her appointment as a step forward not so much for herself as for the women who would come after her: "It will make the way easier for some better one who will come after me—for Crystal or some other beautiful girl who ought to be a minister."[13]

As Annis began to take over more and more of his ministerial duties, Sam faded into the background, spending an increasing amount of time on a succession of farms, first closer to home, then more than thirty miles away, at a farm in Glenora on Lake Seneca, where he cultivated a cherry orchard, tended to sundry livestock, and planted a grove of pine trees. His cottage he named Cherith, after the brook near which the prophet Elijah (Samuel's middle name!) hid from the wicked Jezebel, waiting for the food that ravens would bring him (Kings 17:3). There was much indeed that appeared hidden, secretive, inaccessible to others about Sam. To Max, his father seemed remote, distant even from his God. What he passed on to his children, more by example than by precept, was a childlike love of nature, a joyful, pagan delight in small things growing and flourishing: themes that recur in Max's poetry, too. And he left Max with a permanent unease about standard definitions of masculinity. His son remembered a short, awkward poem about a little flower that Sam had composed and loved to recite in company. "Pretty little aster!," it began. "Can't you grow a little faster?"[14]

As gentle as Sam seemed, his son was always a little afraid of him. Reverend Eastman despised all "self-conscious literariness," perhaps one of the chief reasons for the emotional distance between him and his writer-son.[15] Sam followed his own rules; what things looked like inside him one could only guess. In a later sonnet dedicated to his taciturn father, Eastman imagined him impatiently rising with the sun, after a fitful night of sleep (regarded as "penance" rather than relaxation), to toil in his field, where he will "fill / And flood the soil with Summer for a while."[16] Religion offered no reliable consolation to the elder Eastman. "Dad wasn't square with himself," observed Anstice, looking back on his childhood.[17]

Annis, by contrast, seemed more firmly rooted in reality. In *Venture* the mother of the protagonist, Jo Hancock, is described as being stout, with heavy breasts and a round nose and an enormous mouth—an exaggeration of Annis's physical presence, though perhaps not by much. For someone so invested in the life of the soul, Annis ("Babe," "Mamma," or "Mamsey" to her adoring son) seemed afflicted with an insistently solid body. Surviving photographs show a round-faced woman with a prominent nose and a high forehead, her abundant hair done up in a loose, untidy bun, her eyes wide open (fig. 3). She seems intense, alert, focused. Leaning forward as her husband,

Figure 3. Samuel and Annis Eastman. EM.

characteristically, tilts backward, she seems full of curiosity about what the world has to offer her. As if aware of her strong physical presence, Annis throughout her life sought for ways to deny her body its right to an independent existence, even as it acted up in various ways. Many letters to Max are filled with reports about her chronic constipation.[18] Renouncing regular meals, depriving herself of rest, experimenting with all sorts of home remedies, she resolved to "live inwardly," as she described her plan to Max: "I have seemed to win a peace and a power to do better things and to shake off evil propensities—and to face reality—in a way I haven't known before." Not one to ever be content, she immediately interrupted herself: "Is there nothing which answers to my need and really helps me?"[19]

If Annis was smart, versatile, and witty, Sam was silent, worried, intense. The Eastmans' marriage was a puzzle, perhaps even to Sam and Annis themselves. The romantic—if religiously inflected—fantasies of their courtship had long yielded to more pragmatic arrangements. Sam found fulfillment in his farming, Annis in her intellectual pursuits. Soon she would prefer Whitman's poetry to the Bible. The romance had gone, and so had the theology. "I do appreciate you," Annis pointedly told her husband in one of her letters, substituting gratitude for companionship for a declaration of love. But even this companionship was one often in letter only, with Sam choosing his agricultural work at Glenora over his pastoral duties at Park Church.[20]

Annis's strong emotional needs, the full extent of which might have been unknown even to herself, found an outlet in her relationship with her children, whom she treated as if they were friends or even lovers. "O to hear her come singing home," she wrote about Crystal, "to see the radiance and feel the warmth of her and know that she is mine!" And when Crystal was away, missing her became just another reminder of her "blessedness" in having such a daughter. Max was the recipient of similar declarations of boundless love, reminders that the bonds between the Eastmans made them different from the rest of the world. "I'm afraid I'd starve to death if you were my only child," Annis told Max once when she was frustrated that he had not written to her for a while, "and you must remember that I love you just as much as tho you were." Of all the good and blessed things in her life, she said, the best by far was, she told Max, "knowing you—and being loved by you."[21]

If she was forgiving in her private relationships, Annis appeared determined and uncompromising in her public work. People were surprised by the steely assertiveness that was hidden inside her compact body. And they were awed by her intellect: Annis was widely read and had a deep interest in science (later shared by her son, who would make it his mission to expose the "scientific" fallacies of Marxism) as well as philosophy and psychology. She was capable of delivering an entire sermon on a Whitman poem.[22]

But she also had a lighter side, which was not always visible in public. Annis excelled at imitating other people's mannerisms of speech and could be hilariously funny at times. Much of her capacity for humor she reserved for private communications: "Mr. MacNaughton our fat tenor," she wrote to her children after a particularly trying service, "got up and yelled to some angels ever bright and fair to take him unto their care—he yelled it over and over again but they never took a bit of notice as far as I could see—The idea of an angel taking care of Mr. MacNaughton got onto my nerves so that I felt naughty when it came time to preach."[23]

Annis did not spare herself either in the quirky vignettes from the life of her congregation that she shared with her children. A memorable story in a letter written to Max (he was at his preparatory school in Pennsylvania at the time) reveals both the often-precarious ideological position in which Annis found herself even in a relatively liberal congregation and the reasons her parishioners loved her so much. Without ceding an inch of her convictions, even in the presence of the powerful Reverend Beecher, she would readily make fun of her own theological preconceptions. In this story, Annis had led a teachers' meeting at the Park Church (Papa was, predictably, at the farm). The topic of discussion was the devil, and Annis, when called upon to express her views, frankly said she had no use for him: "All the evil in me I felt responsible for," she said and added she couldn't imagine having to deal with *two* supreme powers. But Reverend Beecher, in closing the meeting, despite his well-publicized progressive views, reaffirmed his own faith in the devil, and thus reassured, if perhaps still a tad confused, the teachers dispersed, "good natured and happy," Annis said. When Annis was back in her quarters, a parishioner, Mr. Slee, came up and reported that the lecture room where the meeting had taken place was full of smoke. Annis went down to investigate and "sure enough the air was blue and sulphurous and brimstony so that one immediately began to cough." A search of the building yielded no clues as to the origin of the smoke. The fire department was called, by which time a sizable crowd had formed outside the church. But there was no fire anywhere. "So we all think it must have been his Satanic majesty himself come to *prove* his existence. It's a good joke on me." That was the kind of story Annis could be sure her son would enjoy. They both knew the real devil of Park Church lived somewhere else—in Annis's quick, agile, rebellious mind. And as Annis's son would figure out in the years to come, his own demon resided in his beautiful body, too, a constant threat to whatever home he would construct for himself in his mind.[24]

His Satanic Majesty was able to cause little damage that night, and he certainly couldn't silence Annis Eastman. In countless, outspoken sermons she tried to direct her parishioners to a path of independence from calcified doctrine and outdated traditions. While Reverend Beecher had kept out of theological discussions, Annis made the adoption of a simpler, liberal creed her first priority, despite resistance from some of her parishioners. Adopted on February 17, 1907, the creed celebrated God as revealed in nature and "human experience" and Jesus Christ as the "Embodiment of the Spirit of God in the soul of man, and our Divine Teacher and Guide."[25] As his mother was losing heart in the struggle with her congregation, Max sent supportive letters: "As it is in your nature that you must serve the advance guard, you will have to see people turn away frowning; just as there are those who serve the rear-guard (unequivocally) have to see people turn away toward you. It is only the double-voiced who can preach to everybody in a period of transition."[26] Double-voiced, Annis was not. One of her regrets later in life was that she had never been disciplined enough to become a writer, that, while perhaps she wouldn't have achieved "great things" in literature, she hadn't even worked hard enough to become another Margaret Sangster or Amelia Barr, the former a poet and frequent contributor to the *Ladies' Home Companion,* the latter a popular British-born novelist and perpetrator of such titles as *The Maid of Maiden Lane* and *The Belle of Bowling Green.* "I might have earned a good living and lived a richer life in ever so many ways if I had held myself to what I felt was *my* work."[27] But, although Annis wrote copiously and fluently, the spoken word was her medium. The notes she kept have survived, piles of pages covered with her nearly illegible scrawl, the sentences punctured by dashes and abbreviations, her pencil, often in need of sharpening, trying to keep up with all she wanted to say.

Annis's sermons reveal the source of Max's own skills as an orator, but they also point us to some of the problems that would haunt him in his later life. In "Man's Place in Nature," for example, from a series of Lenten sermons, Annis affirmed the importance and truth of science and, above all, evolution. An appreciation for science, she told her parishioners, will place us in a "more reasonable" relationship with God. It will help us understand the origin of the beauty of the natural world, the grandeur and nobility of the human character, and the awesome, boundless miracle of life itself: "This we have—we are alive," concludes Annis. Her son's lifelong ambition to be admired not just as a writer but as a scientist—or at least as someone who has made contributions to science—is foreshadowed here, as is his irrepressible delight in the pleasures life has to offer. The earth was, explained Annis, "only one of many planets warmed by the sun, and the sun only one of a myriad of similar suns." All of which was reason enough to keep our minds turned toward the Infinite, the all-pervading Universal Intelligence.[28]

But Annis's professed joy in the limitless possibilities of life was not intended as an encouragement to seize the day and follow one's desires. Living, for her, was hard work. An ardent feminist and supporter of women's suffrage, she was filled with the hope that she would be able to vote before she died (she wasn't).[29] However, one of her great worries was that giving women the right to vote would substitute some quick political gains for spiritual progress. In a long sermon titled "Men and Reform," given to the Railroad YMCA in town, she insisted that the "day of woman's awakening" had come, that all doors be opened to the "dignity power and grace of womanhood" and that all men, even the most masculine of them, be supportive of such a development. The situation of women could be reformed only if men were willing to reform themselves. It would be fatal if society ended up being divided into idealist women and materialist men. Annis's argument, invoking as it does a sinful world in dire need of being saved, doesn't seem particularly progressive today, a feminist version perhaps of Booker T. Washington's hope that uplift-by-education will fix racial disparities (Booker T., "mild, soft-spoken, unpretentious, and yet princely," did indeed spend a night at his parents' house, one of Max's most vivid memories). Nevertheless, her interest in the spiritual improvement of men as a condition for the emancipation of women would have ruffled some feathers at the time.[30]

If corruptible men were one of the main obstacles in the path toward a more equitable world, what better place to start God's work than in the education of a young boy? One can easily imagine the impact Annis's preaching of moral purity would have had on the adolescent Max. For all of his mother's progressivism, in matters of religious education she was unrelenting. With Sunday school, family prayers, church services, and meetings of his youth group, the Young People's Society of Christian Endeavor, Max got "too familiar with the sound of the Bible," as he recalled in one of his suffragist speeches. The result was the opposite of what Annis had intended: "I believe I finally became at the age of 15 completely impervious to the *meaning* of a scriptural quotation as the back of an alligator is to a hail storm." And yet years later he still knew his way around scripture: "I could recite the 3 chapters of the Sermon on the Mount in 8 minutes and 42 seconds, coming in with a lead of 6 verses on my older brother, often giving him a handicap of 3 beatitudes."[31]

Elmira, New York, named, depending on whom you trust, after the daughter of a tavern keeper or after the daughter of a general in the War of 1812, was already an important transportation hub when the Eastmans arrived. Crisscrossed by several railroad lines, it was also the site of an important reform prison headed by the legendary Zebulon Brockway, who believed that a prison should offer spiritual guidance to the prisoner and that the purpose of a jail term was rehabilitation rather than punishment. Neither too large nor too small, Elmira, which sported a population of just a bit above thirty thousand in 1890 (about 17 percent of whom were born abroad), was the perfect setting for Annis's evolving blend of feminism and moral uplift.[32]

To the citizens of Elmira, the Eastman children, daring, dark, their good looks enhanced by their ruddy skin, seemed more than "a little outrageous," Max recalled. But, then, so were their parents: "We were all a little outrageous— all disposed to kick over the decorums and try to get at the heart of things in public as in private."[33] Big, brawny Anstice, for example, the oldest, who shared the initials A.F.E. with his mother, had a well-deserved reputation for militancy. He loved to spear frogs and was capable of driving a nail into a pole head first. Full of energy and aggression, he came across as ready to "pounce on you."[34] By contrast, Max, although he too grew up outdoors, was a chronically nervous, high-strung child subject to all sorts of terrors and phobias. But he also became preternaturally attuned to the compensatory pleasures his body could afford him. With Max, the first stirrings of sexual desire took "the form of an intense wish to go into the bedroom where a little brown-haired playmate slept beside my sister, and kiss her in her most secret place. This desire was private to me, and furtive, unrelated to our daytime play, a thing I burned with after I had gone to bed. It seems simple enough now, and my only remorse is that I lacked the dash to do it." Priapic Max was born. Note the dual impact of Max's retrospective account of the event: while acutely aware that, given the prevailing standards of middle-class respectability, such longing must seek the cover of darkness to have its way, his guilt was limited to his failure to act on his impulses.[35]

Both Anstice and Max were expected to work on the family farm in Glenora during the summer, and it is during one of those summers that a rare photograph showing both of them was taken (fig. 4). Anstice is obviously acting a part, that of the headless muscleman all set to eclipse his cerebral brother: Anstice's brawn versus Max's brain. His shoulders are scrunched up high, while his hat is drawn down over his face. He looks bigger than his brother, brutish almost. By contrast, Max's arms dangle slackly on either side of a body that looks as limp as Anstice's appears to be taut. While Max is still facing the camera, his body appears to be turning away from it, as if he were afraid to be trapped into rigidity.

But Max was no wilting wallflower either. One of his first surviving letters to Crystal reports on his exploits as a cyclist. Max, a student at the Elmira Free Academy, was fourteen then, and Crystal, who was attending the Granger Place School, a preparatory school for girls in Canandaigua, was about to turn sixteen. The letter begins rather melodramatically: "I had a terrible accident today." Now that Max had her attention, he proceeded more slowly. In fact, one gets the impression he had written the letter primarily to hone his budding writerly skills. He had spent the morning trying to sell his old bike, without success. So Max and his friend Frank Easton decided to take it for a spin up Gray Street—two boys on one bike, one on the handlebars, the other on the seat. Just after they had crossed Columbia, Frank started getting "wobbly."

Figure 4. "Anstice and I when working on the farm." "Album in College." EMII.

Swaying back forth on the handlebars, Max was beginning to wobble, too. What follows is a richly comical vignette describing an act worthy of circus clowns: "Pretty soon I swayed a little too far forward and went off with my feet sticking out to-wards the pedals. I slide off and the thing that sticks out in front to hold the lamp caught me by the seat of the pants and my nose began to rub the front tire." Frank then regained his balance and they were back going up the street. But the drama was not over yet: "Pretty soon I got tired of my position and tried to get off. But some way in getting off my trousers got torn up half way down the leg up to the suspender buttons with two or three slits torn at right angles;—Of course I hit on the ground in a perfectly proper attitude and was perfectly comfortable when I got up and tried to get home. I shall have to wear long pants to school day after tomorrow."

The Eastmans were accomplished cyclists. Annis, in fact, would comfortably ride her own "wheel" for seven miles in one day, as Max reminded Crystal in the same letter. But somehow trouble would follow Max around when he was on his bike. When he was taking his apparently unsellable bike to school, he came up behind two Elmira girls, Emily Dexter and Bertha Long. The problem was the cracks in the sidewalk. He was getting closer to the girls when all of a sudden, in Max's own words, "a hand reached out from behind and gave me a push—as is shown in the illustration." Here Max inserted a picture of a giant, detached hand pushing him forward. Thus propelled by forces beyond his control, Max had no choice but to insert himself between the two ladies: "As you might imagine it was a close gauge." Once again he came close to falling off: "I lost my balance and began to fall some way but I balanced up again and I saw that if I ever fell it would cause an awful spill, so instead of letting her rip I gave a great jump up into the air." Holding on to the handlebars, Max nevertheless managed a graceful landing on the sidewalk, "right side up." Collecting himself, he got back on his bike and caught up with "the Girls" and told them it had all been an accident.[36]

Sifting his correspondence later in life, Max, who had in the interim established himself as an authority on laughter, penciled a note on the envelope of that letter: "Example young humor." But the episode also shows quite a few things about Max's character: the combination of recklessness, circumspection, and sheer luck. Rather than taking a fall, he keeps his balance for as long as possible. A reader familiar with Max's future erotic exploits would be more than tempted to attach some symbolic importance to the fact that Max's balance-keeping involves two girls.

Really, though, the one girl he wanted to impress more than anybody else was Crystal. For her, he switched easily from the role of loving brother to rascal, and it was for her he wanted to stress his bad-boy credentials. In the same letter, after sharing how wild he was at Thanksgiving and Christmas, he detailed for her a very un-Christmas-like activity he pursued, again with the famous Frank at his side and with a prop supplied by Anstice. "Frank and I went up the river with A's revolver and shot at a target he has up there." This was not the first time Max had tried his hand at shooting: "We stood the regulation distance—10 paces, and at first we did not hit it at all but finally I just mad [sic] half a hole on the outside edge, which is red then I got one of the white and then on the black which is the Bulls eye. Then Frank got one on the Bulls eye and then one on the white and then I got another one on the white." The future pacifist apparently knew how to handle a gun: "I got 45 and he got 30."[37]

Max's previous biographer has suggested that Max and Crystal had an incestuous relationship, but such a label only inadequately captures the elaborate games both played, especially when they were separated. Not content with being known as a crack shot and irrepressible prankster, Max wanted Crystal to understand he was quite a success with the girls of Elmira, too. At the end of the day, though, he was still his Mama's boy, so much so that Annis, along with her benefactress Mrs. Beecher, controlled even his choice of dance part-ners: "I promised Miss Beecher I'd dance with a Wall Flower and promised Mama I'd dance with another. So I struck a happy medium and danced with three," he cheerfully informed Crystal.[38]

Thus, the brilliant Annis Ford Eastman, without using much force or force-ful words, retained her hold over her children. On the rare occasions when punishments *were* administered, a rationale was given, as when, for example, Annis grabbed Max and bit into his shoulder, a gesture so surprising in its animality that he looked at her in sheer terror. "I just wanted you to know what it felt like . . . when you bit Crystal's arm yesterday," explained Annis. But normally any kind of violence was shunned in the Eastman family: "It is im-portant if you want to know me, to understand that I come of people who were very gentle with each other," wrote Max late in life. "Children were not spoiled in the Eastman family, but they were more than adequately appreciated. Home life was tender and a little utopian, so that by contrast the world, when you stepped into it, seemed rough and harsh."[39]

Annis did her best to disabuse them of any sense that there were innate differences between boys and girls, a message eagerly embraced by Crystal, whose tomboyish behavior Annis praised in her sermon to the seasoned YMCA Railroaders: "I went out into a shed one day when my children were little," she reported, "and found my small daughter climbing about overhead on some beams in what seemed to be a very dangerous position—I said—'Why my dear—what are you doing!' Well she said. 'Brother said I couldn't do this—so I'm doing it!' " While the anecdote was meant to illustrate, to an audi-ence of skeptical men, that the days in which only boys did reckless things were over, it also let them know that Annis, a modern mother, would leave her little children to their own devices rather than scold them for taking risks. Note, too, her reaction to finding Crystal in this precarious situation: instead of telling her to get down right away, Annis first and foremost wanted to know why she was doing what she was doing.[40]

Annis's utopian ideas found a perfect manifestation in the alternative com-munity at Glenora, the site of the Eastman farm. The logbooks from the sum-mers spent at Cherith have survived, several hefty volumes bound in green. Most of the entries are by Crystal and Max or Annis, interspersed with notes from visitors and, occasionally, contributions by Reverend Eastman himself. Starting with the second volume, photographs glued onto the now-brittle pages of the logbooks carry some of the narrative. A few of these show Annis and Sam, but the vast majority are of lovely, athletic, tanned young people sitting on rocks or diving into the water from a springboard, their beautiful, slim bodies flying through the sky, arched in the summer sun, a blur on their rapid descent down. Max, strong and healthy, his skin darkened by the sun, looks as if he enjoyed the attention paid to him. The girls wear their hair down and seem as capable and muscular as the men.

The labor of the Cherithites was usually shared, without any special consideration for gender. Men would work as housecleaners, just as the girls could be found doing carpentry. While Sam was felling trees and towing the logs to the sawmill, others were pulling weeds, planting vines, or tending to the beds of sweet peas and nasturtiums. The poetry Max left in the logbooks was mostly bad—in one particularly egregious example, Max wrote about the music of the woods, played by Pan on a reed that once was a nymph—whereas Annis is often more successful in capturing the magic of the place, the warm, windless days when the whole landscape seems to stand still, the shiny lake, the scent of honeysuckle, the sounds of katydids around the cottage, the fields brimming with Queen Anne's lace and goldenrod, the baskets of peaches and Catawba grapes ready for eating. At Glenora, Crystal, too, found great pleasure, but some of it came from watching Max at work, commemorating one night in early September 1901, shortly before their departure from Cherith, when he was outside in the moonlight digging a ditch: "I hung out of my window and conversed with him till I fell asleep in the act." Cherith was an unreal world of unlimited freedom, a fantasy collectively produced by the various voices represented in the logbooks, as floatingly unreal as the pageants in a Shakespeare play.[41]

And a fantasy it was. Not everyone was always at peace out there. "One seems much nearer the sky up here," wrote Annis in the log on July 7, 1901, and then went on to explain that such closeness afforded her insights into her own self that weren't always comfortable. Consider her tribute to Seneca Lake, in the form of a sonnet written straight into the logbook: "Sheer rising cliffs and vine-clad hills embrace / The yielding body of the restless lake. / And even her expressions changing take / The hue of clouds that float above her face." Remarkably, the lake is pictured as a woman charged with the task of satisfying her environment: "Her tiniest ripples in a laughing race / Forever vainly seek to climb, and slake / The thirst of hills above—as vainly break / Her wildest waves, wind lashed in furious chase." The sestet spells out the comparison between the female lake and the female poet and hints at deeper longings present in both:

Mirror of thine environment, like me,
Art weary of it? Wind and rain and sun
And clouds, all bind their fickle moods on thee—
Thy hopeless strife, like mine, will ne'er be won,
Yet in us both, we dare not dream how deep,
Unruffled, unconquerable currents sleep.[42]

But such feelings were not to be indulged. By sheer force of personality as well as explicit reminders in letters and conversation, Annis left no doubt in her children's minds as to the things an Eastman should and shouldn't do. In one of her letters to Max, Annis defined religion as "man's sense" that "the universe is more than an anthill."[43] Inevitably, Annis's moralism, her rejection of bodily pleasure in favor of spiritual self-transcendence, became a tremendous problem for Max, who would spend his adolescence and early adulthood alternating between physical exuberance and periods when he was too sick to leave the house. While Anstice removed himself from Annis's direct influence, becoming first a fearless athlete and then a rather indifferent Princeton student, the more delicately formed Max succumbed to Mamsey's regimen, in which his precarious health dictated what he could and couldn't do: "Can you imagine where I am now?" he wrote to Crystal in May 1899. "All the rest of the family have gone to church, but I am too 'feeble,' you know. Dr. Stuart prescribes that I sit around and eat and sleep all I can, and not exert myself even in amusing myself. Strange as it may seem I find that prescription very easy to carry out." At least he had been able to avoid church. In Max's impressionable imagination, Annis had replaced God with her own dominant presence. Whatever guilt he felt was related to Annis. Caught between his mother's controlling love and helpless admiration for his more daring siblings, Max drifted into semi-invalidism, settling for a life in which he did not have to act on his impulses because his health wouldn't allow him to do so.[44]

In the fall of 1898 Max left Elmira to attend Mercersburg Academy, an elite preparatory school in Pennsylvania, ninety miles northwest of Washington, D.C., which was associated with the Reformed Church. William Mann Irvine, the visionary principal of Mercersburg, had come to Elmira to recruit suitable boys for his fledgling school. The Eastmans were offered special "minister's terms."[45] Even so, Mercersburg was a stretch for Max's family, and not only in financial terms. Annis's letters to Max are filled with laments over his absence. "I hope you are happy and hopeful and know that I love you *so much*," she scribbled on a note she slipped into his luggage.[46] His going away had paralyzed her, she said dramatically, so much so that all they'd left to do was sit around the house and wait for Max's letters to arrive. "We devoured your letter last night and felt hungry when we got through."[47]

When Annis was in a more practical mood, she would remind her Max to be frugal. Don't put cookies or nails in your pockets, she would admonish him, since his best suit had to last till Christmas at least. On other occasions she worried about his diet, telling him to sleep more instead of having breakfast ("What would it cost extra for you to room alone"?) and to go for walks every day. She sent peaches, grapes, and watermelons as well as newspapers, along with malted milk tablets for "ease of digestion" and underwear and shirts she had ironed herself. Max in turn gave her a green fern for Christmas. The little plant sent Annis into fits of ecstasy: "It smiled up at me and opened out all its little hands and promised to try to live till June. . . . It will be a daily comforter speaking of you and your thoughtful love and understanding of me."[48]

Not all the teachers at Mercersburg were top-notch, but Max, after some initial troubles, went on to achieve the highest academic distinctions of any student in the history of Mercersburg, however short, an average of 97.[49] His mother had been relentless, reminding him, at the slightest evidence of slacking, that his outstanding academic performance sustained her and that, given Anstice's "don't care attitude," she depended on Max just as much as he depended on her. Max complied. Although, much to Annis's regret, he gave up his violin playing, he studied Greek, Latin, and French, and he was soon tutoring other boys. He read Virgil and regularly shared his writing with Annis.[50] He also began to hone his skills as a debater—one topic was whether telephone and telegraph and the railroads should be run by the government or not[51]—and participated in mock trials. Annis began to send him suggestions for speakers and speeches he should study to become a better orator: Daniel Webster, Charles Sumner, a passage from a Ben Jonson play. When Max was chosen as the valedictorian of his class and found himself in need of examples of "unrewarded heroism," Annis didn't have to think long and gave him her favorite one: Jesus. Max also delivered the class prophecy, a tongue-in-cheek prediction of what the future held for them, an exercise he dispatched with bravado and that he would remember for the rest of his life as one of the most joyful moments he ever experienced.[52]

A group photo taken during Max's Mercersburg days shows him among the members of his track team (fig. 5). His dark, brooding face is turned toward the camera, while his left leg is wedged awkwardly between the two classmates in front of him. Annis worried about the periods of despair Max experienced while away at his boarding school. One of the original reasons she

Figure 5. The Mercersburg Academy Track Team. Max is in the second row, far left. "Album in College." EMII.

had sent him away or, rather, why she had agreed to have him sent away was that she had her own bouts of depression and that, around her, Max was, in her opinion, too susceptible to similar afflictions. Melancholy was her "fatal gift" to him, but it was, she assured him, not an incurable illness: "Don't yield an inch to that spirit of despair, darling. If ever a life was worth living yours is." Max had a fine mind and a healthy body, she reminded him. He was "swimming in seas of love" and would be just fine if he remembered only one thing: chew your food![53]

Max had expected to go from Mercersburg to Princeton.[54] Imagine his surprise when Annis told him, in a tone that brooked no dissent, "You are to go to Williams in the fall." A family friend from Canandaigua, Mrs. Thompson, had offered to pay his expenses at Williams College, and Annis was taking no chances. As a present for graduating from the academy, Max was allowed to visit Anstice at Princeton, getting a glimpse of the college where he wasn't going to be allowed to study. "Unrewarded Heroism" suddenly had become a topic that seemed to characterize Max's own life.[55]

2 • Dearest of All Lovers

In 1899 Max, Crystal, and their cousin Adra Ash were enjoying their summer vacation on the family farm in Glenora. They had gone to a nearby glen to swim. Crystal found Adra beautiful and made no secret of her attraction to her when she saw her naked. And she didn't hesitate to share that fact with her mother: "She was so beautiful to look at." She had never seen anything prettier than when "she was standing there with the water dripping from her hair, and red cheeks and sparkling eyes, and to crown all her dimples and fetching smiles." If she had been a man, said Crystal, "I should have lost my heart then and there by just looking at her and having her smile at me. And she was so utterly unconscious of it, that is where the charm came in."

Ironically, walking back from the glen, Adra and Crystal came across two men who were bathing in the nude, too, and here Crystal's reaction wasn't a positive one: "It disgusted me for the rest of the day, and does yet. I think it is an outrage, and that's mild." At the same time, she knew those men could have been her brothers, too: "I know it isn't right. It was dreadful enough just for Adra and me together but just suppose I had been up there with a man? I never shall feel like going up there again, I am afraid, with anyone. Adra said she felt like shooting those men, and my feelings were similar. When I told her that all the boys did it without a thought, she said she couldn't hate her cousins, but she hated all other men and boys."[1]

Crystal's reaction, taking up an entire paragraph in her letter, seems exaggerated. No doubt she was genuinely shocked. But the episode of the nude bathers (so reminiscent of a scene in Whitman's "Song of Myself") also helped her justify her rather ambivalent sexual position in the letter. The impropriety of the nude men spoiling the landscape of the glen for her and Adra (and potentially for other visitors, too) made her manifest desire for her cousin's beautiful body seem respectable. While she wasn't like those irresponsible male bathers, she knew what it meant to be and to feel like a man. And so, apparently, did Adra, who wanted to shoot the nude offenders, a feeling endorsed by Crystal. It's an extraordinary sign of the unconventional relationship she had with Annis that Crystal was able to share these complicated emotions with her: she was confident Annis would understand both her desire for her cousin as well as her outrage over inappropriate male behavior.

The rest of Crystal's letter was chatty—she had finished *Pride and Prejudice* (which she liked very much), had gone out to buy butter with Max (whom she also liked very much), and she missed her mother dreadfully (obviously she liked her, too). Crystal's letter conveys a sense of the difficult balance between radicalism and propriety the Eastman children felt required to maintain and the complex ways in which they reimagined their sexuality.

After that memorable summer in Glenora, Crystal began college at Vassar, an experience in which she allowed Max to take part, at least vicariously, through the many letters she sent to her "dear, dear boy" at Mercersburg (fig. 6). Founded in 1869, Vassar had quickly emerged as one of the colleges of choice for the daughters of the Protestant elite. Contemporary accounts say little about academics and much about parties and other social events. And Crystal did enjoy these extracurricular activities, sharing vivid images of life at a girls' college with Max: "It is impossible for me to tell you about it in the least bit of a way. My first impression when I went over to the campus and in to the college buildings, was an overwhelming but pleasing sense of an endless amount of *girls*. The first night I was here, I went over to chapel, and enjoyed the sight of the girls meeting each other after the summer. It was one of the most fascinating scenes I ever saw. These dear pretty girls grabbing each other and hugging and kissing frantically."[2]

If Max hadn't picked up on the innuendo, if he hadn't understood that Crystal was imagining him looking at these girls and putting herself in his place, Crystal was ready to spell it out for him: "You would have enjoyed watching them, I think, only you would have been crazy to do the grabbing etc. yourself, instead of letting another girl do it. I know you." This was a deliberately sexualized scene. Pretending to understand his desires, Crystal used her letter to arouse Max, all under the cover of her role as voyeur: "Of course I was a mere spectator, but I thoroughly enjoyed it. Some of the girls are tall and stunning." While she was like Max, she was, after all, *unlike* the girls they were

Figure 6. Crystal Eastman. Crystal Eastman Papers.
Courtesy of Schlesinger Library, Radcliffe Institute,
Harvard University.

both watching and, at least in their imaginations, grabbing: "Why for size I am nowhere beside lots of them." For good measure, just in case Max would find it hard to get excited over girls in groups, she switched to a close-up of a beautiful roommate of hers: "She is a brunette, with sparkling eyes, good features, pretty black hair and the most beautiful complexion and coloring I have *ever* seen. I wish you could see her." Or how about any of the other girls she got to be with every day? "There are lots of nice and interesting girls here, but no other real beauty in the house." Do write, she reminded Max.[3]

From then on Crystal's letters from Vassar would contain regular updates, for Max's benefit, about the girls she favored, among them, for example, Lucy: "If only she liked me as much as I like her. My cup of bliss would be brimming for a while." Lucy had walked over in the rain without a coat, and when Crystal saw her, her "beautiful hair" was "all wet and curly," with "little sparkles of rain" on it, while her eyes were aglow and "scintillating." She was "a sight to see," and it seemed important to Crystal that Max see that sight, too. "When I like people I like them *awfully*."[4] A highlight in these shareable fantasies came when Crystal attended a Vassar ball in male attire, which, given the lack of available boys, was a perfectly acceptable practice. Decked out in a three-inch collar and a borrowed dress suit, she showed up with her "fiancée," Miss Janice, on her arm. Mentioning a college mate of hers who had seen Max's picture and instantly fallen in love with him, she delightedly painted an image of compulsively cross-dressing Vassar for Max: "There were about 50 or 60 girls last night who wore dress-suits. Very few of them were rented." Rather than presenting herself as the object of Max's wishes, she put herself in his place, desiring what she imagines he would.[5]

Such gender fluidity yielded some extraordinary results. When Crystal, exceptionally, went to one of these balls as who she really was, she found out that, paradoxically, even more effort was required: "Think of it! You see I didn't have time to get together a man's costume. Everyone said I looked grand." She had an immense pompadour "and two little pieces of black court plaster on my face, and a low necked thing off the shoulders. I am going to have a dress made that way someday." A girl named Clara was her man, and, as she was walking with her, Crystal suddenly found herself switching back to a boy's point of view: "I kept patting her because it made me think of you boys. We had flash lights taken. I'll send you one if they are good." But then Crystal changed gears again. Having impersonated a boy like Max, patting women because it's what the boys do, she nimbly switched back to the role of lustful girl: "The only trouble is that where I see so many sham men around I do *so* long for a real one. Oh dear!"[6]

When Max arrived at Williams College in the fall of 1900, he saw nothing but men, or rather boys who wanted to pass as such. "Williams is great," he reported to Crystal, shortly after his arrival on campus. But the entrance exams dampened this enthusiasm quite a bit: while he was "hot stuff" in Latin and Greek, he failed questions in English, one of which had the prompt "Write on Dryden's religious life." In the end he did respectably enough, "enough to let them know that I wasn't so dumb as I might be."[7] In his dorm room he kept Crystal's photograph over his desk: "I look up and love you every minute."[8]

Nestled in the Berkshires, with the famous purple hills for a background (at dusk they looked like great big hulks standing up into the darkening sky),[9] Williams College was a congenial enough environment for someone like Max, whose interests, despite his successes at Mercersburg, weren't exclusively

academic ones. He threw himself into collegiate life, participating in Freshman Rush, which consisted in swiping a sweater from the sophomores and
trying to hold on to it as they tried to get it back, and joining the exclusive
fraternity-cum-literary society, St. Anthony Hall, also known as Delta Psi. He
was prominently involved in stealing a donkey from a Williams faculty member so that the freshman class president could ride on it—an activity that was
criminal by anyone's standards since it included breaking and entering, van-
dalism, cruelty to animals, and likely a number of other offenses. The reader
feels sorry mostly for the scared little donkey, which had never asked to be part
of the prank. "We got to the Profs barn and founded it locked tight. It was only
about 50 feet from the home and the back windows were open, with people in
the rooms. We got an old piece of iron and pried open the door. It was a door
that wasn't meant to be opened, and there were leaves piled up against it about
five feet high with boards nailed up back of them. I climbed in over these first
and there was the little ass up in a corner scared to death." There was no way
out of the barn that wouldn't have involved breaking down a door, so Max and
his friends decided to lift the donkey up and move it out the way they had
come in, a maneuver that was not an unqualified success. "We got him four
feet up on them and it made him stand almost straight up in the air. . . . We
pulled the boards off or broke them and then pitched away the leaves (and all
this within about fifty feet of the house). Then we had the ass out and gave him
to the Senior who was waiting for him." Max barely made it home that night,
but, as he was glad to report, excelled in his first three periods in the morning,
Greek, English, and German.[10]

As casual as Max seems in his letter to Crystal, his private journal tells a
slightly different story, that of someone who felt almost driven to show his
capacity for naughtiness. "When they come together, and push, and sweat,
and swear, and lose their tempers, then, although I always put on a bold bad
look and act as though I were ready to eat the first man I meet, I really feel
much more like lying back and laughing at the whole thing." He spectacularly
failed his hazing experience, which involved posing as a corpse while his
roommate delivered a funeral oration over his body and another freshman, by
squeezing out a wet sponge, wept copious tears over him. During his mock
funeral, Max, aka "our most noted and illustrious statesman and friend, who
has but recently taken the light of his presence from among us," couldn't wipe
the smile off his face. Regrettably, wrote Max, making fun of his apparent inability to stay in character, that smile escaped and became a living thing: "And
I had to spend the rest of the evening chasing it in and out among chairs,

desks, and tables, under beds and back of bureaus, out of the campus and through the dormitories, in the vain attempt to catch it and drown it in a wash-bowl full of water which I carried for the purpose." A great occasion for Max the budding humorist to flex his muscles.[11]

Wherever there was trouble at Williams, Max was to be found, too, and his freshman journal and the letters to Crystal from his first two years there are filled with gleeful reports on his exploits. Once, for example, he visited a country school during the daytime and had himself introduced as a delegate from South Carolina studying public education in Massachusetts. Another prank involved taking a horse from a farmer's barn during the night, leading it around in circles, and then tying it up in front of the farmer's house, after setting off a firecracker to attract the sleeping man's attention. Or the boys would interrupt choir practice in country churches by loudly singing serenades outside. A pretty waitress became the occasion for the theft of a drumstick and chicken sandwich from the kitchen of a North Adams restaurant.

At the beginning of his second semester Max got himself into serious trouble by participating in a staged kidnapping of a fellow student—all in good fun, he insisted. The whole college and many townspeople had spent the night looking for the perpetrators of that brazen act. Somewhat fictionalized, the episode shows up in Max's novel, *Venture*.[12] Max was, he calmly informed Crystal, one of the villains, and more than that: "I was the *chief* of the villainous gang."[13] The pleasure Max derived from these pranks came not from doing them but from running away afterward, with heart pounding, temples throbbing, and adrenaline pumping through his veins. To him, the likelihood of discovery, the chance of him, Max Eastman, Reverend Annis Eastman's son, being found out and exposed as a worthless scoundrel was infinitely more exciting than the deed itself.[14]

More immediately productive perhaps were the stump speeches Max gave for the Williams Republican Club, presided over by his friend Sidney Wood. His first experience, at East Greenbush, just outside of Albany, was so compelling that a district attorney came up to him afterward to shake his hand. Max soon began to dream of a bright future as a public speaker: "Wasn't that a great experience—to get up before this roomful of rubes and spout forth far fetched figures and absurd similes after the fashion of the regulation 'stump speaker'?"[15] That Max would get such accolades for some of the most absurd nonsense ever spoken was close to a life-changing event for him. One key rhetorical moment from his performance he conveyed to his journal. It consisted of contrasting "our heroic forefathers" with the "hordes of ignorant barbarians who prefer to wallow in the filth and gore of fruitless war rather than to come forth from their state of uncivilized stagnation and learn to govern and be governed." Max had discovered the power of words.[16]

Although they were one hundred miles or more apart from each other, Max and Crystal seemed closer than ever. In their letters they continued their role-play, a mix of semi-incestuous yearnings and juvenile hyperbole. Verbally at least they made love to each other, Crystal, the older one, a little more expertly than Max, but both were delighted by their ability to make the words on the page say what they wanted without saying it too openly. Crystal, who displayed a Williams College flag in her dorm room window at Vassar, would skip her Greek class to write to Max (fig. 7). And her brother would in turn read her letters "instead of the Bible" during morning services in church.[17]

Whether or not writing to Crystal helped him discover his talent, Max began to think of himself as a literary figure. A poem he had written about Mount Greylock caught the attention of the poetry editor of the Williams College literary magazine, and his journal gave him endless pleasure: "It's great to write

Figure 7. Crystal Eastman in her dorm room at Vassar. "Album in College." EMII.

something every night. There is no pleasure in the world like the pleasure of writing things—no matter how poor they are." The pages of his journal now became cluttered with poetic sketches, many of them influenced by the authors he was reading at the time, among them Tennyson and the rapturous, florid Sidney Lanier, who offered just the right combination of chivalry and prudery. However, even at the time, Max viewed these efforts with a degree of irony. One of his sketches began by painting a rather vague image of "the mighty majesty of rolling waves that moan and crash and roar and wildly dash themselves to spray in music to the soul that deeply mourns, or that rejoices with wild restless joy." Such indecisiveness wasn't tolerable, so the waves say to the hapless poet: "Choose! The thrill thou feelest in our . . . inspiring presence, will surely rouse thee from thy doubtful stupor." And as if the alternatives weren't clear, Max elaborated: "Either thou must shout and leap and run for joy. Or thou must weep and tear thy hair in grief." His sketch, commented Max, had started out "with the admirable intention of becoming a poem," but, due to all that mist generated by the wild waves, had failed. Yet it was not in vain that Max spilled all that ink. "Mount Greylock" was published, and in the spring of 1902 Max became the editor of the Williams annual, the *Gulielmensian,* or "Gul," as it was affectionately known.[18]

But Max wasn't always posing. Beside the naughty Max and Max the literary gadfly, a new Max emerged, one that took pleasure in his body's infinite capacity for enjoyment. Along with the more private pleasures of writing, Max, for example, discovered the joys of skiing and ecstatically described them to Crystal: "I am spending all my spare time skeeing. There is no fun in the world like flying down a long hill for half a mile, standing up, and going so fast that you cant breathe. And when you fall you fly forever. . . . I slid right through the snow on level ground, with nothing but momentum to propell [sic] me, and utterly unable to stop, for forty feet. A little dive of ten feet without leaving a track is a matter of everyday occurrence" (fig. 8).[19] Meanwhile, Crystal poured her own desire for ecstasy and sensual gratification into her singing: "My longing to sing is sometimes almost more than I can stand." It made her feel all "queer inside."[20]

In his second year at Williams Max was taking advanced French and German, physics, biology, English, and elocution. He was running track, going faster in a quarter-mile race than his brother Anstice had ever gone, finishing in less than fifty-five seconds. Ralph Erskine, a classmate, would remember later how Max seemed to be better than everybody else at virtually everything

Figure 8. "Jump! (Max—at College)." "Album in College." EMII.

he undertook. He ran faster, shouted more loudly when he gave speeches, tossed stones farther, and once threw a javelin at him with more strength and accuracy than Erskine would have been able to: "My one desire in life for the next five minutes was to brain you with a club." Not having bothered to do his homework, Max would immerse himself in *Antigone* or *Faust* fifteen minutes before class, amid all the noise a roomful of college students inevitably generated, and would then deliver the most beautiful translations imaginable.[21]

And yet, in his letters to Crystal Max reported feeling melancholy at times. He missed his sister. Her photograph was right over his desk at his dorm, next to pictures of Cleopatra and Gustave Flaubert's seductive princess Salammbô. Crystal's would-be boyfriends were fair game between the siblings: "Oh what fools these mortal men seem to be when they are infatuated," observed Max about a suitor named Mr. Rawlings. "Do his letters speak lovingly of moonlit nights on the placid lake, or are they matter-of-fact?" Maybe Max should have a little summer affair too? He had been reading the novel *Graustark*, the first of a series of extremely popular novels by George Barr McCutcheon, set in an imaginary kingdom, a novel that had given him a taste for adventure and romance. "I begin to think it would be a good thing for me to cut loose next summer and get up a romance of my own. How I do long for adventures after I read a novel like that! Life doesn't seem worthwhile without them. But alas! You have to have money."[22]

Instead of adventure, however, Max was headed for the infirmary. A fever he had caught turned into bronchitis, a situation that stymied the college doctor, who gave him, Max said, "some capsules of white dust" that accomplished nothing at all.[23] After two weeks in the infirmary Max was "negotiating for sympathy from all my friends and relatives," writing copious letters, propped up by pillows. Now he really wanted Crystal to come and visit: "I would get out of bed now and take you driving first thing, and call it the greatest event of the year." For what else was there to look forward to? "College is composed mostly of dopes."[24] But Crystal never came, and Max did not have enough money to travel home, so he spent Thanksgiving in the company of the "ancestors and descendants" of the head nurse of the Williams College infirmary, the "funniest Thanksgiving dinner in the history of the family."[25]

The next year Max moved into private housing on Hoxsey Street in Williamstown, where he finally had a room of his own: "It is a nice English family with some dear little white-haired kids—old enough so I don't hate 'em—and terribly neat and clean. I feel like a property owner when I stalk around my room—also like a hermit. I am so glad to be alone again." His college work was still not marked by much dedication. He made such a show of reading the *Rubáiyát* during lectures on Greek philosophy that the professor threatened to send him home: "I said 'Well' and smiled as if I would be perfectly willing [and] then promised to be good next time."[26]

Max became so popular that his class chose him as the orator for the traditional March 13 celebration, a position that required the usual college fanfare, including sequestration in his room while being guarded by the class president and four football players, so that he would not be kidnapped by the freshman class before he had the chance to give his speech. "You can imagine how conducive it was to the development of a speech to have four men in the room all the time smoking and roughhousing." When the moment came, Max was accompanied outside by a dozen other students and introduced by the president of the senior class. Max spoke from the top of a carriage with students from the whole college to the left by a blazing bonfire and people from Williamstown and North Adams assembled on a steep hill to the right. Williams College had turned into Max's city upon a hill, and he enjoyed the power he had as a speaker. Talking to his fellow students and the citizens of Williamstown was different from stumping for the Republicans: "It was so thrilling a situation that it went way beyond the point of stage-fright. O it was great! I felt as if my voice could reach to the end of the earth. It was the greatest success I ever had, I think. Afterward when each class gathered together by the embers and gave a cheer for the other 3 classes, mine carried me on their shoulders. Of course everybody is worked up to a great state of excitement by the smokes that precede the speeches, so that it is the greatest opportunity for a speech that ever could be." Max's only disappointment: the freshman speaker was a failure. His voice so was weak no one could hear him. Max had wanted better competition. Nevertheless, he relished the sense of importance his guards and his vast audience were giving him. "There is nothing in the world that can be compared to making a speech!"[27]

Max was on top of the world. When Annis visited him at Williams in April, she worried that he had lost his humility. Afterward, she sent him a note reminding him that he needed a "vital" religion, one that came from the heart, not the brain, an "experimental faith" that would give his life meaning: "To know God as a friend. Have you ever tried it? Do you pray?" Next on her list was worry about Max's posture: "Gain and keep an erect carriage. Hold your head high—you can do that even if your heart is low—and look straight into everyone's face," even when sitting at a table.[28]

Crystal, traveling by train to meet Max in Williamstown just a little later, was less worried about Max than about herself, or rather about the feelings she had for her brother, which had become more intense than ever. Men lacked finesse, she wrote in her journal, in fact *all* men did, except for Max: "I don't believe there is a feeling in the world too refined and imagined for him to appreciate." It was Max's femininity that made him so unique: "I think it's the highest compliment you can pay a man," observed Crystal, "to say that he has the finesse of feeling and sympathy of a woman." If she ever were to marry a man, he would have to be like Max, exactly like him. She'd rather have a penniless philosopher for a husband and be forced to earn her living herself than bore herself to death with "a practical man" lacking those finer traits. "No amount of worldly disappointment and poverty could be as soul-destroying as to discover a poverty of finer feeling and appreciativeness in the man you must live with all your life, and whose children would be yours also."[29]

Max wouldn't have liked to hear Crystal say such things about him. He was neither a boy in need of maternal instruction nor a man who would rather be a woman. Barely a month after Crystal's visit, Max escaped. He joined Sidney Wood, the accomplice of his freshman pranks, in a crazy journey out West, first to Idaho and then on to the Sierra Nevada, Salt Lake City, Los Angeles, Flagstaff, and, finally, San Francisco. The ostensible purpose was to make money, but it turns out that neither Max nor Sid was quite equipped for the jobs they took on. If Max did not keep a regular journal during the trip, he wrote down his impressions after his return, fusing them into a text that was half fiction, half autobiography and must have given him the clearest sense yet of his potential as a writer. He would later quote some passages from that 1902 notebook in the first volume of his autobiography, *Enjoyment of Living*. But he omitted the dramatic beginning. As soon as they had arrived in Chicago, and with a great deal of ceremony, Max and Sid divested themselves of their college attire, the "emblems of respectability" that stifled them, their collars and neckties, their starched shirts and creased pants, stowing them away in their suitcases: "We put on in their places black cotton shirts, jumpers, overalls, and a red bandanna."[30] What follows is a tribute to the magical properties of the bandanna, with Max pretending to be a member of the working class, a role that even later in life he could never fulfill without a certain degree of self-consciousness or theatricality. The bandanna, Max explained, became his friend, and the prose poem in praise of the bandanna he offered reads as if an advertising agency had commissioned it:

> There is something peculiar about a bandanna, something almost magical, so that I don't think a laborer could live without one. It is not because it may be a suit-case, or a pillow, or a hat, or a neck-tie, or a glove, or a towel, as the need arises; nor even because it is always cool and soothing to the brow and plenty large enough for its own peculiar use. But there is something else about it, something that goes with its being red, some strange quality, so that it becomes a dear friend, and he is glad when he can feel it in his pocket. Surely nobody ever felt so about a white handkerchief, and surely he never could about a blue one! I wonder who discovered red bandannas—for I cannot feel that they were invented.

In Chicago Max and Sid went to the stockyards. They were "watching every bloody operation, beginning with the taking off of their skins, until finally there was only a row of tongues left." After signing with an employment agency, Max and Sid took a train bound for Nevada. Nothing in Max's life had prepared him for his two memorable travel companions, the Boss and the Captain, whom he described with a satirical skill honed on his reading of Mark Twain. Instead of luggage, each man carried a dirty bundle fashioned out of newspapers. Max developed a clinical interest in the more dangerous looking of the two: "The Boss was coarse and low in appearance and speech, and he had seemingly just one idea—that in San Francisco if you don't cheat everybody will cheat you." He was coming from Hoboken, New Jersey, where his family resided, and he pointed out that if any of his relatives ever decided to come live in San Francisco, he would be obliged to cheat on them too and rob them before they could take away his things. Max was surprised that such a troglodyte had family somewhere: "It was pathetic, and something more than pathetic, to think of him as stopping after twelve years of such living among men as he described in San Francisco and taking the long journey home with his earnings."

Traveling across the Great Plains, having opened the window so he could feel the air and watch the clouds and the sunset, Max experienced a moment of self-conscious Emersonian transcendence: "I thought of home and the world and myself and a thousand things but it was not my thoughts but my emotions, my mood that I enjoyed, not my mind, but my frame of mind. The picture is the same in a black frame as in a gilt frame, and yet how different it is! My heart was great, and full of love, and I grew, in those hours." In between raptures, Max read his "Spanish Self-Taught" book. He slept well, even though they were traveling in the lowest class and could not lie down to rest. He had truly begun the worker's life.

Max and Sid got off in Ogden, Utah. The jobs in Nevada were forgotten, and they found themselves headed instead to Salt Lake City, where they went for a dip in the Great Salt Lake—"You feel so much like a bopper that you expect to be jerked under in a minute"—and saw their first authentic Indians. On the way back to Ogden the train ran over an old man who was crossing the tracks with a staff and a dinner pail in his hand. As they started moving again, Max saw the old man's body under a blanket. This was the first dead body he had ever seen, and it had a powerful effect on him.

Back in Ogden, they signed on for jobs in Los Angeles. En route to California, Max was temporarily separated from Sid, an unexpectedly exhilarating experience. Stranded in Reno, Nevada, without a cent in his pocket, hoping to find a hotel room he didn't have to pay for right away, Max got a taste of Bret Harte's West. Nine out of ten stores in town were liquor stores, and there seemed to be more prairie dogs than people. As he was bargaining with the hotel keeper, the latter stepped out to prevent two men from engaging in fisticuffs outside. Max enjoyed his first glimpse of frontier life: "The drunkard wanted to fight with a man with a long red moustache, and the man with the moustache was all ready, and neither could see why they shouldn't begin. The Innkeeper didn't try to tell him it wasn't considered proper to fight on the street, or that anybody would object or interfere, he simply convinced him that he was too drunk to put up a good fight and it wasn't worth while." Max also enjoyed the view he had from the train going through the Sierra Nevada Mountains. The winding lakes, banks full of green pine trees, blue gorges, "a great wideness and loftiness." And he liked the waving cornfields once he was headed to California. Somewhat randomly, Max and Sid got off in Lowell, California, an unincorporated community on the Southern Pacific Railroad no longer in existence today, where everyone promised them work "in the fruit" but no one would give them any. When they finally made it to their destination, a construction camp in Chatsworth Park in the San Fernando Valley, they discovered it was really little more than a black hole: a tunnel, in other words. They chose to seek employment in a nearby stone quarry instead. Putting chains on rocks and hauling them was not a natural fit for Annis Eastman's son: "Four men must carry the largest chain, and it is an enormous effort to lift it to one's shoulder, and you cannot imagine how those big links dig down into your shoulder, and hook into your collar bone." When they asked the superintendent how long the job would last, he told them, "a good deal longer than we would." The sleeping arrangements at the quarry horrified Max. It didn't help that a Mexican laborer was carried out in a box dripping blood just before they came. But Max found it gratifying that the Mexican workers thought he was one of their own, thanks to his dark looks. He told them, "Mi padre es Mejicano y mi madre Americana," a lie that, from then on, led to his being called "cuñado" (brother-in-law) by the Mexican workers.

Max and Sid set up their camp on a nearby hill, on the bare ground baked into hardness by the sun, where they spread their blankets and read Byron until it got too dark. Early in the morning they woke again, their makeshift beds soaked by the California mist. They took a bath in a pond, among frogs, after removing a dead mouse. Sid, whose arm hurt, threw in the towel before Max, who lasted for two more days before it became clear to everyone he was not a "chain man," and he was demoted to pick-and-shovel work, the lowest job in the camp. A Mexican, a genuine one, took Max's place at the chain.

Back home, Crystal was deeply worried. She fired off another "Max letter" of the kind that had become her specialty. Continuing her semierotic game with Max, she mentioned her intention to go on a date with Willie Linn, a strapping fifteen-year-old. "When I get back to Glenora to-night I am going out on the lake with Willie Linn. Isn't that killing? He is six feet two and quite grown up in spite of his fifteen years." And Crystal impishly likened her dealings with Willie to Max's dalliances with one of his would-be girlfriends in Elmira: "My going with him reminds me of your little love affairs with Ethel Cooke. I believe the ages are about the same aren't they?" There was plenty of innuendo in those sentences. While it was socially acceptable for Max to date Ethel, Crystal's going out with a much younger boy would be considered scandalous, as she very well knew. But she wanted to provoke Max. In the same letter Crystal admitted she was fond of other men, too, among them, again, the persistent Mr. Rawlings and their mutual friend Fritz Updegraff, with his penchant for salty language like "By Gad" and "The Devil knows."[31]

The problem became apparent rather quickly, and what Crystal went on to say served as a reaffirmation of her bond with Max: all these men were terribly unoriginal. Fritz, she said, "would have been altogether refreshing if he had not said the same things that he has said so many times before over again." The implication was clear: the Eastmans were something special, more original, unfailingly brighter than the rest. Here is Crystal's account of an outing with Fritz: "In the afternoon we went canoeing, finally landed on Pulpit Rock at about seven. We stayed there till about nine. It was beautiful—all the changing from daylight to moonlight. Fritz told two or three long stories—very interesting and one of them rather disgusting, and then we talked some." Crystal then switched to the real business of the letter, reasserting her bond with Max: "Have you ever thought how few people are original thinkers, even in a small way? I have decided that very few people do any *independent* thinking. Now Mr. R[awlings] is a bright, rather interesting fellow and likes to talk seriously, but his ideas are perfectly conventional. He is perfectly happy in them, but actually, he can't even take in or grasp an original or out of the way thought. For instance Mamma and he and I were talking once, Mamma said in some connection, 'Why, people can be so self-sacrificing as to make perfect beasts of selfishness of everyone around them.' " Obviously, this is a typical Eastman thought, unconventional, against the grain, smart, funny. Predictably, Mr. Rawlings failed the test: "Then up pipes brother—says he knows a fine example of that—tells us about a cousin of his who was always doing things for people—she died—then they appreciated her—final sentiment— 'You never appreciate what people are until they are taken away from you.' "

One can virtually sense Crystal's merriment rising, along with her wonder that anyone could actually be that stupid: "Doesn't that seem to you a remarkable lack of thoughtful grasp," she asks Max (and the beautifully tense way the sentence is constructed is revelatory), "a strong tendency to wander from the point in hand?" Mr. Rawlings was history: "He never lacks something to say and he thinks it is pat, but it seldom is, and no matter what interesting line of speculation or theory (those aren't the words I want) you may suggest, he brings it back to the common place, to well worn platitudes, in his first remark." Rawlings had wasted no time displaying his mediocrity. Since Crystal was on a roll now, poor Fritz became her next target: "Fritz is no independent thinker either." The conclusion was inevitable: there really was no other man but the "boy I love best and like best in all the world." Concluded Crystal: "Oh, it's positively abject, the way I am fond of you!" The future belonged to the Eastman children, and Max's prospective line of business seemed clear to her: "*Real* literature if you'll only get at it and stick to it. That is exactly what I think. No exaggeration. You must feel it and know it yourself. I wish you would acknowledge it and glory in it, with some *real* purpose. Yours with great love and longing, Crystal."[32]

But Crystal's longing for Max was nothing compared to Annis's, who was upset to no end about Max's western adventure. Max himself regretted the escapade, which ended ingloriously with a night spent in prison in San Francisco for disturbing the peace, and he was embarrassed by how selfish he had been. His not coming straight home had created a barrier between him and Mamsey—only the shadow of a barrier but one that was real enough to linger in his mind, a reminder of the basic guilt he, the son of two ministers, would carry for the rest of his life.[33]

Things were soon back to normal again. In the fall of 1902 Max returned to Williams. He was taking courses in political science, government in the fall, economics in the spring, and he was enjoying "German 5," basically a course devoted to the study of Goethe's *Faust*. He was also reading Dante, with the help of an Italian grammar—this on top of French assignments and "a few chapters of Tacitus every week."[34] College had become exciting again, even for a slacker like Max. He was all in favor of Rousseau, he informed Crystal, as long as this didn't involve having to get the book from the library: "If I had that book here I would be wildly enthusiastic over reading it, reading more than is assigned, but someway the process of getting over into the library and searching it out and getting settled down to read it seems a task vague and vast enough to overbalance any possible pleasure in reading it. I know it isn't but I can't persuade myself of it."[35] In a preview of his future interests, he tended to get more excited about the heroes themselves than about the heroic work they had done. When the writer and liberal Unitarian Edward Everett Hale came to preach at Williams, Max went to church and worshiped him instead of God: "I always do when they have a great man." To Max, literature, too, was form rather than substance. It required not sincerity but talent. Not everything needed to be expressed: "If I could put it in a letter that I love you and think of you always, without quite saying it, I would be happy."[36] From that point of view, adhering to Mamsey's expectations for the good life was not particularly difficult: a matter of "just simply up and plunging into the Rubicon—or rather swimming out—and then you are out once [and] for all, and dry right off."[37] Max had never felt closer to Annis than he was feeling now: "I believe Mamma and I would be almost exactly alike if we had lived the same life."[38]

But Crystal's very different way of approaching life increasingly caused him problems: "You give me a new eagerness to be perfectly honest, and open, and straight, with people," wrote Max. "Your clear way of saying a thing is weighing on your conscience, and wanting to take it up and remove it, and never thinking that you can bend a little and let it slide off—O, it really makes me want to stand straight too!" Crystal was Max's "angel of light," the model of perfection he could dream of but not emulate: "You have never built up a mist around yourself, and that is why you always see right and wrong, and the rest of us can't—even Mamma and Papa."[39]

A model of perfection she might have been, but she wasn't a perfect model. Max didn't drink and had never done so, except once or twice, when he wanted to prove to himself that he could do without it and "that there is no battle."[40] Crystal, by contrast, liked to party. She danced and drank and stayed up all night, and when her younger brother criticized her for her behavior, encouraging her to open up to "the Divine Spirit, if you can believe in it," Crystal gave him a taste of that honesty he normally valued so much in her.[41] Even as she assured Max that he was "everything I could ask from a friend and lover" and that she loved him ("I can't really tell you what I mean, but I mean much"), she made no apologies for her wilder side. The appeal of dancing to Crystal, apart from the intoxicating lights, the lateness, the strange conversations and, yes, the alcohol, was "really the attraction of the other sex," the sheer sensation that came from being near men, "with the added delight of rhythm in motion and music." The rhythm of dance music was a way of keeping the animal instincts in us at bay, of making sex civilized, "or fine or uplifting." She knew that dear old terminally repressed Max wouldn't like her for being so explicit, "because you don't like people to talk of anything except beautiful things." The fatal Eastman code of conduct, well known to her, too, was "perfect self control."[42]

Crystal's rebellion against that code had at least some effect on Max. Unleashing his wild side, in a manner of speaking, he purposely flunked an exam at Williams, taking pleasure in not knowing the answers: "I just enjoyed going to pieces on that exam, the wind was blowing in the back of my head, and I was coughing and sneezing and didn't care and I didn't put down lots of things I knew just on purpose."[43] Deep down, he agreed with Crystal that there was too much emphasis on the intellect in education and not enough on the body: "We are working against nature all the time with our 'mind over matter.' " How could anyone be unhappy in a world that had Crystal in it, a "beautiful girl" to stir him up?[44] Max even tried to jump-start his dormant love life by considering the prospect of falling in love with a girl he had met at an alumni dinner, where he had "managed to shine a little." The girl did all the right things: she picked a bunch of violets for him and gave him a pin, which Max wore dutifully next to his heart for a bit. Yet there was something missing: "It doesn't all work out as it might, I must confess." What was wrong with him? It was quite upsetting that he felt nothing, as if he were observing his own life from a distance: "A girl sits down and talks to you on the steps for two hours and then gives you a bunch of violets, and it doesn't fit on to Political Science and Logic at all, yet there is something wanting. I feel that I'm not quite up to the standard." The girl left him cold. Everyone at college thought he had a "sunny disposition," but in reality he was just covering up his feelings really well: "I've learned to let the storms rage underneath instead of on top."[45] Even when she partied, Crystal remained the embodiment of perfection for Max, a woman better than any he was likely to meet. That sentiment, incidentally, was shared also by the much less complexly wired Anstice, now an English instructor in the Philippines, from where he was sending passionate tributes to his "rabbit-girl" or "Bunny," a girl he loved more than anyone else.[46]

While Max was procrastinating in college, spending money as if there were money to spend, and Crystal was dancing the nights away, Annis and Sam were living in virtual poverty, scrimping on food and wearing threadbare clothes.[47] But Annis never complained. They had been too worried about Max this spring to find fault with him, she told Anstice. "He is more and more subject to those awful glooms which paralyse all effort and make him just 'sit still' as he says." She wanted Max to work, but not for her sake: "I wanted him to give up college for a year and go to work, partly because of his debts, and partly for an entire change of thought and interest." But Max easily persuaded her otherwise. "He did not want it, and it was encouraging to see him interested enough in *anything*—to argue for it. His eyes were so pathetic and beautiful."

If Max was too preoccupied with himself to even notice his parents, Annis didn't mind. Crystal seemed forever ready to step in: "She is more and more an angel of light for us all. She takes such tender care of me that I'm sadly tempted to become a complainer, just because her sympathy is so sweet. I'm sure there never were such children as mine!" Note that Annis used the same phrase about Crystal that Max had used.[48]

Crystal, Max, and Annis Eastman had, it seems, wrapped themselves in a cocoon of need—with the mother needing her children, the children needing the mother as well as each other—that protected them from the outside world, whose main fault was that it wasn't related to the Eastmans. Their letters became the medium by which these bonds could be reaffirmed. Anstice was at best an infrequent participant in their conversations, while Sam had long since removed himself from that tangle of needs and demands, burying his own desires deep inside himself, lavishing affection on his fields and garden instead. "He cannot dash off a letter as quickly as I can," Annis had told Max early on.[49] In the triangular relationship of mother, daughter, and son, Crystal, the flawed "angel of light," seemed to model a way in which it was possible to be an Eastman and yet have fun, too. To Max, that was a dangerous prospect, not only but at least partly due to the fact that Crystal was his sister.

By the fall of 1903 Crystal was studying sociology at Columbia, surrounded by desirable men but also uncomfortably conscious of the fact that she was the only female in the classroom. She found reassurance in her continuing love for Max. Thank God for letters: "It seems to me that it is often possible to say the 'real' things in a letter, when it is perfectly impossible in conversation." And she put her theory into practice, adding a postscript that was for Max's eyes only: "I am sending you a note I wrote you about a week before I came home for Christmas. I sealed it and addressed it and then decided not to send it. I kept it, hoping for a time when I could. You see, I was afraid you would feel it too intimate a thing to say even in a letter . . . It is true what I said in the note, and I want you to know it and feel it. You needn't mention it ever." And here was Crystal's note: "Boy, I have just picked out your letters from the pile of received and answered ones, and read them one after another in the order that they came in. I am so filled with the joy of loving you and the sweet happiness of knowing that you love me, that I must tell you. I could give a hundred reasons why I like you. But my love for you is too big and overwhelming to explain. I think it is a glad mystery, connected with God and infinite love. I hope we can both be better and stronger for the power of it." Crystal added,

"Don't let anyone see this, will you?" She must have felt that attaching divine meaning and purpose to her feelings for Max, as her mother once did when writing to Sam, would render them respectable, and yet she also knew they weren't—hence the sealed, never-to-be-spoken-of note.[50]

For Max, though, the pressure coming from his family finally proved too much. Plagued by mysterious nerve pains, a modern version of Henry James's "obscure hurt," he took a break from college and stayed home. The family would not have been able to pay for both Crystal's and Max's college expenses anyway. Wrapped in a steel brace prescribed by the orthopedist Dr. Goldthwaite, Max helped out by tutoring a reluctant Elmira boy. He also participated in an amateur production of Charles Dickens's *Cricket on the Hearth,* where he confused the emotions of his character with his own lustful longing for his costar, Gretchen Fassett.[51]

Max returned to college the following year, his mind restored but his body still hurting for reasons not clear to him or his doctors. Much to the dismay of Ralph Erskine, who had always consoled himself with the thought that at least his musical skills were superior to those of his dazzling classmate, Max had meanwhile learned to play the piano and surprised everyone with a beautiful rendition of a piece by Edvard Grieg.[52] Crystal now took her turn at living in Elmira. She had accepted a teaching appointment at the Elmira Free Academy, though she kept her independent ways: dating men, taking singing lessons, smoking cigarettes, and leaving for weekends in New York City, where she had "a man at hand all the time." And she developed a taste for Greenwich House, a place full of "cranks and reformers," a haven for all self-respecting radicals new to the country. She was also dreaming about living jointly in New York City with Max: "I doubt if I should care to ever see another man."[53] As Max settled into a state of semi-invalidity, Crystal never ceased to encourage him: "Persist in thinking of yourself *perfectly well* only a few years ahead." In her eyes, Max was destined to be a preacher or a writer: "You have beautiful true thoughts, you can write and speak, you are good and yet a struggler—and above all you *understand.* Don't you see that all those things should make a great preacher and minister of you?" It will be, she concludes, "something to work for," even if the road to success was paved with disappointments.[54]

Max did graduate from Williams in the spring of 1905. He was elected to Phi Beta Kappa, too. Theodore Roosevelt was in the audience during Max's graduation. The event was made even sweeter by the fact that Max had won the oratorical contest with a speech on Giordano Bruno, whom he celebrated for having chosen philosophy over the church, heresy over religious orthodoxy.

Although the subject of his speech had been suggested to him by the brilliant Asa H. Morton, professor of Romance languages at Williams, a man who had introduced him to Dante as well as Claude Monet, Max would later claim he had learned but little in college. In 1915, when asked to contribute to the *Decennial Record of the Class of 1905*, Max defined his current occupation as "writing and lecturing on social problems" and added, with a mixture of irony and condescension, "My education, which began in nineteen hundred and five, is progressing rapidly, and I can report excellent prospects of knowing what it's all about when I get through."[55]

3 · A Village Apollo

With college done and all barriers removed between him and the fulfillment of his desires Max promptly balked, and his health collapsed once more. His persistent backache became his career. But at least he was now getting published, too. An essay he composed during this period of prolonged prostration, "On the Folly of Growing Up," shows that some of the major elements of Max's style were already in place. Max begins with a commonplace idea (that the young constantly are put in their place by the elders) and then sends it through the wringer of a loosely dialectic method, with a few luminous epigrams thrown in along the way ("Most people have had too much experience to be wise"), before ending on a provocative, if not entirely unexpected, note: let's grow old without growing old. Hidden beneath the surface of the smooth rhetoric and wrapped in a tissue of references ranging from Aristotle and Empedocles to Saint Benedict, buried among sentences that sound as if quoted from somewhere else, although they probably weren't, was Max's plea—the plea of the youngest child in the Eastman household—to be left alone: "We have a superstition prevailing in our homes that the first thing to do upon the appearance of a child is to bring it up." And: "There is no use in being born unless you are willing to make an honest effort not to grow up." Max's essay reveals an almost frighteningly mature voice: while the paratactic piling on of pronouncements seems to be modeled on Emerson, Max's biting irony and penchant for learned metaphor ("The Senate must be templed upon the Acropolis") are entirely his own: a kind of narcissistic Erasmus of the modern age, praising folly as the new smart.[1]

Max's essay, published with some delay in the *Christian Register,* was a plea for the beauty of arrested development, and he certainly did his best to honor his own injunctions. As his classmates fanned out in search of employment or graduate training, Max hung around Williamstown, spending time with an invalid minister, John Denison, and developing a close friendship with a literate spinster of New England pedigree, Miss Suzie Hopkins. Another product of these months of genteel laissez-faire was an essay in which Max sought to define the nature of poetry. Published in the *North American Review* under the title "The Poet's Mind," the essay is a curious mixture of Emersonian grandstanding and aestheticist snobbishness. It also marks the official beginning of Max's long, complicated love affair with Walt Whitman.

Max's argument was that traditional explanations of poetry had failed: it could be defined neither by its subject matter—hadn't Whitman shown that there were no limits to the things poets could write about?—nor by its mode, which, in Max's understanding, was a poem's meter. A more helpful approach to understanding poetry was to recognize the difference between processes in our mind, between logical thinking and the type of thinking in which the imagination dominates. The former was prose, and the latter was poetry. "Last April," says the prosaic mind. "When lilacs last in the dooryard bloom'd," says the poet, aka Walt Whitman. Consider, for example, this sentence, which sounds as if it had been taken from one of Annis's sermons: "Let there be a junction between your ideals and your daily life." As we think about what the sentence might mean, "something light touches upon something drab-colored, or a vagueness from heaven swims over the picture of yourself in practical costume." Why, then, not choose a better, more poetic phrase right away? "Hitch your wagon to a star." The new sentence gives thought its own natural, visionary form rather than merely putting it into words. The goal of poetry was not to explain life but to make it manifest: "It was not abstract ideas of health and beauty and lightness, but visible Apollo, who moulded Greek life."[2]

But Apollo did not rule over Williamstown. In Max's case, the concrete manifestation of the "junction" between mind and body was his lack of health or, more concretely, his ever-worsening back pain. In late January he found himself in Dr. Charles Oliver Sahler's New Thought Sanitarium in Kingston-on-the-Hudson. Sahler had been a general practice physician in the Catskills when he discovered the power of mental suggestion. Now he was running a facility for all kinds of nervous wrecks, although he drew the line at actual insanity. While Sahler's therapeutic plan included assorted baths, "Turkish, Russian, and Electric," as he advertised, the main preoccupation of the patients at the "Sahler San" seems to have been to do nothing at all.[3] Max quickly lost faith in the doctor's system, which after an initial treatment was limited to one of Sahler's assistants laying her hand on his forehead. His decision not to quit was probably related to the presence of two bewitching girls among the sanitarium staff, Rosanna and Charlotte, who inhabited a cottage in a nearby valley. Romping around with them, in that half-desiring, half-shy-virginal way that made young Max forever popular with the girls while it also effectively prevented him from consummating any of his affairs, he found out that he had hypnotic powers himself, as he bragged in a letter to Annis.[4]

In May 1906 Max, anticipating a full recovery, was back in Williamstown again, with a new zest for life that made him turn down an offer by one of his former Williams College professors, Henry Loomis Nelson, that he become his teaching assistant—a proposition he dismissed even more loftily because it confirmed his idea of what "a scholar ought not to be, a man for whom his subject was never more palpable than paper."[5] He didn't want money, he didn't want a wife, he didn't want dignity, he informed his mother. Max hankered for activity and even contemplated going west again, inviting his worried mother to come along: "We can raise everything from ginseng to the devil out there. There's so much room." In the meantime Max stayed by himself at Glenora, eating raw food (one of his mother's ideas), reading Whitman and other books his mother handed him out of the window of her train car while rejecting her suggestion that she could join him at the cottage: "I am conscious of your caring so much about my being sick." Max talked himself into being "unspeakably happy," but it turned out he really wasn't. A note, written later on one of the envelopes from that time, sums up the experience: "I gave up and ran home to mother June 15."[6]

As Max seemed forever stuck in late adolescence, Crystal dove into adult life in New York City, dating men, sometimes several at a time, as if this were an athletic exercise, letting them come close to her and then keeping them at arm's length, just as they were about to claim the prize. And then she would write Max or Annis to let them know what had or hadn't happened. Paul Kellogg, a journalist and editor of *Charities* magazine, was one of the most persistent. In September 1906, after spending a day with Kellogg on a deserted Coney Island beach, Crystal reported back to Elmira: "The water was great. After that my hair was wet and we walked way up the beach to a place where there are no pavilions and no houses, while my hair blew dry in the wind." Just before they left, "the moon came out clear and we ran and danced close to the waves on the long brown beach." Crystal was so in love with life that her boyfriend lost all excitement for her: "I guess I am not in love with him. I'm half sorry and half glad . . . I'd love to be in love with somebody someday, *hard* so there wouldn't be any doubt about it." Ostensibly more adjusted than Max, Crystal was experiencing a similar kind of loneliness as he did.[7]

In October 1906 Max checked into Dr. John George Gehring's sanitarium for the treatment of nervous disorders in Bethel, Maine, to seek help for his constantly ailing back. Reverend Denison, Max's Williamstown mentor, had discussed his case with Gehring, who had agreed to treat Max for free, on an outpatient basis.[8] This was not an ordinary hospital. Known as the "Harvard of the North" after its prominent clientele, Gehring's clinic even became the subject of a novel, *The Master of the Inn,* which first appeared in *Scribner's* in 1907 and came from the pen of Robert Herrick, a former patient. Gehring, who had a degree from Case Western and had also done some postgraduate work in neurology in Berlin, was a kindly man perennially enveloped in cigar smoke who lived in constant fear of his powerful wife, Marian. His method was simple: let the sick work as hard as they can and get physically strong again, and then all mental problems will vanish. Max, who did not live at the clinic but rented a room in town, had to agree to a regimen of outdoor activities, such as chopping or sawing wood, interrupted by fixed periods of nap time, which the doctor progressively shortened as Max became less and less aware of his pain. He told Max that his back trouble was a mental obsession and that the less he thought about it the better he would get.[9] By November Max was able to work again, if only for two hours a day.[10] Crystal was radiant with happiness over the news: "Oh, if you knew how that thought sends me out thro' the dreary streets with a happy smiling face. . . . There is nothing I wouldn't do for that adorable man, your doctor. He can have my heart and hand for the asking, to say nothing of my brain, purse, and influence."[11]

What might have helped more than the doctor's regimen, however, was the presence in Bethel of Miss Anna Carlson, a "peach of a girl," as he told Crystal.[12] Swedish, blond, strong, and slim, she worked for the Gehrings as a combination maid and nurse and left an indelible impression on Max. Anna's letters to Max have survived, bundles of them, written with a smudgy pen on small, yellowish bifolds of paper in large, confident handwriting. Some of them were in Swedish, a language Max picked up in passing during his infatuation with Anna. (Max the lover would always serve as an inspiration to Max the linguist; this is precisely how he would begin his study of Russian a decade later.) In his autobiography, Max remembered Anna fondly, if somewhat casually. The letters, however, don't seen incidental at all, and neither does the fact that someone had evidently attempted to burn them.

The truth is that Anna and Max were infatuated with each other, to a degree that made Mrs. Gehring nervous. On a hastily penciled, folded-up sheet of paper from sometime in 1906 Max reported to Anna, "Mrs G. saw us start off yesterday afternoon & that we were on the way to the woods—she said so to the Dr—who presently saw us come back." Max was taken to task for his behavior, but more because of what such surreptitious escapes into the woods would have looked like to other people than because of what had actually happened. Anna responded, on the same sheet, that the Gehrings were often "inconsistent" and that she found herself "in strange positions" with them. Most of Anna's letters date from the time *after* Max's departure from Bethel, but if they are to be trusted, Anna's therapeutic value to him must have been tremendous: "Dear unconventional," "big-souled" Max was her "Hero Maximus" or "hero prophet."[13] At the same time, it seems Max also helped Anna, most specifically by encouraging her and her brother Gothard to leave the Gehring household and strike out for themselves in Boston.

In his autobiography Max recalls that Anna was too good a girl to agree to what Max, not a good boy in his own hopeful thinking, clearly wanted from her. But she certainly knew how to string him along, dangling the prospect of gratification before him, never ever taking it quite away from him but never letting him get any closer either. Anna was no Annis, and that was enough to keep Max going. In her letters she re-created for his benefit and excitement, one may presume, their near-intimate encounters in the woods: "And off we are over the dam, running over holes and stones and then tumble down in a breathless heap on the other side—'Oh dear there goes my hair'—'it's no use I can never keep it up'—'eight minutes?' 'oh bother, wait, one pin more, there!' And we're off again. 'Mercy, it's getting dark, no, I don't know that path well enough—I wouldn't dare take it'—so back to our old log and the starting place and now we're at the shack." And she would end suggestively, "It was exciting and fun wasn't it?"[14]

The hints—the tumble, the flowing hair, the dark path almost, yet not quite, taken—would have been enough to rope wayward Max back into a relationship he otherwise might have quit. Anna's letters preserved her lifeline to Max, who, as it turned out, was far from cured and was suffering some of the same symptoms again. In her missives that seemed to grow inexorably longer, Anna dwelled mostly on her own problems, bewailing her lot and the abuse she was suffering from Mrs. Gehring, and thus kept Max at bay. When Max made demands on her, he was swiftly and artfully rejected: "Let us pray for that Christ-spirit that maketh us to live noblest and that will give us the peace

of having done that which is good in the eyes of the Lord," the implication being that what Max wanted them to do was not so good.[15] Anna continued her
role-play, in which Max was alternately naughty boy, wise prophet, or a stern
substitute "daddy" shaking his "hoary locks" at her and "commanding" her to
do things, until she had moved to Boston, where she no longer needed him:
"Perhaps I . . . have been practicing a little inconstancy," she taunted him in
her last letter. One outcome was clear: Max could never go back to Dr. Gehring
again. "Mrs. Gehring is so 'set against' you on my account . . . that she will
make it *impossible* for you to ever be helped by the Dr. again."[16]

In helping Anna Carlson shake off her shackles, Max had tried out the role
Crystal had so far assumed in his life, and that fact did prove to have some
therapeutic value at last. Although his back pain lingered, Max now felt emotionally well enough to join Crystal in New York: "You are a wonderful sister
and I think about you half the time. I want to live with you."[17] His arrival, long
delayed, changed his sister's life, as she had hoped. When Max told her of his
intention to come to New York, she was ecstatic: "Your news came like a sudden great light into my life. My head is whirling with it now, and yet I am so
peacefully glad." All he had to do was come with enough money for a month,
and her lovers would take care of him: Dr. Vladimir Simkhovitch, a recent
acquisition of hers from Greenwich House who "would raise heaven and
earth to get me what I want," or the indefatigable Paul, "with his newspaper
and editorial acquaintances," would help him get on his feet. The prospect of
living with Max again was a "dream of joy." Crystal disliked her roommate,
Madeleine Doty.[18]

Delighted to be able to introduce Max to her friends and the city, she first
put him up at Greenwich House and then found a room elsewhere for him,
small but clean and neat and cheap and with "good air."[19] Crystal threw herself into this new, joint life with the beloved, much-missed brother, who soon
seemed to be spending more time at 12 Charles Street, the apartment Crystal
shared with Doty, than anywhere else. Dr. Simkhovitch took them out to the
theater: "We laughed a great deal and had a silly good time. It solves a good
many things to have Max here." At the bottom of her letter to Annis, Crystal
scribbled, "The sun shines at last."[20] For Max, too, Crystal was "the centre and
hub upon which my life turns."[21] He loved and wanted her so much that a moment of unanticipated solitude almost crushed him: "My heart was just com-
fortless and empty."[22] Although they initially maintained separate quarters,
Max and Crystal were always together, sharing meals, laughs, and friends.

Slowly Max was getting better; he was able to sit for longer periods of time, and when he had to lie down it seemed in line with family tradition: "All the Eastmans, you know, are natural sprawlers."[23] Even then, New York would have seemed big to a boy from Elmira. Between 1900 and 1910 the population of Manhattan grew by 50 percent. Over two million people lived in the city, about half of them foreign-born. At night Max fell asleep amid the cacophony of all the usual New York noises, the streetcars, cat fights, drunken brawls, and random songs that could be heard at any time, night and day.[24]

Back in Elmira, Annis, the "foolish little girl," as her daughter called her, carried on her minister's life, pushing forward with church reforms, delivering progressive sermons, and writing letters to her children that reminded them why Mamsey was "the most *interesting* person" they had ever known.[25] She also continued to do the laundry for both siblings; on rare occasions she sent some cash.[26] The Eastman children really were, Crystal admitted in a moment of introspection, noncontributors, "the poorest 'props' considering our age and sex and 'eddication.' "[27] But things were beginning to look up for Max. Dr. Simkhovitch, who taught economic history, helped him get a position as a teaching assistant in the Department of Philosophy and Psychology at Columbia University. Max's class was "The Principles of Science," a topic about which he knew absolutely nothing. Professor John Dewey, who had come to Columbia from Chicago just three years earlier, didn't care. To him it mattered not what Max knew about a subject but that he *wanted* to know something about it—perhaps Max's first introduction to an important pragmatist principle, namely, that knowledge arises from the adaptation of the human organism to its environment.[28]

Dewey was in his late forties then, a careless dresser, his unkempt hair a perfect match for his torn clothing, and completely uninterested in the usual trappings of professorial authority: an unconventional figure even at Columbia. Like Max, the Vermont-born Dewey was the son of Congregationalists. A lanky, intense, painfully repressed boy as he was growing up, he was saved from a life of religious boredom and Sunday school teaching by discovering science. At Columbia, Dewey ranged freely across various fields, logic, education, psychology, science, and politics, developing his ideas as he was talking, giving each of his students the feeling that they mattered. Dewey thought best when there was noise around him. Filled with multiple fully entitled children, one of them an adopted boy from Italy, the Dewey household was an image of the egalitarianism the Eastmans, for all their outrageousness, had never achieved. According to Max, Dewey embodied in his life and attitudes what

Whitman had done in a book, namely, "the essence of democracy."[29] Max also began to work as an assistant to Dickinson S. Miller, a former student of William James and perhaps the most idiosyncratic philosopher on the Columbia faculty. Part of Max's work with Miller consisted in taking him out in a canoe on the Hudson every day, for the sake of the philosopher's health.[30] He was flooded with papers to correct, although this wasn't a problem for Annis's son, equipped with a "mental deftness" he had inherited from her and that enabled him to read any kind of handwriting with dispatch.[31]

The pay for the instructorship was meager, around $500 a year, so Max still had to borrow money from Crystal, who was really not in a position to be generous. But she simply couldn't say no to Max, who remained "the one I wanted to marry always."[32] He seemed to be growing "more beautiful to look at" by the day, and he surrounded himself with so many girls that Crystal found it hard to keep track of them.[33] It was hard not to be envious of that gorgeous boy with the perfect skin and face full of "light and animation," and oh so perfectly unself-conscious about it all.[34] "Lovely to look upon," Max had not learned how to be careful with the limited financial resources he had, unlike Crystal, who appreciated how fortunate she was to have Annis as her mother: "Oh, the unhappy people who do not have you for a mother!"[35]

Crystal was now closer to Max than ever. To Annis she said this was the greatest year of her life.[36] From about that time stems a short passionate note to Max, thanking him for some unknown favor: "Oh, thank you, my mind and heart are most distracted with vague and conflicting longings and sudden desires. But, with all of me, poor and uncertain as I am, I know that I love you. I thank God for you as I thank God for the sun and wind, for the mountains and the sea,—for all the songs of birds, for green fields,—for moonlight and the wonderful stars; because as it is with all these,—you are very near my soul." Max was making her life "full and rich and joyous"; life without him had become difficult to imagine. Crystal was so full of happiness that she went out to the beach one afternoon and made a fire, "fantastic and beautiful with all sorts of queer things burning." Whenever she broke up with her lovers, she knew there would always be Max, standing bareheaded in the sunshine, looking handsome, smiling, prompting Crystal to say out loud: "Ah, here is a *Man!*" Crystal knew she was a "queer one" when it came to men, as she told Annis.[37] Max was her god, her savior, and she saw nothing amiss in comparing him to Jesus Christ, another young man who had chosen "thoughts and words" as his profession, as she thought Max would do, rather than a more sedate, respectable way of life.[38]

Max's teaching further helped in the self-confidence department. He took to it like a fish to water. "I gave a great lecture Monday," he reported home, boasting that in order to deliver it he had needed only "a note or two on the desk." He had read Whitman to them, "as the culmination and ideal attitude to nature and natural science."[39] Being able to work again was a fantastic feeling. "I am going to lecture the heads off of my class this morning." Quoting Mary Baker Eddy (whom he had been reading recently) on "holy inspiration," he declared, "*I am About to Combust!*"[40] He looked good and felt good. The students liked his candor. Once during one of his classes, when he was attempting to expound Aristotelian syllogisms to his undergraduates with the help of blackboard diagrams, a hand shot up in the back of the room: "Professor, what's the use of all this?" Max put down his chalk, drew a long breath, and answered: "I'm ashamed to say it nets me only five hundred dollars a year." He felt, he said, much better after that. And so did his sophomores. Incidentally, the student who had asked the question was Joseph O'Mahoney, who would serve four terms as a senator for Wyoming in the U.S. Senate, a New Dealer and fierce opponent of big business.[41]

Max was also attending lectures on socialism at the Rand School, taking weekend trips to Croton-on-Hudson and elsewhere, and when Buffalo Bill's Wild West show came to town he went to see it.[42] Dewey would become the kind of father to him he never had—interested in his ideas, without wanting to influence him—a true pragmatist. Max worked in an office next to Dewey, with the door open between the two. Sundays he dined at Dewey's house, and then they would spend most of the afternoon and sometimes the evening together. Max also helped Dewey, never known to be a dazzling stylist, with his writing, improving both style and clarity in the ethics textbooks Dewey was preparing with his former Chicago colleague James Tufts. If the famously dull Dewey wrote a quotable sentence, a possibility Max questioned, and it appears in his 1908 textbook on *Ethics,* it is possible that Max had lent a hand.[43]

Max spent the summer of 1907 at Glenora working on his plan to get published by a major magazine. Looking for suitable topics, he focused on his recent medical adventures. The result was "The New Art of Healing," an essay in which he contrasted the charlatans of Christian Science and the faux magicians of the "New Thought" school with "suggestive therapeutics," as practiced by Dr. Gehring, an approach that relied on "fixing an idea" in the patient's mind and thus effecting a cure of his or her physical ailment. In this method the patient relinquished herself to the doctor, not out of weakness but as an "act of will." The strongest patients were the best ones, observed Max, who had learned his lesson well: "A great deal of alleged physical suffering is primarily mental." That didn't mean these afflictions weren't real. But they did not result from any physical infirmity, and there was no pill that could cure them. Instead of leaving these wretched sufferers shuddering under the noxious influence of a misconception, exposed to "a thousand house-grown maladies of the imagination," the doctor trained in suggestive therapeutics would try to replace the wrong idea with the right one. Max's essay is marked by both personal urgency and a delight in the force of epigram: "The chief value of many pills lies in the satisfaction of taking them." And, in a closing gesture aimed at those who had already been helped by the new science, Max encouraged patients to speak up: "So long as the unprejudiced are cowards we are wholly damned by prejudice." To his delight, the *Atlantic Monthly* accepted the piece and ran it the next year.[44]

There was no lack of women who were interested in relationships with Max, but, paralyzed by a nagging sense of inadequacy, Max made a mess of one potential relationship after another. In the summer of 1907 he read Whitman's "Song of the Open Road" with Florence Wyckoff, a lumber merchant's daughter and his riding buddy during the long summer weeks he spent at Glenora. He came as close to her as anyone could, riding next to her during long trips, but he never touched her, though decades later he would still remember her satiny skin.[45] Not for him Whitman's famous "adhesiveness." Annis sensed that not everything was right with her son: "With all my joy in you I do not love the feeling of sadness about you and when that exists I'm pretty sure there is reason. You seemed to lack buoyancy—and your face *was* sad." She suspected that Max's melancholy was connected to Florence ("Are you at peace with yourself about Florence?"), although she quickly shifted to more organic reasons for his hangdog appearance ("indigestion malaria or just weariness"). Trust God, she advised, "but watch yourself a little more." On the envelope of Annis's letter, Max much later, when he was reviewing the correspondence from those years, noted the real reason for his malaise: "The problem of sexual intercourse."[46] Filled with desire, he was too afraid to act upon it, too afraid to fail if he did.

The summers he spent at Glenora would have offered lots of opportunities for Max to divest himself of his inhibitions. The logbooks for those weeks record an endless cycle of swims, hikes, house repairs, picnics, canoe paddles, porch parties, baseball games, concerts, naps, and huddles around the fireplace, punctuated by the arrivals and departures of summer residents and their guests, the Langdons, McDowells, and Pickerings, and the wistful saying of good-byes at the end of the season. Even Anstice was not immune to the special atmosphere at Glenora, the mix of athletic competitiveness and drowsy laissez-faire that made city life seem so far away. After a rather secular Sunday morning service conducted by Max himself (the topic was Emerson on heroism), Anstice contributed a rare entry to the family log, made even more peculiar by the touches of poetry he added: Max's sermon had "crystallized the whole life of the summer into a jewel which we shall carry with us, our most precious memory, and an unending inspiration."[47]

Surrounded by powerful women not afraid to flaunt their joy in life and to (sometimes literally) let their hair down, such as the "Amazon" Muriel ("Mooley") Bowman, Max did feel instantly rejuvenated whenever he returned to Glenora (figs. 9, 10). "Oh the wild joys of living," he intoned in one of his many ecstatic logbook entries, "the leaping from rock up to rock, / The strong rending of boughs from the fir-tree, the cool silver shock / Of the plunge in a pool's living water!"[48] Inspired by the Australian swimming champion Annette Kellerman, Max discovered the joys of diving. Soon "natatory festivals"

Figure 9. "Mooley" (Muriel Bowman) at
Glenora, 1909. *Cherith-Log*, 1909. EMIIA2.

Figure 10. Max Eastman at Glenora. *Cherith-Log*, 1909. EMIIA2.

became the main preoccupation of the Glenora folks: "Mary and Muriel each turn a flipper amid cheers," Max noted on July 24, 1909, "and the 'standing-sitting dive' (in loving memory of Annette Kellerman) gives the spring-board a chance to get back at us."[49]

Max's signature dive was the Flying Dutchman, a combination of front spring and one-half backward somersault.[50] But he also pioneered a jump called "the running-dream-dive-from both feet," an innovative athletic feat that won him the admiration of all. "Nothing permanent in this world but swimming parties," the philosopher wrote smugly in the logbook (fig. 11).[51] He went from sporting dark sweaters and white shirts and looking, according to Crystal, like a cross of Hamlet and Lord Byron to walking the trails in whatever garments he pleased. "It's a good thing the trees are growing tall around Cherith—for the Cherithites are coming about as near the Simple Life as it is possible to get," opined a still somewhat baffled old friend, Ruth Pickering, on July 8, 1908. "Each morning when I see Max he has discarded some article of clothing which he has decided is *positively unnecessary*." He was now strolling around wearing khaki trousers, which, by the old Max's standards, would have

Figure 11. "All In," August 11, 1909. *Cherith-Log*, 1909. EMIIA2.

been close to being naked. Interestingly, Ruth, the abiding object of Max's furtive desires during those years, could be seen around Glenora chopping wood in her bathing suit.[52]

Sam and Annis Eastman viewed this paradise of whirling, wheeling, flying, diving, swimming, and, more troublingly, skimpily clothed bodies—one they had originally helped create—with mounting skepticism. Sam especially was perturbed by so much freedom: "Grand fight in the afternoon on going back to nature precipitated by Dad," Max noted in the log. Crystal and Adra, who had by then gotten past their earlier reservations about nudity, had been sitting in the parlor in their bathing suits, and Sam took exception to their appearance. They were, he decided, "too bare." The self-appointed apostles of nakedness shot back, and a verbal skirmish ensued that didn't end until Annis, brilliant but bedraggled, returned from Elmira amid a rainstorm and wanted to know what was going on. "You started it," complained Max, pointing at Reverend Eastman. "I made one solitary remark," answered Sam, defensively. "That's all the Lord made at the beginning of the world," interjected Annis, who disapproved of loudness even more than nudity. "And look at all the trouble he caused," concluded Crystal. However, Annis herself was not in favor of the "skin-craze" either, as she freely admitted two weeks later when the family was again "angryin'," the Eastman word for fighting. Again, Dad had brought on the debate, this time by arguing against tea and beer, which provoked Baldwin Mann, Adra's husband, into proclaiming, loudly, his support for Anheuser Busch.[53]

There is no doubt these summers did a lot of good things for Max. But they also instilled a lifelong sense of frustration in him: he was so near the forbidden fruit yet unable to pick it. Max wanted to have fun, but he was also enough of a Puritan to be haunted by the feeling, injected into him by his painfully repressed father, that one maybe shouldn't be having fun at all. Max's constant desire to be elsewhere, doing something else, with somebody else, with *anybody* else, would prove to be a source of never-ending agony, to both him and the people around him.

It was not easy for Max to define the exact kind of liberation he craved. Ever since Miss Julia Beecher had read Whitman's "Calamus" poems to him when he was a mere child, Whitman had hovered over Max's life like the shadow of an ancestor one would rather forget. Whitman's promise of spiritual fulfillment was sanctioned by Max's own mother, who based an entire sermon on a passage from *Leaves of Grass* that made spiritual health contingent on finding God not in some faraway transcendent realm but all around us: "I see something of God each hour of the twenty-four and each moment then / In the faces of the men and women I see God."[54] Max's copy of *The Wound-Dresser,* a compilation of Whitman's essays and letters about the Civil War he acquired in June 1908, is heavily marked, at least at the beginning, especially next to a passage about the "magnetic touch" of mothers and their healing influence.[55]

The idea of healing was prominent in the two essays on Whitman Max undertook to write in July of that year, working for three to four hours a day on them. In "Walt Whitman's Art" he took issue with a statement the Scottish metaphysician William Hamilton had inscribed on the wall of his classroom at Edinburgh University: "In the world there is nothing great but man; in man there is nothing great but mind." Max considered that aphorism entirely "unserviceable" because it negated "our bodies and the gods around us." Max wanted—and it is clear he was speaking mostly for himself here—to "open the doors of our senses and go out through them." Max's essay is less analysis than poetic invocation: "Perhaps the wisest mind is the child's. Once we were not indifferent to the morning. We did not wake at the greeting last night's proposition in commerce or logic, but at the smile of the sun. The stuff of our thoughts was not sentence and numbers, but grass and apples and brown honey." Whitman had kindled Max's dormant pagan sensibility, prompting him to imagine himself dancing "in the dew with naked feet." Poetry was the adult's return ticket to childhood and the urban person's reminder that the country exists. "The universe does not exist in the abstract, nor in general, nor in any classification, but in concrete and heterogeneous detail." Thus, Whitman's poet was a master of many perspectives: he sees the world of adults with the eyes of a child, and the world of the city with the eyes of the "countryman."

These were two perspectives Max thought he was well equipped to understand. From his higher vantage point he felt able to judge not only the way Whitman judged others but also Whitman himself and to separate the wheat from the chaff. Max described his method of reading *Leaves of Grass* as a "thrashing out" and "winnowing out" of Whitman. His essay was not about Whitman, but a document of his own intuitive understanding of the poet, a record of how he had felt his way into Whitman's poetic universe, his "divine and barbaric fore-showing of wonderful material." And such foreshowing was what Max aimed for in his work, too, by *demonstrating* to his readers, rather than merely explaining to them, the difference between poetry and prose: "Prose is telling people what you have in mind, poetry is putting it into their minds." The point of Whitman's poetry, as Max understood it, was not to tell readers that the poet had crossed Brooklyn Ferry but that he had *experienced* crossing it. In Max's idiosyncratic terms, Whitman's poetry creates a *character*, not an idea. It works by direction—selecting a part or an attribute of the thing to be represented, such as the "malformed limbs" the surgeon in *Leaves of Grass* amputates and drops into a barrel—or by indirection, association by resemblance, as happens in Whitman's "Passage to India," where the speaker invokes the "temples fairer than lilies." Poetry embodies the ideals of the spirit in the life of the senses. As in trigonometry, it allows us to take measure of the unknown through the things we know and thus to "nail our diagram to the stars."

But Max also knew that his own sensibilities were quite different from Whitman's. He didn't like Whitman's famous catalogues, "so many pages full of words," which, he felt, turned the poem into a kind of drunken dictionary. Nature does not make lists, and it does not keep books. Still, gems gleamed out of the unrefined ore of Whitman's writing with a luster that made it difficult to reject him, as "persons of soaped and sweetened culture" are apt to do. Half prose and half poetry, Whitman's work was much like Whitman himself: "His book has a rank flavor like the presence of a man."[56]

But was there enough of that man in Whitman's poetry? In his second essay on the poet, "Whitman's Morals," Max celebrated Whitman's obvious sanity and balance, the fact that he was the "moral engineer" for the people around him as well as for the nation, including the Civil War wounded he tended to.[57] Yes, he had a demonic side too: he was irresponsible, selfish, insincere. His candor and love would, at a moment's notice, turn into self-deception and egotism. But that was precisely what made him human. Disliking him meant disliking the person next to you: "Know that your distaste for these pages is your distaste for the man next to you." What some readers hated about the good gray poet Max in fact admired: that he was "as certain about the universe as a boy with an orange." In his "cosmic bravado," Whitman made no attempt to fit the evil he recognized in himself into a larger moral philosophy that would preach the eternal perfection of all things in the mind of God. The road to the Divine begins with an acceptance of the importance of our instincts: "Man will ride to heaven on an animal," Max exclaimed. The "house of culture" was not "set on stilts." At this point in the essay, Max was talking more to himself than to his imaginary audience. From his mother's letters we know Max had kept a picture of Father Time on the wall of his room at school.[58] Now the vision of Time running after us, cracking his whip, resurfaces as Max celebrates Whitman's optimistic rejection of any kind of philosophical pessimism. "We have the power to choose between these attitudes." To Max, Whitman's poetry rises above the many creeds of the time that offer hope for salvation. "There is wildness in it, for it is the return of man to his rights as an animal." Max wasn't yet riding to salvation on the back of an animal. But Whitman had at least allowed him to dream about doing so. Against his mother's vision of Whitman the spiritual guide, he set his own version of the poet as the prophet of sexual healing. Nevertheless, Whitman's open road still seemed closed to Max, except for occasional glimpses: closed by his own shyness and by a debilitating fear of sexual failure.

Max proudly offered both Whitman essays to Richard Watson Gilder, the editor of *Century* magazine, because he had known the poet. Gilder was shocked. "We are a family magazine," he told Max, quickly placing the manuscripts back in his hand "as though I had handed him a turtle."[59]

Religion and philosophy "may prove well in lecture-rooms," Whitman had chanted as he was traversing the wide-open landscapes of his America, "yet not prove at all under the spacious clouds and along the landscape and flowing currents."[60] But associate instructor Max Eastman was hopelessly stuck in the lecture rooms of Columbia, with no end in sight. By contrast, Crystal had ventured out into real life, and with a vengeance. In the fall of 1907, after passing her law exams at New York University, Crystal moved to Pittsburgh, where she worked as an investigator for the Russell Sage Foundation, examining the death certificates of workers. The so-called Pittsburgh Survey, directed by Crystal's discarded lover Paul Kellogg, was one of the most wide-ranging investigations of working-class life in the modern city ever undertaken. Crystal threw herself into workers' compensation law and the stories of those victimized by corporate greed. But no excitement could make up for Max's absence. "I am *so* homesick for a word from you," she complained. "Aren't you going to write me soon?"[61]

Crystal still needed Max to hold her hand when life got too exciting for her, and she kept thinking, with more than a touch of jealousy, of his girls, especially when they happened to be the ones she had had her eye on, too: "I want to jump on a train and drag you from Alice Barrow's clutches instanter. She is the one I told you about, you know,—my great enthusiasm. Isn't she wonderful?" What a curious situation: Max and she were competing for the same girl, but at the same time Crystal was also competing, with that girl, for Max's affection: "Oh, I know you'll like her better than you do me!" She also just *had* to tell him about the picnic she would go on, an "all day picnic in the woods with two girls and their recently acquired husbands. The husbands, Jim and John, are both very fond of me and I of them." And, like a true lover, she kissed the little feather Max had included with one of his letters: "Did this little blue and black feather flutter into your hand from a bird that was flying over Morningside Heights? It is a sweet feather, and I am kissing it."[62]

Crystal's new responsibilities did not diminish her sense that Max was superior to her. He had the gift of the gab, the power to make others care—a future preacher, maybe, or, more likely, a writer: someone people would listen to. She told him so in a letter written from Jacob's Creek, the site of the worst mining accident in Pennsylvania history, the Darr disaster, which killed 239 men and boys on December 19, 1907. "It is strange to think of a little village in which there are almost two hundred and fifty families in mourning." While Max buried his head in philosophy books, Crystal was inspecting bridges, wire plants, and railroad yards to help workers in the fight for their rights, and she nevertheless felt inadequate: "It's hard to be the stupid member of such a brilliant family."[63] But at least they were both making money now, though it wasn't enough yet. "It's time we cut loose from the apron strings," declared Crystal, even if this meant walking into the future "hand in hand in poverty."[64] But if Crystal was ready to cut those strings, Max was not. He still had his laundry done by Annis, and it seems he was a tough customer:

"Please try to think of some way to fold, or do up my shirts, so that collars won't get wrinkled and double back funny in the journey."[65]

Word of Crystal's legal expertise reached the governor of New York, Charles Evans Hughes, who appointed her to serve, as the only female member, on his Employers' Liability Commission. Returning to New York City in the fall of 1908, Crystal had suddenly become the most visible and the most overtly radical of the Eastman siblings. "Now I pick you for the illustrious one," griped Max. Should he now give up all his own aspirations to greatness and settle down with her in "governmental luxury"?[66]

Well, not quite: Max and Crystal moved into a fourth-floor apartment on Eleventh Street, with two bedrooms, two living rooms, and a kitchen, for $33 a month. "No elevator, but good legs on the both of us," Max reassured his mother. They liked the neighborhood, a "respectable quiet peaceable home-going house-cleaning neighborhood of general Americans." And they acquired new furniture, including, for Max, a worm-eaten desk for $2.50 and a couch-bed with a hair mattress for $15.[67]

Living and working together proved beneficial for both of them. Max's teaching commitments at Columbia left all but one of his mornings and Tuesday, Thursday, and Saturday entirely free for his writing and gave him time for other things too, such as swimming.[68] Newly excited about his prospects, he registered for a doctoral degree at Columbia, with a thesis—yet to be written, of course—titled "The Sense of Humor."[69] His intention was to address the "science of laughter laughingly," a tall order for someone so early in his career.[70] No wonder the project for many years remained what it was then—a good idea. Years later he returned to it. In 1922 Max published *The Sense of Humor,* followed, in 1935, by the best-selling *Enjoyment of Laughter.* It could be said that Max kept on writing, for over twenty years, the dissertation he never even started.

In addition to his academic duties Max took on the coaching of a boys' athletic club on the Lower East Side, in one of the rougher areas of town. His letters tell of his efforts to impress youngsters who were physically much stronger than he was but didn't know the wrestling moves Max had somehow acquired. The club was sponsored by the Hamilton-Madison Settlement House, and a compelling reason Max took on the new job was the fact that it was paid. But he also liked the challenge, the opportunity it gave him to bolster his rumpled sense of masculinity. "It was the only job I ever tackled harder than teaching logic to sophomores."[71] Hamilton House had begun running clubs for boys and girls around 1902 with the aim of getting the offspring of impoverished immigrants off the streets. Max found a gymnasium he could use and seems to have done everything else right, especially when he set out to organize the club, making the boys elect their own president and a treasurer. There were some bumps in the road, as he reported to Mamsey. During a particularly tumultuous meeting "the chairman poked the secretary under the ear and almost knocked him out of office!" But this wasn't anything Max couldn't master: "I took the chair—after an hour of roughhouse—and held them down to an orderly meeting for another hour."[72]

Max enjoyed the validation New York seemed to give his desire to be more than a bookworm. The city and its surroundings certainly had much to offer, from the octopus in Battery Park, unfortunately already dead by the time Max got around to visiting it, to spectacles such as the car races on Long Island, and, in October 1909, Wilbur and Orville Wright's madcap flight from Governor's Island to the Statue of Liberty. The swimmer Annette Kellerman, dubbed the most "perfect woman in the world" by a Harvard professor thanks to the assumed similarity of her proportions to those of the Venus de Milo, joined the Eastman siblings for lunch. After the meal, Max offered to teach Kellerman how to skate.[73]

Max also tried his hand at performing. The British actor and director Ben Greet, whose troupe was impressing Americans that season with Shakespeare plays, had invited him to be one of the Wise Men in a miracle play (only three rehearsals, sighed Max). In a more momentous development, the photographer Alice Boughton asked Max to pose, alongside the professional actor Walter Hampden, in a variety of biblical scenes she was taking for *Good Housekeeping* (figs. 12, 13). Max's classically handsome dark looks provided an effective contrast with the hirsute Hampden's Jesus, lending an unexpected air of authenticity to these supposedly Mediterranean scenes. Max the recovering invalid and refugee from religious morality must have relished the challenge to play a character awakened to new life by divine healing. Appearing as one of the blind men from Matthew 9:27–30 and as the man with the withered hand from Mark 3:3–5, Max played the part he knew best: that of the gorgeous, passive, imperiled male, alone or almost alone but at the center of attention, while a family dressed in rags watches from the sidelines, their faces frozen in an expression that reflects their wonder at and distance from what is about to befall Max.

In many ways Crystal's and Max's joint life was a parody of a marriage. It absolved them of the obligations that came with real marriage or any kind of romantic partnership and allowed them to cultivate their neuroses on their

Figures 12 and 13. Alice Boughton, *The Healing Miracles of Jesus the Christ* (1909).
Source: Boughton, "The Healing Miracles of Jesus the Christ: Studies in Artistic
Photography. Illustrating Scenes from the New Testament. Posed for by Walter
Hampden and Others." *Good Housekeeping,* December 1909.

own. But the arrangement gave each of them a modicum of economic security: one was likely to have some money if the other didn't. Most important,
they could have fun together.

Their letters are full of intimate details from their shared life: Crystal coming home to Max drying his hair in the bathroom; Max nursing Crystal through
one of her fevers; both of them going out, either jointly or separately, to theater
performances or for a tennis match. One evening, on a whim the siblings invited everyone they came across to dinner at a little Jewish restaurant on Sixth
Avenue. Max arrived with four men and two girls, while Crystal came with a
man and a girl. "Practically none of them had seen each other before," Max
wrote, "and it was the funniest jolliest thing now." After dinner the group ad-
journed to the room of one of the girls. By then Max and Crystal had gone on
to a suffrage meeting, heavily attended by Vassar girls. Apparently they re-
joined the party later and "fooled around the fire for the rest of the evening."[74]

In October 1909 Crystal and Max moved to 118 Waverly Place. They went about the move, including the selection and placement of the furniture, like any married couple would. The place was expensive: $20 for each of them, not counting the $15 they hoped to receive from a yet-to-be-found boarder. But the rooms were so fine that Max and Crystal couldn't resist. The bond between them was stronger than ever, despite fits of envy, especially on Max's part. Max once defined the basis of their intimacy as a form of "emotional richness" that found no outlet in traditional romance. The reasons for their dissatisfaction with conventional love relationships were slightly different ones. In Crystal's case, the "man-thing" she craved rarely went with the kind of character her intellect demanded from a man. Put more crudely, Crystal wanted both refinement and sex from a man, and that was impossible. As for Max, he was just a "sauce-pan full of superficial sex feelings," a drifter without the power of concentration Crystal had. As both Max and Crystal realized, they were just right for each other. "Free, equal, unpitied by each other," they were able to make the best of their shared frustrations, enjoying the "richness of outer life" the city had to offer them.[75] In a hilarious poem drafted at the time, Max reflected on the fate of a "suffragette hen," a "female cock," made more domestic by the infusion of blood "from a more domestic stock," until she was filled with the "peace of saints above" and renounced her disposition to roam around the landscape. Max rejected such a fate for himself:

> But as for me, I'd rather be
> A poulet to eternity
> And die in lonesome liberty,
>   Without begetting,
> Than lose my own identity
> For the salve of setting.[76]

A proud chicken ("poulet") rather than a rooster, he didn't need (yes, that was the rhyme he opted for) a booster, preferring the fake domesticity of Waverly Place to the responsibilities of adult life, or what Annis, in a rare moment of overt criticism, defined as her ideal, a "life of doing things."[77]

Small wonder that Max, in his daytime existence as a philosophy student at Columbia, opted for an equally unconventional approach to the field. Systematic study was not his thing. He took and passed his exam in German philosophy after barely getting beyond the letter A in his encyclopedia, and he found reading Schopenhauer in the original less than energizing.[78] But then he also had little patience for traditional metaphysics. Under the guidance of Dewey,

Max developed a version of pragmatism that accepts life as it is and finds purpose in the things that immediately surround us. "If pragmatism means anything," he wrote, "it means to lay 'Reality at large' in the lap of the metaphysicians and go about your business. If the pragmatist will not let Reality with a large 'R' alone, his troubles will never cease." To Max, the pragmatic hypothesis is "an interpretation of human thinking as science finds it" and as it would appear to a "dispassionate mind." The systems we develop as humans are entirely random, the products of our struggle for survival. They become systems only because we study them as such: "The beautiful technique of [man's] arbitrary endeavors becomes itself arbitrarily an object of endeavor. That is, he [man] *likes* great systems of ideas with a certain coherence, and he uses the same technique in attaining these systems and quarreling over them that he did in attaining and quarreling over food."[79] Understanding such arbitrariness, to Max, was the hallmark of "modern and scientific attitude." For the pragmatist, religion, philosophy, all attempts to attach lasting significance to life are thus efforts comparable to procuring dinner for the family. Pragmatism was, he concluded, no "sugar-plum" theory but a serious, iconoclastic endeavor, the business of strong souls. It was a philosophy that remained in touch with the demands of daily life, privileging immediate experience over abstract morality—philosophy for the plain man, Max's version of a "life of doing things."[80] Some of these ideas found their way into a long paper on Plato's philosophy that Max began to draft in November 1908 for the Philosophy Club at Columbia he had helped found.[81]

There was more than a note of wishful thinking in Max's new philosophy. Looking at Max's notes from his Columbia years, one gets the sense that his philosophical training was intended as a means of sorting through and then dumping the religious baggage Annis had left him with. The Greeks didn't have churches, Max reminded Annis. "Perhaps churches aren't the final resting place of great minds and hearts."[82] That Max's escape was happening as Annis, too, was discarding her own theological baggage seems richly ironical: she had started reading Thales and Heraclitus two years earlier. She had been taking summer classes at Harvard for several years, where she also heard Santayana and James lecture.[83] Poor Max. Wherever he found himself in life, Annis had either been keeping up with him or was several steps ahead.

A page of proposed exam questions gives us an inkling of how interconnected such philosophical issues were with Max's own life: "I. Distinguish 2 uses of the word empirical. II. If all knowledge derives from experience, what is the use of deduction as a priori reasoning? III. Give outline showing the rise of scientific induction. IV. 2 Reasons why astronomy was the first science. V. Define Miracle." One can imagine the answers he would have expected for the final question. In his lecture notes he offered a succinct, memorable definition of theology: "What could be deduced from what somebody said." The "modern spirit," by contrast, was "the finding of facts."[84]

Such finding of facts had been Crystal's business, too. She was now working the evidence she had gathered as an investigator into a book, *Work-Accidents and the Law*. "If adequate investigation reveals," she wrote, with the withering irony her brother had mastered, too, "that most work-accidents happen because workmen are fools . . . then there is no warrant for direct interference by society in the hope of preventing them." But if proper investigation showed that a considerable portion of accidents was due to insufficient concern for the safety of workmen on the part of their employers, then intervention in some form was surely warranted.[85] Crystal's book went on to document numerous individual cases of workplace injury and death combined with a look at the subsequent impoverishment of their families, thereby establishing irrefutable links between the callousness of the rich and the disenfranchisement of the poor and rooting in real life what for Max still was philosophical play.

The suffragette "hen cock" that wouldn't settle down was more than a casual metaphor for Max. Although he claimed this had happened more or less by accident, Max in 1909 became one of the founders of the Men's League for Woman Suffrage of New York State. The way he recalled it later, Max had, at a suffrage meeting, suggested that such an organization would be a good idea and that he would establish one, a statement that made it into the *New York Herald*.[86] He now had to make good on his foolish promise. But the proposed league seemed like a good way for Max to do what Annis and Crystal were doing, too, and yet make use of his own unique talents as a speaker. As it turned out, others, notably the influential journalist, editor, and owner of the *Nation* and the *New York Evening Post*, Oswald Garrison Villard, had already been in conversation with Anna Howard Shaw, the leader of the American suffragettes, about the creation of such an institution. Max appointed himself treasurer and secretary of the new league and soon enlisted Annis's and even Sam's help in managing his correspondence and the checks that came in. When Annis came to New York in November 1909 to seek psychoanalytic treatment from Abraham Brill, the first analyst in the United States to have his own practice, she spent her spare time in Max's apartment writing addresses on envelopes for the league.[87]

Max proved to be quite adept at harnessing the different advocates for the cause into supporting his new organization, assembling an impressive list of vice presidents, chairmen, board members, and so forth. But he, too, knew he couldn't have gotten anywhere without his mother's support. "Thank God you helped me with this," he sighed in a letter to Annis, surveying the "secretarial debris" that surrounded him at his desk.[88] According to its charter, published the following year in pamphlet form, the purpose of the new organization was "to express approval of the movement of women to attain the full suffrage in this country, and to aid them in their efforts toward that end by public appearances in behalf of the cause, by the circulation of literature, the holding of meetings, and such ways as may from time to time seem desirable." The membership fee was one dollar per year. The progressive millionaire and philanthropist George Foster Peabody was president, John Dewey chaired the executive committee, of which Villard was a member, while Zebulon Brockway from Elmira, William Dean Howells, and the reformist Rabbi Wise served as vice presidents. Among the chartered members were many familiar names from Max's and Crystal's lives: apart from Samuel and Annis Eastman, there were "Baldy" Mann, Max's classmate Ralph Erskine, Crystal's erstwhile lover Paul Kellogg, Max's former professor Dickinson Miller, and the ubiquitous Vladimir Simkhovitch.[89] Max had some impressive stationery engraved and printed and aggressively pursued invitations to speak, while also soliciting new memberships. Send me those membership requests, Max never tired of saying at his events: "It is one thing to support a movement, and another thing to lick a stamp to advance it."[90]

The rationale for the Men's League for Woman Suffrage, spelled out in many speeches Max would give over the next years, was crystal clear. The one way to get results in America is to threaten a politician that you won't vote for them, Max would explain. But if you are a woman and you don't have the vote, what do you do? Answer: "You are in an extreme predicament. You are unable to wake up our legislators at all. The end towards which you are striving is itself the means by which you may attain it." Hence the league. "The League has for charter members about a hundred and fifty of the best men in the state," and their most important objective was to "make equal franchise an issue at the polls."[91]

Max's first official appearance in his new capacity was at the Monroe County suffrage convention in Ontario, New York, on June 14, 1909. Max later called the speech his purgatory: too learned and too long, it nevertheless earned him $15, although, he quipped, any audience, had they been adequately warned, would have paid $500 to avoid having to sit through it.[92] He went on to memorize his speeches and learned to compress his arguments, adapting them to the occasion and the audience. Many of his lecture notes have survived among his papers, and several of them Max had retyped later, perhaps as he was working on *Enjoyment of Living*. Max identified a voluminous package of notes as the text of that first speech, although he also noted that he reused his script when he spoke in Rochester more than a year later.[93]

The speech—newspaper accounts of the Rochester event confirm that Max stuck pretty closely to his draft—shows why he became such a sought-after speaker.[94] He very cleverly began by questioning his right to speak about woman suffrage. He was young, a man, and an academic, the last person who should be holding forth about the issue before an audience of battle-hardened women "most ardently convinced of the righteousness of this cause." Moreover, he was speaking in Rochester, the home of Susan B. Anthony. Maybe there were a few "inanimate males" in the audience (Max actually crossed out this very funny phrase, probably a wise decision). But even those were likely in full agreement with his argument. Max then very adroitly brought his personal history, as the son of two ministers, into play: "This was exactly the way I used to feel about going to church. It seemed to me that if we were fairly well agreed upon the Bible, and the minister, and a handful of familiar hymns, we could let it go at that. There was no use getting together every Sunday and shouting about it." And yet meet his congregation did, Sunday after Sunday, and there was good reason for that. Why not adopt the same method for a worthier cause?

Max then changed gears and spoke as a philosopher. Hadn't Aristotle argued that man was an animal equipped with reason? Both men and dogs were able to stand on their legs, but men, unlike dogs, talk and can hold and exchange opinions. Now what one would have to add to that philosophical definition was a psychological one. For man was also a suggestible animal, as Ambroise-Auguste Liébeault, the father of hypnotherapy, had shown as early as 1866. Max was speaking not only as a student of psychology but also as a former patient when he went on: "The fundamental, first, forcible, and eternal way to get an opinion into a man's head and keep it there is to say it to him *often* and *loud*." And wasn't that precisely the purpose of a meeting such as this one? To say, often and loudly, what everyone knew to be true anyway, that women should have the right to vote? At that point in Max's delivery, hardly any woman in the audience would have doubted his authority to speak on behalf of her rights.

To his credentials as a minister's son, philosopher, psychologist, and hyp-
notist, Max added yet another element—that of the teacher. He explained that
he regularly exposed his sophomores at Columbia to arguments in favor of
woman suffrage, regardless of their indifference: "They think I am queer to
introduce such a matter into the classroom to begin with, and they think I am
queerer still to lecture them on the result." Max went on to give his listeners a
brilliant example of the kind of problem he would discuss in the classroom
and in passing proved what a skilled logician he was. As everyone knew, the
governor of Tennessee, Malcolm R. Patterson, had recently opposed a prohibition bill with the argument that it would bring women, who had been pushing
for the law, "into the poisonous atmosphere of political strife."[95] Now this
could be interpreted to mean two things: either that Governor Patterson enjoyed the poisonous atmosphere of political strife and did not want to see it
diluted by the presence of women, or that he liked the women of Tennessee so
much he wanted to protect them against such toxicity. Either way, there was
only one conclusion to be drawn from this: "*The present state of Tennessee politics is somehow incompatible with the present state of Tennessee women.* You can't
bring them together without changing one or the other, or both." The inevitable question: were the government of Tennessee, in all its venerable poison-
ousness, and the women of Tennessee, in all their holy innocence, really well
served by the status quo? The answer was evident: change was needed. As Max
put it, "I would like to see the air of politics cleared up by the introduction into
it of all the moral idealism of which the community is capable, and I would
like to see women's ideals, and the 'ideal of woman,' unburdened of senti-
mentality and hitched up into some sort of working contract with reality."
Women deserved better than "a life of futile and neurotic sainthood," and
politics, in Tennessee and elsewhere, was more important than to be left to the
poison-mongers. One-fifth of women had entered the workforce anyway, and
the political arena needed nothing more than their expertise now, as new areas of concern like sanitation, factory regulations, unemployment, and wage
inequality had emerged. The socialists already understood that. And that was
perhaps one of Max's most effective points. Giving women the right to vote,
and thus completing the government, as it were, was a way of preventing a
full-scale revolution. Clearly, Max wasn't yet a socialist.

Over the next two or three years Max would speak at the state suffrage convention in Troy, New York, and the national convention in the District of
Columbia as well as in Albany, Boston, Buffalo, Ithaca, Philadelphia, and

Pittsburgh. The Men's League for Woman Suffrage gave Max the opportunity to do what he had long known he was especially good at, public speaking, and get paid for it, a prospect attractive to someone who at times couldn't even afford his rent.[96] In February 1910, for example, he claimed he made $225 in addition to his measly salary as a Columbia University teaching assistant. "I can get 100 a month out of my league," he predicted, "and have half of my time free."[97] He also met some of the most courageous reformers of his time, such as the British suffragettes Ethel Snowden and Alice Paul.[98]

Most important, Max's self-created responsibilities allowed him to spend more time with a girl, the "large-featured," entrancingly liberated, courageous Inez Milholland, Crystal's friend from Vassar. Inez would drive him to some of the events while also holding on to her own independent suffragist career that would get her arrested more than once. Turned into a tigress by Max's virginal reticence, Inez extracted a declaration of love from him as well as an invitation to spend some of the Christmas holidays with him, which is when Inez apparently first figured out that she preferred, as Max feared she would, a more athletic lover. Over the next few months their love, by all appearances never consummated, fizzled out. Max blamed the breakup on the different things each of them wanted to get out of their relationship. But what indeed would Inez have thought about a lover who gave her six big roses while secretly wishing he had, in fact, put three of them upon his mother's pillow while she slept? One just hopes he didn't say any of that to her. Even Annis now felt her son had gone too far, though the reason she gave chillingly reveals just how closely knit the Eastmans really were: "I say that the 3 thus bestowed in your intent are always (the imperishable part of them) on my pillow when I wake so that Inez had only the bodies of the 3." In other words, why did Max worry? If he didn't understand what she meant, why, then love had really clouded his intellect.[99]

Some of Max's suffrage events also went less than smoothly. In Poughkeepsie, for example, Max was getting ready to address a "wedge-shaped audience" at the Collingwood Opera House. After an incredibly tedious lecture by Ethel Arnold, whose main claim to fame was that she was a niece of the more famous Matthew, the editor of the *Poughkeepsie Free Press,* who had previously declared his allegiance to the local suffrage movement, stood up, and surprised everyone by speaking out against it: "O it was awful!" But Max saved the day by giving an impromptu speech that kept the audience on the edge of their seats and even motivated some to stand up—yet not for the right reasons. Talking about the ongoing strike of the shirtwaist factory workers in New York, Max discussed the fact that some had been tried in court "in company with harlots," and though this reference had been intended in support of one of Max's favorite themes in these speeches, the sanctity of womanhood, the mere mention of harlots induced some elderly participants to leave. If not exactly a "handsome" audience, that is, an audience not reluctant to use their hands for applause, the Poughkeepsians rewarded Max with frequent giggles, which he took to mean they liked his off-the-cuff manner.[100]

Reports in the newspapers show just how circumspect Max was during his public appearances. There was, for example, the event in Baltimore, at the Academy of Music on Howard Street on February 27, 1910. According to the *Baltimore American*, "several thousand men and women interested in the cause of equal suffrage" came and listened to Alice Paul, the American suffragist known for her role in the British fight for the women's vote (so Max was, which he did not mention, not the main attraction). The event was held under the auspices of the Just Government League. Alice Paul set the tone for the event by comparing the fight for the women's vote to the struggle for American independence and denounced those who regarded the methods of the British suffragettes as extreme: "We have broken windows for a cause, yet we've been classed as criminals while fighting for a principle." When Max came on, introduced to the crowd as Professor Eastman, his message was conciliatory. No windows needed to be broken over here, he reassured his audience. Class was not really a problem in the United States, and there was nothing to be militant against over here. Of the four reasons usually given for women's suffrage, reasons that he, too, had recited in every one of his speeches—justice, the purification of politics, the idea of democracy, and the full development of the personality of women—Max emphasized democracy. He said he pitied those, referring specifically to Presidents Roosevelt and Taft, who supported the women's cause only out of a lukewarm sense of justice.

Democracy meant equal rights for all people. Max then used his favorite example, the shirtwaist strike, to demonstrate how widely accepted the different treatment of men and women was and how such inequality was directly related to suffrage: "Over 35,000 women appealed to the police commissioner for protection and were given no satisfaction. . . . If it had been 35,000 men with votes I know their demands would have received attention." This was a clever and bold move. The shirtwaist strike had just ended, and while Max inflated the number of women involved (20,000, not 35,000), the facts were scary enough to employers and would have been fresh on people's minds. Led by the immigrant garment worker Clara Lemlich and supported by the National Women's

Trade Union League, the strike, despite the thugs hired to attack the pickets, had led to vastly improved working conditions and higher wages for the mostly Jewish workers in the industry (though not at the New York Triangle Shirtwaist Factory, where a deadly fire a year later would kill 146).

But Max then somewhat reduced the force of his example by pointing out, as he was so fond of doing, that the right to vote would benefit the women themselves: "It is not a question of chivalry in giving the women their rights, but a heroic step in the evolution of a great race." But hadn't Lemlich's example just shown that women were quite capable of evolving on their own? The truth is that Max had a keen sense of audience, and while talking about the strike had taken courage, he made sure he wasn't going to bite the hand that fed him, or at least not too much. While he was answering questions a collection was taken. Obviously, by tailoring his message to the mainstream, Max kept his audiences with him: people *were* listening to him. Max was a full-fledged pragmatist now: expediency mattered to him more than being right on every single issue. And what an enormous validation for Professor Eastman, technically still an instructional assistant at Columbia University! A dinner in Max's honor took place on Saturday night at the Hotel Belvedere. The attendees listed in the paper, including a federal judge, two renowned doctors from Johns Hopkins, politicians, and lawyers, were all men.[101]

Not all attendees at Max's events were equally enthusiastic. The *Gazette-Times* of Pittsburgh caustically observed about one of his speeches: "No new arguments were advanced."[102] And a frequent guest at suffragist meetings sent Max a bluntly worded note in which she took him to task for speaking a lot without saying much. Paula Jakobi, a member of the Heterodoxy Club, a loose association of New York women with radical views, found Max unconvincing: "Always when you rose I had hopes—always I was disappointed. You looked strong, young, self-confident, thoughtful, and you would begin and ramble on in an amiable, nonchalante way but you had no message—your words meant nothing." Did he think the public was so easily fooled? "Give it your best and it would respond to the echo."[103]

To his credit, Max never pretended he had original insights to share. He firmly believed that saying them at all was what mattered more than *what* he said. In a 1911 essay for the *North American Review* he gave a kind of summary of the ideas he had been discussing and would continue to discuss on the lecture trail: that it was high time to end a political system that turns women into stuck-up saints, even though they have long entered the workforce, and that the need for reform had been known to humankind since Plato, who had criticized the legislator bent on making the male sex happy when he had the capacity of "making the whole state happy." Giving women the right to vote was nothing one could or even should have to argue for; the need for such a measure was as self-evident as the fact that women were mothers and men were not. We must not only give the ballot to those women who want it but also get those involved who do not yet know enough to want it.[104]

In his speeches Max made such self-evidence his main theme, turning the fact that he had nothing new to say into a kind of performance art, switching between a self-conscious display of boredom with the issues (do I really have to go on?) and a highly effective form of sarcasm. Sure, he didn't have anything new to say, he conceded. But then the old problems persisted. Take the woman who had invented the detachable shirt collar, "that well known device for saving a man the trouble of changing his shirt." While men had "gobbled up" this woman's invention "and saved themselves no end of bother and effort to keep clean, for over fifty years," they wouldn't dream of allowing a woman to wear one. Women invent things for men, who, instead of being grateful to them, don't do anything for them in return: "They won't even give her political liberty in recognition of the invention, although she stands ready to make all sorts of other changes equally important to the progress of civilization." Thundered Max, "That's the only original idea on woman suffrage I've heard since I came into the business." No need, really, to go over the other 2,780 reasons in favor of woman suffrage.[105]

Note that Max refers to the making of suffrage speeches as a business. In part this is certainly what it was for him. However, what sounds like cockiness and even laziness in Max's speeches was really a tool, and an effective one at that: watching Max perform circles around that which needn't even be said and which never needed to have been said in the first place, listeners initially not convinced would finally be overwhelmed by the realization of how outdated their objections were. Max lent his handsome face, youthful appearance, intellectual authority, and oratorical skills to a cause that, in part because of him, dominated the newspapers. And audiences, for the most part, loved their Max, the Columbia "professor" turned suffragette, a "hen cock" if ever there was one.

Which is not to say Max wasn't deeply impressed by those who did have new things to say. After Inez, Max's would-be girlfriend, died on November 25, 1916, of a blood-related illness, Max wrote a touching tribute to her "flashing and heroic beauty" for the *Masses,* in which he tacitly acknowledged the limitations of his own position. "There was," he wrote, "something almost superhuman in the way this young and beautiful girl passed among all the classes and kinds of people, sowing and reaping the joys of life, and yet never losing her *self*, never shaping or coloring her true nature and her true purpose and belief for a smooth half hour with anybody." Not afraid to make people uncomfortable, she also knew how to be happy and to make others happy. "If everyone of us who believe were possessed of that drastic courage she had to make our belief known and felt in our words and acts always, how much more quickly we should win the world."[106]

The fact that all-too-human Max made money with his lecturing did not bother him greatly. He even quipped rather shamelessly, "As long as the women don't get their votes I'm all right!" But Inez's example wasn't lost on him. He did care about the women whose cause he had joined. Working with them, the "finest in the land," gave him the confidence that the "prophets of democracy" had not erred about this country and that one didn't have to be a "one-eyed jackass" to want political change.[107] But it is also clear that his new job mattered to him personally. Max wanted to live "without froth and senti-mentality, like a big river," and stumping for a glorious cause gave him a glimpse of such a big life. If being a gym instructor had made him feel like a man among men, Max's work on behalf of the league permitted him to display his more feminine side and yet seem sufficiently masculine and assertive, "brave enough," as the *Buffalo Courier* asserted, to "help the women in a cause that is generally unpopular among men."[108] Max was a "man suffragette," as the *New York Daily Tribune* dubbed him, and he was good at it, he told Annis: "I answered questions in Baltimore, and O I just had a flow of wit and wonder that would astonish you! We laughed and enjoyed each other for an hour and a quarter—15 or 1800 [of] us. I will tell you the whole tale—the whole de-tale—when you come!" Obviously, he was so much more now than just Annis's apprentice.[109] "I am doing something that I believe in and care about in my healthiest moods," he wrote to Annis. "*Please* back me up."[110]

Academically, things were looking up for Max, too. Much to his surprise his professors had accepted his long Plato essay in lieu of a dissertation. Max wasn't about to dispute their decision: "I guess I shall pull thro' in my usual way." And that "usual way" was to rely on past achievements.[111] Max's final exam took place on May 17, an occasion he did not remember too fondly after-ward. He had passed his exam *and* survived Halley's comet, he reported.[112] And as if the fact that he had survived the procedure were more important than being allowed to flaunt his degree, he never filed his dissertation. Techni-cally, Dr. Max Eastman never got his Ph.D.[113]

Max's essay-turned-dissertation, first titled "The Quality of Plato" and then "The Paradox of Plato," was a little under seventy pages long in typescript. While Max's ideas might not be entirely original, the form in which he presents them is unusual, beginning with a short preamble in which he lays out his goal. And it is not an academic one: "This essay aims to reproduce, in a medium of modern words and ideas, the flavor of Platonic discourse, and the procedure of Platonic thought." Max wants to promote, he explains, "a free and human understanding" of Plato's philosophy and help those "who find it difficult to attain, without special education, the high pleasure of reading Plato." Note that Max is already imagining himself as speaking to a wider audience.

The Plato he recovers is a bit like Max's Whitman but even more like Max himself: his senses wide awake to the beauty that surrounds him, he can never forget about the larger moral framework either. But if Max is haunted by the moral values that had been instilled in him when he was a child, Plato was *devoted* to them. "A lover and advocate of immediate values," eager to "linger and behold and recklessly enjoy the innumerable things that he likes," Plato would at the same time always think about the consequences of his behavior and then perhaps end up condemning the very thing he likes. Max's criticism of Plato is muted but effective: while Plato denounces all imitative art as inferior to philosophy, his *Republic* is itself a supreme example of literary art. Plato made fun of poetry, and yet the *Republic,* in its beauty, smiles at his efforts to contain art: "No image-breaking morality appears in its plan, nor in the infinite pains taken to make it a true and natural dialogue." In fact, observes Max, Plato makes of philosophy a work of art.[114]

Rather than criticizing Plato, Max wants to make him his spiritual brother, subject to the same warring impulses that were tearing Max apart. And as Plato had done with his *Republic,* Max strives to make his dissertation a work of art, too, illustrating the conflicting tendencies in Plato's thought instead of merely explaining them. Max takes his cue from the two dialogues that exemplify the opposing sides of Plato's battle: the *Gorgias,* according to which the pleasant needs to be pursued for the sake of the good, and the *Protagoras,* in which the good is only meaningful dependent on the pleasure it generates or the pain it avoids. Then Max constructs a dialogue between the two books, as if they were two people talking. If his theory were right, asks *Gorgias,* would not all things be valuable that satisfy "the will of a baboon"? Bring in whatever animal you like, responds *Protagoras,* coolly. Desire is what introduces value into the world. Even stones have needs: they "desire to get near the earth, and the only time you need be afraid of them is when you get between them and what they desire." Human beings are at once minds and bodies, angels and baboons. Plato's failure to keep the angel separate from the baboon mirrors our own confusion, which is why he is ultimately not convincing, "just as we are never quite convinced by the world, which genially and eternally continues to lay before us its variety and disorder." Plato had *not* found the key to the world; what's more, he knew, "in his heart," that it couldn't be found.

Hence Max's redefinition of the point of philosophical inquiry. If we consider philosophy a journey, an ongoing conversation that never resolves anything at all, even a doctoral thesis like Max's "does not need to be apologized for," especially if it, Max adds wittily, "gave its author no pain in the birth" and does "no injury to anyone else." Traditionally, philosophers have focused on following their original scheme, avoiding all intellectual detours and coercing "every remark that is made" into conformity with their argument. Which is precisely what Max won't do. Just a few pages later, he abandons all pretense of an argument and launches into a fable in which some hypothetical observer looks down on the world as it once was, big and scary, with the elements raging. From the vantage point of his steep mountain, the man sees little creatures running around in it and using the mechanisms of their minds to combat the elements or, for that matter, to think up something like God or a "Divine Science." From the observer's mountaintop all ideas look the same—they are facts, like the weather. And if anyone should ask who that observer might be, why, says Max, he is one of those creatures too, as we all are, "running after the things we want, and blown one way or another by the wind."[115]

Max's dissertation thus carried in itself the seeds of its own destruction as an academic enterprise. But it was precisely that move that insured the writer's survival: "For if there is anyone whom the relentless flux of things and opinions in this world, will shipwreck and overwhelm, it is he who essays to pass through it with his mind intent upon abstractions and his body drawn up into his mind." Max, for one, hoped he would find a way of drawing his body *out* of his mind.[116]

As Max the male suffragette was taking off in new directions, Annis (fig. 14) worked to reassert her bond with him. "You are too much like me to shine *steadily*," she told him, with perhaps just a hint of malice. She, for one, could never be a "propagandist," since she was "always more than half convinced that I have no case." Did Max have one? Absent an abiding light in their

Figure 14. Annis Ford Eastman, 1908. *Cherith-Log*, 1904–1908.
EMIIA2.

lives, a distinct hope for a distinctly better future, what choice did Max and she have but to finish their jobs "until the bell rings for letting out?"[117]

Whether she knew it or not, the bell was about to ring for her. The year before, after years of digestive troubles and increasing problems with her circulation, she had subjected herself to a painful operation carried out by Dr. A. W. Booth of Elmira. Weeks of home care by nurses followed. The procedure left her feeling, as she noted with characteristic self-irony, "like a pancake that has risen too high and fallen."[118] Now, in January 1910, the operation had to be repeated, this time at the Arnold Ogden Hospital in Elmira. Anstice, who was working as a doctor at New York City Hospital on Blackwell's Island, a hospital for prisoners and the poor, was involved from the beginning. If the surgery was easier than the previous one, Annis now underwent a more difficult convalescence—nights racked with pain and days spent lying down. "Every few hours they do some hurting thing to me," she complained about her nurses.[119] During her ordeal she drew inspiration from reading Helen Keller, a person "with no sensations to speak of" who had overcome the limitations of her body.[120]

Annis's health remained precarious afterward. By April 1910 she was sick again, too sick to officiate at Mark Twain's funeral in April. In accordance with

Twain's wishes, the simple ceremony at the Elmira estate of the Langdons had consisted of nothing but Samuel Eastman's address and a brief prayer. "We are here to weep with those that weep," said Sam and went on to invoke the kinds of ties that had become so precarious in his own life, asking the assembled mourners of Twain "to give thanks with those whose own he was in the sacred bonds of human kinship and family affection."[121] Max made light of Annis's affliction, expressing his relief that she had given up her mad desire to walk upright: "Parenthetically, I can't refrain from wondering if God, with all the images he had before him, could possibly have *chosen* to be a biped. I don't see how anybody but a fool could really *want* to stand on his hind legs. It makes me doubt the whole story." The subtext was that Annis, being ill, had joined the circle of all those who spend their lives lying mostly on their backs, a group of which the ailing Max had become a member years ago. In reality, though, Max was broken-hearted that Annis had missed her opportunity to celebrate a truly great man, someone from the days when heroes counted for something and not everyone was bent on showing "social consciousness." Max himself was a "grief-stricken baby" over Twain's death: "I loved him so."[122]

In one of her last long letters to Max a mortified Annis reported that she had misplaced Max's Plato essay-turned-dissertation, which she had been planning to read. "I have *not* the ms. of your thesis!" What an awful blow to her as well as Max! "It convinces me that I am not *fit for affairs* anymore. I must find a little hole somewhere and creep into it." Would Max have to write it over or else lose his degree? "Just think of your having to remember such a thing as that about me all my life!" Annis complained about "the mountain of blue tension" that was weighing on her. Dimly she was aware of a "real thing" that was coming her way.[123]

On October 22, 1910, a heartbreakingly beautiful day, that thing came, and it was terrifyingly real.[124] Annis suffered a stroke, and her dramatic death struggle—not that she had lost her son's manuscript, which in any case turned up within a week—stuck with Max for a lifetime. For forty-eight hours Annis fought to stay alive, making sounds Max remembered as "loud and raucous and resistless as the detonations of an airplane motor."[125] It seemed to Max that few bodies would have fought so hard for survival as Annis's did. The woman who had spent her life as a minister trying to control her body, to forget that she even had one, in death had become nothing but body, a pumping, sputtering, noisy machine. The tireless suffragette Annis Ford Eastman, perhaps one of the smartest American women of her time and certainly in the state of New York, died—and this is precisely what she had feared—before she had been allowed to vote.[126]

Annis's death left the family stricken. The most direct, most moving statement came, many months after the event, not from Max but from Crystal: "All these days since it happened," she wrote to Max, "I have thought of Mamma and realized that she is dead almost every hour."[127] She was longing for Max to be with her. But sorrow is a lonely business. In a pattern of behavior that would repeat itself again and again when people close to him died, Max did not know just what to say about his own feelings.

Annis's miserable end threw into turmoil Crystal's plans for the future, which included getting married to a handsome insurance salesman named Wallace Benedict from Milwaukee, "Bennie" for short. Suddenly, staying with Max seemed more important. "Getting back to N.Y. and living with you was the hope I fed my drooping spirits on—not Milwaukee and the married state," she wrote. But Max insisted she give marriage a try—if she couldn't stand it, she'd know it was not because of him, a suggestion Crystal said gave her "humorous courage." Perhaps, said Crystal, virtually admitting the true nature of their relationship even as she made fun of it, "after we've both experimented around for a few years—we may end up living together again. That's a delightful alternative to the story book end—'and they lived happily together forever after.' "[128]

4 · The Flea from Tangier

Seven months after Annis's traumatic death, on May 5, 1911, Crystal did marry Wallace Benedict. Although her father had been expecting it, the wedding hit him "awfully hard." Samuel Eastman was, as Max heard, "feeling blue" about having been left out. Max reassured him by saying he had extended "a family blessing" to them, the last vestige of the religious routines of his childhood. But he himself had an even bigger surprise in store for "Daddie."[1]

Crystal had introduced Ida Rauh to Max in 1907. Six years older than Max, Ida was a determined, fearless woman with a big, triangular face, penetrating eyes, prominent cheekbones, and a full head of dark hair. Physically she was quite the opposite of Max's mother. Her friends thought she resembled the lions outside the New York Public Library.[2] She wore, as the writer Robert ("Bob") Carleton Brown remembered, the first horn-rimmed glasses ever glimpsed in Greenwich Village.[3] Trained as a lawyer, Ida had been the secretary of the Women's Trade Union League, an organization intended to educate women about the benefits of trade union membership. It was Ida, not Dewey, who introduced Max to the writings of Marx and Engels, perhaps in the hope that dialectical materialism offered a way out of the dislike of philosophical systems he had formed under Dewey. Max later insisted that even then he recognized the quasi-religious nature behind Marx's and Engels's confidence that the future would unfold the way they wanted it to: "I found them cloudy and couched in an idiom alien to my kind." (His kind: the Columbia "professor" of philosophy.) Although Marx and Engels called their doctrine scientific socialism, they obviously did not know what science was. But what he liked about their approach was that it offered a method for revolutionary change. As a hypothesis to be verified in action, socialism made sense.[4]

Before he got any further in his study of Marxism, Max verified another hypothesis in action by marrying Ida. He later speculated on the effects that his early "psychological impotence," the crippling performance anxiety he felt whenever he was with a girl, might have had on his life.[5] There is indeed reason to believe that at the time of his wedding Max was, at least technically, a virgin.[6] That was both good and bad—good in the sense that years of repression had finally, finally come to an end; bad in that Ida unwittingly and ultimately to her detriment opened a whole new world of sexual satisfaction to him, from which, at least for Max, there was no turning back. They were married in Paterson, New Jersey, on May 4, 1911. Max did not mention the wedding to anybody, especially not his father. The morning after the ceremony, he regretted his decision. He felt the course of his life had been irrevocably altered: "I had lost, in marrying Ida, my irrational joy in life."[7] The horror over the mistake he had made overshadowed the trip to Europe, a kind of honeymoon, on which the couple almost immediately embarked, boarding the *Königin Louise* for Gibraltar on May 6.

Max did everything to hide the fact that he was now married. The note written on the eve of his departure for Europe, while he was still in New York, is remarkably evasive and refers only to Crystal's recent union with Bennie. "There was nothing for them to do, but get married," Max wrote to Sam and tried to console him. "I hope you caught a little of the spirit of love and youth and simplicity of purpose with which they went and did it. I am so *happy* over them. I sail away joyfully—though with lingering and always returning sadness, as you know." Almost as an afterthought he added, "Ida is going on the same boat with me, so you can think I will not be weeping—Max." Crystal, now in Milwaukee, did suspect that her beloved brother had taken the plunge, too, although she wasn't sure: "Of course it doesn't make a difference, but it would have been fun to know." The new "strange wives and husbands" weren't going to pull them apart anyway. Crystal was imagining some utopian free-for-all where they could all live together, according to "some Seneca Lake plan with a few children playing around." If she was thinking of the Seneca Lake prophetess Jemima Wilkinson, she probably didn't realize that the latter's plan had included complete sexual abstinence.[8]

Bound for Europe, Max seemed determined to treat the fact of his marriage as entirely incidental. En route to Gibraltar he took refuge in marathon sleeping ("I haven't had a thought or made a voluntary motion since we started") and got some perverse satisfaction out of the fact that he hadn't seen any whales, though everyone else had: "I missed the whale. Of course, I missed the whale," he told Sam in a letter sent from Gibraltar. "I was asleep. Everybody else saw him. And nobody wants to talk to me anymore. That's one good thing about missing a whale." He included the descriptions of scenery he thought Sam would have expected (the Azores looked, he wrote, more "like magnified lichens on an old log than real vegetation") and closed his letter with another reference to sleep: "With which apt description of the natural scenery I lapse into my normal state of somnolent disregard for everything I came to see."[9] No mention of Ida.

That changed once Max got to Tangier, that mad mix of all the cultures in the world, a city both Mediterranean and distinctly African, where the painter Eugène Delacroix had once discovered a symphony of colors that would preoccupy him for the rest of his life. On letterhead of the Hotel Cavilla in Morocco, a place Crystal would stay at just two years later, Max shared the news with Sam: "You will not be surprised now that Ida and I are married" (fig. 15). He had written to Crystal and Anstice, too. However, he warned Sam, "I don't

Figure 15. Hotel Cavilla, Tangier. "Doesn't that make you feel homesick, old boy?"
From postcard sent by Crystal Eastman to Max Eastman, March 18, 1913. Schlesinger
Library, Radcliffe Institute, Harvard University.

even want to think of it as 'settling down' and all the rest of the ideas I don't like." Ida regarded their marriage as casually as he did and was going to keep her name "in all relations in which it is possible." Sam was welcome to think of them as "crazy birds." But Ida and he were very happy.[10] Sam was so shaken by Crystal's wedding that he took Max's news calmly, though with a certain degree of bewilderment: why on earth did his two younger children insist on not being married even though they were? But then he resigned himself, said Crystal, to "not understanding."[11]

Max's happiness with Ida remained an assertion rather than a self-evident fact. Tangier proved to be a strange backdrop for their torturous honeymoon. "No imagination would paint the colors, no imagination could add" to the sights and sounds one saw and heard in this city. It seemed as if one had stepped right into scenes from the Bible: "Moses holds the stirrup for you, and Elijah beats your mule from behind." At night Max lay awake listening to the city. Once he got up and pocketed a small gun—where he got it he doesn't mention—and lost himself in the streets: "You can imagine the excitement, parting those cowled figures that resented me," he wrote to his father, "much more excitement than the situation called for really." But *could* Sam imagine it? Max described how, in a state of nervous ecstasy, he pushed his way past the veiled bodies that thronged Tangier even at night. His blood rushing and his heart beating to the accompaniment of drums, the wailing tunes, he found his way to a rooftop garden somewhere, full of fragrance and beauty. A nightingale was singing, while in the city below the muezzins on their minarets began chanting their *adhan,* or call to prayer. At home, Ida was asleep.[12]

The longest of Max's letters from abroad, as it turns out, dealt with—a flea. Writing from Sorrento on June 19, 1911, in a long epistle that looked more like a draft of a short story than an actual letter, Max recounted his travels not with Ida but with a pesky insect he had "taken in" at Tangier. When he first saw the flea, it was in the middle of the night, and Max, who claimed he had never seen or dealt with such an animal, was convinced he had killed it: "I squeezed him between my fingers until he was flat, and then I set him on a smooth board in the floor and rolled him. I didn't bury him. I just left him there when he was dead and went back to bed." Imagine, then, Max's surprise the next morning when he woke up and, glancing at the board, "just to make sure of my night's work," found the flea gone. As Max was just about to learn, to his infinite dismay, endeavoring to kill a flea was an incentive to the animal rather than a deterrent: "He likes you all the better for it."

Over the next few days Max's personal flea survived multiple other attempts on its life, such as the application of ammonia; being talked at in a frantic voice ("they will never hear you out"); and the violent shaking out of the window of "every rag and scrap of goods that I or the room possessed." Nothing worked. The resilient flea followed Max across the Mediterranean to Naples and now to Sorrento, where Max spotted it sitting on the mattress, getting ready for his day's work: "I peeled off my coat and dove into that mattress like a dog after a wood-chuck, tore through a large pile of bed-clothes and pillows, wiped the spring, scoured the bed-stead, moved the bed away and scrutinized about ten square feet of floor, tearing up the carpet as I went—But no good. He was just gone." When Max got ready to put his coat on again, there the flea was, sitting on his lapel! Max tiptoed back to the window, and, with a jubilant shout, "snapped the thing way out in the open air clear of the house about six times the way you would snap a whip. Then I brought it back, with a sigh of almost divine satisfaction and laid it over the back of a chair." As Max's coattails came into view, so did the flea, apparently unharmed. Max dangled the coat out the window again, holding it upside down, at arm's length, and slowly unfolding it as he continued to shake it, as vigorously as he could. For just a moment Max thought he got a glimpse of the flea as it was tumbling out of the coat. But experience had taught him not only to double-check but also to shed his clothes: "That, by the way, is the only way an experienced sportsman will go flea-hunting—naked. It's the only safe way and the only profitable way. It's the only way you can be sure whether you're hunting him or he's hunting you."

A careful inspection of body and room yielded no signs of the wretched flea. Max got dressed, putting on a new set of clothes. But as he was just about ready to tie his shoes, the flea reappeared, sitting on his pant leg as if it had always been there: "For a moment I couldn't move. I just looked at him. And he jumped." The flea was gone. But was it? As Max resumed his shoe tying, there the flea sat, in exactly the same spot! Resigned to accepting it into his life, Max went to dinner, joining a "highly attractive and respectable" family from Naples that had arrived the week before. And lo and behold, something unbelievable happened. When the dinner was done, the flea was gone, too. "While writing this I feel alone for the first time in a month." Far be it from him to pry into the affairs of that highly respectable family from Naples. But the moral of the flea story was clear: "There is only one way in this world to get rid of a flea—Be sociable!"[13]

Nowhere in the story, one of the most extensive, self-contained ones ever told in Max's letters, is there any mention of Ida, and the resolution it offers (Max's jubilant embrace of solitude after a month of enforced companionship) is hardly what one would expect from a newlywed. The reader is tempted to attach a different moral to the tale of the flea that made Max's travels so miserable. If the point of sociability is the sharing of vermin, then being alone (as opposed to being married?) emerges as the supreme goal of one's life. Max's flea story is the opposite of John Donne's tongue-in-cheek tribute to the flea swollen "with one blood made of two," a place "where we almost, yea more than married are."[14]

Another text about animals conceived during Max's Italian sojourn, the sonnet "At the Aquarium," offers a different glimpse of his complicated inner state. In Naples, Max and Ida visited the Stazione Zoologica, the public aquarium created by the German zoologist Anton Dohrn, and were impressed by the large tanks filled with water pumped in from the bay. Illuminated only by the sunlight streaming in from above, the Stazione's aquaria were lined with volcanic rock from Mount Vesuvius. In this dusklike setting visitors would look straight at the fish, at eye level, as if they were in fact with them at the bottom of the sea. The first two lines of the poem Max composed on the spot, at the Stazione, whereas the rest of the sonnet came to him when he was back in New York in a room he had rented, apart from his family, so he could concentrate on his poetry. There he tranquilly recollected the emotion he once had in Naples, staring through the glass at a world he found surprisingly similar to his own. Despite the nod to Wordsworth, this was hardly a sublime experience:

> Serene the silver fishes glide,
> Stern-lipped, and pale, and wonder-eyed;
> As through the agèd deeps of ocean,
> They glide with wan and wavy motion!
> They have no pathway where they go,
> They flow like water to and fro.
> They watch with never winking eyes,
> They watch with staring, cold surprise,
> The level people in the air,
> The people peering, peering there,
> Who wander also to and fro,
> And know not why or where they go,
> Yet have a wonder in their eyes,
> Sometimes a pale and cold surprise.[15]

The poem's overriding sensation is coldness. Its serenity comes from the absence of emotion, an effect achieved by making the reader view the world as a fish would, which, like water, goes where it must, not where it wants to go. The "wonder[ing]" eyes in the final couplet are those of the people, not of the fish, but at that point identities are so blurred it doesn't really matter. Where humans, from the point of view of the fish, look surprisingly like fish, all that is left for us to feel is, indeed, a "pale and cold surprise." It is no longer clear who is inside or outside the tank. The glass of the aquarium wall becomes a mirror of sorts. The "wonder" conjured by Max's sonnet has nothing wonderful about it, as the speaker is asking a question that he fears the fish have already answered. "At the Aquarium" became Max's most reprinted poem.

With fleas and fish as his companions, Max found little pleasure in the usual pursuits of the tourist. In Florence he paid dutiful tribute to the "greatness of the great pictures" he saw, but what really excited him was the fresh milk he was able to drink there. Not for him the sparkling wine of the Italians, who were, incidentally, ignorant enough to boil their milk as soon as it came out of the cow. "O for a beaker full of the warm cow!" That was, Max joked, his "hymn for about two months, as Ida will more than testify." Here, finally, Ida shows up in his correspondence, if only parenthetically. And just as Max asserted—much to his father's delight—his rural credentials ("I'm really a country clod"), he mentioned Ida's artistic inclinations, which were "to surpass the books." But Ida's artistic bent was, he observed not without malice, more than offset by her "fanatical devotion to the five-cent moving picture show." They virtually hadn't skipped "a single available cinematograph since we struck Naples," and now they knew all the latest popular dramas in Europe. It appears that Max was very much trying to represent himself as one of Twain's innocents abroad. The landscapes of Italy, including the "famous lakes" (Como, Lugano, Maggiore), weren't really beautiful—where, oh where were the meadows and "amiable trees" he knew from home? It was all "scene-painting" to him, no reason to linger anywhere. "It is nowhere the big rough natural pure earth with reality of life in it." Venice they skipped. And after visiting Milan, he felt ever more drawn to Glenora.

Sam had done Max a particular favor by addressing a letter to both of them ("Dear Max, dear Ida too"), making him hopeful his father would finally come around to his view of the marriage question. "Dad, maybe you'll understand me better if I say that I straight out disbelieve in and dislike marriage, the whole idea, significance, consequence, and specific result of it." What he wanted was friendship, and no artificial ceremony could generate that or, for that matter, ensure that love would last if it wasn't meant to be. In one of his letters Sam had mistakenly assumed they had gotten married at Sorrento—but what did it

matter? As long as one could laugh about such things and make fun of the irrelevance of such rituals, there was hope, "for it is laughter or disgust with me."
Max ended his letter by asking his father not to forget to water his garden: "I
don't want Glenora to be all dried up when Ida comes! Please pour on water!"[16]

All in all, Max's reports from what he strenuously avoided calling his honeymoon leave the reader with a more than ambivalent picture of his marriage-
that-wasn't-one. The enforced looseness of their arrangement had backfired
almost as soon as it had been accomplished, and Max seemed set on *not* enjoying Europe—whether he was out, revolver in his pocket, courting danger in
Tangier, killing a flea in Sorrento, or spurning Italian wine in Florence. While
Ida, restricted to a cameo appearance in Max's letters home, discovered the
delights of early European cinema, Max hankered after the meadows and cows
of Glenora. Having alienated his father by not including him in his marriage
plans, he now was doing his best to assure him of his continuing loyalty to the
pastures of home, as if his marriage had never happened. The happiness their
casual marriage bond was supposed to ensure was conspicuously absent from
Max's letters, smothered by all the defensive rhetoric Max employed to justify
something he had claimed needed no justification. If the idea of marriage
disgusted or amused him, why engage in it at all? Max was about to find out
that mere resistance against an institution didn't do away with the power of
that institution itself, as long as one adhered to its rituals.

On the way back from Europe, Max's insomnia came back. He was wandering the deck at night, the reluctant prodigal son returning to a father who had
never much wanted to be included yet felt left out when he really wasn't.

After their return, the young couple set up residence in Glenora, where Ida
embarked on a new career as a sculptor. She transformed a leaky shed, affectionately christened Barneycastle for reasons long lost to history, into a studio
of sorts and was soon gathering local children around her as potential models.
Somewhat to Max's surprise and Sam's delight Ida appeared to embrace the
challenges of the rural life and was not above hauling groceries from the train
station in a wheelbarrow. Her slips and one-piece bathing suits brought the
sophistication of Village life to rural New York (fig. 16). At the same time,
given her willingness to lend a hand whenever necessary, no one could accuse
her of haughtiness.[17]

Crystal and her insurance salesman husband Bennie came for a couple of
weeks. Crystal had found a modicum of fulfillment in working for women's
rights in Wisconsin, but she had continued to "ache" for Max, his place in her

Figure 16. Ida Rauh, 1911. *Cherith-Log,* 1911. EMIIA2.

heart not getting smaller but bigger "as I go on learning things."[18] The visit was a great success from the perspective of Crystal herself, who found it "as completely happy a time as I have ever had." Wasn't it great that the four of them all got along so well?[19] Perhaps Crystal was telling herself and Max these things hoping that the mere act of saying them would somehow *make* them true. Perhaps she was also relieved to see Max married and therefore rendered forever inaccessible to her. In a letter written a month later she spoke of her "half-sad yearnings" for Max, her wish that she'd done more for him when they were still living together—coded language, perhaps?[20] As Ida was still trying to fit in, Max was increasingly getting distracted by the ghosts of his past and, more particularly, by the enticing figure of Ruth Pickering. Max was proud that he was still the smartest kid in the neighborhood, able to beat everyone around him at Twenty Questions. His new brother-in-law was especially impressed when Max was able to guess, in eighteen questions, the word "fourscore" from Lincoln's Gettysburg speech. Noted Bennie: "That's going some."[21]

After Ida and Max established themselves in their first joint New York apartment, they put her name first on the mailbox, as Ida Rauh, not Mrs. Eastman. Their unconventional union unleashed a storm of prurient curiosity and public comments in the press, from the *New York World* to the *Elmira Star-Gazette,* which quoted the pastor of Elmira's First Methodist Church with the plea that "every man's hand be raised" against "the entrance of this serpent of lust and falsehood." Sam Eastman, who had moved beyond his initial disappointment over having been left out of the marital plans of his younger children, tried to help Max by preaching a sermon advocating the complete equality of men and women, pointing out that if one took the Bible literally, one would have to assume that God had recommended polygamy as the way for men and women to live together.[22]

According to the *World*, Ida viewed their marriage-that-wasn't-one as a mere "placating of convention." If they hadn't done it, it would have hindered their work. "It seems to me that the world should be interested in the work people are doing, what they are, not whether they are bound by a legal tie or not, but as people choose to interest themselves in that tie, we are willing to conform and satisfy them." When asked if hers was a trial marriage, Ida responded tartly that everything in life was a trial. If the reporter meant, however, that there was a time limit for it, "I should answer, decidedly not." She simply wanted to be with Max, and he with her, and to live "naturally" together. Max, who was also interviewed for the article, pointed out that Ida ("my wife," he called her) works "just as regularly at the Women's Trade Union League for the things she is interested in as she did before her marriage." When the reporter asked whether or not that conflicted with her duties at home, Max asserted that if men were able to carry on their work without being charged with neglecting their homes, women should enjoy the same right. And Ida left the reporter with a memorable image: "Women were not born with pans tied around their necks and a sign that it was their destiny to wash them."[23]

The *New York World* article referred to Max as a "professor of Philosophy at Columbia," but that was wishful thinking at best. In truth, Max was unemployed. "I reckon you'll have to work for a living when you get back," Crystal had observed, somewhat acidly, in a letter sent to him while he was still traveling.[24] But Max was more interested in finishing his book on poetry. To that end, he rented—from what funds was unclear—a small farmhouse in Waterford, Connecticut, as a summer retreat. It was there that Sam came to visit him. Even he was impressed by how remote the couple's new home was, reachable only via a narrow road with mullein, yarrow, and chokecherry growing wild beside it. The 150-year-old house was right next to an inlet opening up to the wide, endless ocean: "Here they were living by themselves cozy as kittens in a basket, not a house in sight barring the spiritualist camp across the inlet." Max had already built his own diving tower, from where, when the tide was in, he could jump headfirst into ten or twelve feet of water.[25]

While Max was out at the inlet diving or working on his book, Ida was, "rather unexpectedly," producing a baby. In his recollection of that summer,

Max almost made a show of his indifference toward fatherhood, expressing, among other things, his hope that, as a consequence of the new addition, his duties as a husband might be lessened: "I dreamed fitfully, as many a fondly expectant father has, that a fine, bouncing baby, by diverting a portion of its mother's libido, might make me less precisely a husband."[26] But Ida's love for Max, despite her growing awareness that her husband's commitment to her was a lackluster one, remained undiminished. In a touching little poem written during the summer at Waterford, when she was carrying Max's child, she surrounded her husband with an almost mythical aura. His deep mind contained, she wrote, all that makes up souls in other, conventional people. Her Max is an almost primeval force, striding on toward a future she fears might not include her. Max's extracurricular interests in all women not his wife are represented by the smiles he plants in the hearts of all those ready to receive them. Left behind are the truth-seekers, the ponderers, the fearful ones—in other words, people like Ida Rauh:

> Sending swift smiles deep into hearts of those who
> Have a waiting Eye to catch the beams of light
> A heart that searches for the vibrant truth,
> Look toward me twice so I may be assured
> That you and I are more than passers-by.[27]

Perhaps Max was flattered by the image of his alter ego moving so confidently forward on the road of life. He obviously liked the poem, so much so that he copied it and stuffed it in an envelope marked with the words: "Ida's Love." If Max's marriage was destined to fail, it was not for want of effort on Ida's part.

While he was at Waterford Max received an invitation to become the new editor of the *Masses,* a bolt out of the blue. "No pay," the note said, written in brush by the artist John Sloan. The founder of the magazine, the Dutchman Piet Vlag, had moved to Florida and left it in the hands of an outstanding group of artists and writers, including Sloan and Art Young, Charles and Alison Beach Winter, and Maurice Becker as well as Louis Untermeyer, Mary Heaton Vorse, and Inez Haynes Gillmore. Max wasn't too excited about the "yellow" version of socialism and do-goodism the *Masses* seemed to espouse. But he couldn't help but be impressed by the fact that the magazine was cooperatively owned. He probably also realized it would take his mind off his other problems as he was reluctantly sliding into married life. And even as a boy he had admired Young, combing through the comic weeklies to find drawings by him. Appropriately, it was Young who, after a dinner with Max at a Turkish restaurant on Lexington Avenue, had identified Max to his colleagues as a likely prospect for the position of editor.[28] Here, finally, was Max's chance to embrace a life of action rather than continuing to marinate in his own stale poetic juices; here was his invitation to become a "full-sized man."[29]

Max was proud that his editorship led to a reinvention of the magazine, in intent as well as design. The *Masses* had been "a mild voice speaking mainly for the cooperative," he wrote in an autobiographical fragment. "I transformed it into a voice of the revolutionary class struggle."[30] This wasn't too far from the truth. Max's first editorial in the first issue under his leadership trumpeted a "radical change of policy" and asked for the cooperation of readers: "We are going to make THE MASSES a *popular* Socialist magazine—a magazine of pictures and lively writing." The plan was to stay out of fractious political debates ("We are opposed to the dogmatic spirit which creates and sustains these disputes") and instead to exemplify what other magazines only preach: "Life as a whole from a Socialist standpoint."[31] The fusion of illustration and text, of fact, fiction, and poetry, made the *Masses* the embodiment of a better, more exciting future, a utopian one perhaps, but one that was just within reach.

The bohemian journalist John ("Jack") Reed, soon to be arrested for his work with the silk strikers of Paterson, New Jersey, joined the staff and spurred Max on to an even more radical redefinition of the magazine's politics. The *Masses* would be, announced Max in the second issue, "a revolutionary and not a reform magazine; a magazine with no dividends to pay; a free magazine; frank, arrogant, impertinent, searching for the true causes; a magazine directed against rigidity and dogma wherever it is found; printing what is too naked or true for a moneymaking press; a magazine whose final policy is to do as it pleases and conciliate nobody, not even its readers."[32] If one listened closely, there were overtones of Whitman in this description: the poet sauntering through his city, speaking the password primeval, allowing the "dumb words" of the masses to resonate through him. Conventional magazine art, Max explained in a little book he called *Journalism Versus Art,* was "business art," focused on knowledge, not on experience, upon "ease of recognition" rather than on the more difficult process of making their individual vision available to the viewer. The same was true of magazine writing, produced so that its author may *make a living* and not so he and his readers may *live* and embrace life. His publication was different. To him, the *Masses* would herald precisely the "deeper change" in magazine culture Max felt ought to happen: it offered a place for the "best talents of the country" to come together and present their individual perspectives on life, politics, and culture, free from the pressures of an "insanely competitive market."[33]

Over the next few years, editing the *Masses* would take up all Max's time. "Mr. Eastman is not robust physically," warned the veteran publisher E. W. Scripps, in a note to Max's patroness, the California millionaire and supporter of radical causes Kate Crane Gartz. "His nervous system is such that it should not and cannot safely be submitted to the strains inevitably attendant on such a business as the publication of 'The Masses.' " Calling Max a maker of the "finest literature," he cautioned that his "excellencies and his finest qualities are just those which unfit him for the task he has imposed upon himself."[34] But that statement was spectacularly untrue. Max as an editor was an inspired choice, for several reasons. It was his ear for linguistic nuance, his insistence on rigorous artistic standards as well as beauty of execution, his considerable charisma, the aura of inscrutability he cultivated (no one could ever be entirely sure what he thought), and the none-too-trivial fact that he was himself beautiful that made him so well-suited to reconcile the many diverse interests that had attached themselves to the magazine and to be an effective fund-raiser with wealthy, left-leaning donors.[35]

Gone was the mediocre mix of kindly feeling and genteel socialism that had characterized the previous *Masses*. Every issue offered an explosive mix of good writing and art. Some of the names, including Jack London, Upton Sinclair, Sherwood Anderson, Art Young, George Bellows, and Boardman Robinson, have weathered the vicissitudes of literary and artistic fashion, while others are forgotten, often unjustifiably so. The rambling book reviews of the magazine's managing editor Floyd Dell, the sharp commentary of the anthropologist Elsie Clews Parsons, the fiery, in-your-face articles of John Reed against war ("And you, gentle reader, will be the first to get shot") helped create a publication unlike anything Americans had seen before.[36]

Inevitably, Max's writing changed, too, although he did stay true to his aversion to dogma. In a March 1913 column for the *Masses* he staged a conversation between himself and an unknown acquaintance riding with him on the subway who wanted to know what he was: A Party Member? A Syndicalist? A Direct Actionist? A Sabotist? A Laborist? Industrialist? Anarchist? Invariably his answer was, "O no!" He was, he said at the end of the little article, a "Get-offist," which he defined as someone who was "going to get off at this station."[37] But invariably, too, he had to take positions both in and beyond the magazine, positions that went beyond a noble support for letting women take part in the democratic process. There was no getting off at the next station when matters of life and death, such as workers' rights or a looming European war, were about to be discussed. In May 1913 Max addressed the striking silk workers in Paterson as "the most important people in the world" and declared categorically that "the people who wear the silk have got to work just as hard as those people that make it."[38] It was his hope that the struggle for women's rights and labor rights could be merged. A year later, at a meeting in Cooper Union, when asked to define what feminism was to him, he reiterated his support for workers, distancing himself from what he called the "Middle Class Idealists." There was, he said, "more real feminism in Paterson, New Jersey last spring than all New York and Greenwich Village put together ever dreamed of."[39]

Personally, Max's life was getting more complicated, too. Daniel Eastman's birth on September 6, 1912, in a New York hospital, bewildered rather than exhilarated his father. An unpublished poetic sketch comments on Max's jaundiced view of procreation and presents a Darwinian view of underwater life in which things perish almost as soon as they get born. Once again Max is descending into the world of slimy, fishy things to find analogies for his confusion:

> The net brings up, how long and languidly
> A million vivid quiverings of life.
> Keen-finned and gleaming like a steely knife,
> All colors, green and silver of the sea,
> All forms of skill and eagerness to be,—
> Who die and wither of the very breath
> That sounds your pity of their lavish death
> While they are leaping starlike to be free.

Like the fish, humans live to die, obliterated by their irrelevance among the thousands of births that have happened right before and will happen after theirs:

> They die and wither, but the aged sea,
> Insane old salty womb of mystery,
> Is pregnant with a million million more,
> Whom she will suckle in her oozy floor,
> Whom she will vomit on a heedless shore,
> As we were vomitted [sic] in days of yore.[40]

The ocean described in this poem was not Whitman's ancient crone rocking the cradle, humming words both seductive and beautiful, but the primal ooze uselessly spitting out one slimy thing after another.[41] The existence of his son mystified him, and although Max learned to become a somewhat better father than contemporaries and biographers have given him credit for, his embrace of parenthood remained lackluster throughout his life. Never convinced, in the words of the Philip Larkin poem, that "he should be added to," Max inwardly rebelled against the religious implications of fatherhood, the biblical "begat" and "begetting" that ascribed to sex a teleological purpose, a justification that superseded the mere pleasure of the act.[42] The irony of Max's life was that he would continue to stumble into the very arrangements he professed to despise: marriage, fatherhood, writing for money.

Perhaps more important for Max was another birth that took place a few months later, in June 1913, the publication of his first book, *Enjoyment of Poetry*, one of his most enduringly successful titles. The enjoyment of poetry Max wanted to impart was, first and foremost, his own enjoyment of it. Distancing himself from the scholars of poetry, Max said he wanted to restore poetry to its central place in everyday life. Poetry was not practical: "A man in the pressure of affairs bent upon taking life poetically, is like a mule trying to browse while he is driven." But that didn't mean that poetry exists in a distant realm, entirely removed from our daily concerns. Max was adamantly opposed to the barriers scholars had erected between ordinary readers and poetry as an elitist discourse. Instead of classifying images as metaphors or metonymies, he distinguished between figures that merely illuminate and those that move us away from the subject of the comparison and push us in new directions. "I am poured out like water" (Psalm 22:14) was an example of the former, while "The Lord is my shepherd" served Max as an example of the latter, because here the Lord is almost forgotten in the pastoral idyll. While poetry does not ask us to change our life, it enhances and heightens it. It allows us, wrote Max, to experience emotions for their own sake, something the ancient writers understood better than the moderns who are so eager to produce important works that they risk being misunderstood by their readers. Not so Virgil or Theocritus: "We take delight in this free-hearted poetry as we might in the rippling of a stream where it spreads out among little stones." Poetry is the poet's gesture toward the world. It gives presence and power and physical reality to ideas and yet also points beyond them, at something that lies outside the "poet's chamber." True poetry runs "along the verge of infinity."[43]

While Max was willing to grant poems their music—their physical, tangible reality—he did not want to make poetry into an event by itself, an experience superior to the lower-level experience it is supposed to portray. If you wish to compose poetry, let the words flow the way the waves do, remembering that each word, made new by you, enters alive and vivid into the stream that constitutes the enjoyment of poetry—of the poetry of life, that is. The rapturous last pages of Max's book combine Whitmanian fervor with an earnestness that must have come naturally to the lapsed son of a minister: "The poet, the restorer, is the prophet of a greater thing than faith. All creeds and theories serve him, for he goes behind them all, and imparts by a straighter line from his mind to yours the spirit of bounteous living." Awakening readers to the untapped reservoir of joy inside them is Max's avowed goal: "A world laughs and bleeds for us all the time"—the world of poetry—"but our response in this meteoric theatre we suffer to be drugged with business and decorum." The final paragraph of the book, which celebrates man's return "to his rights as an animal," was a riff on the praise Whitman, in "Song of Myself," had lavished on the animals that do not "whine about their condition" and do not weep for their sins or "lie awake at night . . . discussing their duty to God."[44]

Crystal was utterly absorbed in the book, she told Max, and she found herself thinking about it even when she was not actively reading it: "It makes me cry not to be a poet." Hearing Max hold forth on poetry was like going back to school again. She was crazy about his ideas and wondered how he could have kept them to himself for so long: "I think you're probably the first poet with a really analytical mind. That's why you can take poetry & explain it with the result that the explanation instead of taking the life out of the poetry—puts life into it." Unlike other writers on poetry Max had written a book that appealed to the reader's intelligence as well as to his or her more visceral impulses. Crystal was now finding poetry everywhere and, most important, wanted to write it herself. Max was "a great boy, as Anstice would say."[45]

In Glen Allen, California, Jack London showed himself similarly energized. There was none of the usual balderdash in *Enjoyment,* none of the "absurd notions about poetry" he had encountered elsewhere. What he had found in Max's *Enjoyment* was good common sense as well as "delicacy and distinction."[46] Generations of readers agreed. In 1961 the book was in its twenty-fifth printing and had been, as Max boasted in an interview, selling "at the rate of about one every two days for almost 50 years."[47]

Staying behind in Glenora, taking care of her infant son while Max was in the city putting his magazine together, Ida tried to persuade herself she was made for the role of the stay-at-home mother. But things were harder than she expected. Some letters from those early weeks when she was trying to adjust to her new life have survived: small sheets filled with her large scrawl, folded into tiny envelopes that would have just fit into her hand as she carried them to the train station to be dispatched. So there she was, on a warm morning in late June, wistfully watching from her porch as Max left for the city, scanning the fields for signs of him for as long as she could, even though it was only hay she was able to see: "I went to the side of the porch where the wisteria is growing and between the tops of the vines I could see a stretch of the road, first about opposite Henderson's, and there you were, and then I thought I could see a piece beyond again but no it was just the field, yellow with hay and not the road at all." The so-called pleasures of the country life could not reconcile her to the fact that she felt abandoned by him: "I miss you, miss you, miss you, miss you, miss you. Last night just after you went, Glenora seemed bare and ugly—truly it did. It was an absolutely new aspect, just for a few minutes and then minutes lapped over again in the past and it was the same again only awful empty." Hers was not the Glenora of the carefree summer revels Max had known since his young adulthood. Too small to be company, Daniel had not "voiced any heroic sentiment yet for me to repeat" (fig. 17). Ida found herself imagining all the places Max went to in the city: "Please write about everywhere you go—so I can follow you about with my mind's eye and *don't* be rash or careless." Composing her little notes, sometimes several a day, gave her a vicarious sense of participating in Max's "other" life. By making her accounts intentionally "stupid" she hoped to force him to be similarly literal in his writing and tell her everything he did while he was away: "I only want to tell you everything as it happens, so that you will do the same. . . . I have the same feeling one has waiting for a train—patience and a feeling of forced self-control because it won't help to hurry events if you fret. Anyway don't stay longer than you have to."[48]

To Ida, mailing these notes from Glenora was no casual affair. They had to be written fast, when the baby was down for one of his infrequent naps, for example, and she had to run them down to the station in time for the daily mail pickup. But such trips were a welcome distraction on days when picking peas in the garden and watching little Daniel trying to sit up by himself were the absolute highlights. On her envelopes she wrote, "special delivery," wishing that this instruction would have "some occult influence on the postman" and make him carry her words faster to him.

The picture of her marriage that emerges from the letters Ida wrote during the first summer of her son's life differs markedly from the one Max gave his readers when he remembered those days in his autobiography. They show Ida determined to put up with the discomforts of a life that had little to offer her: the house was drafty, the neighbors annoying, and, though Max hired a girl

Figure 17. Daniel Eastman, with nurse,
September 2, 1913. From *Cherith-Log*, 1911.
EMIIA2.

named Laura to assist her, she was largely left to her own devices with a new
baby that wasn't always easy to take care of. A "perversely" big baby, Daniel did
not feel the need to sleep during the day and seemed impervious to the tem-
peratures that soared to ninety-eight degrees. That said, Ida was certainly
proud that Max's work on the *Masses* was going so well: "You have done
wonders—It is because you are so sweet and just and patient and tolerant—
that has gone—I think you have made them all feel some of the same spirit of
mutual appreciation."[49] Max's letters to her she celebrated as if they were the
last ones she would ever get from him: "I read them first very hurriedly and
then I browse in them every little while, or nibble at them like a rabbit."[50]

In August 1913 Max's first volume of poetry, *Child of the Amazons*, appeared. The title poem, the product of Max's classical learning acquired at

Williams, he had begun years earlier during one of the wild Glenora summers when he was romping through the woods and rowing across the lake with lovely, wild-haired Muriel Bowman. It told the story of Thyone, who had defied Amazonian law by wishing to live with her lover, shirking the "enterprise of soldiery." Given to "languid talk," Thyone, at least at the beginning of the poem, is a poet, not a warrior, as the Queen of the Amazons observes: "Dost / Thou hope to whirl a spear with lovelorn muscle?" The Queen asks her to consult her heart, and Thyone reconsiders, bidding farewell to "Romance, idle, sweet, and transitory" but not before reminding the Queen how she, like all other Amazons, had her baby torn from her, "a very little body like thine own," one she had touched and loved for his dimple and "the ring of blue between his half-wide lids." Ordered to cease her "woeful eloquence," Thyone once again commits herself to a "life of action upon God" and resolves to prove herself "equal to the world." Motherhood can wait:

> No Amazon shall enter motherhood
> Until she hath performed such deeds, and wrought
> Such impact on the energetic world,
> That thou canst it behold and name her thine.[51]

And no Max Eastman, dissatisfied as he was with his own accomplishments, should have entered fatherhood, Ida might have been tempted to add.

Certainly, the *Masses* was Max's chance to have an impact on the "energetic world." Throughout the volume, however, the alternative world of wild nature, represented especially by birds, from thrushes to meadowlarks to yellow-birds to Canada geese, is pitted against the always incomplete desires and schemes of humans. In "The Thought of Protagoras," a philosopher, characterized as "a man born regal to the realms of thought," is shot just as he is about to reveal the infinite Substance of which all other things are merely attributes. Max's "cold surprise"—a phrase from "At the Aquarium"—at the sobering realities of human life underlies the entire collection, despite the fact that it ends with a rather self-consciously optimistic tribute to a hero of action, Leif Ericson: "They sing thee, O Leif the Lucky, they sing thee sublime."[52]

If one bears in mind that 1913 was the year Ezra Pound's "A Few Don'ts by an Imagiste" appeared in Harriet Monroe's magazine *Poetry,* Max's early verse, with its labored images and "thous" and "thines," strikes one as mired in the poetic idioms of yesteryear. The reviewers were certainly puzzled that the co-founder of the Men's League for Woman Suffrage would be writing such contrived, traditional poetry. The Wellesley professor and Socialist Vida Scudder, who had come to Max's book fresh from supporting the striking textile workers in Lawrence, Massachusetts, admitted as much right at the outset of her review of *Child of the Amazons*. But she went on to suggest it was a good thing there was so "little social stress" in Max's poems. Max's new volume would help readers understand that a radical was "a very normal person" after all. As she saw it, his poetry could only benefit her fellow fighters in the cause of women's rights: "We rise from reading, emancipate [*sic*] and adventurous."[53]

Those on the other side of the political spectrum also found plenty that was political in Max's poems, although they viewed it differently. A writer for the *Minneapolis Journal*, for example, thought the title poem was nothing short of a call for the temporary elimination of men: "The upshot of the discussion seems to be that by the lockout method the belligerent ladies hope to bring about the perfect union of man and woman." The reviewer concluded, in a line showing more than ordinary wit, that Max's poetry was likely "to frighten father [i.e., men in general] half out of his wits."[54]

Vida Scudder's positive review did little to lift Max's spirits, especially after he learned that Crystal's former boyfriend Paul Kellogg had made her write it.[55] Throughout his life Max worried that he wasn't a real poet and that his concern with technique had pushed aside any genuine emotions he had wanted to express. The poetry notebooks he was keeping in the mid-1910s do show that Max did tone down such personal connections when he decided to publish a poem. A good example is "A Visitor," a poem not printed until a few years later, in Max's second volume of verse, *Colors of Life* (1918), and then under a new title ("A Visit"). With all the cross-outs restored, the poem depicts two human panthers mating, after the female, "hot and quiet," has roused the male into action:

> You came with your young body lithe and silent
> Like a panther to my den, where I
> Though powerful lay velvet in the shadows
> Sleeping, and you drew me like a magnet,
> Your slim muscles moving hot and quiet
> In the darkness drew me, till my veins
> Erect and burning woke me and I rose,
> And stole upon you like a panther, and
> You held me, and gave back your strength to mine.[56]

Was this the dream Ida couldn't fulfill for Max—the fantasy of a strong, desirous woman who would call forth his own desires in a sexual encounter?

A dream so scandalous that Max had to rewrite the poem for publication? "You came with your small tapering flame of passion" begins the revised version, in which the woman is little and snakelike, if still troublesome.

Ida's influence is visible in these notebooks in a more unexpected way, too: as a reader, cocreator, and editor of Max's work. For example, at the end of an untitled poem beginning "The timid morn lies quiet on the earth" we find the short but revelatory note, "Made for I. R. who supplied the first line and the feeling."[57] And another entry shows Ida correcting Max's language. For understandable reasons, "To My Maltine with Cod-Liver Oil," a tribute to the concoction that relieved Max from what one may assume was constipation, remained unpublished. Which, in a way, is a shame, because it points to a side of Max the poet not usually evident from the published record, namely, his capacity for humor:

> Foul-smelling flask of liquid glue
> I lift my lyre in praise of you!
> Fish-oil and bilge of salty beer,
> I give you hallelujah cheer!
> Of all the galled and greasy saints,
> And mangy angels, dressed in paints,
> And gods of wry and righteous face,
> Who've blessed my trouble-haunted race,
> And given their groaning guts relief
> Beyond all natural belief,
> You, vile concoction, are the chief![58]

The "hallelujah cheer" is a particularly appropriate and hilarious accompaniment to Max's bowel music. Interestingly, the adjective "trouble-haunted" in line eight was Ida's addition: she replaced Max's ponderous "idol-hunting" with a much funnier alternative.

Child of the Amazons, in conjunction with *Enjoyment of Poetry*, helped establish Max as a poet-philosopher of sorts, a public authority on subjects that extended beyond the issue of universal franchise. He was now represented by William B. Feakins in New York, who printed flyers showing an impeccably dressed Max wrapped in thought, next to an endorsement from none other than Woodrow Wilson himself: "His talk on humor was the most brilliant combination of thought and humor I have ever listened to." Blurbs on the reverse of the sheet ranged from the *Buffalo Express* ("He had his audience laughing almost from the outset") to his ex-girlfriend Inez Milholland, an authentic Amazon herself ("The idea of the woman of the future is best expressed by Max Eastman in his very beautiful poem, *Child of the Amazons*"). Max not only had something to say, potential clients were told, but he knew how to say it so that it mattered to the general public, while also keeping them entertained.

In the fall of 1915 Max published two highly visible articles in *Everybody's Magazine* in which he presented psychoanalysis as a quick and surefire method of coping with the challenges of everyday life—from failed relationships due to an excessive fixation on one's mother, to unexpected falls, to embarrassing slips of the tongue.[59] The spiffy illustrations accompanying the articles showed well-dressed people in more or less embarrassing situations, taking surprising falls, embarrassing themselves in relationships, or misspeaking in social settings, with captions touting the relief that would come from knowing the causes of such behavior: "People of neurotic constitution are just people who have never broken away, in the depth of their hearts, from the family situation. They are still dominated in all that they do and feel by a repressed love, or a repressed hate, toward mother, or father, . . . or sister, or brother—a passion which possessed them when they were little children."[60] In case Max's readers didn't get the point, the editors of *Everybody's Magazine* included a picture of a round-cheeked, well-fed baby on the same page. "What we call a 'nervous' person is a grown-up infant," suggested Max.[61]

Only those who had known Max for a long time would have detected an urgency in these sentences not entirely justified by the purposes of a magazine article. Certainly, everyone, as Max assured his readers, suffers from a "family complex of sorts," and we spend our lives reliving these "old passions of childhood, to our utter undoing as grown-up and efficient human beings." But the truth is that some of us are more liable to do this than others, namely, those among us who had been "excessively sensitive children, and were too closely adored, or too hideously nagged."[62] The fidgety, hypochondriac child of Annis Eastman was speaking about himself. But Max stopped himself before he gave away too much. Most people, he assured his readers, are not much affected by their neuroses. They'll forget a name or an appointment (as Freud himself had admitted he occasionally would, especially when he was supposed to meet with patients he was treating for free). What a relief, then, for them to know that such slips were not due to any "supernatural powers."[63] Max's main intent in these articles was to normalize psychoanalysis, to represent it not as a scary process by which your id gets ripped out from under the layers of censorship, but as a sensible explanation of the concealed causes of odd behavior, as the ultimate confirmation that there was nothing really wrong with you.

Max knew that psychoanalysis was more than a quick fix for the annoying goofs and gaffes of everyday life. But nowhere in these two articles does he admit that he himself had been seeking therapy because of his growing problems with Ida. Max's analyst, Dr. Smith Ely Jelliffe, mentioned by name and pictured, next to a cigar-smoking Freud, in Max's first article, had diagnosed him as suffering from the aftereffects of a lingering Oedipus complex. He attributed Max's socialist leanings to latent hostility toward his minister-father and his problems with Ida to an unresolved incestuous desire for his sister. A "Niagara talker" to Max's "Lake Ontario listener," Jelliffe subjected Max to a crash course in Freudian doctrine. Max read every book by Freud and about Freud he could find. But therapy turned up no new memories of Max's childhood, and all the fixations mentioned by Jelliffe, from fetishism to homosexuality, seemed equally plausible to him. But there was no healing pain, no revelation, and though he developed a strange, troubling affection for his round-bodied and friendly analyst—Freudian transference, as he noted with his newly acquired knowledge of psychoanalysis—nothing was accomplished.[64]

Max was too much interested in the women out there who he felt were waiting for him, women who wanted to receive him with open arms, to accept Jelliffe's verdict as the truth about his inner mechanisms. Ida, not ready to give up on him, in the summer of 1914 decided to take matters into her own hands. As the world elsewhere was inching closer to war, she took a train to New York and left Max and Daniel alone in the old boathouse in Tenafly, New Jersey, where they had moved in an attempt to escape from the noise and pressures of life in Manhattan. While she was gone Max engaged in Freudian self-analysis. He filled three composition books with often self-pitying and sometimes acute reflections on his current situation, notes about dreams he had and attempts at analyzing them, and plans for getting his life back on course. Daniel doesn't play much of a role in these entries, except as a whimpering presence in the next room.

His thoughts focused on Ida, Max alternately lamented her absence and then celebrated it, as the necessary condition for the release of his polyamory. The problem was not that Max didn't desire Ida—several passages extol her beautiful body—but that Ida desired no one else but Max. As loose as their marriage was, Ida was still expecting Max to be there for her, to be her mate.

But Max's sense of himself as an author, as a creator, depended on being free to do what he wanted rather than being limited to his identity as a husband or as a father: "Plato celebrates the love that does not beget children, except such children as the Iliad and the Odyssey."[65]

At least at this early point in his self-analysis Max was still trying to convince himself that sex wasn't the reason he felt the way he did: "Perhaps the true sublimation of the animal hunger for me is a modern platonic one—not especially, or only, a love of ideas, but a love of the whole world, a wondering love of the whole world. I felt that Ida would be (if she would!) a friend in the world, but the world would be my lover." Ida had deprived him socially rather than just sexually. Unlike Annis or Crystal, she did not care about other people and had, directly or indirectly, kept him away from his friends, he complained, and, "suggestible" and "pliant" as he was, he had subjected himself to her view of life.[66]

As he went on with his analytic navel gazing Max diagnosed himself as suffering from exhibitionism, given his "frequent dreams of bodily exposure, as well as the exposure of various forms of nobility and heroism in my soul." Freud, in a passage about exhibitionism from *Three Contributions to the Sexual Theory* that would have been familiar to Max, had linked the desire to expose one's genitals to the confused wish to make someone else do the same thing and thus to be reassured that men are men and women are women.[67] Lo and behold, one of the most disconcerting dreams Max records is of a "beautiful, white-bodied woman" in a bathtub with perfect breasts and, would you believe it, a most beautiful penis. Was Max's rampant desire to imagine women naked rooted in the haunting fear that they might not be women at all?

A bit unexpectedly, homosexuality becomes a key motif in these notebooks. In yet another dream—like the previous one omitted when Max reprinted passages from his self-analysis in his autobiography—Max and his father are headed for a swim. They walk, accompanied by Max's would-be lover Inez Milholland, through a village full of "curious black people" to get to a bathhouse, where, Max hopes, they will undress in each other's presence. But in Max's dream, the river (a "slot," really) where Max and his father were going to swim suddenly fills with ashes: "We gave it up and went on further." The ashes Max himself, in the analytic part of his dream re-creation, attributes to his fear of homosexuality: though he clearly desired it, he was spared the sight of his naked father.[68]

In another dream he reports, Max wakes up alone in a room and at first cannot, try as he might, open his eyes. Under his bed he then finds a rakish little hat with a pink and red headband that he immediately wants to wear, although he knows such headbands have been banned by the government. Not coincidentally, Ida would never fix her hats the way Max would have liked her to. Max now realizes that his desire for the inappropriate, illegal, feminine hat, of a kind his wife wouldn't wear, coupled with his inability to open his eyes, once again points in the direction of repressed homosexuality. Just a day before, Max had met a man "who really attracted me."[69]

Max's sense of his masculinity was far from robust, as these dreams confirm. They also hint that the Reverend Samuel Eastman, a diffident father at best, had something to do with that. His cousin Adra would later tell him how she constantly had to fend off the elder Eastman's advances when he was staying with her, an indication of how painfully repressed Sam himself was. While Max might not have been aware of Adra's predicament, his father's demons were well familiar to him even when he was young, and lest the same fate befall him, he actively transformed himself into one of the most famously or, depending on one's point of view, notoriously unrepressed lovers of the American Left.[70] And that indeed was the self-image Max felt most comfortable with when he reached the end of his self-analysis. "Unsublimated heterosexual lust," not worry about his masculinity, was responsible for all his troubles, he noted with relief. All his problems came from his unfulfilled wish to make love to someone not his wife.[71]

In the summer of 1915 Max, Ida, and Dan made their way to Provincetown, where Max spent much time strolling around the wharfs while Ida threw herself into a new project, the Provincetown Players, which she cofounded. As a member of the Washington Square Players, she had theater experience; as an activist, she was a master improviser. The casual atmosphere in Provincetown was ideal for what she had in mind: "There were no actors and nobody in show business around. There were just painters and sculptors and writers and a few intelligent people who liked theater and thought it was in an awful mess, and there was nothing they wanted to go see. Well, we thought it would be nice to have a theater of our own and to put on our own plays."[72] The radical journalists Hutchins Hapgood and Jack Reed were there, as were the playwright George Cram Cook and his wife, Susan Glaspell, and Eugene O'Neill, Just the group of people to start a new chapter in the history of American theater. Max's colleague from the *Masses* Mary Heaton Vorse owned a wharf in Provincetown, with a fish house at the end, not more than an old shack, but it seemed good enough to serve as a theater. In the absence of seats or benches, people brought cushions and sat on the floor. Two movable doors behind the ten-by-twelve-foot stage could be rolled back to reveal the ultimate stage set, the ocean itself. The Provincetown Players were born. After a second season in Provincetown, in the summer of 1916, a charter was written, and Ida's group moved the whole enterprise to MacDougal Street in New York.

Max wasn't involved. Or so he said in his autobiography. The truth is he participated in both plays performed during the first season at Lewis Wharf, Cook's *Change Your Style* and Wilbur Daniel Steele's *Contemporaries.* The former was a play about the dilemma of a young student in art school, bankrolled by his wealthy father, who, instead of working with the respectable artist his family has picked for him, an adherent of the academic style of painting, decides to study with his revolutionary, post-Impressionist colleague. The rebellious art student was played by the painter Charles Demuth and the reactionary art professor, in a bit of delicious irony, by Max, whose traditional aesthetic preferences would not have escaped notice even in 1915. Ida played a wealthy art patroness who changes her mind about purchasing the young student's first and rather abstract work. In *Contemporaries,* a more overtly political play about an Industrial Workers of the World (IWW) organizer's protest on behalf of the homeless, Max performed the part of the crotchety landlord.[73]

Max did not like Provincetown. "A summer town where all the folks are old," he called it in an unpublished poem, "The fishers old with labor, and the rest / With life, or art or some exotic thing." He felt "lonely-hearted" there. Even the seagulls appeared to pick up on his misery: "The gulls cry sadly / As their shadows drift across the sand."[74] Max had his mind set on a more congenial place. In the autumn of 1915 he acquired a small, yellow clapboard house at 70 Mount Airy Road in Croton-on-Hudson, a picturesque village about forty miles north of Manhattan. A former cider mill, the house was the second oldest in the village. The purchase price came to $1,500, but Max could manage the minimal down payment of $20 that was required. He had maintained a special attachment to Croton ever since, during his first months in New York, he had taken a "slim, strong-bodied, brown-skinned" nurse named Nancy there and unsuccessfully tried to kiss her.[75] Now he had come back as a resident.

Max's house is still there today, close to the top of a hill, accessible by a steep, narrow, leafy road that must have been pretty precarious to navigate in those days, especially in Max's temperamental Ford. The house had four small rooms and a roofless porch, and it came with a barn (now gone), part of which Max converted into a study. While he planted some Japanese iris from his mother's garden in Glenora, Max left the property largely to its own devices.[76]

Inevitably, the entire neighborhood has undergone a facelift since the days when Mount Airy Road was, according to fellow socialist Joseph Freeman, nothing more than a stretch of "brown, hilly earth."[77] But visitors still get the feeling that the outside world didn't matter much, as if New York weren't just a half-hour train ride away. And the two-mile walk from the Harmon train station is as daunting today as it was then.

Croton and the surrounding areas had been popular for a while with artists seeking respite from the noisy environment of the city, and Max quickly understood why. The presence of other writers promised inspiration, while the remoteness of the place guaranteed privacy. For more than two decades Max's little house on the hill would serve as his writing retreat, love nest, and general refuge (at least until government agents began to show up there as well). It also kept him connected with the kinds of places he had loved so much when he was a child. Mount Airy was Max's Glenora, offering all the pleasures of a rural existence but without the demands that came with living on a farm. No one in Croton did any gardening. Tangled bushes, tall grass, and weeds long gone out of control gave the community a delightfully neglected look: a kind of communist pastoral, a workers' paradise without any workers. At the top of Max's hill there was a meadow with grass so high that the British painter Clare Sheridan, who had come for a visit in May 1921, felt like an insect when she lay down in it, "with the buttercups so much higher than ourselves, and the tall seed grasses like slender trees above our heads."[78] Reinvigorated by the experience of Croton, Max's poetry brimmed with celebrations of thistles, clover, butterflies, and birds, tokens of his pagan delight in nature, an antidote to the post-Puritan sense of propriety and the institutionalized religion that had dominated his childhood and was still wreaking havoc on his marriage. He took great pride in the tennis court he installed in his backyard, which became the unofficial center of an expanding radical community.

Max had by now become a celebrity, a socialist with a country home. It was in this capacity that he was featured in the December 1916 issue of *Countryside* magazine in a segment titled "The Country of Some Interesting People" (fig. 18). A portrait by Paul Thompson, who would acquire some fame as a World War I photographer, showed Max by the fireside in his country home, reading an issue of what might be his own magazine, the *Masses,* wearing impressive boots with rustically scuffed tips. Behind Max is a bookshelf, on the floor some carelessly strewn correspondence. His dark shirt goes nicely with his salt-and-pepper hair, giving him an air both of youthful, iconoclastic energy and genteel wisdom. The caption accurately summarized the conflicts

Copyright, Paul Thompson
Max Eastman belonged to the most exclusive fraternity at Columbia, but is editor
of "The Masses" and one of the hottest of the radicals today

Figure 18. Max Eastman in Croton, 1916. Photograph by Paul
Thompson. From "The Country of Some Interesting People,"
Countryside (December 1916).

in the personality of that country-loving drawing-room radical. "Max Eastman
belonged to the most exclusive fraternity at Columbia, but is editor of 'The
Masses' and one of the hottest radicals today." The *Countryside* folks reprinted
Max's poem "The City," a kind of post-Baudelairean fantasy in which the
speaker moves through alien city streets, past blue faces and piercing whis-
pers, realizing his solitude, for the country is where he really belongs. Max's
Greenwich Village buddies, had they bothered to read the magazine, would
have been mightily surprised to see him relaxing in a wicker chair, looking
like a self-satisfied country squire. There was no mention of Max's family.

As the United States was lumbering toward participation in a war no one
wanted, Woodrow Wilson's wavering attitude to the war in Europe confused
and annoyed Max. As a member of a delegation of the American Union
Against Militarism led by Crystal, Max got a chance to speak with Wilson at
the White House, an experience on which he reflected in an essay for the July
1916 issue of the *Masses.* He had known Wilson since 1912, when he met him

at a banquet organized by the New York Chamber of Commerce in Syracuse and came to appreciate his verbal dexterity. At the time, they discussed women's suffrage, and Max prided himself on having persuaded the president that this was a worthy cause. Now, even more was at stake. But Max came back from his White House meeting with the disconcerting feeling that he had been "beautifully handled." He was still convinced that Wilson personally did not want war. But, as if to prove he wasn't in the president's pocket, he took Wilson to task for neglecting the working class, the skeleton in America's closet. It had to be said that Wilson was in cahoots with the capitalists: "Some day this skeleton will walk. It is not dead or decayed. More offensive than that—it is true." This was the new Max, a master of the clipped, declarative sentence, the folksy but effective metaphor.[79]

When Wilson ran in the November 1916 elections as the "Peace President," Max supported him. Along with Randolph Bourne, Paul Kellogg, Amos Pinchot, and others, Max established a small Emergency Office (later renamed Committee for Democratic Control) at 70 Fifth Avenue, whose main purpose was to agitate, in New York and elsewhere, against the possibility of the United States being dragged into the European war. Max and his fellow activists took out newspaper advertisements, printed handbills, and gave lectures. Petition your president, they urged, wire him if necessary but make sure he keeps his promise of neutrality. An advertisement they published in the New York Times on February 2, 1917, struck a conciliatory tone: "We recognize the perplexity of the problem before you," wrote the signers. "The men and women who elected you will back you in the most extreme measures for keeping this country clear of any ignominious eleventh-hour participation in a struggle for mastery which is not their own."[80] On April 1, 1917, Max addressed a crowd in Detroit: "You cannot," he explained, "destroy German militarism by making war on Germany."[81] But it was all in vain. A few days after Max's speech, responding to Wilson's demand for a "war to end all wars," a war that would make the world safe for democracy, Congress voted to declare war on Germany on April 6, 1917. Had Wilson just been stalling for time?

Max's magazine responded swiftly. Wilson's war wasn't our war, declared Reed, and Max wrote an editorial encouraging people to refuse to be drafted: "For my part I do not recognize the right of a government to draft me to a war whose purposes I do not believe in." Wilson's government had added another turn of the screw by not even communicating the purposes of the war they wanted—"an act of tyranny," said Max, "discordant with the memory even of the decent kings."[82]

Appropriately, the artist Henry Glintenkamp's cartoon on the topic, published in Max's August 1917 issue, had a Goyaesque intensity that underscored this devastating assessment (fig. 19). It showed the allegorical figures of Youth, Labor, and Democracy chained to a war cannon, with a wailing mother, her dead child on the ground, sunk to her knees on the barren ground. Some readers might have remembered that the wheel was a notorious medieval torture device. But the figures in the cartoon are beyond the reach of torture: their suffering is over. Youth, Labor, and Democracy are dead. Conscription is not a beginning, but an end.

Max received his notice to appear for a physical examination in mid-October 1918. At thirty-five, he was well within the age bracket of the third registration held on September 12. He immediately dashed off a note to the

Conscription

Figure 19. H. J. Glintenkamp, "Conscription," *The Masses* (August 1917). Courtesy of The Modernist Journal Project, Brown and Tulsa Universities.

War Department's local board in which he apprised them of his state of mind: "I do not believe in international wars, and I do not recognize the right of the government to conscript the bodies of its citizens for service upon foreign soil." Well aware that the conscription law did not allow any exceptions, Max said his motive in sending the card had been merely to keep his record clear and to reiterate his principles, which were "more sacred and of more value to the country than any religious scruple, or any membership in any antimilitary sect, could possibly be." He was not expecting a deferment, and indeed he didn't get one. But surely everyone involved realized that drafting Max Eastman would have been a very bad idea.[83]

Meanwhile, at the *Masses* Max had his own internal war to deal with. Resenting his firm editorial hand, the artists among the editors, led by John Sloan, lamented that the magazine had now developed a "policy," a development at odds with the spirit of its founders. They demanded that the position of editor and managing editor be abolished and that decisions on pictures and text be made by separate committees. Max recognized that this initiative was directed against him personally. He went on the offensive and reasserted his editorial privilege to make the final decisions. Max's view was that the cooperative principle had outlived its usefulness. In a note read at an informal meeting of the editors and stockholders on March 23, 1916, he explained that the editing of a magazine such as the *Masses* was too complex to be done in meetings, especially if the contributors didn't show up. Max emphasized that, since he was doing all the fund-raising, he was "the boss" of the magazine. If they wouldn't let him edit, then he would leave.[84]

Impressed by Max's threat to resign, the artists in attendance offered a compromise, namely, that "their plan should apply only to the pictures and that the literary side of the magazine and the conduct of the business should continue as before." But Max wasn't having any of it: "I said that the reasons which induced me to despair of the cooperative plan applied equally to the pictures and text." A vote taken on Sloan's elimination proposal ended inconclusively; Art Young joined Max's camp.[85] At the annual meeting of all the stockholders on April 6, a motion proposed by Max's camp, to drop the rebels from the list of editors, failed. But Sloan's original elimination plan was also voted down, certainly with the help of a clever marshaling of proxy votes from absentee stockholders. A majority reelected Max as both editor and president of the *Masses* Publishing Company and, in a surprise move, added Sloan as vice president.[86]

Clearly, there was trouble in the socialist paradise. The press loved it. When a reporter for the *New York World* showed up at Max's Washington Square apartment, he was greeted not by Max the power wielder but by Max the languid, "seen-it-all" poet, clad, as the paper reported the next day in a classic example of bad journalistic prose, "in pajamas, a raincoat and an ample yawn." Nothing had happened, really. "It was our semi-annual scrap. We live on scraps. Twenty fellows can't get together to paste up a magazine without scrapping about it." The same reporter subsequently went to Sloan's apartment in Washington Place, where he had a very different experience. Sloan welcomed him "wearing a vivid green flannel shirt and an even vivider scarlet necktie." And he was angry about what had happened: "It just proves that real democracy doesn't work—yet." He added ominously, "I don't think you'll see my name in the Masses for a long time." Barely an hour later Sloan called in his resignation letter, reading it to the *New York World* before Max had even seen it: "Dear Max, 'If thy right hand offend thee, cut it off.' This afternoon I played the part of one of the five fingers"—Sloan was referring to the other artists who had rebelled against Max—"in the above-suggested tragedy, and foolishly resisted amputation. Now, alone at night, I have decided to submit to the operation." Three of the other fingers, the artists Stuart Davis, Glenn Coleman, and Maurice Becker, followed Sloan's example and left, as did the writer Bob Brown. Glintenkamp stayed on. Max had won.[87]

The postrebellion *Masses* had become, as Floyd Dell observed, a "practical dictatorship," an ungenerous statement since Dell, as Max's "faithful lieutenant," was at the very least one of the facilitators of Max's empire.[88] But, as Max saw it, he had dealt a deathblow to the kind of self-indulgent bohemianism that he believed all serious socialists should oppose. "Personal revolt," as manifested in Sloan's self-pitying resignation letter, had to yield to the scientific discipline the revolution demanded. The artists were hoping to use the *Masses* for artistic self-expression, whereas Max, as editor, wanted to see its pages devoted to the hard work of political analysis.[89]

However, as Max's appearance before the *New York World* reporter suggested, behind the mask of Max the hard-nosed political analyst and merciless ruler of the paste-up room, the old, poetic, pajama-clad Max had lingered on. A mock-up parody of an issue of the *Masses* found among Max's papers pokes fun at the purpose-driven political writing that seemed to have taken over his life (fig. 20). Max's parodistic cover showed, under the title "Knowledge and Revolution," one of his columns in the *Masses*, a languid, tousled-haired poet, tall like Max himself, lying on the bank of a river, writing in a notebook, one

Figure 20. Max Eastman, mock-up for *The Masses*.
Undated. EMIIA1.

impossibly long leg draped casually over the fork of a tree, the other one dangling into the water below, where the fish from Max's poem "At the Aquarium," "stern-lipped, and pale, and wonder-eyed," seem to be nipping at the poet's naked foot. This cartoon was more about knowledge than revolution, more about rest than action. On his right foot the poet is wearing a slipper.

On December 15, 1916, the *Masses* held a fund-raising ball for itself in Tammany Hall, which was then on East Fourteenth Street. It was there that Max Eastman, the hottest of radicals today, met a girl who was also considered a hot commodity in her world, the exceedingly beautiful twenty-one-year-old movie and stage actress Florence Deshon, and fell in love. News traveled fast even in those days, especially in New York, and Max's newfound happiness did not remain a secret for long. Ida was incensed. Unpleasant words were said, accusations leveled, fiery notes exchanged. Max's and Ida's letters from that unhappy period, with their misspent verbal brilliance, remind the reader of the sheer potential, the raw intellectual power that had resided in this relationship. When Max finally left Ida for good he found it necessary to tell her he had never loved her, words that crushed Ida more than any fight they had ever had.[90] In an undated note, written perhaps as much as a year after the final breakup, Ida made no secret of her surprise over what had happened. All her effort, she said, all her professions of sympathy had finally proved to be insufficient. As she was groping for words to express her disappointment over Max's behavior, she inadvertently revealed just how much she had been under his influence. "Fantastic" had been one of Max's favorite expressions of dismay: "O Max how can you look and say such ruthless things. What has got into your mind that the whole past of effort and sympathy seems to have left you with this cold condemnation of me. How strangely fantastic of you to act as if I had wronged you and to act as if—because you had never loved me as I had loved you—you must ignore that fact and treat us as a case in a category of domestic disagreements—How strange it all is to me—."[91] Max retaliated by saying that she had produced the situation in which they now found themselves. It was all her fault! He accused Ida of not wanting to understand him, of having "shut the gates of sympathy," a rather outlandish charge given that he had just told her he had never loved her. In a passage he then crossed out, he blamed her for ignoring Dan's rights and predicted that their son would judge her harshly later.[92]

In many ways Max's behavior was incomprehensible. Ida was brilliant, courageous, independent, and free-spirited, the very woman he should have wanted at his side as he took on the establishment. As a lawyer, she had defended him in court when the *Masses* was sued for libel. As a fearless artist, with her own studio at 5 West Sixteenth Street, where models would, scandalously, pose for her in the nude, she had crossed boundaries. And as a fellow activist she defied the law by publicly distributing birth control pamphlets at a mass gathering in Union Square, "right under the noses of 50 policemen," and gotten herself arrested.[93]

Max realized that by abandoning Ida he had lost all purchase on nobility and wisdom. But he still felt compelled to take *her* to task for the failure of their marriage. Ida was, he charged, determined to hate him, so any reasonable attempt he'd make to defend himself was bound to fail.[94] Ida categorically rejected his reading. "It is not hate, Max, that makes me feel that way," she told him. "This is not true and never was true. I believe you of course, if you assure me again that you hate me, and you may want to think that I do you— but this is not true—your letters still fill me with amazement."[95]

Max wrote back the very next day, assuring her that his response was not fantastic. She had gone around saying, to his face as well as in the presence of his friends, that he was "absolutely selfish" and "absolutely egotistical." This had made it easy for him to hate her. He had given her as much of himself as he could, had offered her his soul daily, but Ida had wanted more: "I always thought that the avidity with which you could drink up the blood of sacrifice and devotion and still be unsatisfied was truly terrible." Max's rhetorical powers now got the better of him: "Your conception of what must be given to you seems colossal and hideous, and you rise in my eyes as an unslakable monster of selfishness." Her desire that he give up Dan was an indicator of Ida's vampirical nature. Since she had chosen to be hard and contemptuous, it was his right to be so, too. He was enclosing a letter for Dan, to be read by him when he was grown up, "in which I tell him that, although I love him and think of him always, I have left him completely to you, because I have hurt you beyond measure, and the only thing I have that I can give you in compensation is my complete absence from your life and from your love for him."[96]

Ida's reply came in the form of a note scratched out on a train. If she had behaved badly since their separation, it was all justified by Max's unspeakable cruelty in telling her he had never actually loved her. With the memory of Dan's face before her, she pleaded with Max to give her any sign that inflicting all this pain on her had really been necessary. Speaking of her "terrible sense of betrayal," she pointed out that all the words of affection and tenderness he had found for her before their separation now seemed hollow and untrue. To add insult to injury, Max had immediately afterward embraced his new, liberated life right in front of her: "Hardly had you gone from my house than you began your life of joyous loving on my doorstep almost and even in the places where our friends and old associates were, flaunted your sense of glorious relief and utter indifference to the very places of my most intimate feeling." If he was able to say to Dan that he had hurt her "beyond measure," why couldn't he say that to her face, too? Max's callous claim that he had never loved her had made a mockery of their life together, a "terrible nightmare lacking every kind of feeling." It was not the case that she took no responsibility for what happened: "Many gross faults I have, many weaknesses. I mean this in all humility." But to accuse her now of self-righteousness wasn't fair. Had she not given him all the freedom he wanted, and had she not done so entirely unselfishly? Her letter was not meant to accuse Max, only to give him—and Ida goes on to offer a memorable phrase—"some deep colors of my mind" and to tell Max exactly what her feelings were since he had never bothered to find out. And those feelings were, to be sure, complicated: "I don't think life expresses itself clearly or simply for me."[97]

Amid all the accusations traded between his parents, a drawing by the five-year-old Daniel Eastman, sent to Max in January 1917, stands out as a poignant reminder of the real sacrifice at stake in this failed marriage (fig. 21). It is Daniel's self-portrait as a kind of giant human sponge wearing footsies, his mouth wide open in surprise. Interestingly, Dan's hands appear as part of his assorted facial features. Gartered and stuck into footsies and with his fin-like hands glued to his face, Little Dan seems bereft of agency—an impression he would have easily gotten from his fighting parents.

Max believed he had atoned for all he had done to Ida by giving up any right to play a part in his son's life. Neither he nor Ida pushed for an immediate divorce. But he still felt guilty about what he had done or, rather, failed to do for Dan. "I love you and long for you," Max had written in the letter he wrote to Dan during the breakup, "and I have cried in the night for the sound of your

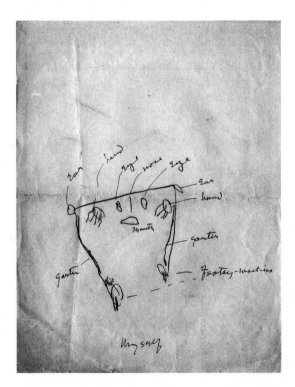

Figure 21. Daniel Eastman, self-portrait, 1917, with additions in green ink by Ida Rauh. EMII.

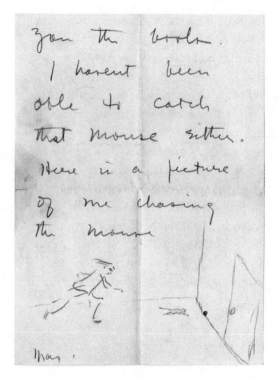

you the books.
I havent been
able to catch
that mouse either.
Here is a picture
of me chasing
the mouse

Max.

Figure 22. Max Eastman to Daniel Eastman,
undated. EMII.

voice, and your wonderful endless questions that I would answer, and for the trusting of your little hand in mine." We don't know much about Max's relationship with Dan in the years after he left Ida. But an undated letter in Max's papers offers a tantalizing clue that he remained involved in his little son's life (fig. 22). Apparently Max had promised to deliver some books to Dan but had been unable to do so since he was sick. He referred to a mouse in his apartment—a mouse known to Dan from the time he had spent with him—and admitted he hadn't been able to catch it either. And then Max entertained his son with a charming picture of himself, hair flowing, in hot pursuit of that mouse as it was heading for a hole in the wall. He must have known that Dan would have been receptive to stories of parental incompetence.

5 • We Were Beautiful Gods

When Max ran into Florence Deshon on that fateful night in Tammany Hall in December 1916, he knew instantly that there was no turning back. Florence had come to the ball with her current lover, John Fox Jr., the author of the best-selling western novel *Trail of the Lonesome Pine* and a donor to the magazine, but he was quickly forgotten. Equipped with abundant brown hair, large, dark, smoldering eyes, and a heart-shaped face that appeared radiant on the screen and indeed must have seemed so to Max that night, the twenty-one-year-old Florence, "a girl of the Leonardo type," was hard to resist, for both men and women. As he danced with Florence, Max's previous life faded away as if in a dream. Their minds and bodies flowed into each other, a "joyous overflowing of bounds." Unbelievably, Max realized he had seen her once before, walking east on Thirty-fourth Street and holding a painted Japanese parasol over her head. She seemed to him then "by far the most beautiful being I had ever seen." When the ball ended, Max stumbled home as if in a trance; within days he had left his family for good and moved in with the very tolerant Eugen Boissevain at 12 East Eighth Street. A month later Max turned thirty-four.[1]

Florence Danks (Deshon's original name) was born on July 19, 1893, in Tacoma, Washington, to Samuel Danks from England and Florence ("Flora") Spitzer from Austria. An aura of mystery and obfuscation surrounds her from the beginning. Her parents were not married; when they registered their daughter's birth, Samuel pretended he was a clerk from Denmark, while Flora, in the Pierce County registry, gave "Walter" as her last name.[2] When their daughter created her own last name, she was only continuing a family habit. By 1900, the U.S. Census shows Florence, her brother Walter, and her parents living in Manhattan, on Eighth Avenue. Both parents made their living in music-related fields, Samuel as an arranger for a New York music publisher and Flora as a music teacher.[3] At one point the family lived in suburban New Jersey, but by 1915 the parents seem to have broken up, Florence's brother continuing to live with Samuel, while Flora, who would soon begin to call herself a widow, and Florence struck out on their own.

Florence had inherited her parents' artistic inclinations, and she was as clever as she was beautiful. When and why she took up acting is not known, but it is clear she systematically reinvented herself to fit the type Americans wanted to see on the screen: a sultry combination of ingénue and femme fatale. Her dark looks gave rise to persistent rumors, actively encouraged by Florence, that her mother was a gypsy. Perhaps a convenient way for her to hide her mother's Jewish heritage? Her vaguely French-sounding, entirely fabricated name served only to increase her exotic appeal. When Max and Florence crossed paths she had already appeared in several films with Vitagraph Studios in Brooklyn and was considered a rising star, as famous for her willfulness as for her beauty.[4]

A month after the ball Max called on Florence at her apartment on East Thirty-fourth Street and made perfunctory conversation with her mother. Then, his eyes resting on Florence's clingy silk gown, he took her out to dinner to Mouquin's on Sixth Avenue, a longtime and very popular gathering place for artists, famous for its imported wines and authentic French kitchen. Max was so enraptured by Florence's presence that he felt like "Pan dancing with the dryads." Afterward he drove her in his beat-up Ford Model T, the overworked engine sounding like the Battle of Gettysburg, to his house in Croton, and it was there, later that night, that "the ideal rapture and the physical achievement of love were so blended as to be indistinguishable."[5] In other words, Max slept with Florence Deshon. And sleeping with Florence—a woman as free and liberated as Max was constrained and fenced in by years of repression, imagined illnesses, and self-doubt—to him was something akin to a religious revelation.

In the next few weeks a flurry of notes, sometimes accompanied by bouquets of flowers, went back and forth between Max's residence on 6 East Eighth Street and the apartment Florence shared with her mother at 49 East Thirty-fourth Street. Fortunately for Max, Florence was as taken with him as he was with her. "My love," he told her, "I would give my soul to lie in your arms tonight."[6]

No biographer could do justice to the intensity of this relationship, manifested in many little, hurriedly written notes, alternating between longing ("I miss you so tonight I cannot sleep"), impatience ("my love, there is no hour but the hour when you come back"), gratitude ("I loved being at the opera with you"), and disappointment ("You left me so coldly today"). Two intense human beings had found each other. To Max, Florence was no awkward mother substitute, as Ida Rauh had been. She had the same capacity for enjoyment that had lain dormant in him, the same urgent need for pleasure paired with a contrary push for self-assertion. That combination would, in Florence's case, prove lethal. Unlike Max, Florence, who had already reinvented herself several times before she met him, was reckless and not averse to taking risks, even foolish ones. Max survived their relationship, but he emerged from it a changed man. Before he met Florence he had hunted for shades of Annis and Crystal in every woman he met. After he had lost her, he would spend the rest of his adult life reliving that loss.

When Roi Cooper Megrue's *Seven Chances*, the comedy in which Deshon played the part of the lustful Florence Jones (fig. 23), went on tour to DC in

Figure 23. Florence Deshon as Florence Jones, 1916.
Photograph by Jean de Strelecki. EMII.

February 1917, Florence saw members of the Women's Peace Party shivering in the cold outside. They were standing on boards and straw mats because the ground was frozen solid, clutching banners demanding liberty for women. Angered by President Wilson's lackluster support of the suffrage amendment, they had been picketing the White House for months, sometimes burning copies of the president's speeches. Many of them were arrested and ended up in workhouses, a stark reminder to both Florence and Max that their relationship was unfolding against a backdrop of legal inequality and constant threats to people who shared their political convictions. No wonder Florence was dreaming of how she and Max, going "as fast as lightning," would skate their problems away.[7] Max didn't hesitate, took a train, and showed up in DC, skates in hand: "Must I be with you every second?"[8]

With the possibility of American involvement in the war looming, Max was delivering antiwar speeches at a flurry of mass meetings. But his mind was always on Florence and the next time he would see her again. He felt loved, vindicated. Poetry effortlessly flowed from his pen: "You are thinking of me— you are coming back to me—and when you come you will be all that the impossible beautiful dream of you is. And so my throat is relaxed and my breath flows quietly and I wait for you, with joy. I want you to know this, and so I let myself so into the sweet music of saying it."[9] But the outside world continued to distract him. In June 1917 the Espionage Act was passed, and the *Masses* became a natural target of the authorities. Designed to curb, on the eve of America's entry into World War I, the influence of foreigners on American politics, the new legislation became a useful tool in eliminating internal dissent. One immediate consequence was renewed attention on the use of the U.S. Postal Service for the dissemination of ideas that might be considered anti-American. On July 5 the postmaster general of New York, Albert Burleson, declared the August 1917 issue of the *Masses* "unmailable" under the newly established law, the beginning of legal troubles for Max and his magazine that would continue through two trials. When Max protested and asked that the offensive material be identified, the postmaster refused.

Max sought an injunction and had the great good fortune to end up before Judge Learned Hand of the New York Federal District Court. The objectionable material from the August 17 issue included Henry Glintenkamp's "Conscription" (see fig. 19), a cartoon by Boardman Robinson ("Making the World Safe for Capitalism") as well as an Art Young drawing of a group of businessmen making war plans while a timid representative of Congress wanted to know, "Where do I come in?," the answer to which was, "Run along!" Also deemed offensive were an editorial by Max himself, in which he called for funds to defend Alexander Berkman and Emma Goldman after their arrest for advocating that men not register for the draft, and an article by Dell about conscientious objectors. No one was bothered by Max's "The Lonely Bather," a fairly explicit poem in which Max projected the frustrations of unfulfilled desire onto the "slim and sallow" body of a woman lying beside a stream.

Judge Hand was not convinced. The incriminating entries were, he determined, examples of American citizens exercising their right to freedom of speech. Incensed, the postmaster general turned to a helpful judge in Windsor, Vermont, who did as asked and forbade the distribution of the August issue until an appeal of Judge Hand's decision could be heard.[10] Max was undeterred. When a massive storm raged through Croton, taking out a "glorious big elm tree" near the train station, Max ran out into the yard, tore his clothes off, and, as he told Florence, "*drank* it." Let us see who shall be master. The storm "couldn't blow *me* down!"[11]

Max had begun traveling on behalf of the People's Council of America for Democracy and Peace, a product of the First American Conference for Democracy and Terms of Peace, held in New York in May 1917. "It's fun to travel with your expenses paid," Max wrote to Florence, as he was enjoying the view from his open train window. He was dreaming about his speeches but even more "about you-and-me."[12]

Max's activities were now garnering national attention. He was pleased to see how many people turned up to support his pacifist or, rather, antimilitary message (fig. 24). "I am more than ever sure 'the people' (whoever they are) are against the war." A clear sign of that was the nervousness Max generated in the cops who showed up at his events. In Chicago, for example, a "hard shell" of policemen surrounded him wherever he went: "They patted me on the back and mock-arrested me when I left the building, and I noticed they were listening more attentively than anybody else." The *New York Times* covered his speech, quoting his inflammatory remark, "We are not yet so excited over German atrocities that we can't see the atrocities of our own people." It seemed everyone was taking notice except Florence, who wasn't writing to Max as frequently as he wished.[13]

But Florence was distracted. Her Vitagraph appearances had caught the eye of Samuel Goldwyn, and though her interview with him and Goldwyn Pictures cofounder Edgar Selwyn did not lead to a contract (the salary was too small), Florence had her mind set on success in Hollywood. She went to see

Figure 24. Crowd at one of Max's speeches, Cleveland, December 1918. Undated postcard, EM.

Jaffery again, one of her Vitagraph movies, and was appalled by her performance. Writing to Max, who was by now in Oakston, South Dakota, she sighed, "The picture is very old, and it looked terrible. I looked all right, but my work looked very amateurish. A year certainly makes a difference."[14] Max responded that she shouldn't think about the film too much: "You know it made a hit." Movies, literature, war, and workers' rights seemed forgotten when he missed her, and more than once he thought of canceling the entire tour. From Kansas City he wrote, "I find myself continually playing with the idea of telegraphing Miss Secor that I'm dying, or that I've joined the army, or that I can't find South Dakota, and just flying home to you."[15] This from the same man who had, a few days before, filled an entire opera house in St. Louis, with people standing up and cheering him. "I never saw such an audience."[16]

The strain of the tour, combined with his nervous longing for Florence, finally proved too much for Max, and he began to suffer from insomnia. "I have had a funny time with myself," he wrote to Florence. Staying with friends a little outside of Kansas City, Max couldn't settle down, slid into his clothes and out of their house, followed by his hosts' barking dog. Running to the gate in stockinged feet and then on for another half mile through the prairie grass, he managed to catch the last trolley car to Kansas City, where his hotel room beckoned. When Max called his hosts the next morning they had not realized he was no longer at their house: "They were all still going around on tip-toe congratulating themselves that I had slept so long—they knew I hadn't been sleeping—and he had climbed a tree in the night to catch a rooster so it wouldn't wake me up crowing at dawn!" Max feared for his sanity, so much so that he picked a nerve doctor at random from the Kansas City phone book. The doc pronounced him sane and sound, noted his excellent blood pressure, and then went on to perform "a minor operation" on Max's wallet, sending him away with the observation that "if I would go to bed intending to rest, instead of to sleep I would both rest and sleep, but if I went to bed intending to sleep I would neither." That night Max slept like a lamb.[17]

The image of Florence's body stayed with him as he traveled by car through the "dull, flat, characterless towns" of North Dakota, towns that dulled his consciousness.[18] While the people adored him, the authorities cranked up their pressure on him. In Fargo, where Max had gone at the invitation of the antiwar Non-Partisan League of North Dakota, things got downright dangerous. Max was staying at the Gardner, a "Modern European Hotel" offering "Cleanliness, Courtesy, and Comfort," according to its letterhead. But the hotel's proprietor apparently felt not too bound by the promises made on his stationery. Max had been banned, by police orders, from every available hall in Fargo, and a military drill had been scheduled for exactly the time he was supposed to speak outdoors and on the very same block. Max was informed that the rifles used during that exercise would in fact be loaded. Casually, the hotel owner mentioned he would hang Max if he decided to speak in front of his hotel instead. Cleanliness, courtesy, and comfort. Max realized that this speech was going to be the most difficult thing he had ever done in his life.[19]

Max, the minister's son from Elmira, was afraid. Afraid of what the police might do to him, afraid that Florence, in his absence, was in love with someone else, sick in "heart and body" that no one in the world might care about whether he lived or died.[20] Mark Twain, his hero, might have been comfortable among these brash-talking, wisecracking men, but Max was not. He didn't know that Florence had in fact sent him a supportive letter, in which she told him, among other things, that she thought he was the man the nation needed: "Everybody in other countries is crying for a leader. In America I think you are the leader."[21] However, her letter went to Minneapolis, Max's next stop, in anticipation of his arrival there.

Stuck in Fargo, Max found himself very much alone when he came, in his own considered opinion, closer to death than he had ever been before. All the "money and power" in Fargo were against him, but, unwilling to simply cancel the Fargo meeting ("I am a man"), he asked two boys in an automobile to drive through the streets of town and to spread the word that he would hold his rally in a building near the outskirts of town. When Max got there, over two hundred people had gathered inside the building, with several hundred more assembled outside. Soon the soldiers had arrived, too. Everybody was waiting to see what would happen next. Max walked to the platform and began to speak when a group of six soldiers burst into the hall, knocking people down. "There was some commotion, and I told them to come down in front, there were seats on the platform. Cold-eyed, coarse, professional fighters—low in the brow, big in the torso—I knew them, I feared them, and I hated them. They were nonplussed a little at my politeness and quietness and their public position. I told them I wanted to go back a few sentences so they could get the thread of my argument." After Max resumed his lecture, the astonished soldiers listened for a few minutes before they remembered why they had been sent and started yelling. Max asked the audience if they wanted him to continue, and all but a handful rose in a show of support. But it was too late— more soldiers were pouring in, and Max noticed about fifteen of them standing right behind him. They were getting more confident and drawing closer as the noise prevented Max from being heard by anyone. A soldier was turning off the lights when a woman in the audience intervened: "For God's sake don't do that, there are women and children here!" Meanwhile, another woman, who had, as Max learned, driven thirty miles to see him because she was such a fan of the *Masses,* stepped up and began arguing vociferously with the soldiers, hoping to distract them. When the woman who had invited Max motioned for him to follow her to a side exit, Max initially complied, but, seized with an absurd desire not to show his fear in public, he changed his mind and walked out through the crowd instead. Many of them shook his hand and told him how sorry they were and that "they had come a long way to hear me."

Once safely outside, Max and supporters ran through the dark streets until they had reached the house of Max's hostess, where she quickly pulled down the shades. Soon the phone rang. The soldiers were on their way! When his hostess asked him "if she hadn't better take me in the automobile down to the station to take a train," Max responded quickly, "Yes, you had." What followed was like a scene from a movie: slipping out of the house and hiding behind a bush till a car had pulled up, clutching a revolver that someone had pressed into his reluctant hand, Max the self-declared antimilitarist, wearing a borrowed hat and raincoat, was whisked out of Fargo. As he was hunkering down in his getaway car, Max was shivering: "It was cold, and my fear was physical now—I was sick, chilly, I wanted to be alone, it was hard to talk naturally, I felt weak, but I loved that six-shooter as I never loved any inanimate thing before!"

Once Max was safely in Minneapolis, the attorney general of North Dakota, William Langer, phoned him to offer his protection. A member of the Non-Partisan League and, as it happened, a former student of Max's at Columbia (Max had given him a grade of 100 in a logic class), "Wild Bill" would go on to become one of the most colorful figures in North Dakota and national politics. A fervent isolationist, he kept his antiwar stance during his two full terms as governor of the state and in the U.S. Senate. But his assurances were not enough to entice Max back, especially after the woman who had so courageously intervened by arguing with the soldiers that were about to seize him and had thus probably saved his life, told him she had seen the soldiers camped outside his hotel, promising themselves a "necktie party" when Max arrived.

Max ended his account of the incident with a textbook regressive fantasy. He had done all that to prove he was a man, but he really wasn't. In truth, he was back to where he began. "I am baby and I yearn for your breast," he informed Florence. "Oh my beautiful and my beloved I want to lie down in your arms." If ever in his life Max was entitled to such a dream, it was after that nearly lethal summer night in Fargo.[22]

Upon his return to New York Max threw himself back into his relationship with Florence. It was then he composed one of the most vivid tributes to her, "Sweet Lovely Night":

> Sweet lovely night, O bring me to my love,
> To drink the liquor of her shining eyes,
> And catch her colored laughter with my lips,
> To kiss her arms, and cling to her warm breasts
> Erect and rosey-pointed up to meet
> My cupping hand, to feel the intimate,
> The self-touch in another's passioned flesh,
> And run my pure bold fingers lightly on,
> And through the coarse sweet hairs & lips, until
> Hot inward flesh cries out against their tips,
> And in her thighs as in a nest
> Of Eagerness, and all along her body
> Live and leaping, I lie close and cling,

And plunge my throbbing to the hilt, and take
Her happy panting passion through my blood,
And in the pulse and color of her being,
Noble, tender, all trusted in,
Pour out my being to the utter last
That my flesh faints and falls upon her flesh,
With lovely and enamoured death,
And our sweet spirits mingle,
And we are one at last.[23]

As explicit a description of a shared sexual climax as one is likely to encounter in a text that can still pass for poetry, Max's unpublished poem tells us much about him, though little about Florence. Perhaps unusually so for a love poem, she appears only in the third person, as "she" and "her," the willing recipient of the pleasure the speaker is able to give her, which will then again translate into pleasure for him ("my flesh faints"). Living, leaping, throbbing, and dissolving, Max, above all, discovers himself (fig. 25).

But Max didn't have much time to savor his reunion with Florence. For one thing, he had seriously underestimated the postmaster general of New York, who wanted the *Masses* to be not just censored but terminated. The successful suppression of the August issue allowed Burleson to argue that the *Masses* was no longer a true periodical, a strategy that finally had the desired effect. In November 1917 the Second Court of Appeals overturned Learned Hand's earlier decision. The loss of second-class mailing privileges meant that Max's magazine would have to cease publication. Max was without a job. The irony was that the very moment the court killed his magazine Max received news of the successful revolution in Russia. Closer to home, Morris Hillquit, a founder of the Socialist Party of America and a prominent labor lawyer in New York City's Lower East Side, shocked the New York establishment by garnering an unprecedented 22 percent of the vote in the mayoral elections. "O you don't know how happy I am about that," wrote Max, "almost more than if Hillquit had won."[24] In the same election, with over 6,300 women serving as poll watchers, New York voters passed woman suffrage by a majority of 102,353 votes. Commented Florence, "It is very good for a beginning. I guess the pickets in Washington must be very happy. I think the victory is due to them. They put Suffrage back on the map after a long silence."[25]

But none of this could save Max. Only a few days after the decision of the appeals court he and several of his contributors, including Josephine Bell,

Figure 25. Max Eastman, ca. 1918. Photograph by
Marjorie Jones. EMIIA1.

Dell, Glintenkamp, Reed, and Young as well as the magazine's business editor, Merrill Rogers, were officially indicted for seeking to "unlawfully and will-
fully obstruct the recruiting and enlistment service of the United States." The
charges carried possible sentences of up to twenty years and a fine of $10,000.
The trial opened on April 15, 1918, with Hillquit in charge of the defense. "You
look so worried dearest," wrote Florence. "My heart aches for you. Please forgive me but the trial is a strain to me also and I miss you so much."[26] Two
months earlier, on February 12, Lincoln's birthday, Crystal and Max had jointly
launched their new magazine, the *Liberator*, named after William Lloyd Garrison's antislavery publication. With Lincoln and Garrison hovering behind
him, Max announced a change in his views of the war, although the reason he
gave seemed hardly suitable to sway a jury in his favor. The *Liberator* was en-
dorsing America's "war aims," declared Max in his first editorial, insofar as
they had been "outlined by the Russian people and expounded by President

Wilson," in that order. The goal was not war but peace, "a peace without forcible annexations, without punitive indemnities, with free development and self-determination for all peoples"—read: the Bolsheviks, as Max's enemies would have immediately added.[27]

The trial, which took place on the third floor of the old Post Office building, was a farce. Presiding over *United States v. Eastman et al.* was August Hand, Learned's older and "less genial" brother. A marching band performing outside the window forced the assembled group, including the defendants and therefore also a reluctant Max, to rise to their feet whenever the "Star-Spangled Banner" was intoned. Was he not patriotic?, Prosecutor Earl Barnes wanted to know once proceedings were under way, prompting Max to remind him that he had risen for the anthem and to mumble a declaration of respect for the boys "dying for liberty."[28] Art Young fell asleep during the proceedings, a clear violation of courtroom etiquette, and, when roused, drew a portrait of himself resting comfortably on his chair with his eyes closed. "Art Young on Trial for His Life," as he called the little sketch, was perhaps the sanest commentary on what was happening around him.[29] Dell, however, who had already been drafted and emphasized that by profession he was a soldier, embraced his chance to testify so that he could rail against militarism and "related subjects." He seemed ecstatic to have a captive audience, twelve men who had "to sit there and listen to me." And Hillquit, arguing for the defense, pointed out that constitutional rights were not a gift but a hard-won accomplishment of the American nation and therefore could not and should not be taken lightly away.[30]

But in the end it seems that none of that mattered all that much. Max noticed that one juror, a square-shouldered young man from the Bronx, seemed to have made his mind up from the beginning and apparently went on to convince two others to adopt his point of view. Max dashed off a complimentary sonnet to that twelfth juror, a factory manager from the Bronx. There was no "heat of conscience" in him and no "pious care / For points in virtue to be lost or won." He was, in other words, like Max, skeptical of all that jingoistic rhetoric used to justify the American war effort: "I felt that to be with you would be fun." With three jurors voting to acquit, the government's case collapsed.[31]

A second trial in the fall of 1918 ended anticlimactically as well. Prosecutor Barnes had chosen to dedicate his final words to a friend who had died on the battlefields abroad, a powerful tribute: "Somewhere in France he lies dead, and he died for you and he died for me. He died for Max Eastman. He died for John Reed. He died for Floyd Dell. . . . His voice is but one of the thousand silent voices that demand that these men be punished." Whereupon Art Young, who had been napping once again, awoke and whispered, "Didn't he die for me, too?" The courtroom exploded with laughter. Reed, freshly returned from Moscow, assured him, "Cheer up, Art, Jesus died for you."[32]

Jesus played an unexpected role at that second trial. He showed up, too, in Max's speech to the jury, a memorable performance. It was published, all forty-four pages of it, by the *Liberator* as a separate pamphlet, and rightly so: Max's defense of socialism as a position that demanded respect even from those who didn't share its goals was a masterpiece of political rhetoric as well as of courtroom diplomacy. Socialism was, said Max, "either the most beautiful and courageous mistake that hundreds of millions of mankind ever made, or else it is really the truth that will lead us out of misery, anxiety, and poverty, and war, and strife and hatred between classes, into a free and happy world. In either case it deserves your respect." What a clever idea to give the members of the jury a choice between socialism as a "beautiful mistake" or as the embodiment of a life-saving truth! Max also invoked Samuel and Annis Eastman. His parents had taught him, he said, to admire the man from Nazareth, whose faith and influence were much closer to the message of Socialism than to the message of "any other political body of men." And once again, this time with only four jurors voting for conviction and eight against, the jury was unable to reach a verdict.[33]

Perhaps because he had been so preoccupied during the year, Max felt that Florence had become more distant, too: "You used to love my gentleness and aspire to it a little, as I love and aspire to your impetuous strength. You used to be moved when I showed you my ideals, as I am moved by yours, and we grew together." She seemed to resent him, and Max feared she was pushing him out "on the edge of her world."[34] But he himself had contributed to that process with a small volume of poetry, *Colors of Life,* published by Alfred Knopf in October 1918. His poems were dedicated to her, although, perhaps out of respect for her public status, he had refrained from mentioning her by name: "To One Who Loves Them / And Whose Beauty Crowned Their Dreams."

Colors of Life paints a rather complex picture of Max's relationship with Florence. In "To an Actress," the poem that supplies the collection's title, Max celebrates Florence as a life-giving force—though not without also imagining the eyes of desiring men that rest on her approvingly. Somewhere in the back of Max's mind was the biblical Susannah from the book of Daniel, chapter 13. But his Susannah is a demonic force, fully conscious of her power over the wilting, panting elders who spy on her: "You walk as vivid as a sunny storm / Across the drinking meadows, through the eyes / Of stricken men." In the sonnet titled "Those You Dined With" Max contrasts the view of Florence's suitors, those who want to see her as a kind of pagan queen, a gemlike Cleopatra surrounded by glittering gold, "the mistress of a pale king," with his own favorite image of her as a gypsy, "free / As windy morning in the sunny air," a carefree spirit driven only by her natural impulses. The deeper levels of Florence's being, the poem suggests, are known only to Max.

Here, as elsewhere in the book, the studied formality of Max's poetic language, poured into the inflexible mold of fixed poetic forms, contrasts oddly with the undercurrent of real emotion seething below the surface.[35] In a poem with the Elizabethan-sounding title of "A Praiseful Complaint" we get an agonized Max bemoaning his lover's elusiveness. A coldhearted dominatrix despite her "crimson lips" and "burning fingertips," Florence wields her elusiveness over him like a whip and recoils from his naked passion like a plant, tendrils furled (Max is obviously not afraid of mixing his metaphors when necessary). Rather than just Max, she wants "all the world" as her mate. Arguably the most successful poem in the collection is "X Rays," where Max, for once, finds an objective correlative for the overflow of emotion that makes some of the other poems almost a little embarrassing to read. The occasion for "X Rays" is unknown. Did Florence have an X-ray taken with Max present? Did Max merely imagine the scene? No matter, the metaphor finally allows Max to separate the lover from the poet, and with great success. Countering fears about the invasiveness of X-rays, the machine makes Florence seem more naked than just naked: a virginal, vivid skeleton in the green light, startled into an intense purity, stripped of the flesh Max so desires, a "naked and pale . . . wonder," a slim-hipped, exquisitely boned spectacle, luminous, fragile, and self-sufficient against the dark screen of Max's life.[36]

Max's erotic fantasy, "Sweet Lovely Night," did not make it into *Colors of Life*, though Max reworked it for a private manuscript he titled "To My Love," intended as a New Year's gift for Florence. Among the poems in this little booklet are several unpublished ones, notably "A Telegram," which is in many ways the most charming, unaffected love poem Max ever wrote. It tells of a cold, wintery Christmas day he spent in Croton when the sky was "a cold grey metal" and the ponds were as frozen as Max's mood. But all of this changed, and sleep came easily to him, as "breasts to a thirsting baby," after Florence sent him a telegram, "five sweet words" that helped him find peace because they were "words that remembered."[37]

Colors of Life came equipped with a preface in which Max admitted that the struggle for the future of the world occupied his thoughts but not his heart. Life was greater than revolution, he exclaimed, and "life is what I love." Unabashedly, he revealed where his real interests lay: "Though I love life for all men and women, and so inevitably stand in the ranks of revolution against the cruel system of these times, I love it also for myself. And its essence—the essence of life—is variety and specific depth. It can not be found in the monotonous consecration of a general principle." Anyone who would later accuse Max of unpredictability had obviously not read these sentences. The remainder of the preface was devoted to Max's battle with Whitman, whose allegedly artless celebration of life Max sought to unmask as in reality more self-conscious and artificial than his own stiffly formalist verse. Whitman's poetry was, he argued, little more than the willful extension of the very private form of the love letter—"too individual" to be intended for public consumption—into the shared realm of poetry. Whitman wasn't playful and in fact had less direct access to nature than, say, the Greeks, who, content in their "sun-loved" world, would have never been able to understand what Whitman, with his contrived chants to the body electric, was trying to accomplish.[38]

Once again reviewers were confused by the lack of revolutionary fervor in Max's poetry. In her magazine, *Poetry,* Harriet Monroe mocked Max's "shocked conservatism." And in the pages of Max's own *Liberator,* Floyd Dell wrote that he couldn't believe these poems had been written by the same man who had sat next to him in the courtroom as they were being tried for espionage. But such critiques depended on a partial reading of Max's new poems, which, despite their formal conventionality, talked about sexual attraction in ways that violated social decorum.[39] The iconoclastic Los Angeles photographer Edward Weston, for one, who was then embarked on his own exploration of light, form, and beauty, understood Max's intentions. He took his copy of *Colors of Life,* given to him by Max himself, and heavily marked the passage about the Greeks not requiring any cosmic preparation to be able to enjoy life for what it is.[40]

In February 1919 Max departed for the West Coast to gather funds for the *Liberator.* He left Florence behind in Croton, where she lay awake at night and tried to make the time pass faster by playing their favorite songs on the Victrola, reading Plato's *Dialogues* ("they remind me of you"), and driving his car "all over."[41] The *Masses* trials had made Max's name a household word wherever he went, and his relationship with the beautiful Florence was no longer a secret either. When he arrived in Hollywood, Max's reputation had preceded him, to the extent that he began to worry that he might be the reason Florence had not been able to score a major movie deal yet. The director Cecil B. De-Mille, for example, "an ugly fat fool," had been rather nasty to him. A "screaming patriot," he believed everything the papers had said about Max. But not all Hollywood types were so intractable. Another director, D. W. Griffith, often regarded as the inventor of Hollywood, expressed admiration for Max's activities: "You are a braver man than I am," he said to Max. "I take my hat off to you." He also admitted that he never really believed in his own propaganda film, *Hearts of the World* (1918). War was, said Griffith, equally atrocious on both sides. "He seemed to have a real liking for me—which as usual in such cases I pretended to reciprocate. I urged him to do a picture of the history of the class struggle, and I'm going to send him the Communist Manifesto and that book we've talked about reading, 'The Ancient Lowly.' "[42] Max also met Charlie Chaplin, already "the most famous man in the world." Chaplin had asked to be introduced to the young socialist firebrand. They went for a walk, and Max impressed Chaplin by hitting the top of an evergreen tree with a green apple as if he had never done anything else in his life—a gesture so perfect in its random, understated, casually masculine bravado that it was bound to have an effect on the man Max would later characterize as an eternal child driven by the need to be the boss. On his way back Max stopped to give a speech in San Francisco, after which a "smoldering," blue-eyed beauty from Russia, Vera Zaliasnik, introduced herself to him. The meeting was a prelude to several sessions of passionate lovemaking, perhaps made more intense by Max's knowledge that Vera, besides being the girlfriend of the *Masses* contributor Robert Minor, had once killed a man (she was fourteen and he had sexually assaulted her). For all his dedication to nonexclusive, free love relationships, Max did not share news of this amorous detour with Florence.[43]

Meeting Chaplin in Hollywood reinforced Max's intention to finish writing the book on humor that had been on his mind for a long time. After his return he spent mornings in his barn in Croton poring over his notes, and thoughts of the book accompanied him even on the days he had to be in New York putting the next issue of the *Liberator* together: "Tomorrow and Monday—my book again," he informed Florence. "Tuesday we make up the magazine, maybe Wednesday—then toward the end of the week the deep dive for a masterpiece!"[44] Florence was off doing new things, too. She had accepted an engagement in another Megrue comedy, *Among the Girls,* with Percy Knight in the lead, a Scottish-born actor and notorious drunk who drove her crazy: "I am very disappointed in him," Florence wrote from DC. "I can never tell how my scenes with him will go, he is just as liable to kill them as not, and not through meanness, but just inability." Her attitude toward acting was every bit as professional as Max's toward his writing. Working with the shiftless Percy had reminded her that "nobody can arrive any where no matter how great their natural talent if they don't work seriously." After each performance Percy would get drunk with the chorus girls, while Florence worried about how her scenes with him would turn out the next day.[45] When the company was in Boston, at the Park Square Theatre, Florence reported that she had to walk the streets at night "threateningly" carrying a big stick in her hand. "The men here ought to be all shot at sunrise, they are so tough," she opined. "But they all shy away when they see the stick and by the time we land home our anger has turned to fits of laughing to see them all react the same way."[46]

Despite Knight's unpredictability, the tour was a success, and Florence's letters once again sparkled with the wit that had first attracted Max to her; perhaps they also had an influence on his evolving book on humor.[47] His days were now taken up by writing and by thinking about when he would next see Florence. At night, he went to sleep holding her letters in his hand.[48]

With Florence away, Max spent most of his time in his Croton house, traveling to the city only when *Liberator* business demanded it. He cashed in some bonds to bail George Andreytchine out of prison, a Bulgarian-Russian immigrant with a penchant for getting himself in trouble and who was nicknamed "the human torch."[49] Max offered him a temporary refuge at his Croton house: "Things are getting so hot that it is exciting."[50] Money remained scarce, but life on Mount Airy Road seemed like an everlasting party. For dinner he would invite Floyd Dell and his much taller, larger, and louder wife "B. Marie" or his other neighbors, Jack Reed and Louise Bryant. He didn't seem to mind that Jack had withdrawn his name from the editorial page of the *Liberator* in protest over what he saw as the magazine's continuing kowtowing to the Wilson government.[51] He also spent much time on the tennis court, playing singles or doubles with other radical friends, the lawyer Dudley Field Malone and the artist Boardman Robinson. Nothing seemed an obstacle, and Max was not averse to playing a game of tennis in the rain at midnight: "It was good to play and my 'members' feel limbered up and better reconciled to their membership."[52] And yet he missed Florence: "Much smoke and ashes and lively unimportant talking, but there is no gay pleasure in those things without you."[53]

Inspired by his new confidence in his body and its powers and openly desirous of Florence, Max included an erotic, even pornographic fantasy in his letter, which was plainly intended to arouse her. The beginning sets the scene:

I love you. I want you. Darling if you were here now—the yellow lights are shining just in the dark edge of twilight, and we would soon pull the curtains and lock the door, and all the sweet quiet little house would be ours, and I would stand before you and kiss you and put my hands in your hair, and then I would try to unfasten your dress and you would help me, and your clothes would slip down, and you would laugh and put your arms around me, and I would take my clothes off too, and then I would fix the bed for you, and we would slip in there together, shivering a little at the cold sheets but warm in the touch of each other.

From there, Max gives free rein to his feverish imagination. One wonders where, in an age still under the shadow of that tireless guardian of American morality, Anthony Comstock, he got the courage to send this through the mails:

My lips would cling to your lips quivering, beloved; until your thighs throbbed under me, and all the warm color and wonder of your beautiful lips thirsted to receive me, and every nerve and muscle of my being stood full of the fierce will to thrust in to the deeps of you. And then for madness I would leave your kiss and creep down to bury my lips and sensitive tongue in the hot salt flame of the folds of your body, and you would find my body too, and those sweet delicate lips of your love would burn against the very intimate essence of myself, until we could bear no longer any separation, and with your eyes closed and your lips curved intensely and your white thighs open, you would lie one second til I seized and clung to you all one, and my hot muscle plunged up through you to the inmost thirsting nerve, and we were lost, lost, lost in madness of each other's life.

The passage is unusual in its explicitness, allowing us to reconstruct the specific sexual acts from the descriptions given. And though it is certainly written from the man's perspective, Max's emphasis is on the mutuality of the pleasure he and Florence would enjoy if they only could be together now. More than anything, Max's letter vividly illustrates what had increasingly become important to Max: the right to do with one's body what one wanted, unencumbered by social convention or rules imposed by the state. Sexual liberation, for Max, had become inseparable from political liberation.[54]

In his humor manuscript Max freely acknowledged his debt to Sigmund Freud. But he also took him to task for still perpetuating the idea that sex was a furtive, subterranean thing. Freud had forced people, complained Max, "to confess that their bodies are great surging tanks full of lust and suppressed carnal hungers" and to look at all we produce in our waking hours—thoughts, poems, works of art—as covers for such unacceptable desires. But what if there was nothing to confess? In Freud's view the most hilarious, casual jokes, once the analyst has had his or her way with them, "declare themselves as fundamentally sexual." What bothered Max was less Freud's theory as such— and certainly not the idea that sex makes us do things that, on the surface, don't appear sexual—but his rhetoric that still seemed beholden to the idea that lust is something that must be revealed, confessed, dragged out into the open light of day as if it were a criminal that needed to be punished. Freud had lifted "a great incubus of shame from the shoulders of humanity," but in explaining to us how our minds always worked, he had not addressed the question if ever they could work differently, too. Max was looking forward to a time when sex would assume its role among the many factors that make up, as he wonderfully described it, "the companionable variety of nature."[55]

Thus, if Max was thinking about sex when he was writing to Florence, that didn't mean he was always thinking about it but that sex was what was on his mind at that particular time. Florence certainly got the message. "I loved your letter," she replied from Boston. "I read it over and over. I can almost feel your sweet body close to mine, you write so vividly. . . . I must see you, I must touch you and hear you, if I am to live."[56] In Max's view Florence and he were "beautiful gods," living in a space entirely of their own making, newly consecrated each time Florence was able to travel back to Croton.[57] The world revolved around them: Max the unafraid moral conscience of a nation rocked by the recent war and the ongoing revolutionary developments in Russia; Florence the epitome of beauty and grace, harbinger of a new society in which sexual relationships were no longer constrained by the heavy burden of American Protestantism that, for so long, had loomed over Max's life. Max felt invulnerable. When a secret State Department message was leaked regarding American support for anti-Bolshevik coalitions in Russia, Max, his voice strong with moral outrage, read it out loud in Madison Square Garden.[58]

Max must have been surprised, then, when Florence rejected the narrative he had been sketching out for both of them. Accepting an offer from Samuel Goldwyn, she departed New York for Hollywood in July, leaving Max howling with loneliness. Despite the subject of his work in progress, a sense of humor was not what sustained him as he tried to cope with his abandonment. For months at a time theirs became a relationship conducted chiefly through letters and telegrams, a realm in which Max, master of the well-placed word and subtle phrase, should have had the upper hand. That this was not so is one of the remarkable features of their correspondence. While Max reflected on his loneliness, describing how he would dash around in his Ford "crying like a baby," how he would open the closet in his house at Croton to sniff Florence's lingering scent in the clothes she had left behind, and how he had moved his bed into the barn so he wouldn't have to face his empty house, Florence typically talked more about her environment, the people she met, the plans she had for her career.[59]

Yet being separated from Max was hard for her, too. She was "steeped in melancholy," she wrote from the train to Los Angeles. "You are so beautiful to look at and to touch." The reading she had brought along for the ride seemed hardly suitable to lift her spirits: Robert Burton's *Anatomy of Melancholy*.[60] Once in Hollywood, she added a biography of Milton to her reading list because the poet, in his desire for perfection, reminded her so much of Max. But she was already in love with Hollywood ("the sun shines so beautifully"), and she adored her new dressing room at the Goldwyn studios in Culver City.[61] She had taken a room at the Hotel Alexandria, which boasted the city's most fabulous ballroom and was really the place to be in downtown Los Angeles, frequented by the rich and the beautiful and those who wanted to be seen as such: silent movie stars, Hollywood moguls, and the inevitable hangers-on. It was in the lobby of the Alexandria, during the exact same month Florence was living there, that Chaplin, whose infant son had just died, met the four-year-old child performer Jackie Coogan, the child star in *The Kid,* still considered one of his finest films.[62]

Max's letters to Hollywood overflowed with unfocused desire. The green ink he preferred made them seem almost feminine, but the words leap out boldly at the reader, yearning to be more than words. They become a way of touching her, as Florence realized: "I sighed for you to be really there so I could feel your sweet touch."[63] While Florence seemed to grab whatever was handy—a pencil Max left behind, a scrap of hotel letterhead—to pour out her emotions, unfiltered, onto the sheet in front of her, Max's letters are those of an editor: the lines are straight, the words correctly spelled, and new paragraphs helpfully indented. More often than not Max would cover both the front and the back of his sheets so as not to waste paper, as Florence was apt to do. Emotionally, though, Max came across as more unrestrained, ranging from abject declarations of misery to orgasmic displays of joy to blatant expressions of neediness and the desire to exert control over Florence. He warned her not to let go of her "beautiful gipsy color on the screen" in exchange for some generic Hollywood ideal of perfection. In a 137-word telegram Max elaborated: "I WORRY CONTINUALLY ABOUT YOUR CHANGING THE MAKE UP YOU USED IN JAFFERY AND AUCTION BLOCK YOUR COLOR WAS EVERYTHING IN THOSE PICTURES THEIR SUCCESS HAS BROUGHT YOU THIS OPPORTUNITY WHY TAMPER WITH ONE OF THE CHIEF ELEMENTS OF THIS SUCCESS?"[64]

But Florence did not need his advice: she was finally doing work that met her high standards. Her first major film was *The Loves of Letty*, produced by Samuel Goldwyn and directed by Frank Lloyd. The star of the movie was Pauline Frederick, a seasoned stage actress who had made her film debut in 1915. Florence had been cast as her best friend, Marion Allardyce. Frederick was openly jealous of her, but Florence liked her part, and Lloyd was, she told Max, just lovely.[65] Only one copy of the *Loves of Letty* has survived, and although it is in rather poor shape, Florence's acting has lost none of its appeal.[66] She looks stylish and graceful, if slightly somber and, indeed, pale, her heart-shaped face glowing in the mostly dark rooms where the action takes place. Tall and slim, she towers over the shorter Frederick. Her dark eyes burn themselves into the viewer's mind; ultimately they make her character more inscrutable than Frederick's rather transparent Letty. *The Loves of Letty* occupied a special place in Florence's portfolio: "There is never a moment I look strange like I sometimes did in Vitagraph pictures," she said after she saw the finished production: "I always look like myself."[67]

In August 1919 Florence moved into an apartment at 1824 Highland Avenue, the "prettiest little" place, with a porch and more space for herself and her mother, who had joined her.[68] While Max buried himself in the stacks of the Columbia University library or retreated to the privacy of his Croton house, deploring, quite unhumorously, the slow progress of his book and the interruptions caused by his editorial responsibilities, Florence sought public recognition in Hollywood. She tried to keep up with Max's life in the East, reading the New York papers—"childish with their red terror"—as well as Scripps's *Los Angeles Record* for the labor news.[69] Max and his friend Marie Howe sent letters to people they knew in Los Angeles to help Florence settle in, including the painter and writer Rob Wagner, the wealthy socialite and patron of left-wing causes Kate Gartz, and the labor organizer Joe O'Carroll.[70]

But Florence's Big Break never came, not then, not afterward. She did get a few roles in films now considered lost, and out of the little she made she kept sending money to Max, a fact that almost seems to have turned him on.[71] "At this studio they think of me as a lovely sweet girl," she complained to Max, "and only want to cast me in sympathetic parts." Her "big fight" to get the lead in a movie based on *The Perch of the Devil* failed when the author of the book, Gertrude Atherton, personally intervened and said she was certainly beautiful enough but much too young.[72] In August 1919 she was cast in *The Cup of Fury,* directed by T. Hayes Hunter and based on a novel by Rupert Hughes, who melted when he met Florence and told her she was "one of the most beautiful girls he had ever seen."[73] Goldwyn did invite her to have dinner with him and other executives in the business, among them Frank Joseph Godsol, the "eminence grise" at Goldwyn Pictures. Everyone liked her, and Florence's beauty was compared to that of Mona Lisa, as she proudly told Max. But money remained scarce all the same.[74]

If Florence was fighting to establish herself as a Hollywood actress, Max back in Croton was also trying to figure out what to do with himself. Sharing his small Croton house with the "blundering" George Andreytchine didn't help. Once his impulsive housemate lopped off the lower branches of the trees that formed Max's hedge, and Max blew up. "Now they stand there all trimmed up like long-legged chickens," he lamented, surveying the damage done to his trees. Gone was "the sweetness of seclusion and the beauty of all that I have watched and watered for those four years since I planted them." Andreytchine was entirely apologetic and, with tears in his eyes, offered to make amends. "It's too bad that I have this interior revolt against intimacy," observed Max.[75] In the same letter Max included one of the longest, most coherent stories he shared with Florence, and the care with which he narrates it suggests it had hit a raw nerve.

A few days before, he was driving around uptown with Floyd Dell and George in the car. They had just picked up the poet Claude McKay in Harlem when Max found himself on 153rd Street, on the wrong side of the bridge over the Harlem River. He turned around. Since the street was empty, he was driving faster than usual. He was chatting animatedly with his passengers, just as he had always told Florence not to do. Suddenly a little boy, "just about the size of Dan when I left him," seemed to appear right in front of the car. The situation was surreal, a complete reversal of the sane order of things. Running "from clear across the street," with his head down and his arms pumping, the little boy was coming toward them at a fast clip, as if he was determined to get hit. "He was running toward death in the same haste that one would run away from it." Dell uttered a surprised "Why look at this!" Max knew that hitting the brake would accomplish nothing, since the car would slide into the boy and probably kill him, so he abruptly jerked his steering wheel to the right. Swinging the vehicle up the curb, he smashed it, with a loud crash, straight into a tree. The Ford's mudguard just grazed the boy, who fell on the pavement, scraping his shoulder and elbow. Max got out and picked the boy up and carried him to where he said his home was. Once there, Max was in for another surprise. He found an apartment swarming with "a thousand other kids" and an overwhelmed mother who took only a mild interest in Max's account of the tragedy he had barely averted. When Max returned to his smashed Ford, the full extent of what had happened began to dawn on him. He had to hire a truck so that the "tin remnant of our long suffering Ford" could be dragged away from the street. Everyone was relieved, however, that the kid had survived. Drifting off to sleep in his bed at night, Max was playing through the scene again in his mind: "I guess I could never have slept if I had hurt him."

If this had been a dream rather than a real experience, Freud would have had a field day with it. At any rate, Max's behavior before, during, and after the accident proved he was quick on his feet in an emergency and not afraid to act if necessary, something that couldn't fail to impress Florence as she was slowly drifting away from him into a new world where Max feared he no longer mattered. But the story also cast cold water on the demands of the traditional family structure: while the boy's mother didn't much care, Max had shown himself ready to sacrifice his car and perhaps the lives of himself and his friends in order to protect the life of a child not his own. Max might have failed as a biological father, but by protecting that strange little boy, he had, if only for a moment, become everyone's father.

The very next day Max challenged fate again. Going out in his boat on the Tappan Zee with Claude, Eugen Boissevain, and George on board, he ended up in the middle of a great big storm. Claude and George were convinced they were all going to die, as was Dudley Malone on the shore, who kept saying Ave Marias for them while his wife, Doris, was running around the house repeating to herself, "They are drowned, they are drowned." At the helm of the boat, Max, however, was "wildly happy." It was a fantastic sight: "The boat rolling half over, the sail creaking and booming, dipping in the water and flying into the sky, sheets of water from the sky and great waves crashing over the boat drenching and pounding us, the river so full of white caps that it looked like a grave under the black wind, and great cracks of lightning rending the sky with terrific thunder no further off than the top of the mast." Giving orders in a steady voice, Max got them out of danger. "I enjoy being a hero," he said to Florence. But he also admitted that, being an experienced sailor, he knew they were relatively safe. "If we had been way out at sea, I would have been sick with fear." Max, the limited liability hero.[76]

The topic of Max's editorials in the August 1919 issue of the *Liberator* just so happened to be the importance of courage. Taking aim at President Wilson once again for violating his promise to the American people to keep them out of the war, Max imagined how Wilson would be heckled by courageous pro-testers at public appearances, something that would be unthinkable in the United States but more than possible in Europe, where there was a tradition of social and military courage. And Max slammed Wilson's secret campaign— a private war without an actual declaration of war—against Soviet Russia, re-printing the intercepted cable he had read at Madison Square Garden. Even if there was no tradition of social courage in the United States there was plenty of room for personal bravery—such as Max's.[77] Florence bought her copy of the *Liberator* in Hollywood, "the finest number I ever read." She liked the cover, a drawing of Crystal by Maurice Sterne, and the "lovely poetry," but above all she admired Max's editorial, so "brilliant and witty."[78] Indeed, Max's confidence was on the rise again, politically, personally, intellectually, and he kept postponing his long-planned visit to Hollywood, pointing out that he had to wait for Crystal to come back from her trip to Hungary. Inside his study he was, he said, "slinging Plato Aristotle Hegel Bergson Voltaire Schopenhauer and many more pompous professors around my head and through my legs and up over, twirling and turning them like a juggler."[79]

Incidentally, the "lovely poetry" in Florence's *Liberator* issue included a handful of works by Max's new friend Claude McKay. Max rarely allowed men to get as close to him as Claude did. Claude was smitten with Max and Max's life from the moment he visited him in his Croton house. As far as he was concerned, even the storm on the Tappan Zee that had nearly capsized their boat was part of the beautiful existence Max had created for himself: "I *love* your life!" Max became a mentor of sorts to the younger man, reading his work and offering suggestions for improvement.[80] In the *Liberator* Max celebrated the "fine clear flame of life" he had found burning in Claude's work. But in the best-known poem of the series, the sonnet "If We Must Die," that fine flame threated to become a conflagration. Alluding to Longfellow's famous injunc-tion, in "A Psalm of Life," not to go through life "like dumb cattle," McKay exhorted his black brothers not to die like hogs in the battle for survival,

"Hunted and penned in an inglorious spot / While round us bark the mad and hungry dogs." Unsurprisingly, the concluding couplet, "Like men we'll face the murderous, cowardly pack, / Pressed to the wall, dying, but fighting back," put McKay on the radar of the Justice Department.[81] Later that year he left the United States for England.

Max arrived in Hollywood on September 28, a visit heralded by a flurry of telegrams, as if he were the Queen of Sheba. After sending her mother back to New York, Florence had found a new apartment at 6220 De Longpre Avenue, just one block away from Sunset Boulevard. They lived on the ground floor, surrounded by palm trees, overlooking green meadows. The house is still there today, though Hollywood, of course, has changed considerably, as indicated by the gated windows and the "No Trespassing" signs that are now attached to the house. But the huge palm trees fanning the desert winds might still be the same, and the mild smell of marijuana lingering over De Longpre serves as a reminder of a different era of social experimentation. This is where Max and Florence met again and where they spent their nights, the windows open to the soft air.

After they had been separated for so long and by so many miles, kept apart by a "great cold wall," as Max put it, they were hoping they could simply pick up where they had left off.[82] But Max had waited too long, for a thousand different reasons explained in many letters and, when he had the money, telegrams. An even greater mistake was to introduce Florence to Chaplin that fall. Unwittingly, he had become the agent of his own destruction as Florence's lover. Soon both he and Florence were spending evenings at Chaplin's house, participating in charades that got ever more complicated, expanding from cues for speeches picked out of a hat to themes for one-act plays, improvised at a moment's notice with costumes pilfered for the occasion from the wardrobes of guests who had come to stay for the night.

Neither Max Eastman nor Charlie Chaplin got much work done that fall; both Chaplin's *The Kid* and Max's *The Sense of Humor* suffered as a result. It's unclear how much their competition for Florence's favors played into the frenzied energy the two friends put into their charades, as if a life of play would keep the looming storm at bay. In *Heroes I Have Known* (1942), Max called Charlie an "actor of one role only," a man unknowable yet somehow predictable, too: beautiful to look at but without any principles to speak of. Chaplin has, wrote Max, "no unity of character, . . . nothing in his head that, when he lays it on the pillow, you can sensibly expect will be there in the morning."

Leading so many people to believe he was their "intimate friend," Chaplin in fact kept everyone at arm's length. Never sorry for what he did, the Chaplin Max re-created for his readers was an essentially amoral creature: instinctive, rapacious, self-involved. He was his mother's son: deeply unhinged, she had been charming enough to convince immigration officials she was sane and should be allowed inside the country. If Charlie had any integrity at all, it lay in his art. Harder to live with than "Lord Byron or a kaleidoscope," as Max brilliantly put it, the chameleonic Chaplin treated women the way one buys and then immediately throws away a cheap pen. Too busy with himself, Chaplin had never given the world the full measure of his talents and had poured them instead into that one little creature with baggy pants, oversized shoes, and the too-tight jacket familiar from the screen, a predatory child, as bewitching as he was dangerous. Chaplin was Max minus the remnants of religious scruples. It is obvious that Max's portrait of him, for all the self-conscious literary posturing, was shaped by deep affection as well as by envy and a long-suppressed desire to take revenge on the guy who had taken his girl.[83]

Max celebrated the end of his Hollywood stay by accidentally taking Florence's car keys with him, leaving her stranded at the train station, at the mercy of a dubious mechanic who took the vehicle apart, strewing sundry parts over the floor, before admitting he couldn't start it. Interestingly, he didn't have the tools either to put it all back together again, so Florence had to hail a cab and arrange for her car to be towed. Having no money at all, she wrote bad checks right and left. Notably, she never once berated Max for the inconvenience he had caused her. Instead, she baldly stated the facts and then wrote about her longing for him: "I shall hold you in my arms close to me and keep you warm, and won't mind the lions roaring and the winds howling."[84]

As Florence was wondering where he was and why he wasn't writing, Max found himself in San Francisco in the arms of an admiring "girl poet" he had felt compelled to visit. That poet was, although Max doesn't reveal her name even in his almost-tell-all autobiography, Genevieve Taggard, who would go on to acquire some reputation as a poet in her own right. Not classically beautiful, she reminded Max of another hero of his: "I declare you could dress her up in a beard and take a picture of Walt Whitman." A perhaps more potent aphrodisiac for Max was that she adored his work: "She made me very happy by showing me a volume of my poems almost all worn out, and the passages marked that I know best." Concluded Max, "It was wonderful to find that my poems were to a stranger who read them just the same thing they are to me." He didn't tell Florence he also slept with Taggard.[85]

His dalliance with Taggard over, he exchanged her embrace for that of another admirer, his "stormy-haired love" from his earlier visit to the Bay area, Vera Zaliasnik. As he was bedding Vera, Max wouldn't stop babbling about Florence, so much so, in fact, that he afterward apologized, unnecessarily so, as Vera felt: "I am not hurt when you talk to me of Florence." Her love for Max, she said poetically, was "so absolutely clean and beautiful, so almost heavenly in its calm, love, that I cannot relate myself or a single of my thoughts of you to pain and a sense of unpleasantness." But when Max's train pulled out of the station in San Francisco, Vera was seized by a powerful impulse to throw her body before it so that it could not take her lover of one day away from her: "And I will never forget the lovely image of your waving to me from the observation, just as I was running away from the unbearable scene of separation."[86] Anyone still baffled by Max's serial philandering might want to remember that the shadow of Elmira's Park Church was still looming over him—and that Florence, in the preceding months, had also freely mentioned men that interested her, from the screenwriter Louis Sherwin to a movie director she had gone swimming with and, finally, an unidentified man she thought she "might like."[87]

Max returned to a New York gripped by hysteria. On January 2, 1920, vowing to rid America of its "moral perverts," federal agents carried out the so-called Palmer Raids. Under the direction of U.S. Attorney General A. Mitchell Palmer, they raided pool halls, restaurants, and private homes in thirty-five cities and, without warrants, arrested more than six thousand alleged radicals. In faraway California Florence read about the commotion in the papers, hoping that the jails could not hold all those taken into custody. But that was not the case: many of those arrested were held for weeks or months without access to legal counsel, sometimes in deserted army encampments. Among the federal agents who participated in the Palmer raids was a young J. Edgar Hoover.

Max's work on the *Liberator* had become even more important now. Rather inconveniently, Crystal had, Max felt, pretty much abandoned him. As a co-editor, she was forever in a position of inferiority—the brilliant writing was his, and that's what the public cared about, he observed. "Restless, insatiable girl—self-assertive, yet utterly dependent on others."[88] Florence might have taken that rather smug characterization as applicable to herself, too. The new film in which she had gotten a part, *Dollars and Sense,* directed by Harry Beaumont, bored her to no end.[89] She knew she was not the only one in Hollywood who was disappointed with her situation. Other "movie people" felt exactly the same: "There is absolutely no poetry or beauty in their lives. . . . There is no artistic reward or material."[90] This wasn't art but business.

There was some hope, though. Somewhat puzzlingly she informed Max, "The only art is that of photography."[91] That sentiment did not come from nowhere. Through Max, Florence had met the photographer Margrethe Mather, seven years older than Florence and originally from Salt Lake City, a "slim, quietly magnetic girl, snub-nosed, grey-eyed, with this-way and that-way floating ash-blond hair." She struck up a friendship with Mather that likely became more than that. At least temporarily Florence also shared her apartment with Mather, who was a bit of a waif, too. Like Florence, she had changed her name: born Emma Caroline Youngren, the daughter of Danish converts to Mormonism, she chose for herself the last name of a man for whom her aunt worked as a housekeeper. Mather, who was by inclination a lesbian, though she was also embroiled in a torturous relationship with the married Edward Weston, fell in love with Florence and took more photographs of her than of anybody else in her career. Max instantly knew something was afoot: "Don't love Margaret too much," he warned Florence. "I have no other home but where you are."[92]

Into this volatile situation ambled Charlie Chaplin. He had dinner with Florence on Christmas Eve and gave her a box of lovely, handmade handkerchiefs as well as, more important, a small role in his new film, *A Day's Pleasure*, where she was seen in the now-famous Los Angeles traffic jam. Driving her own Ford onto the set, Florence got, in her own account, caught between two cars and cried out to the traffic policeman, presumably the same one who, in the version we know, ends up in the manhole, "Are you going to let them kill me?" But she got no sympathy from the copper. "Keep out of the way can't you, was all he said."[93]

Chaplin made sure Florence did not keep out of *his* way. He is "always very sweet to me," she told Max.[94] Soon he was a fixture at 6220 De Longpre. Florence gave him Max's *Colors of Life* as a gift, perhaps as a reminder to both of them not to go any further. "He was so happy to get it." Then she revealed that she had been to Chaplin's projection room to see *The Kid:* "It is wonderful wonderful. I cried and laughed and smiled and was so worried some of the terrible policemen in the picture would get him. It was the most exciting thing I ever saw."[95]

This was a good time to distract Chaplin. Although he was already separated from her, Mildred Harris had refused to grant him a divorce, and the production of *The Kid* had cost him a half million dollars. No wonder Charlie wanted to get away from it all, a proposal Florence readily embraced: "As soon as he finishes this picture he asked me if I wouldn't take a trip in his car." They felt, she wrote, "the wanderlust very strongly and were flying all over the world at a great rate." While Max was hunkering down in Croton and tinkering with the *Liberator,* which by now seemed more like an albatross around his neck than a harbinger of freedom, Chaplin was promising Max's girlfriend car rides "all over the world." Evidently, Florence wanted to make Max jealous; disarmingly, she even disclosed why: "I fear in each letter I receive that you will describe somebody you have fallen in love with." Max took the bait. He was frightened about Charlie, he told her. "Do you think he is as nice as I am?"[96]

Max never revealed much about the ménage à trois in which he, Florence, and Charlie found themselves, except to say that "a lot of unusual emotions were given a place in the sun."[97] But it didn't take Florence long to realize that Chaplin wasn't too unlike the character he played on screen: "Charlie ever speaks of going away," she complained to Max, "but it all depends on the picture he is making, and at the rate he is working, he will never finish it." He was vain and easily jealous of others, like the brilliant French comedian Max Linder, whom Florence met at Charlie's studio, a "smart little fellow." Afraid to be upstaged by Linder, Charlie ran for his dressing room, pulled off his hat, and roughed up his hair, a look he knew would make him appear charming: "So he caught a fleeting vision of himself in the mirror and all was well in the world again." If anyone needed psychoanalysis, decided Florence, it was Chaplin, who seemed incapable of disentangling himself from his domestic nightmare yet couldn't stop talking about it: "I know I am naughty, but I become tired of Charlie's troubles. He stays in that frightful situation at his home, and his powerlessness to move wears me out."[98]

Meanwhile, Florence's professional situation had steadily worsened. By Hollywood standards she had not worked much, and so it must not have come as a complete surprise to her when Cliff Robertson, Goldwyn's studio manager, took it upon himself to tell her she was no longer wanted.[99] Her career at a standstill, and the man she still cared most about far away, Florence drove her Ford to a Hollywood airfield, perhaps the Aerodrome owned by Chaplin's half brother Syd on Crescent and Wiltshire Boulevards, and convinced a pilot to take her flying. "Don't be jealous," she told Max, as if she wanted him to be. Suited up and wearing goggles, Florence loved being high up in the air, seeing the world the way a bird would, reduced to happy insignificance. There were the tiny houses, reminders of the boxed-in life she wanted to leave behind.

Florence's cleverness is evident in how she plays with the word "adventure," using it as a description of her flying experience—and an adventure it certainly was—as well as of the way she now viewed her future with Max. "Only come if it is an adventure." And she mapped out the kind of communications she wanted to have with him, words exchanged on the go, in scribbled notes, telegrams, in automobiles going full speed to some unknown destination: "Let us have conversations together as if we were riding in the Ford." Florence was signaling to Max that she wanted to be spontaneous, on the move, unpredictable. While Max strove to fix her in place—as his gypsy girl, pining away in California, immune to the fatal attractions of Hollywood, yet still successful as an actress—she told him not to come and visit for the wrong reasons. She needed to find herself first.[100]

Days later Goldwyn ended Florence's contract, confirming what she had feared. Speaking about herself in the third person, she offered an unsparing view of herself and announced she was not coming back to join Max in his socialist utopia on Mount Airy:

> I who began the race for success so well equipped, now stand completely stripped with no vision before my eyes but one of mediocrity. I cannot force it. I cannot give up all my bright hopes. I would die first. Utter utter despair fills my heart. It is my self I have to live with always, it was my self I wanted to love, how can I care about this dark girl, she is no longer lovely to me, no longer beautiful. Do not think I mean I did not love you. That is not so, but I cannot be happy with you unless I am happy about my self. You understand that don't you. I am not coming back to the little house on the hill. I have given up that dream completely. I cannot go back.[101]

But back she went, or at least she was hoping to. Within days she had landed a new job in New York, working, for $350 a week, with the French director Maurice Tourneur.[102]

She had barely put the letter in the mail when she heard that Max had become otherwise preoccupied. Disaster had struck. She telegraphed Max immediately regarding the "RUMOURS WHICH HAD HURT MY HEART." Max telegraphed back: "I WOULD TELL YOU IF SUCH A THING WERE TRUE, YOU KNOW THAT DONT YOU" and then supplied the following self-assessment, enhanced by a hilarious misunderstanding that must have happened at the Western Union office, where the clerk obviously was not familiar with Wordsworth's poetry: "AM LONELY AS A CLOWN."[103] Had Max been responsible for the mistake, what a Freudian slip

Figure 26. "A picture of the little brown sandals. And Lisa swimming
like mad!" Lisa Duncan in Venice, 1920. EM.

this would have been—the very kind of linguistic mishap that would have
been great material for his work on humor. But no amount of self-pity could
have helped Max out of the situation he himself had created. He finally had to
confess that he had done what Florence had always feared he would and begun a relationship with another woman, Lisa Duncan (fig. 26), one of the
"Isadorables," the six German-born pupils of Isadora Duncan whom the famous dancer had formally adopted so she could import them to the United
States.[104]

Max had been helplessly attracted to all of them. On stage, the Duncan girls
were a whirlwind of muscular legs, bare feet, and flowing garments. But Lisa
was the one he had fallen in love with. When Florence confronted him, Max at
first made a clumsy move to pretend that nothing catastrophic had happened
and praised the article about her he had seen in *Picture-Play:* "Your portraits
. . . are rich and gypsy—warm and beautiful as the world's desire." But if Max
had hoped he could thus maintain what he now called his friendship with
Florence as well as continue to enjoy the new sexual high to which his relationship with Lisa had brought him, he was wrong: "I do not care if you are in
love with Lisa," Florence fired back. "I feel like one who has walked and trotted
and run a long way, and now I can rest."[105] The damage was done.

But Lisa, younger than Max by fifteen years and at the beginning of her
dancing career, had even less reason than Max to commit to a relationship. She
had just emerged from one, in fact, with a man she called Arnold, presumably

the photographer Arnold Genthe. By mid-April she was in Philadelphia, and two months later she had left the country, along with the other Isadorables. Her letters to Max were almost orgasmic in their intensity and liberated even from the mild constraints imposed by English grammar: "My lips durst for your sweet delirious kisses—my body trembles with the memory of you—my heart longs for our cruel unkind love. . . . Max don't you remember our kisses—madness—passion—my shyly whispered trembling words—my tears—my love—my complete happily-pining All."[106]

He had evidently not told Florence the truth when he claimed, in the sheepish letter he had sent when she found out, that he never desecrated their shared memories at Croton, since Lisa explicitly thanked him for what she had experienced there. "All my heart is with you in the little gaycoloured leaves, on the green hill—where I experienced the most exquisite wildest ecstasy of love," wrote Lisa while already on her way to Europe with the rest of Isadora's troupe. During the transatlantic passage even the ocean reminded her of Max. Its undulating colors and flowing waves offered her an image of their shared, wildly flowing love, as she stated in a rhapsodic letter written to Max in her native language.[107]

Lisa's letters kept coming, from Paris, Versailles, Venice, and Athens, written in her big, scrawly, virtually illegible handwriting, conjuring the "aching sweet memory" of Max and, soon enough, the new, liberating experience of dancing under the hot sun of Greece, all beauty and music, which made her "dizzily happy" and which she felt Max needed to share, too.[108] From there, as well as later on from Paris, she sent encouragements to Max to come and visit her: "We could read and play to-gether and will speak French."[109] Isadora's demands on her and the other members of the group were inhuman. But unlike Florence Deshon, Lisa Duncan was completely happy in her art. She wanted to "expand and breathe freely," which seemed to be especially easy in Greece, "where the air is so light that one just wants to fly-fly-fly."[110] If she couldn't have Max with her, well, then, she would dance him into existence: "There are moments when you seem so very near to me and that is when I dance—the memory of those starry nights and your warm sweet kisses comes to life again and with their tender influence and ecstatic joy I move—love—and live. . . . I love you most when I dance—when you are infinitely more closer [sic] to me than even in your wildest sweetest embrace."[111]

One of Max's best poems, "To Lisa in Summer," catches some of the excitement Lisa had generated in him. It is quite a feat to evoke a liquid, flowing world of sexual excitement in the stiff mold of a Petrarchan sonnet, but this is precisely what Max does. Lisa is absent, a memory only, but to Max—who represents himself doing what he loved to do so much: swimming, diving, bathing—she is present everywhere in nature, in the waves that touch him, the flowers, birds, and leaping butterflies, the wind. The poem consecrates Lisa's memory, turning nature into an altar to her beauty, an icon of grace, cool, deep, silver, still:

> All things that move are memories of you,
> The waves that linger glimmering and slim
> Along my body when I dive and swim,
> The daisies bathing with me in the dew,
> The nimble swallows in the limpid blue,
> The leaping butterflies above the trim
> Wild yellow lilies dancing in the brim
> Of winds that are but naked motion too.
> There is no wing or willow in this place
> So swift or slender it can bend and bless
> But in remembrance of your kindling grace,
> And even the deep cool waiting water knows
> How liquid is the depth of your repose,
> How silver still a pool your quietness.[112]

More than forty years after their fateful first encounter, Max, who had lost touch with her, located Lisa again. Living in poverty in communist Dresden, she was delighted to hear from Max: "Your letter made me shed sweet tears." Whatever had changed, she was still, she told Max, entranced by the "ecstasy of a pose," and she had never stopped dancing. "Your memory is very precious to me," she added, and revealed that she had been reading "To Lisa in Summer" to herself over the decades to sustain her "in moments of doubts or disappointments."[113]

Left behind by leaping, flying, laughing Lisa, Max found himself crawling back to Florence only to discover she had moved on, too. "Just talk to me as though we were riding in the Ford," he pleaded, appealing to their shared enthusiasm for cars.[114] He faulted his upbringing and his marriage—"I was bound falsely and outrageously by my relations to Ida"—and said they simply had met too soon after he left Ida: "Just twenty-five days after I escaped from her, love conquered me, putting down in pain and cruelty the terrible rebellion in my soul." And now the rebel had arisen again, rearing his ugly head.[115]

Florence said nothing, except for a short note sent almost ten days after Max's letter, in which she reiterated that she wanted love, not friendship.[116] Sitting at his desk in Croton, Max filled half a notebook with scrawls, using his characteristic green ink. He deplored Florence's coldness, her alleged contempt for him, her tossing him off as if he were a dead dog.[117]

But Florence was not well. Feeling worse and worse during the first weeks of summer, she ended up in bed at her house, cared for by a nurse. She was lonely and scared. Chaplin, still running away from his wife, Mildred, had left town. When Max found out, he urged her to come to Croton.[118] He wired money and saw to it that the preferred physician of Greenwich Village dwellers, the infinitely tolerant Dr. Lorber, examined her when she came out. Lorber diagnosed an abortive pregnancy and had the dead fetus—Charlie's child, Max assumed—removed. As soon as Chaplin heard the news, he also found his way to Croton, where he checked into the Tumbleweed Inn and did his best to complicate whatever rekindling of intimacy seemed to have taken place between the star-crossed ex-lovers. Instead of fiery passion, however, their love merely flashed and then sputtered on. Although she was grateful for what he had done for her, Florence would not allow Max to dissuade her from returning to California. After her departure, a restless Max went to watch Florence's last movie, *The Twins of Suffering Creek*, at the Village Theatre on 8th Avenue and became foolishly proud of Florence when a big fat man next to him burst into tears during one of her scenes.[119] The tears were really *his* tears, tears about what he had come to, as he told Florence in one of his green-inked, smudged notes.[120] "I once was your lover and now am nothing," he wrote. Desperate for any kind of reaction from her, he even sat down and calculated the money she owed him ($400).[121]

In November Florence mailed him a series of portraits Margrethe had taken of her. But Max found the photographs artificial, devoid of the "light that shines in your eyes": beautiful pictures but not pictures of Florence's beauty.[122] The problem wasn't Margrethe's. The life had gone out not of Florence's eyes but of her relationship with Max. On November 30, 1920, she cut off much of her brunette, very fine hair that Max had liked so much and sent a shock of it to him in New York—stuffed, without an accompanying note, into an envelope from the Friday Morning Club, a suffragist association founded in April 1891 by Caroline Seymour Severance, the first president of the New England Women's Club in Boston and a friend of Susan B. Anthony. This was not a Victorian-style memento of her love for him but an assertion of her independence, especially given the fact that Max had always tried to control her appearance, down to the very makeup he thought she should use. She had bobbed the hair he liked so much, and she wanted Max to know what she had done.[123]

Max did come out to visit Florence once again, at the end of February 1921. Crystal, plagued by ill health, had permanently left the *Liberator*, and Max had passed on his daily editorial responsibilities to a team of editors willing to take turns, Floyd Dell, Bob Minor, and Claude McKay, and he was finally free to work on his book. But things went badly wrong once he was in Hollywood. Words were exchanged—Florence said he was "depriving her of life" without giving anything in return to her—and Max found himself out on the street: "I know there is nothing left I can do for you but take my terrible self out of the way of your beautiful brave life. I am trying in tears and agony to pick up my things." An "ocean of blackness," wrote Max, in a melodramatic, self-pitying note he left in her mailbox, encompassed him.[124] He left Hollywood for good on June 7.

Florence was now without Max and also without Charlie, about whose complicated affairs—involving a seventeen-year-old aspiring actress named May Collins, much in love with Chaplin, though he wasn't with her—she continued to report in letters to Max.[125] Croton was deserted. There were strangers living in Crystal's and Floyd's houses on Mount Airy Road, and no one seemed interested in challenging Max on the tennis court. Andreytchine had escaped to Russia, and Jane Burr, the proprietor of the once-hip Drowsy Saint Inn, living by herself in the house above Max's, puttered around the neighborhood like a parody of Croton's glory days: "She is *not* going to turn that house into an inn," joked Max.[126]

In Hollywood Florence was doing some acting on the stage. She was also reading Van Wyck Brooks's new book, *The Ordeal of Mark Twain,* and was bothered by the author's apparent misogyny. Nevertheless, some of Brooks's observations on humor she felt could be useful to Max.[127] Was she trying to move their relationship to a new level, that of colleagues sharing ideas? Max, at any rate, was pleased by Florence's newfound interest in his work. With her as an audience his book had come to life again, a "beautiful thing." Most notably, Florence saved Max and his readers from the very awkward title Max had been contemplating, "What and Why Is Humor?"[128]

It was just at that time that the proof sheets for the most recent portraits of Florence and Max taken by Mather arrived in Max's mailbox. The images, as Max realized, fictionalized their identities, lifting onto the higher plane of art what in life had remained stubbornly imperfect and difficult. "It is fine model-ing," quipped Max. He thought the photographs of him against the infinite dunes, taken likely on Redondo Beach, outside the home of Weston's friend Ramiel McGehee, highlighted his best features—his nose and his raincoat.[129] But that is not really true: in one of the best shots from that series (fig. 27), the most clearly defined thing is not Max or his coat but the wooden railing that divides the image diagonally. The relatively shallow depth of field keeps the dunes in the upper half of the picture in soft focus, with sand filling its lower half. In the middle ground, the post to which the slats are attached (we discern even the heads of the nails that were used) appears to slightly lift the railing so that it almost buckles. That this occurs close to what normally would be considered the compositional center of the photograph is evidence of Mather's genius. Obviously, this is not intended to be a photograph of a

Figure 27. *Max Eastman.* 1921. Photograph by Margrethe Mather and Edward Weston, Museum of Modern Art. Digital Image © The Museum of Modern Art/ Licensed by SCALA /Art Resource, NY; © 2016 Center for Creative Photography, Arizona Board of Regents/Artists Rights Society (ARS), New York.

wooden structure in the sand. But, then, Max is not where he should be in this portrait, a feeling reinforced by the two or three indentations in the sand in the foreground. Was that where he had been sitting earlier? Mather's decision to have Max perch on a railing and then to push him away from the center is perhaps a commentary on something she had experienced firsthand in his volatile relationship with the woman she loved, too, a relationship in which he had done a lot of fence sitting. But she also might have intended her portrait as a more political reflection on the forever unpredictable Max, someone who always wanted to belong and never quite did, who was as little in agreement with his environment as a guy wearing a suit and tie was equipped for a walk on the beach. Max, in this photograph, recedes from us and our attempts to understand him.

In Mather's eyes Florence (fig. 28) was also turning away into a space to be inhabited only by herself, although she remains close to us, so close we feel we can touch her. Mather's series included one of the most remarkable portraits

Figure 28. *Florence Deshon*, 1921. Photograph by
Margrethe Mather. EMII.

of Florence ever taken, quite unlike the earlier images Max had objected to. It's a startlingly effective and erotic photograph, utterly devoted to capturing Florence's beauty, as the light, which seems to be coming from the right, travels over her face, sculpting her features, emphasizing the cheekbones, her chin, her right shoulder. Florence is turning away from us, yet not quite: her head is somewhat tilted toward the left, as her dark eyes seem to be pulling her into the dark background. While on the right Florence's bobbed hair is still distinguishable from the background, the left half of her face is fading into blackness.

Mather has the camera making love to Florence's face, caressing it as if she wanted to remember its beauty. The intimacy of that gesture is enhanced by the stray lock of hair on Florence's forehead that seems to be touching her left eyebrow, as if to encourage us to appreciate even more the strong, bold contours of her face. This is a portrait not so much of Florence Deshon as of our desire to possess what we cannot own.

Yet another portrait from Mather's series, *Nude Study*, also known as *Nude with Shawl* (fig. 29), features Florence naked, with her back toward the viewer. Her head is tilted to the right, with one side of her hair, bobbed but thick, falling down into the empty space created by Mather's decision to have Florence pose in the left half of the picture. The shawl she is holding is an elaborate, clever joke. Since Florence is turned away from us, it covers the body precisely where there is no need for cover, or not so much need for it—as if Mather had wanted to highlight the voyeuristic aspect of the photograph. And yet, since the cloth does conceal part of Florence's left buttock, something of a barrier remains between us, the viewers, and the sitter, allowing Florence a modicum of privacy even in the act of exposing herself to us. Normally, one would place a shawl around one's shoulders. That Florence doesn't draws our attention to her upper torso and makes it seem stronger, broader than it would normally appear. And the simple trick of having her lift her right foot adds a sort of balletic intensity to the image, emphasizing the lightness with which Florence carries herself. This is a portrait of someone who, even when naked, reveals little to us, a gesture of farewell performed by a woman turned inward and with no place to go: she is facing a wall.

Florence never read the letter in which Max held forth about his beautiful nose and favorite raincoat in Mather's photograph. On July 25, 1921, she sent it back to him, unopened. In a separate note she blasted him for his "neurotic selfishness."[130] The end had come: the "Black Panther" inside Florence had

Figure 29. *Nude with Shawl*, 1921.
Photograph by Margrethe Mather.
Courtesy of the George Eastman
Museum.

arisen, despite the attempts Florence and Max had made to move on with their respective lives.[131] Florence had moved back to New York by then, but not to be with Max. By all accounts she was spiraling further and further downward. She had, as her friend Marie Howe described it, "no work, no hope of work, nothing but discouragement." Instead of success, there was blackness around her, the blackness her friend and likely lover Margrethe had identified in her photographs of her. After Hollywood and Chaplin there was nothing but the prospect of a job somewhere in an office. "She was falling down down down until she struck bottom," said Howe. And though Florence occasionally saw Max, she never confided her sense of despair to him.[132] One of the last surviving notes from Florence to him, written in ink on speckled blue paper, acknowledges the appearance of *The Sense of Humor* and the dedication of the book to her: "Nothing ever made me so deeply happy as my name in your book."[133]

The end came ingloriously for Florence on February 4, 1922, in a third-floor apartment she had subleased from Dudley Field Malone and Doris Stevens at the Rhinelander Gardens complex on West Eleventh Street. A neighbor, Minnie Morris, found her lying on the bed, with the gas turned on, even though the apartment had recently been electrified. The window was wide open. She had last been seen the night before, returning home at around midnight.[134] Max was at a theater when he learned what had happened. He rushed to St. Vincent's Hospital to give blood, but it was too late. In a terrible parody of their life together, Max lay next to Florence's lifeless body on a stretcher. At 11 p.m. that night she died. She was twenty-eight years old. The assistant medical examiner of the Borough of Manhattan found no evidence that Florence had taken her life, giving "illuminant gas poisoning (accidental)" as the cause of death.[135] But questions lingered, especially after word got out that Florence had had a male visitor the day before and that a quarrel had taken place. Confronted by a *Times* reporter, Max adamantly denied there had been a rift between him and Florence and asked that he be left alone.[136] But her friends did not doubt that she had killed herself and that Max was at least partly responsible. "Florence made a suicide," McKay observed. Amid the "silly rumor flying across the Village," a worried Crystal sent Claude to console Max, but there was nothing for him to do except keep his mouth shut: "What else could I do before such a big trouble."[137]

Florence's mother hired Frank Campbell's "Funeral Church" on Broadway to take care of all the arrangements. Campbell's company had made a specialty of the funerals of actors, acquiring a reputation that continues to this day: the celebrities they have buried range from Rudolph Valentino to Lauren Bacall.[138] Max nearly lost his mind during those days. He wanted to go to Campbell's parlor, where Florence's body was, and had to be restrained by Crystal, who also convinced him not to attend the funeral. "I lay still in my room as though paralyzed until it was over," he wrote in his autobiography.[139] At least he did not have to wait long. Florence was buried on February 6 in Mount Zion Cemetery in Maspeth, Queens, the only real acknowledgment we have of her Jewish ancestry. In fact, the speed with which the funeral took place—Florence had died during the Shabbat, on a Saturday afternoon, and was buried the following Monday—suggests at least an attempt to adhere to Jewish custom. Her grave was in the section reserved for the burial society Chevra Kadisha, also known as the Independent Order of Free Sons of Judah. According to her burial card she was interred in grave 23 on Path 10L Road 3 of Mount Zion. No care for her grave was arranged, and no map of the section has survived. The inscriptions marking the simpler graves in that section are now mostly faded. Florence's final resting place could be anywhere under these withered stones.[140]

In the days after Florence died Max received a card in the mail from the nurse who had taken care of her when she was carrying Chaplin's dead fetus inside her. "I just read of the terrible news of my beautiful Florence Deshon's death," wrote Marie Alamo Thomas from Grand Junction, Colorado. "I am heart broken! It seems too tragic to think of all her beauty—gone!"[141] Unbeknownst to Max, Marie Thomas had continued to live with Florence even after she had returned from Croton. But Max ought to have remembered a poem Marie Thomas had sent to Florence, care of Max Eastman, when she was recovering in Croton two years earlier: a rapturous song of praise for her that left little doubt Marie had loved Florence, too, with a simplicity of feeling that had been unavailable to Max and, it seems, other men. To Marie Thomas, RN, Florence Deshon was a dark-eyed gypsy, too, but one destined to live forever: "Beautiful girl that you are, dear. / Girl full of life and freedom and cheer, / With slender form and gypsy-like grace, / The eternal spirit of youth in your face!"[142] Now, she said, the pain was greater than she could bear.[143]

When Max went through Florence's belongings after her death he found a copy, in his own hand, of the poem he had written during the first year of their tempestuous relationship, "Sweet Lovely Night." Folded many times over, the little piece of paper would have easily fit into Florence's purse, and maybe that's where she had carried it during the past few years.[144] He found something else, too, a poem written by Florence herself, in pencil (as she preferred)—a poem fit to dispel, once and for all, the myth of the childlike, vaguely gypsylike Florence he might have chosen to cultivate. In these lines Florence sounds like an early incarnation of Sylvia Plath, rising from the ashes of her life to eat men like air—or, in this case, to press down her high-heeled shoe on her faithless lover's twitching throat:

> I once said I would not stand
>   by and watch love dying
> I did not think
> that with burning tongue
> and brain seething with hate
> I would kill him
> I did not think

that I would press my heel
upon his throat
I did not think that I would bend
down and pick up a
beach stone
and put it inside my
bosom,
and carry it for a heart
All the days of my life
I did not know.
I only said I would not stand
By and watch love dying

And stand by she certainly did not. Max himself believed she *had* killed him, or something inside him. "You do possess me, yes, you have your will," begins a poem found among his papers, titled "To One Who Died." He felt as if he had been put in the grave alongside her: "Your dear dark hand is on me everywhere. / My life is buried in the earth with you." In her absence the dead Florence continued to control him: "My mind finds back the way from everything to you." Then again, realizing that he was, after all, still alive, he was seized with guilt: "If I were brave, like you, who loved and hated me, / I would lie down beside you, whom I loved and feared."[145] In Max's mind there was no doubt Florence had wanted to die, whether or not she had technically killed herself. Now she owned him forever.

Max's book *The Sense of Humor* was officially released just a few weeks after the death of the one to whom it was dedicated. In the very first chapter Max evoked the smile that had inspired him, the smile that had filled his imagination for so long. That smile would begin, he wrote, "with a flash, because the motion of the upper lip comes first and so strongly, and yet the lip broadens a little as it rises so that while all the teeth shine the mouth is only redder than it was—the cheeks curve, and the eyes gather light and attract the brows and lashes toward them just infinitesimally, warming their vivid glitter with those radiant soft lines of good nature and good-will." Such a hospitable smile transforms the entire face into an open invitation to feel welcome. A smile, writes Max in the same chapter, "is the path along which two selves approach." It is finer than a good wine or a bouquet of flowers or the colors the sun paints onto the clouds in heaven. It is the source of light toward which men struggle "through so much pain and blind anxious endeavor." Poignantly, the smile Max evokes is a smile that no longer exists, except as a memory or, now, as an object of study. It had been, of course, Florence's smile. Describing it in such physiological detail had allowed him to detach it from its owner, whom he never names, and to forget that terrifying poem he had found. With Florence gone from his life, Max had made her, or part of her, into an artifact.[146]

Given the personal impetus behind his work, the sheer range and depth of interests Max displays throughout the twenty-two chapters of the book is doubly impressive. Although he had tried to make his book enjoyable, Max said in his preface, and "keep it alive to the qualities of its subject," his overall purpose had been scientific. Gone was the relatively narrow scope of *Enjoyment of Poetry*. In the book's first, general part Max offered his views on subjects ranging from the "Laughter of Pleasure" to "Good and Bad Jokes," while in the second part he reviewed theories of humor and human behavior ranging from the Greeks to Freud and the Harvard psychologist William McDougall. The poet Richard Le Gallienne, in a lengthy review for the *New York Times*, expressed his surprise at Max's versatility and marveled that this advocate of Bolshevism had, for the purposes of this book, exchanged the red tie for the doctor's gown.[147] He remained skeptical of Max's attempt to probe, once and for all, the mystery of laughter and to substitute science for intuitive or impressionistic explanations that had so far been offered. To him, *The Sense of Humor* was not science but a "fool's errand into the unknown." Yet it offered good fun along the way.

As far as Le Gallienne was concerned, the most interesting passages in the book occurred when Max was writing about "poetic humor" or the capacity to see the world "in many different ways" and to choose laughter over tears whenever possible. In the book Max's primary example of that ability was an image created by Florence's erstwhile lover and Max's competitor for her heart, Charlie Chaplin. In the dream sequence from *The Kid*, the Chaplin movie Florence had loved so much, the world is briefly transformed into a paradise where even cops and dogs have wings and float freely around the set. As the Tramp, played by Chaplin, discovers his new wings, he briefly reaches back and plucks out a few feathers—a complex gesture, Max said, reminding the viewer that these wings are just a prop and dreams are nothing but dreams. The very quickness of the gesture is the essence of humor, in Max's reading: it's over almost as soon as it has happened. It constitutes, wrote Max, the acceptance of our failure to transform ourselves into something other than what we are.[148]

Max's theory of humor was indebted to Chaplin as much as it was to Twain, and, as was the case with both of his models, there was more than a bit of wishful thinking behind it that the world can indeed become a better place. Max saw laughter as joyful, childlike play and not the fulfilling of some dark, sinister tendency in us of which we ourselves are hardly aware. What irked him most about Freud was his repeated assertion that children have no sense of humor. To Max, this was patently wrong. "Children have," he wrote, "a more lively though crude sense of what is comical than we have, . . . and their pleasure in nonsense is the pure evidence of this trait." As they mature and become more self-conscious they learn to attach more positive meanings to their childish play instinct and make it palatable to their adult taste.[149] But the impulse remains the same: we laugh because we want to laugh, not because we really want to have sex.

If only it were true. In an undated note to Max Florence acutely observed that the tragedy of the relationship between Max and herself had been the sheer weight they had both attached to it. Entangled in their own neuroses, they had never been able to laugh together. "If you could laugh at the little mule in me," she wrote, "instead of expecting it to have horse sense, I know I could laugh at you, and we could be happy friends."[150] While Charlie *performed* humor and Max *wrote* about it, neither of the two men had known or been able to teach Florence how to *live* it.

6 · Malyutochka

Still reeling from the shock of Florence's death, Max, in April 1922, left the United States for the medieval city of Genoa. At the initiative of Prime Minister Lloyd George of Britain, the representatives of more than thirty-five countries had gathered in the old Palazzo San Giorgio to figure out a way forward for the world after the devastations caused by World War I. What was at stake was the relationship between the newly formed Bolshevik regime in Russia and the Western, capitalist countries. Max was not the only writer who had shown up in Genoa. Hemingway was there, too, equipped with "the most beautiful row of teeth I ever saw in man, woman, or child," as well as the notorious writer Frank Harris, now in his dotage, who had just published his notorious pornographic autobiography, *My Lives and Loves*. "Every wild man of the decade was there who could get there," observed Max.[1] Who knew economics could be so sexy? This was the first time that Max, after writing so many articles about them, came face to face with real Bolsheviks. At the age of thirty-nine he had divested himself of most of the responsibilities others entering middle age have accumulated, and he was eager for new adventures.

Before he left for Europe, Max, at the urging of the IWW organizer and communist activist Jim Cannon, had joined the Workers Party of America, the legal organization established by the Communist Party of America. At the time, he was convinced this was a true party for workers, not part of a larger international communist network. At least that is what he told the FBI later.[2] He also hoped being a card-carrying communist would help him make connections abroad more easily. His "not very lofty motive" relieved the conscience of the proud "Get-offist": since he wasn't serious about being a member, joining the Workers Party didn't really count. He placed the card in his suitcase and then forgot it was there. Or so he claimed. "My reputation as editor of the *Masses* and the *Liberator*—John Reed's editor—was credential enough with the Bolshevik leaders." More immediately useful was the document from the *New York World* that made Max a special correspondent and gave him direct access to the conference, though it seems he did very little journalistic work. His one semiofficial task, other than compiling reports for the *Liberator,* came when, briefly, he filled in for a British journalist dispatched to the conference, George Slocombe of the *London Daily Herald,* who had impressed Max with his red, "dagger-shaped" beard. Other than that, Max was content to be a hanger-on and to help out when needed, as he did when the Russian foreign minister Georgy Chicherin needed a lengthy French document translated. Max soon found out that his French was not nearly as good as he had thought. But at least he had managed to wheedle his way into the Imperial Hotel in Santa Margherita, about twenty miles down the coast from Genoa, where the Russian delegation was staying.[3]

It was there he met, on a later visit, the woman who would share his life for more than three decades. On the balcony on the hotel's second floor (fig. 30),

Figure 30. Albergo Palazzo Imperiale, Santa Margherita. "Where Eliena and I met in 1922." Green arrow drawn by Max. Undated postcard by Fotoedizioni Brunner & C. Como. EMII.

Max had watched the sculptor Jo Davidson at work on a bust of the Russian diplomat Maxim Litvinov. Bored with the proceedings, Max was leaning against the balustrade when a rose fluttered down and landed at his feet, thrown from the floor above where the secretaries with their typewriters were staying. Max wasn't sure which of the four girls whose heads he had seen peeking out of a window above him was responsible for the rose. When one of the girls—"not exactly pretty" but cheerful, sturdy, muscular—came skipping down the stairs, Slocombe introduced her to Max. She was Eliena Krylenko, the sister of Nikolai Vassilyevich Krylenko, who was as well established and well connected a member of the new Bolshevik power structure as one could imagine: the former head of the Red Army, he was now in charge of the Prosecuting Collegium of the Revolutionary Tribunal of the Soviet Republic. Later he would serve as the commissar of justice, or chief prosecutor, for Russia and then the entire USSR. A fiend at the chessboard, he became the mastermind behind the expansion of Russian chess into a national, state-sponsored propaganda machine. When Max began to take an interest in Eliena, he was, whether he immediately realized it or not, truly entering the inner circle of Bolshevik power.[4]

Twelve years younger than Max, Elena (later Eliena) was born on May 4, 1895, in Lublin, Poland, which was then occupied by the Russians.[5] Her father, Vasilii Abramovich Krylenko, had been a *narodnik,* a member of the Russian socialist group that placed their hope for the liberalization of Russia on the peasantry and their willingness to rise up against the ruling classes. The *narodniki* were fiercely persecuted by the authorities, and it is likely his political convictions as well as the needs of an ever-increasing family forced the elder Krylenko to accept a position as a *chinovnik,* a minor government official, in distant Poland.[6] A naturalist and poet who always carried a worn copy of Goethe's *Faust* in his breast pocket, Krylenko senior was not well suited for a life as inspector of liquor taxes. But he was a gentle and peaceful man, a father who had taught his children to be averse to anything "brutal, crude, ugly, cocksure or stupid." He had a large, comprehensive library, and in the afternoons he would read Mark Twain or the *Iliad* to his children. It wasn't a coincidence that they were, at least the way Eliena remembered it, the only Russian family in town the Poles respected. She was convinced that her early years in Lublin, "where the old ghetto still stands," played a part in turning her into the tolerant, socially conscious person she became as an adult: "a humanitarian, a rebel, a fighter against oppression of an individual by another individual, of a nation by a nation," free of any narrow sense of nationalism or chauvinism.[7]

Tragically, her parents' marriage was not a happy one. Older than her husband, Eliena's mother was consumed by jealousy, instilling in her daughter a lifelong aversion to relationships based on force rather than mutual trust. As a punitive measure Vasilii Krylenko was eventually transferred to a godforsaken small town eighty miles from the nearest train station. The loneliness of the place, reinforced by a natural inclination to melancholy and the precarious state of his marriage, led him to take his own life. Miraculously, Eliena emerged from these difficult family circumstances with a sunny temperament that impressed everyone who knew her. Unlike her brother Nikolai and sister Olga, she never became a Bolshevik. Neither red nor white, she described herself as "an onlooker and a skeptical critic of both sides," certain only about the joy she felt when the tsarist regime was overthrown.[8] Energetic, cheerful, blond, and ready to forgive, she was the opposite of Florence Deshon in almost every respect. A lawyer by training, like Ida Rauh, she had similar Slavic features but a much stronger, more athletic build. Walking next to the six-foot Max, Eliena, who was barely over five feet tall, had to jump and skip "trying to fit my short steps with his long stride."[9]

The writer Lillian Mowrer, whose husband, Edgar, was covering the Genoa conference for the *Chicago Daily News*, remembered her as looking like one of "Giotto's emphatic little angels with her long, narrow eyes, high cheek-bones and short, curly hair."[10] And the painter Ione Robinson, who met Eliena in 1927 just after her arrival in the States and subsequently became her art teacher, remarked, "I have often wondered how anyone who has been through so much revolution can be so gay." She was especially charmed by her astonishing ability to laugh and speak at the same time.[11]

Eliena was in Genoa because she was in charge of the staff of Maxim Litvinov, one of the most colorful figures of the Bolshevik revolution and a kind of roving ambassador for the new system. She also worked as his personal secretary. As Max found out, she had been the one behind the rose-toss, even if she had not carried it out herself. Max was intrigued. The next evening he found her outside sitting under a kumquat tree, eating kumquats and crying over the breakup of a relationship. "These tears are not for you," she declared, and Max was enchanted by this combination of vulnerability and cockiness. They shared kumquats and spent the night sitting on the Ligurian shore watching the waves.[12] Although Max was attracted to her—in a note typed later he described her as "not sensual but sexually alert"—he evidently did not think of their "emotional relation," a term he used in his autobiography, as something that would endure.[13]

Eliena became his *malyutochka,* his sweetheart, useful to him in multiple ways—as a secretary, manager of his finances, housekeeper, fellow artist, and mostly tolerant companion. And he became useful to her in one most tangible respect: he helped her survive. Eliena's entire family perished under Stalin, including her powerful brother Nikolai, who had gone on record saying that in order to impress the masses it was important to execute not only the guilty but also the innocent. He certainly lived up to his promise, sending thousands to their deaths. But the revolution eats its own children, as it certainly did in his case: in 1938 he was removed from his post as commissioner of justice of the Soviet Republic, arrested, and forced to confess to engaging in anti-Soviet activities. On July 29, 1838, in a swift trial that lasted about as long as many of those he had himself overseen, namely, twenty minutes, he adamantly disputed what he had confessed, thus presumably hastening his execution. Once Nikolai had defended his tribunal's order to execute Admiral Shchastny despite the Bolshevik opposition to capital punishment by declaring that the admiral was being not executed but shot. Now he himself was—shot.[14]

"No threat or torture ever made you speak," intoned his sister Eliena, who had obviously been misinformed, in a poem (incredibly, a sonnet!) written in October 1950. Eliena and her brother shared more than the same determined jawline: they were tough people and not easily intimidated. But Eliena was right that, regardless of what Stalin's executioners could and would have done to him, Nikolai had inflicted his own worst punishment upon himself:

> By thoughts more sharp than torture you were shamed,
> By your rash deed that could not be repealed,
> The folly of your brave great life revealed.
> You could not cringe—too deep was your defeat.
> You died in silence, stricken, bruised and defamed
> By your own error, not by their deceit.[15]

From Genoa Max traveled on to France, where he sampled the pleasures of the French countryside and the delights of Parisian nightlife. He conversed with Anatole France and engaged in another affair in Paris. It was in Paris that he met the writer Albert Rhys Williams, who had observed the October revolution firsthand and would remain a lifelong convert to communism, unwavering in his support even of Stalin. With Albert as his travel companion, Max finally set off for Moscow, the actual destination of his trip. He later included a detailed account of his journey into postrevolutionary Russia in the second volume of his autobiography, *Love and Revolution,* but the journal he kept during these first months provides a more intimate look at his experiences unfiltered by hindsight.[16]

Albert and Max stopped in Berlin first, where they obtained the necessary papers at the Russian embassy. Traveling to Russia from Germany was an experience in its own right. The Germans had been neat, focused, orderly. Their crops were flourishing, and wherever Max went, someone—men, women, and children—was always at work. How different things were as they got closer to the Russian border. In Lithuania, as their luggage was being inspected, Max and Albert took a little walk through a village where everyone seemed to be asleep, including a fellow with a switch who had been given the task of keeping a pig out of a yard and who was now dozing under a tree, overwhelmed by the magnitude of his responsibility, while the pig was rooting around freely. From time to time the man would wake up and wave the switch perfunctorily, whereupon the pig would take off, presumably just waiting for the moment when the ineffectual watchman had succumbed to sleep again. Max saw this as emblematic of the Slavic mentality in general. If Germany was the hardworking, virtuous brother, Russia was "the lazy poetic philosophizing never do well who gets wonderful ideas, may do great things if he ever gets to work."[17]

In Riga, Latvia, waiting for their connection to Moscow, Albert and Max made a trip to the beach, where Max, with obvious pleasure, watched the beautiful, healthy, strong women in their comical, umbrella-shaped bathing suits. It was here, too, that Max began his study of Russian in earnest. Dictionary in hand and never one to settle for modesty, he celebrated this new phase in his life as a linguist by translating a poem by Mikhail Lermontov, "The Mountain," or "Utyos," an exercise in which he involved his fellow passengers. He was so proud of his crowd-translated poem that he published it later in *Kinds of Love*.[18] Back on the train, a comfortably equipped one, with beds in the compartments, big windows, and tea served "every little while," Max continued to work on his language skills. His first complete sentence, "I want milk," was a complete success: "I got it, rich, clear, creamy, warm, from the cow." Not at all like Italy, where there was no milk to be found. Max was enjoying the signs that life in Russia wouldn't be so bad after all: the beautiful women, the posh train, the leisurely lifestyle, the fresh milk. On April 25 a red guard at the border, blond and blue-eyed like fellow socialist Mike Gold back home, pulled out a piece of white bread to demonstrate the luxuries that awaited them in Russia. Max relished the experience: the red guards in their long coats lined up beside the train, the young, intelligent-looking young man who came through the train to check their passports, the strains of the *International* being sung by the passengers.[19]

There was more singing and more poetry the next day in the village where they disembarked to await the arrival of the train from Moscow. Max was pleased to see the "soft sweet ragged poetic-looking" people on their way to work, noting especially the girls carrying railroad ties. So much for Russian laziness. He noted, too, how fair they all seemed, perhaps inadvertently revealing his American bias, as if he expected physical labor to be done by the darker-skinned. He loved these firm-bodied men and women, the kids hunting for berries in the hedge, the lavender potato blossoms, the cows in the meadows, even the clouds in the sky, and he probably never realized that, writing these lines in the diary, he was already producing social realist kitsch. At night the peasants sat by the lake, enjoying the view—all of them poets in the making.[20]

His arrival in Moscow was less pleasant. The only person to meet them at the train was Jim Cannon of the Workers Party, who took them over to the vermin-infested Hotel Lux, where hulking Bill Haywood, the founder of the IWW and recent fugitive from American justice, also lived. Max counted forty-eight bedbugs his first night in the Russian capital. After his paeans to proletarian productivity, he lapsed into laziness himself, joining other expats for breakfast and dinner, going for walks in the park, and enjoying the architecture. "I have only one purpose in the world—namely to take my time."[21] Through Albert's connections they secured more upscale accommodations in the house of a former "sugar-king" now used for visiting diplomats. Max realized his new abode was "incongruous" and "not suitable," but he did not decline the offer either. In *Love and Revolution,* he later created the impression that everything but the beds and chairs had been carried off, but his journal says otherwise. The "expensive-looking" house was in an incredibly convenient location, and the interior was lavish, with pictures on the walls, stained glass, carved wood, and furniture tastefully arranged throughout the house. "The comfort is ravishing."[22]

Moscow, with its deep blue and golden domes and the green and gray-red towers of the Kremlin, was more appealing than any European city Max had known, and the flamboyant, extravagant colors and unique clustered design of St. Basil's Cathedral, in Max's opinion, made all futurist art seem "green and provincial." It was as if Max had fallen asleep and woken up in some surreal dream, a fairy tale straight from *The Nutcracker,* were it not for the signs of political upheaval around him. The only thing Max couldn't stand about Moscow was the constant ringing of church bells, all with different chimes, as annoying as a gang of boys who had been let loose in a well-furnished kitchen and were trying to see how many different kinds of noise they could make. "I am told they bang them a little oftener and harder since the revolution." From an architectural point of view, though, Max had to admit that the many, many churches added considerably to the attractiveness of the city. As the sun was setting and the moon was rising, the delicate crosses flashed in the light, and the gleaming gold domes began to shimmer like rare flowers that were about to unfold their petals. Moscow appeared lovelier than any other city, most certainly "lovelier in the variety of color and form than Paris."[23]

It was a ravishingly metropolitan, easygoing place, too. There was so much to see! Max admired the kind, sleek, well-behaved cab horses whose equally kind and humorous drivers constantly fed them treats. In Germany, Max remembered, drivers cursed and whipped their horses. Moscow had the smoothest-running streetcars he had ever ridden, and, in the market, one could buy the best-looking vegetables in the world. He found not a trace of snobbishness in the Russian people, who wore what they wanted (no one was expected to don a hat, for example). The red guards, rather than marching with Teutonic precision, walked leisurely, with "leonine grace," using a slow farmer's step that would take them where they wanted, to the beat of their "strong masculine shouting songs." The good-natured traffic policeman, his rifle strung across his back, had nothing to do since the streets were so wide. Even the beggars in their dust-colored rags seemed young and hopeful, their wonderful faces radiating contentment. The people he met were eager to speak Russian with him. They seemed "*interested, alive,* talkative, healthy, never tired." And all the buildings carried signs identifying them as belonging to the people. Max was in a trance.[24]

This was nothing short of a Whitmanian catalogue, down to the phrases Max used. If Whitman had given us an America that never existed, Max was now reinventing Moscow as a larger version of Greenwich Village. Lloyd George had called Russia an "unhealthy country." But Max, relishing the "democracy of manners and aspects and attitudes" he found there, had never felt healthier in his life. Everyone he talked to thought the Bolsheviks were carrying the world to a new and better future, a better civilization. This was the same Russia that, in 1920, had become the first country to legalize abortion, a fact surely not lost on the old feminist Max.[25]

There were some worrying factors, to be sure. The effects of the famine that had affected mostly the Volga and Ural regions the year before and had killed millions of people were still being felt. The cost of living was high, and the prices in the stores were worse than New York. "One can't imagine where people get the money." A newly rich class of traders and speculators was rapidly consolidating itself. How could the workers be in charge when people beside them were enjoying comforts denied to them? "Either the workmen will take it away from them again en masse—or they will yield to the 'influence,'" Max reasoned. "Wealth will rule."[26]

A few months earlier Comrade Stalin, a name that had so far meant little to Max, had been appointed general secretary of the Central Committee of the Communist Party of the Soviet Union. And in May 1922 Vladimir Ilyich Ulyanov, known to the world as Lenin, had suffered the first of his several strokes. The future fate of Russia was unfolding before Max's very eyes, though he likely didn't realize it. He did not know that, just the year before, Yevgeny Zamyatin had completed his antiutopian novel *We*, a relentless analysis of the ideologies underlying totalitarian reform movements such as Bolshevism, which the Russian censors promptly banned. And while poets like Alexander Blok felt they were suffocating under Bolshevik rule—in February 1921 Blok had issued one last, desperate plea for "freedom of creation"—Max comfortably moved among other expatriates. He found the revolutionary activist's life irresistibly charming. He paid a visit to the house of Ludwig Martens, recently deported from the United States after running the Russian Soviet Government Bureau, the informal Russian trade agency, and now a member of the Soviet on National Economy. Everyone there was either just coming from or going to somewhere else. "So much fun having a revolutionary International, it will be a pity when the work is done." All of this was wonderful material for a writer. "Why doesn't somebody write an international novel?" One day even the long-lost buddy from his Croton days, George Andreytchine, showed up at the Hotel Lux, fresh from Paris.[27]

With great enthusiasm Max watched Mikhail Kalenin, the president of the All-Russian Central Executive Committee and nominally the head of the Russian state, receive petitioners at his office, who had come with requests ranging from a new tea set to an education: "They come crying and go away laughing" (fig. 31). Over two hundred people had shown up on that particular day, many of them leaning forward to whisper long tales confidentially into Kalenin's patient ears. The wonderful thing was that everyone who had traveled to Moscow with a petition got to see this "patient friendly alert intelligent little man" with the wide nose, the wavy hair, and the unkempt beard. A dispenser of "good cool moral advice," Kalenin had become a kind of father confessor to those otherwise

Figure 31. Oscar Cesare, "Kalenin, president of Soviet Russia,
Receiving and Listening to the Appeals and Complaints of Workers."
Drawing, 1922. Published in Paxton Hibben, "Lenin's Little Father
Substitute," *New York Times Magazine*, November 12, 1922. Courtesy
of Library of Congress, Prints and Photographs Division.

not listened to: "It seems to me this is one of the most wonderful inventions of
the political intelligentsia of the Bolsheviks." Max recognized the showiness
of the event, but he felt that Kalenin served an important function: "A petitioner
instead of going to some sub-deputy-doorkeeper and gradually working his way
up to someone who can handle his case, goes discreetly to the President of the
Republic, who either handles his case (if it can be settled with a word and a signature) or *directs him* to the proper official." Being able to go and share their
needs with Grandpa Kalenin, as he became known, gave people an intimate
connection with their government that was unknown in capitalist countries.
And it gave the president "something to do besides preside." That was the one
valuable concept behind the antiquated idea of the monarchy.[28]

The great cartoonist Oscar Cesare, known simply as Cesare, who was also
staying at the sugar-king's residence, accompanied Max during his visit. While
he was in Moscow Cesare had managed to gain access to the elusive Lenin and
sketched his portrait, an event he excitedly shared with the readers of the *New
York Times*.[29] At Kalenin's office Cesare drew not only the president but also

his secretary, an overburdened woman who, while talking on the telephone, managed to critique Cesare's portrait, pointing out with a smile ("in that friendly way that Russian girls do") that he had made her nose appear sharper than it was. That indeed was the new Russia.[30]

Outside Kalenin's office Max ran into the journalist Paxton Hibben, who was already disenchanted with his Russian experience, deploring the loss of idealism around him. Russia wasn't "starving the way it was last year," he said reproachfully. Cesare and Hibben came along the next day when Max and Albert, led by a reporter from *Izvestia* and a red guard, toured the Kremlin, a powerful experience. All the literary stereotypes—"gorgeous chambers," "regal splendor," "imperial magnificence"—applied. "You find out what those words mean." The insignia of the Comintern—the banner of the International, the water pitchers, the gavel, the long table, and modern chairs—looked incongruous yet oddly reassuring amid all the ostentatious gold of faded tsarist glory. Almost against his will Max was moved when he saw "the sheltered soft quiet bed" where Nicholas had slept, surrounded by the little pictures he had treasured, and the extravagant bathtub made of pure silver. "Something very pathetic about being a Czar—never having a chance to be humble." But these reminders of Nicholas's life seemed irrelevant now, as everywhere around Max there was "life, energy, movement."[31]

In the evening Max went to see the neofuturist ballet in the Pillar Hall of the House of the Trade Unions, where most recently Lenin's show trials of the members of the Socialist Revolutionary had been held and where a bust of the tsar had been replaced by one of Lenin. Max was sure the music critics of New York would have collapsed in "spasms of indignation." But much to his surprise he discovered he didn't like the ballet either, the first real sign of trouble in Max's developing love affair with communist Russia. Max watched in disbelief as the bodies of young men and women squirmed through convulsions that made as little sense as the stage set, "a series of platforms, ladders, steps, and peculiar things which might be called yard-drums." On this complicated and ultimately meaningless scaffolding, to music by Claude Debussy and others, these beautiful dancers—whether they were naked or not, one couldn't tell—would contort their bodies in ways that lacked all thought and feeling, "like all the distinctively modernist art of the times." This was "cold experimentation with the technique of art," though Max was relieved to see that at least those Russians were no Puritans.[32]

Max was eager to improve his Russian, a language he said was marked by "graceful soft winding and lingering beauty" when spoken the right way but sounded unexciting and toneless when spoken in an ordinary fashion. He met up with Eliena Krylenko again, who not only taught him a few lessons but also cooked for him and told him she couldn't bear watching how the workers had their rights gradually taken away from them while the Bolsheviks stood by and did nothing about the situation. But Max, as always, spread his affections rather evenly, striking up a relationship with a girl named Tonya, the daughter of a tsarist general who was constantly complaining that life in communist Russia had ceased to be life. Tonya put on the national costume, probably for Max's sake, looking utterly beautiful. When she began to dance, her father, forgetting his gripes, joined in, leaving Max with the impression that it was not life in general but, rather, the general's life that had been upset by the revolution and that that was what he had been complaining about.[33]

During his first winter in Russia Max saw the big changes the revolution had brought to the country, but he was still convinced they would all be beneficial. He didn't agree with the bourgeois Russians and their American friends he met at the parties in Moscow, who went around calling the Bolsheviks names. "I wonder why they weren't all summarily shot in the revolution," he exclaimed in a moment of uncharacteristic intolerance. He was at least trying to like the paintings of "big, dramatic, vigorous things" Eliena showed him when she took him to an art gallery. (He made an exception for the "hideous" Lenin Monument.) And he was delighted to see Irma Duncan, of Isadorables fame, and to hear she was teaching Isadora's "great art" to Russian children. Maybe he, too, could create a life for himself in Russia?[34]

Max redoubled his efforts to become fluent in Russian. He tried his hand at another Lermontov poem, this time "The Sail," a poem that had made a deep impression on him. In the lonely white sail on the misty, wide ocean, "flying from what in the homeland / Seeking for what in the new," he certainly recognized aspects of his own situation, and he might have read the speaker's final characterization of the traveler as a prophetic summary of his own daring:

> Beneath him the stream, luminous, azure;
> Above him the sun's golden breast;
> But he, a rebel, invites the storms
> As though in the storms were rest.[35]

As if to make good on Lermontov's endorsement of risky travel, Max obtained passes for himself and Albert to travel to Sevastopol on the southwestern Crimean Peninsula, a thirty-eight-hour train ride, again in a car equipped with all the available luxuries. After his arrival Max was instantly smitten

with the beautiful, permanently tanned Crimean girls. Snippets from Tennyson's "The Charge of the Light Brigade" swirled through his head as he continued on to the famous resort town of Yalta, on the opposite side of the southern
tip of the peninsula, a "wilder and less cozy Italy." There, in the town that had
once seduced Anton Chekhov into building a villa, Max settled down, too, with
the sun-kissed sea in view. He was long convinced there was a direct connection between sex and linguistic proficiency, and he immediately went ahead
and picked a language tutor. Nina Smirnova, an attractive, safely married
woman who was vacationing in Yalta, became his *utchitelnitza,* or teacher.[36]

Studying Russian and "lying in bed all morning" quickly became synony-
mous for Max. Under the influence of the Crimean sun, political pontifica-
tions gave way to idle observations about language and national character.
What, for example, did it really mean that there were no definite articles in
Russian? Lazy mornings were followed by lazier afternoons sunning and
swimming in the nude on their favorite portion of the beach, which Max and
Nina, in honor of their newfound love, christened, perhaps not quite originally, "MaxNina" (МаксНина). Remnants of the old order were still visible.
Max noted with interest that, though joint bathing was permitted, beach areas
reserved for women would be separated by about fifty yards.[37]

It didn't bother Max that his utchitelnitza, self-assured and patient as well
as passionate, was no friend of the Bolsheviks. Her husband was a Social
Democrat, and she was convinced the Communist Party, despite Lenin's obvious intelligence, would stand in the way of progress. Max, by contrast, was still
intent on finding the Bolsheviks likable. On one of their strolls along the coast
Max was eyeing some tasty-looking grapes in one of the tsar's former vineyards near the Imperial Palace in Livadiya, with a guard positioned right in
front. The tsar's grapes protected by the Red Army? "Will you shoot us if we
steal a grape?" The young man turned away from Max and Nina as though he
were going to get his gun. When he emerged again, his hands were full of
grapes, a scene as if from a Murillo painting and no doubt of great symbolic
significance to Max in his quest for the good in Bolshevism.[38]

Chatting with the youth in town, Max heard repeatedly how members of
the bourgeoisie—admirers of the White Russian general Pyotr Wrangel—
were shot or thrown into the sea. But Max also noted how even those opposed
to government did not seem to be afraid to say what they were thinking. And
most of all, he was proud of his ability to understand them. Learning a new
language was easy if people were willing to follow his example and not try
to study "20 different things at once." In a month anyone could learn to

communicate with patient people in any foreign language. That said, the Russian language was certainly special. Max was fascinated by the various aspects of verbs, "one when they intend to finish" something and one "when they don't." Understanding the difference was crucial: "You discuss what you want with a waiter and he goes off in the middle of his discussion. That was the aspect he was talking in." But what seemed confusing to the outsider was in fact a set of clear directives to the native speaker.[39]

Relishing his newly acquired language, warmed by Nina's eager embraces, Max never wanted to leave. Yalta was a holiday of the senses, a vacation not only from the personal complications of his existence in America but also from the political complexities of Moscow. Here was all he wanted: "Study, sunshine, salt-water, swimming and showing off how bright I am. What more can the heart desire?" Watching the lovely nude bodies of women, separated from the men, "lying in heaps on the beach," he gave tribute to the one god left from the pantheon of his youth, the sun: human flesh was so lovely when "colored in the sun." Nina certainly felt that their time was running out, especially in view of the fact that her husband was on his way to Yalta. In letters to Max she found herself arguing with God, who had given her "great love" for Max but not the opportunity to stay with him. "If God would give me one month to be with you in Yalta, I would give him an entire year of my life." She consoled herself with the thought that they would meet again in Moscow or Kharkov. "I am such an optimist, . . . but right now I am sad."[40] On their last evening together the couple had dinner in a restaurant and danced to the languid strains of Sydney Baines's "Destiny Waltz."[41]

Oh, Yalta. Everything seemed possible then. And yet there were people who sowed doubt in Max's mind: the old woman in burlap rags near the Red Army barracks who, with tears streaming down her face, took him to a place where people had been shot and exclaimed, "They did this to Russia—you tell this to the people in America. The world needs to know what we've come to. . . . I pray for Nicolas and I pray for the return of the grand duke." And the peasant who, when asked if he wanted Wrangel back, responded that he did not want any more change: "We want to work the land, that's all. It makes no difference—Czar, Communists, or God. We want peace and a chance to go to work." Or the man on the train who said there were plenty of communists in Russia who did not want to be disciplined by any party.[42]

But then there were highly satisfying experiences, too. On his way back from Yalta, in Kharkov, Max and Albert were cordially received by the first chairman of the Ukrainian government, Christian Rakovsky, who bent over backward to find them an appropriate room, with mixed success. Although the Ukrainian army, railroad, postal service, telegraphs, and telephones were all controlled by Moscow, Rakovsky was following his own independent course. Max was pleased to see that he and Mme Rakovsky had turned the best homes of the bourgeoisie in Kharkov into crèches, hospitals, maternity centers, and orphanages. The shores of the Black Sea were lined with homes for children and workers in need of rest.[43]

Nina continued to long for Max, impatiently awaiting his letters, imagining herself kissing his "beautiful white head" and his oh-so-desirable tanned body. If their relationship, to Max, had been part of the fantastic unreality of the entire Russian experience, to Nina it was painfully real. As she was waiting for him she was learning English. Why had she fallen so deeply in love with him? Hypnosis (perhaps Max had shared his skills with her) didn't help. Did his new teacher—here Nina used the feminine form, an indication she knew Eliena had taken over again—love him as much as she had loved him?[44] A note written around the time of Max's departure shows that, regardless of what would happen to their relationship, Nina was going to be fine. First there was despair: "Our beautiful little fairytale by the sea has come to an end. . . . Tomorrow Max begins a new life, a new fairytale . . . there will be another Nina, and then another, and then another." And then came insight, proof that utchitelnitza was ultimately made of the same material as her Max: "And what is to become of Nina from Yalta? Stupid little Nina. She will love and wait for her Max for a long time; she will treasure the fairytale of the sea; and then, most likely, she too will begin to search for a new fairytale, a new Max."[45]

In December 1922 Max witnessed the Fourth Congress of the Third Communist International, the last one attended by Lenin, who delivered a speech but was too weak to show up for any regular sessions. The resolutions passed were unabashedly self-congratulatory. The delegates affirmed that the predictions of the Third Congress regarding the world economic crisis and the tasks of the Communist International had been completely borne out by the course of events and by the development of the workers' movement. Capitalism had maneuvered itself into a place that was entirely at odds with basic human rights. One of the main dangers confronting a unified communist movement was "democratic pacifism," a defense likely to be used by bourgeois democracies; the adequate response was to be as militant as possible in continuing the spread of the workers' movement. And the main challenge facing every Communist Party was to strengthen its influence in the factories.

Max was more interested in the people than in the theories that were spouted. He was delighted to see again his old friend Claude McKay, the "prince of the revolution," luminous "like a black pearl" among the delegates. McKay assured the communists that "Negro soldiers" would be fighting not only for their own emancipation but for the emancipation of the working classes the world over. The German delegate Clara Zetkin delivered a strong plea on behalf of the women of all classes, not just the workers, and impressed Max greatly: "bluntly mild" in form and face, she was a grandmother with a "tiger's mouth," and she dared to use the word "democracy," which had been banned from the official discourse. The "unfalteringness" of most of the delegates, their confidence in their own rightness, got on Max's nerves, as did their hatred of centrists, an attitude Max felt had diminished and hardened the Comintern. The international workers' movement should be in the hands of big men with big minds, not little guys like Nikolai Bukharin, whom Max compared to a canary. The dogged chanting of party songs ("that terrible Sunday School tune over and over again—stanza after stanza") indicated patience as well as a terrible lack of humor: "Not one shaft of illumination so far." How could Grigory Zinoviev, the president of the Comintern, a "complete stranger to joy," a man with an irritatingly high-pitched voice and a smile in his eyes that never connected with "anything in his lips" and vanished almost as soon as one had perceived it, seriously hope to make, as he said, the world more beautiful? Max couldn't understand how the delegates were able to sit through these uninspired speeches, speeches "without a ray of light in them." They didn't play; they didn't need to play.[46]

Not that Max would have shared these impressions with readers back home. In a note sent back to the *Liberator,* he applauded the "hard-handed, iron-minded men" that were now in charge in Soviet Russia, and Bukharin especially received praise for his "big voice," his trenchant wit, and the subtlety of his political analysis.[47] There is a reason for Max's circumspect reporting. More than most, Max realized the obstacles a genuine radical movement faced back home. Denigrating the only available model would serve no good purpose. In the back of his Russian journal he sketched out some ideas for the future of the American Left written under the influence of the Fourth Congress. A revolution of the kind that had swept through Russia couldn't happen in the United States because people had attempted to *organize* it. "We have formed a party of revolutionary action when no revolutionary action is possible, so like a machine with no work to do, it destroys itself. It will continue to destroy itself." The movement in the United States needed diversity, not homogeneity; Max cited the shutting down of William Foster's Farmer-Labor

Party as a disastrous move on the part of the Communist Party. The premises of the Third International that the breakdown of capitalism was imminent and that the movement had entered the phase of revolutionary action simply did not apply in the United States. The revolution had never even begun, while the counterrevolution was alive and thriving: "They have reached the stage of the guillotine while we were still in the stage of desultory propaganda! They have killed the I.W.W. They have killed the Communist parties." Capitalism was not breaking down in America. "The task in America is not action, is not even organization of action—the task is elementary education," Max explained.

Unlike the Europeans, ordinary Americans had witnessed the war only from a distance. In the European countries the war had, arguably, catalyzed revolutionary action. In the United States the work of the Second International still had to be done. Never having experienced the war, Americans had never really experienced the patriotic story of winning it. Business was flourishing in the United States, and the working class had other things to worry about than revolution. And here Max embarked on a sharp analysis of the American character, pointing out that the "extraordinary brutality" of American life had reinforced the solidity of the American capitalist class. He went on to offer a trenchant list of bullet points, in which he displayed once again the combination of brilliance and sarcasm he had honed during his years editing the *Masses* and the *Liberator*:

1. Other nations are a mixture of all human types. The Americans were bred from a single type—the type that "leaves home."
2. We burn a negro at the stake for the delight of a mob every 4 days.
3. We sentence our agitators to as many years as the other nations do months. We are as brutal in peace as they were in war.

The United States had lived through its own accidental uprising, a bourgeois revolution before there was a distinct bourgeoisie and even a proletariat, an upheaval that had produced "very real freedom and democracy," a successful revolution that had taken place in the past, so that no more revolutions were needed. The importation of foreign or slave labor had perpetuated among American workers the illusion that such freedom and democracy had been extended to them, too, that they were part of a nation of "sovereign citizens." The working-class movement in America was dominated by "collectivist" foreign professors or, in the case of the IWW ("a wonderful flying squadron of rebels"), by foreign or migrant workers. And the American Federation of Labor, unlike other such associations in the world, endorsed capitalism both politically and practically. *"There never was a great native working-class socialist organization in America,"* Max concluded his devastating analysis. When he reworked these notes to submit them to Leon Trotsky, he added that the only way to give the handful of true communists working in the United States a chance was to limit the influence of Slavic immigrants on the movement: "The demand of the Third International for an artificial unity is preventing the growth of an American communist movement."[48]

Naturally, Max was also thinking about his friend McKay as he was jotting down his angry notes. He was aware of Claude's recent departure from the *Liberator,* under less than ideal circumstances. In fact, the falling-out between Claude and Mike Gold, Max's anointed successor at the helm of Max's former magazine, was one of the reasons Max's former protégé had fled to Russia in the first place. But there were other reasons, too, and Claude took advantage of their reunion in Petrograd to lay them out in vivid detail. He added that he wanted to address them in a book on the situation of Negroes in the United States the Bolsheviks had asked him to write. Claude, the only black man on the *Liberator's* editorial board, thought it was self-evident that the future of African Americans would have to be at the center of the class struggle. But no one would agree with him, and no one appeared willing to give race the kind of prominence in the magazine that the proportion of blacks among American workers demanded. Although he was no longer the editor, Max immediately felt he had to defend his magazine. What exactly, he asked, would be the point of alienating the mostly white readers of the *Liberator* by putting the race problem front and center in the magazine? Approach the subscribers carefully, and they will be more likely to support you. But Claude refused to accept Max's insidiously practical argument, pointing out that the real problem lay with the magazine's editors, not with its readers. They had never really discussed race, had they? He remembered a rather telling incident involving Max and himself. Looking for a place to eat on Sixth Avenue, Max and Claude had ended up in a rather seedy establishment. After casting an astonished look around, Max told Claude, "If I were a negro, I couldn't be anything but a revolutionist."[49]

Claude decided that Max, despite their long-standing friendship, was really an opportunist, someone who was always "in search of the safe path and never striking out for the new if there are any signs of danger ahead." He pooh-poohed Max's "romantic notions" about the communist dictatorship, particularly the belief that the successful Bolshevik revolution would automatically end racial and sexual discrimination. Was there really no more anti-Semitism in Russia? Did Max truly believe that the communist leaders could "by a single stroke change the minds of all the fossil-minded, stereotyped and manikin wrecks of humanity that have been warped by hundreds of years of bourgeois traditions and education?"[50]

What was at stake in this exchange was not just the situation of blacks in America. On a more personal level, Claude's letters were objections to his friend's patronizing tone, to his assumption that McKay was a willful child in need of parental guidance. "This everlastingly infectious smile of mine" had kept the real Claude hidden from Max.[51] On some level Max certainly realized their friendship was in jeopardy; hence his decision to include a grainy photograph of a beaming Claude with his report on the angry Russian response to the Curzon Ultimatum, the British demand that the Soviet government scale back its activities in areas close to the British Empire (fig. 32). He wanted to remind the *Liberator* staff and the magazine's readers of a man that some of them would have rather forgotten. At the same time, by deciding to feature McKay with his trademark broad, and, yes, infectious grin, visible even in a blurry newsprint picture, he had inadvertently confirmed his friend's suspicions: Max did not really know much about him.

Figure 32. Claude McKay in Moscow. From Max Eastman, "Moscow's Answer," *The Liberator* 6.7 (July 1923): 23, EMII.

Incidentally, Claude did not mention his problems with the *Liberator* when he published Негры в Америке (*The Negroes in America*) later that year, and Max in turn kept their exchange out of his autobiography.[52] It is obvious that, quite apart from the serious political concerns he had, the bisexual McKay wanted to be loved by his friend. As their correspondence in subsequent years showed, Max did respond, though never as fully as McKay might have hoped.

It was at the Fourth Congress in Petrograd that Max finally saw Lenin, if only from afar: "a granite mountain of sincerity."[53] And it was there, too, that Max summoned the courage to approach Trotsky, the regime's war minister, the beginning of the most consequential political relationship of his life. He found Trotsky gracious and quite unlike the cartoons he himself had published in the *Liberator*. The Russian leader turned out to be most interested in the situation of communism in the United States and pledged his support for a homegrown American workers' movement. Max, in turn, pledged his support for Trotsky and promised to write an account of his life. Max stood out in Moscow, not so much as a foreigner but as a foreigner among foreigners. He was different from the rest: George Grosz, the German artist, during his visit to Moscow remembered vividly Max's beautiful, red-soled boots and the fact that his handsome nose was constantly buried in an English–Russian dictionary. And this difference was precisely Max's ticket to the inner circles of Russian power, which now, as well as in his capacity as Trotsky's biographer, stood open to him.[54]

Eliena found Max a room in Moscow, and it was here Max and she began living together, more by habit than as the result of a deliberate decision. Eliena's unselfish generosity was an ideal complement to Max's innate egotism; even the story of Max's relationship with the infinitely forthcoming Nina of Yalta did not faze her: "I don't want to possess you." In his autobiography Max qualified his description by adding that Eliena was so forgiving only to those she loved. Her flashes of anger, the hardening of her blue-gray eyes into undisguised hatred would be experienced by many of Max's extramarital lovers in later years.[55] Older and more experienced than she, his hair turning white, but equipped with a taste for adventure as well as deep appreciation for her sense of humor, Max was the perfect lover for Eliena, a youthful substitute for the father she was still mourning. What's more, he came from a country that had long interested her. Eliena had been familiar with Mark Twain ever since her beloved father read *Huckleberry Finn* to her, and one can only imagine the effect Max's explanation that he had not only read but also personally *known* Mark Twain would have had on her.

In April 1923 Max attended the Twelfth Congress of the Russian Communist Party. The ablest brains of the establishment were discussing ways in which to make a socialized economy profitable for their citizens, and while the debates confirmed Max's belief in the seriousness of the Bolsheviks, they also intensified his desire to get out of Moscow. In addition, work on his Trotsky biography had been complicated by the fact that he was now also planning to write a novel. He needed time away from the rulers and wanted to experience life among the ruled. Albert recommended Sochi on the Black Sea, Eliena convinced Litvinov that Max as well as the party needed her services, and Max purchased tickets for the train and the trip by steamboat down the Volga in search of the next chapter of his Russian adventure.[56]

Sochi was not as established and storied a resort as Yalta. But the discovery of the curative power of the mineral springs during the last tsar's regime had turned it into a destination of sorts for the middle classes and especially for Jewish tourists, who were not allowed in the Imperial spas. Bathhouses, dachas, and modest inns sprouted along the coast of the Black Sea. In 1919 Lenin nationalized all resorts in an attempt to make them accessible to workers, peasants, and members of the Red Army. Private clinics and villas were transformed into sanatoria, catering to patients with conditions ranging from eczema and digestive disorders to syphilis. Max, Albert, and Eliena arrived in Sochi during a time of unprecedented growth, when the number of patients in search of cures increased from a few dozen in 1920 to several thousands in 1925.[57]

Max and Eliena, who had no money at all, lived in the front room of a sparsely furnished cottage they shared with the landlady and her two lady friends, Ruzha and a girl Max nicknamed Gipsey. "They killed 'em all," the landlady said when asked where the men were. She didn't miss the tsar, but the Bolsheviks had turned out to be much worse: "I want to be free and do what I like and I was free before and did what I liked. Now I'm not." One of her friends interjected that, though she was not a communist, it seemed pretty clear to her they had arrived at "a certain page in history, and we've got to live it." The "Bolsh" had done some terrible things, but conditions hadn't been great before; nobody with a minimum of social consciousness could have been satisfied. But the landlady was not happy: "I hate the Bolsheviks that's all; they are murderers." Max had obviously advanced considerably in his ability to understand idiomatic Russian. Now he was no longer translating

Lermontov; he was transcribing phrases from the conversations he was having with ordinary people, people who would say things like "Russia is the rubbish hole of the world" and "The Bolsh took you by the neck; that's all."[58]

The pages of his journal were beginning to be populated with creatures so
real that one wonders if Max invented them. There is the little man with the
face of a monkey, for example, who tells him he is a monarchist and then immediately corrects himself: "No, I'll tell you I'm a party communist." Max asks
him if he is afraid. No, says the man, he's not afraid, but he'd rather die: "I
don't see anything in life right now. If you can't live *comme il faut,* I don't see
any use living." What did he mean by *comme il faut?* Well, says the man, "I
want to have good meals served to me and good clothes, and 2 servants, and
be free to go and come. I don't want to live the way a soviet tells me to. I want
to be free." But, responds Max, shouldn't those two servants then have a right
to have two servants as well? Things aren't that simple, after all. Well, says
Monkey-face, "I'm not political you see, and I've just told you my feelings, they
aren't what you want after all. I want to go away from Russia." Adds Max, in
his journal, "All of them want to go away from Russia."[59]

It was in Sochi, too, that Max met a cousin of the composer Nikolai Rimsky-
Korsakov, living in the most abject poverty imaginable, a shadow of his former
self, surrounded by his exquisitely mannered, beautiful, emaciated wife, his
partially paralyzed daughter, his mother-in-law, her sister, and a granddaughter. Franz Xaver Winterhalter, a painter popular with the royals of Europe, had
painted Rimsky-Korsakov's mother, Madame Barbe de Rimsky-Korsakov, a
legendary beauty (the portrait was, and still is, in the Louvre). Rimsky-Korsakov spoke English like a native, and Max was struck by the contrast between
the family's aristocratic manners and their torn clothes and dirty surroundings. Their little granddaughter, about five years old, played with the family's
sickly looking cats and rabbits. These people had owned estates in Russia and
Nice, had been friends with the Vanderbilts and the duchess of Marlborough.
He didn't mind the loss of his lands and servants, said Rimsky-Korsakov:
"That's all humbug, I'm glad to be done with it." Their house had no windows,
no carpets, and no water, and the tea they drank was made from chestnuts.
Without friends they would be starving. Would the whole world become socialist? "Somehow we live." In his autobiography, at the end of a more fully
imagined account of the afternoon he spent with the Rimsky-Korsakovs, Max
added he was glad he had "no fixed system of ideas" in his head that would
have prevented him from admiring this once and, as far as he was concerned,
still noble family.[60]

. . .

In August 1923 Max was summoned to Kislovodsk, a spa city in the northern Caucasus, where Trotsky was recovering from the mysterious illness that had removed him—tragically, as Max would come to realize—from any influence of Moscow politics. At about the same time, Eliena went back to her job with Litvinov in Moscow. Max's time in Kislovodsk, where, incidentally, he could have seen the five-year-old Alexander Solzhenitsyn running around in the streets, was a huge disappointment. Max's ego had just gotten a huge boost by the news that Scribner's had sent him a check for $500 in royalties from sales of *The Sense of Humor*. But Trotsky, too busy to see him, treated him as if he didn't exist. Max did, much to his surprise, run into Isadora Duncan, an encounter that made his Caucasus experience even more surreal than it already was. Isadora, accompanied by Irma, had just emerged from her unhappy, brief marriage with Sergei Yesenin, known for both his poetry and his drunken excesses. Max took them to lunch but afterward escaped. Although he was badly in need of company, he disliked her penchant for lecturing. And he did not want to be reminded of his former involvement with Isadora and her girls, preferring instead to wallow in loneliness and depression, a "depression do smierti" (unto death), as he wrote to the now-absent Eliena in the characteristic mix of English and Russian phrases he adopted whenever he was too tired or too frustrated to write in Russian.[61]

He was seized with the acute feeling that he didn't belong there: "My love of the proletarian dictatorship is exactly equaled by my horror at the proletarian table manners," he wrote acidly, after unhappily turning down food in the dining room of a local sanatorium because everyone around him was eating and talking at the same time. To Max, the noisy eaters around him sounded like so many electric ceiling fans gone out of control.[62] After an abortive attempt to buy some raspberries in the market (too expensive!), he sat down and vented his frustration in Russian verse:

> Without Eliena, without berries,
> Without each of these delights,
> There is nothing left for Max here,
> There is only "Trotsky's Life!"

Max added, "I am so lonely and tired, good for absolutely nothing. I am languishing. I am lying on the bed, and I do not know where I am, or why."[63] There were minor irritations. For example, no one in town seemed to know how to properly roast coffee beans. But they loomed large in his mind, and he found himself dreaming of a "plentiful and perfect life" for both himself and Eliena in Sochi. His mastery of Russian was improving, though the finer points of Russian grammar still eluded him. In an encounter both funny and poignant, he found himself chatting up a woman who proved to be a deaf-mute. Drenched in sweat, shrieking Russian phrases at her, he was wondering why she wouldn't respond to him, as an interested audience gathered around them, curious how long it would take that slow-witted, stubborn American to figure out the problem.[64]

Max reached the pinnacle of despair when he ignored the mysterious suggestion made by one of Trotsky's couriers that he board a certain train to Moscow "biez platno" (for free), only to find out later that Trotsky—and a Trotsky willing to talk!—would have been on it. To make matters worse, he learned that Eliena, whom he, if he had only taken that accursed train, could have easily visited in the Russian capital, had come down with malaria: "Why couldn't that fool *tell* me or ask Trotsky's permission to tell me that he was going to Moscow?"[65] Guilt-ridden and despondent about his ability to complete his Trotsky biography, he began to pelt Eliena with missives reminding her to take her quinine: "If you should be sick, then I should die."[66] He was now writing notes to her several times a day. She was his lover-friend, his "mother-child," and, perhaps the most off-putting epithet, his "brown baby-slave." He addressed her as his *liagushka* (лягушка, or frog), his "funny Elena," while referring to himself, in his all-time favorite fantasy of wished-for relief from adult responsibility, as "half-grown." He was Eliena's "egoistic, impatient, impolite, nasty, shrieking . . . infant."[67]

Once he was back in his old digs in Sochi, Max rallied. This was, he realized, a writer's paradise. The flea population had diminished since his last stay, and here he was, in a warm, beautiful place, with direct access to the railroad, but far away from the carpings of his colleagues and the political shenanigans in Moscow. He was ecstatically happy about the "velvety and wild" sea and basked in the sun that was "loving all the animals and birds and the race of man."[68] Thanks to regular swims in the sea Max was in better shape than ever. He felt transformed: wonderful and young and strong and "very handsome," as he concluded after a peek into his little mirror, and he didn't mind anymore that Albert, who had set up camp outside of Sochi, had better clothes.[69] Conveniently, his landlady's friend, the almond-eyed Gipsey, proved to be more than forthcoming, too, as did the girl who came in to clean up his room, experiences he freely shared with Eliena: "Gipsey very much wanted to seduce me, and I said, 'very well.' . . . This was yesterday evening (Wednesday), but today when I reported this news to my Liza, she said, 'That's something of a pity' so sweetly that I repented, and also told her 'very well.' "[70] Although Gipsey was, in her own assessment, "entirely without sexual passion," she seemed eager to please Max, who in turn was, he unashamedly told Eliena, "learning to demand of her what I want just as though I had a right to it."[71] It is hard to tell whether these passages were descriptions of actual events or merely intended to entice Eliena away from Moscow. Either way, it was obvious he missed her.

Max was now hard at work on his novel, which gave him so much more pleasure than that infernal Trotsky biography. "Darling, my love, I have written one chapter of my novel! I have no other thought and no other literary interest now but that novel. It is going to be rich and exciting and wise and wonderful. You must come and help me. Do you still think you would like to be my secretary?" It was high time for her to leave "nice fat young Litvinov" behind and come to work for him.[72] "You told me not too long ago that I was just as important as Litvinov.—Not the biggest compliment I ever received, but I remembered it just the same."[73] His manuscript was progressing faster than he had expected: "I believe in it absolutely *almost* all the time. I realize it so vividly myself that I believe other people must also." Still, Max was being careful. Don't tell anyone I am writing a novel, he warned Eliena: "I don't want people waiting for it the way they did for my humor book." The novel had become his all-consuming purpose in life, and finishing it, "without ever stopping," a matter of life or death. "I want to do something with all my heart once before I die," exclaimed Max, a little dramatically: "I don't know what I will be or what I will do *after* this book, I only know that I will defy every expectation, and betray every duty that people think I have, in order to finish it." He was ready to offer Eliena a contract as a secretary, but without any emotional entanglements "or agreement and responsibility between us even for one minute."[74]

Eliena did come, but Max, falling back into a pattern of behavior that at this point would have seemed numbingly familiar even to him, found he liked her much better when she was away. Infinitely understanding, Eliena went back to Moscow. She returned once more in December, but by mid-January she realized Max needed solitude and left again. Soon, Max's private troubles paled in comparison with the political ones. On January 23, 1924, shouts of "Monsieur Max! Monsieur Max!" interrupted his work. Gipsey stormed into this room to tell him, with some elation, that Lenin was dead. Upset with her behavior, Max became uncharacteristically violent. He grabbed Gipsey and threw her out of the room: "And you greet this rumor with open arms," he exclaimed. "I despise you! I despise you!" Outside, the sea was "silent as a pool," and Max walked around town with sadness in his heart, unable to think or speak, flabbergasted that the world around him went on living as if the greatest man in history hadn't just died.[75] In Moscow Eliena was among those who paid their respects to the dead Lenin, and she went away feeling "quite sick."[76]

As it was for hundreds of thousands of mourners, Lenin's death was a key event for Max. Throughout the meanderings of his political career Max never significantly wavered in his admiration of the leader of the Bolshevik revolution, even after he had long given up on communism. Lenin was a "very great man," he told Harry Schwartz of the *New York Times* in 1963, the one man he had known who was able to be both an "ardent rebel" and a "patient adjuster and teacher," driven by practicality. Lenin had always refused to make a "divinity" out of communism: "Had his premises been scientific, he would have been a social and political engineer par excellence."[77]

When news of Lenin's death reached him, Trotsky was in Tbilisi. He had been ill for most of the winter, after catching cold during a hunt in the marsh country north of Moscow—a wish come true for his rival Stalin, who was busy securing his right to the throne. Stalin advised Trotsky it would be impossible for him to reach Moscow in time for Lenin's funeral, and so Trotsky went on to the coast, to Sukhumi, about ninety miles east of Sochi. When Lenin was buried and radio stations all over the republic broadcast messages asking listeners to stand up, Trotsky hunkered down, wrapped in blankets, on the terrace of his luxury hotel.[78]

In Sochi it was snowing, snowing, snowing. The entire town was now covered by a white, heavy, wet blanket of snow. Max felt lonelier than he had ever been before. There were no new letters from Eliena, and he feared his own letters weren't reaching her either. "I feel . . . as if I cannot survive here," he told Eliena. The situation was made worse by Eliena's hints that she might be pregnant. "I thought that maybe you would say something about the baby in your telegram? No baby?"[79]

At least he was working again. He was reading *Moby-Dick* and writing an essay that threatened to become much larger, "The Wisdom of Lenin," perhaps the germ of *Since Lenin Died*, the book Max would publish a year later. "There is no more important book in the world today," Max observed immodestly.[80] When Trotsky told him by telegram that he could not see him ("in view of my illness, better later in Moscow"), the news came as a great relief to Max, who took it as a sign from on high he didn't have to finish his biography and could settle for a snapshot of his early life.[81]

In his personal life Max saw himself trapped in a vicious circle where he both wanted to be independent and needed someone to take care of him. At the age of forty-one Max felt entirely unprepared to face life's challenges on his own. "There is only one way to get peace, only one way to get my head clear, and that is to leave you forever," he wrote to Eliena in a letter he ultimately decided not to send. He claimed, paradoxically, "I could never do that alone. I could never do that except by falling in love with somebody else." He had, it seemed to him, two alternatives: "One is to struggle towards clearness and creative joy alone, where my obstacle is this dreadful grief accompanied with dim-mindedness and strained feelings in my head. The other is to struggle for it with you, where the obstacle is that emotional coldness accompanied by the same dim-mindedness and strained feelings." He was, alternately, a yearning infant or a rebelling man, or maybe both at the same time: an impossible conflict and one that was going to harm his writing. His only hope consisted of going to Vienna "and asking Freud to recommend me a psychoanalyst." Apparently, Max never expected that the great Freud himself would have time to take him on as a patient. A touchingly domestic image of Eliena mending his pajamas rose before Max's inner eye. He now felt that being with Eliena was really the better of the two options. Besides, Moscow was closer to Freud.[82]

Once he was in Moscow Max took full advantage of the resources of the Library of the Marx–Engels Institute, where he made the mistake of reading Lenin's *Materialism and Empiro-Criticism,* which he found to be joyless to a sobering degree ("a political harangue").[83] He attended the Thirteenth Congress of the Russian Communist Party and watched first Trotsky mount a lackluster, unconvincing defense of his position and then Stalin and Zinoviev dance on the dead body of Trotsky's vanished influence. But Max's major achievement during those months in Moscow was finishing his book about Trotsky, which he had now wisely limited to the revolutionary's early years.

Leon Trotsky: The Portrait of a Youth (1925) is a peculiar work, marked by a quiet and largely unrecognized brilliance. In form and style Max's book is a self-conscious, literary effort to capture some of the qualities of a man who was himself quite a literary person. Max disavowed the American edition, published in New York by the Greenberg brothers. New to publishing, the Greenbergs had been none too careful about seeking their author's final approval for the text they sent to the printer. Max made sure that the British edition, released a year later under the new Faber and Gwyer imprint (where T. S. Eliot was working as an editor), was without the idiosyncrasies that were, from a literary point of view, one of the highlights of the first printing. In the original American text the repertoire of styles Max employs is remarkable. In the early chapters about Trotsky's childhood, for example, he appears to imitate the language of children's books: "And here there were comfortable chairs," the narrator tells us about the hut, with its "fat brown roof," in which Trotsky grew up, "a table, an immense square stove, and on top of the stove a great big sleepy-eyed cat." Outside, the Ukrainian landscape looks as if we had accidentally burst into the middle of a Russian fairy tale: "It is all snowy white outside, and the drifts curve half way upon the low windows, and it is all warm inside, and tender and friendly and unworried." Max's syntax is often deliberately clunky, with the object following after the adverbial phrase, as in this sentence about young Trotsky: "He was printing with his pen a little magazine." Such grammatical idiosyncrasies create a deliberately foreignizing effect, offset, in other passages, by a direct, familiar, even colloquial tone: "What you see in his blue eyes is goodness," writes Max about Trotsky. "His mouth is sensuous and happy in its curve; and there is always the readiness for a social dimple in his cheek."[84]

Throughout this short book Max is able to draw for us, with a few quick strokes of the pen, the key settings in which Trotsky's political evolution takes place, from the school in Odessa to his mentor Franz Shvigovsky's garden in Nikolayev to Trotsky's jail cell and his exile in the Siberian village of Ust-Kut. Like the dimples in Trotsky's face, Max's prose is capable of hardening into "iron ruts," especially when he confronts those who, from the secure position of exile, attack Trotsky. The biographer's special ire is reserved for those who, for tendentious or personal reasons, malign Trotsky in print, as did one of his former fellow revolutionaries: "If a worm could snarl," declares Max, "it would make a noise like Doctor Zif's book." Max's own language, concrete, earthy, direct, with a distinct preference given to Anglo-Saxon words, reflects the continuing influence of Whitman, as when Max informs us that young Trotsky's tongue was "full of the brag of its extreme opinions." Memorable vignettes of characters or scenes in Trotsky's life occur in every chapter. What reader could forget the watery-eyed, bewhiskered police inspector in Verkholensk who can be seen peering, every night around ten, through the slightly lifted trapdoor in Trotsky's attic—that is, until Trotsky vigorously aims his boot in the direction of the policeman's self-important face. The inspector never showed up again.[85]

There is a fair amount of humor in the book, too, leavening the drier passages dealing with Trotsky's political development. Again, Max seems to model his writing after Trotsky's, whose own wit shines through in the excerpts Max inserts: "It was not Neyman but his salary that made the speech," Trotsky is quoted as having said about an engineer who tried to discourage his workers from rebelling. When Trotsky admits his "verses are bad," Max follows suit: "And his critical judgment, I may add, is very good." A highlight is Max's characterization of the corrupt prison guard in Kherson whose face carries "the expression of Christian benevolence with a market value of ten gold rubles"—paid for, naturally, by Trotsky's mother—as he delivers tea, a pillow, and a blanket, and "some good things to eat" to his prisoner. Such humor may turn into cutting irony when Max's own political opinions color his prose. This, for example, is his comment on Trotsky's taking on the postmaster of Ust-Kut for refusing to hand him his mail: "Trotsky is one of those unreasonable beings who never give up the idea that things are supposed to be just."[86]

Max's overall aim in the book was to illustrate Trotsky's development from a "littérateur" to a "social engineer," or Bolshevik, a role he knew his readers would have some trouble comprehending. Thus, whatever passing familiarity with Trotsky this biography generates inevitably collides with a contrary impulse that insists on Trotsky's strangeness: "He has, to be sure, a faculty of burning absorption in problems of mere truth which you and I, chilly Anglo-Saxons, might fail to understand." Max is not, he admits, "a really conscientious biographer," and he has no interest in judging Trotsky for the ways in which he has arranged his romantic life: "Natalia Ivanovna is not Trotsky's wife, if you have a perfectly legal American mind, for Trotsky was never divorced from Alexandra Lvovna." And Alexandra, "to sum up a number of things that are not the business of a contemporary biographer," defies American popular expectations by having remained Trotsky's friend. Max's own lingering disappointment with Trotsky shines through only occasionally. For instance, Trotsky is, he admits, not a good listener, and he lacks a clear sense of the feelings of other people. A brilliant orator and thinker, a charismatic commander and inspirer, Trotsky is "not great as a leader of men."[87]

That said, Trotsky's weaknesses are not unfamiliar to Max: the battle Trotsky had to fight within himself was Max's own. Trotsky started out as a follower of Plato, that first communist, as it were. Ideas were more interesting and real to him than things. For an intellectual of that "static" type, and Max would definitely have been thinking of himself as he wrote these words, ideas become "a kind of daily companion and redeemer of our world, consoling us with an extreme 'belief' about its future and yet leaving us free to patch it up in little ways less disturbing and more ready to our hand." Believing, in this manner, in an idea meant getting stuck on it. It meant resisting those who would undertake to put it into action and thus disturb one's inner equilibrium.

But, noted Max with relief, Trotsky had left that phase behind. He was no Menshevik, a reference to the members of the reformist faction of the Russian socialist movement. A true Bolshevik, he was a scientist of the revolution and a staunch believer in the need for immediate change: "Trotsky means action down to the last letter of every word that comes out of his mouth." Appropriately, Max's book ends not with a glimpse at the current situation in Russia but with Lenin designating Trotsky as the man in whom he had the utmost confidence when faced with the prospect of his death. On the last page of Max's book Trotsky had not yet failed to step up to the task for which history had prepared him. Everything was still possible.[88]

That, however, was a feeling Max no longer shared. His decision to go home was set. Yet implementing it proved difficult, since Max, a persona non grata in his own country, had no valid passport. To complicate things even further, Eliena had, years ago, by carrying a letter for her anarchist sister Sophia, managed to get herself on the blacklist of the GPU, the Russian secret service. When she applied for a diplomatic passport that would help her leave Russia, she was told that her only chance of obtaining such a document was to be willing to accept more such letters and send them on to the secret service. A sympathetic Litvinov advised her to agree: "You don't have to *do* it, you know." But Max quickly realized that while such a piece of paper would get Eliena out of the country it would not allow her to stay abroad unless a way could be found to have her added to Max's passport, if and when he finally got one. On June 3, 1924, Max and Eliena were married. While Max hunted down the required witnesses, Eliena had gone home to pack: "I suppose I am the only man in history that ever got married without a bride."[89]

Max and Eliena arrived in Folkestone, England, armed with an impressive looking but useless temporary document issued by the British trade representative in Moscow, who probably hadn't even been authorized to sign such a thing. With the help of U.S. Senator Robert La Follette's son, "Young Bob," he secured a regular passport, whereupon Max and Eliena relocated to Juan-les-Pins on the French Riviera, a sun-warmed, lush Mediterranean paradise, a Sochi without the communists. Max's hope was that, surrounded by pine trees, fine-grained sand beaches, and spectacular ocean views, he would be able to finish the various projects he had begun in Sochi. They moved into a pension called Martha, where Max commenced his writing regime and Eliena, although still shaky in her command of English, typed his manuscripts and washed his shirts in a well. A hard man to keep on the porch, Max soon embarked on a trip to Paris, ostensibly to seek treatment for a bad case of sciatica he had developed, leaving Eliena at home trying to make the best of a hopeless situation: "Every woman in the dining room tries to ask me some question," she wrote to Max in Paris, "and they all speak so low, and are so far from me, and I do not expect this sudden question or some other invitation for a talk, that I can only say 'what.' " Realizing she shouldn't say, "What?" but "Pardon?," Eliena is too busy to catch the next question, and again "What?" slips out of her lips before she can stop it. Now, yet another lady weighs in and repeats the question. Eliena's response would be instantly familiar to anyone who has tried to learn a foreign language out of a textbook: "I dimly understand that it is something about my being alone, and how it must be dull. I smile to both old ladies and say, 'O, yes, it is very dull, but it is such beautiful weather.' " There were no further questions.[90]

In France, Max formally inaugurated the experiment in free love that was going to preoccupy him for the rest of his life. While poor Eliena, recalling her jealous mother, did her best to keep her part of the deal, allowing herself to be kissed at a party and accepting a ride from a man "so slim and beautiful" that her desire was "quite contradictory to my words," she would inevitably forget to act the libertine and incautiously tell Max she loved him. Max was not amused. "I will not say 'love' again," she apologized. In Juan-les-Pins every day was the same, she told Max in Paris. They were flowing by, she wrote, "like a water in the river; every moment new but always the same, making the same noise around the little stone." Eliena played tennis, went for bicycle rides, and waited for her husband to return, though she would tell him she didn't.[91] Max's Paris excursion had meanwhile changed from a medical mission (the doctor told him that he was a rather "mild case") to a trip down the halls of past erotic exploits. "I love Lisa and I always will," Max told Eliena after reconnecting with the dancer Lisa Duncan. "It is sweet to find her still so exquisite, composed, and tender and slowly wise." If Eliena had had any doubts how serious Max was about his open-marriage concept, there was the proof. "It was a joy to be so loved so well," chirped Max after spending time with Edna St. Vincent Millay and her husband, Eugen Boissevain: "They are darlings together." Everybody was excited by how tanned and healthy Max seemed. "Look at him! Isn't he beautiful?" exclaimed Ganna Walska, the Polish opera singer and new owner of the Théâtre des Champs-Élysées.[92]

Max did return to Eliena, but it became quickly apparent that some radical changes were needed and that Max wasn't the one who would be making them. He did have some income, a "trickle" of royalty checks from his *Enjoyment of Poetry*, even less money from his *Sense of Humor*, and an advance for the American rights to his Trotsky biography. But that was not enough to live on. In December 1924 Eliena took action. She left Juan-les-Pins and went to Paris herself, where she had found a position as a secretary at the Russian embassy. "How terribly hard it is for you to take up that kind of work after our life here," sighed Max in Juan-les-Pins and redoubled his efforts to bed a "bushy-haired" French tennis partner he had his eyes on (he was successful).[93] Not that Max was lazy: following his well-established routine of getting up in the morning and beginning to write come what may, he worked assiduously. But when Eliena unexpectedly sent a large check, Max was just fine with that, too: "Beloved, I just got your telegram your love, love, and the enormous sum of five hundred francs! O my darling, how I love to have you feed and clothe me! I am just like a little selfish animal. And I love you with all my heart and soul and stomach and warm cozy skin, which I have just dressed in a new big thick suit of underwear!"[94] In Paris Eliena pointed out that that was only half of what she was due to receive for two weeks' work at the embassy: "Am I not your molodetzt? Am I not your little zhabochka?" (freely translated, "Am I not doing a good job for you? Am I not your little frog"?).[95]

Newly flush, Max ambled over to the Château des Enfants, a villa owned by the eccentric leftist photographer George Davison, who had formerly worked as a manager for the British branch of Kodak, where he became the largest shareholder after George Eastman himself, the founder of the Eastman Kodak Company. Was Max tickled by this connection to his remote relative? The man who liked to refer to his lovers as children wholeheartedly embraced the notion of a house dedicated to the idea of permanently arrested development and had no problem partaking of Davison's famous hospitality. The Château des Enfants served as an open house for many sorts of washed-up artistic existences and anarchists from all over the world. It helped that the cliffs behind Davison's house were about twelve feet high, towering over a deep blue ocean perfect for swimming and diving.

On Christmas Eve twenty-nine guests from ten nations had assembled at the house, and things quickly got out of hand. Max danced till five in the morning, no doubt working on his romance with "Bushy Hair," who had told him she was the daughter of a marquis, inspiring a fantasy in which Max acted the part of the seedy "Bolshevik Agent" and she that of a besieged, virginal aristocrat. She loved what Max told her about his open marital arrangements and, Max reported to Eliena, said "she would like to take your place when you go away, and then go away when you come back." But not to worry, he added, "*I love you with all my heart.* (And I love my five hundred francs, and I wear it next to my heart all the time.)"[96]

Was that the reason Eliena sought out one of her former lovers in Paris? Except that for her, things didn't go as smoothly as they had for Max. Her former lover (perhaps the man she was crying over when Max met her in Genoa?) was a beautiful boy with daring, sad eyes but now, to her horror, marked by disease. Tears ran from her eyes. Eliena also went to see Max's Lisa Duncan, which did not go well. Yes, conceded Max, she was "really very hard to talk to." Max had never deceived Eliena about his intentions regarding their marriage, but throughout the three decades they spent together it seems the open-marriage concept worked much better for him than for her. Alone in Paris, fending off the advances of Max's friend George Slocombe, she was preoccupied either with what was going on in Russia or with what Max was doing in southeastern France. The attempts to discredit Trotsky that filled the pages of *Pravda* made her heart beat so hard that she thought it would jump out of her chest.[97]

As liberated as Eliena was in some ways, when it came to matters of sexuality she often balked. She even had a preferred term for going to the bathroom, which she called using the Lloyd George, a disparaging reference to the British prime minister.[98] When the French Ministry of Agriculture sent a kind of mobile cinema around the countryside to show the peasants how to work scientifically on their fields, Eliena felt very uncomfortable, not only because she was watching the film surrounded by farmers who had eaten a lot of garlic but also because of the subject matter, which appeared *neprilichny* (improper) to her: "They started showing how to transfer female organs of wheat unto the male organs of it." She added, probably only half-jokingly, that she was "awfully shocked" and had to run home.[99]

Her longing for Max, however, made her bold (figs. 33, 34). Alone in Paris, she was constantly thinking about how he would touch her. "Oh I love you, I love you. My passion to [sic] you is as great as my love," she scribbled on a piece of paper. "Why it doesn't go away, in spite of two years we are together, why you always make my blood flow violently when I see or feel a hint of passion in you, why you always make my flesh alive by only the touch of your

Figures 33 and 34. Eliena and Max in Antibes, ca. 1924. EMIIA1.

darling hand or body. Oh I love you, I am crying now." Here she was, using the dreaded word again. Eliena carried that little note with her for two weeks. But then she sent it anyway, admitting, in a sentence she added, that such talk was "neprilichny." Would he please return the note to her once he had read it? But Eliena's declaration of love, the description of her blood flowing at the mere suggestion of a reciprocal feeling in Max, in all its rawness survives her self-mocking postscript.[100] And Max, despite his antics, despite the aloofness hinted at in Eliena's note, always knew what he had in her, too.

Thanks to Eliena's new income Max was able to join her in Paris and to work on the book that would best express his shock over what he saw as Stalin's hijacking of the Russian revolution. *Since Lenin Died,* published in 1925 by the Labour Publishing Company in London and subsequently by Boni and Liveright in New York, picks up where *Leon Trotsky: The Portrait of a Youth* had ended. A small volume, it went a long way toward establishing Max as a voice in debates about the future of communism. It also warned loyal fans of Bolshevism that Max was going to be trouble. From the first page of his book Max set himself up as the person most suitable to explain Russia to the uncomprehending rest of the world. And he wasted no time either in defining the divisions that would come to haunt Russia for the next few decades and to name the culprit behind that division, the Communist Party of Russia: "Nothing that has happened in Russia has been so misunderstood by the entire Western world as the crisis in the Communist Party which has thrown into a silenced opposition men like Trotsky, Rakovsky, Radek, Antonov, Pitiakov, Krestinsky, Preobrazhensky, and many more of the intimate friends and aides of Lenin, and concentrated the whole ruling power in the hands of a group dominated by Stalin, Zinoviev and Kamenev."[101] As an opening sentence, this was nothing short of brilliant. The phrase "silenced opposition" demonstrated Max's skill as a writer, as did the two lists he created, the first containing the many names of those that had been forced into dissent, the second, of those actually in charge, citing only three names, an effective illustration of the power that was supposed to belong to the people remaining in the hands of a few party leaders. The name-dropping, ranging from the familiar to the unfamiliar and almost unpronounceable, at least for most Western readers, spoke to Max's expertise.

As the book progresses, Stalin emerges as Max's main adversary. It was he who, assisted by the Politburo, branded Trotsky an "enemy of Leninism," even though Lenin had so clearly designated him a successor. Stalin had purposely misrepresented Trotsky's motives. Trotsky had never wanted the old Bolshevik leadership to relinquish power; instead he advocated the gradual introduction of actual proletarians into the party, a vision Stalin ridiculed by admitting, in a deliberately absurd move, two hundred thousand workers at once. Max, for his part, mocks the Communist Party establishment as a "gang of mediocre bad boys" determined to make the world "an impossible place for mature people." People might object that his book was more concerned with the moral character of the revolutionaries than with the fate of the revolution and that his book might be altogether "too personal." But Max won't have any of that: "I have but little interest in personal indignation."[102] Wherever he can, Max insists it is not he who is on a personal vendetta but the Soviet bureaucracy. They are the ones using Marxian ideas as "weapons in a personal fight," a fight that has taken them further and further away from the ideals of Lenin. Listen to Max's description of Lenin, a man he had met only once: "Nobody who has not seen Lenin or read his books can possibly imagine the force of that man's will, and his intellectual authority. It was a phenomenon like Niagara, which the strongest men could not merely stand by and watch." As a father figure, Lenin was almost too powerful, leaving behind a large family of childlike orphans. Among these, Trotsky alone had the capacity to act and think independently. As Leninism became canonized (a development Trotsky described as fatal) and the Communist Party transformed into a church, the task had fallen to Trotsky to keep alive "the thinking of Lenin after his brain is dead and embalmed." Trotsky, rightly, was concerned with concrete situations and the solutions of concrete problems, but now he found himself opposed by "abstract dogmatists." And he was unprepared for that. To Max, Trotsky was a hero, but, unfortunately, a flawed one, an imperfect son, not equipped to take the reins from the Ur-father Lenin, whose only and most powerful weapon had been "the simple device of saying all he thought." When it mattered, when, after Lenin's death, everyone was waiting for a word from him, Trotsky had remained silent. Max said he himself had observed, with great irritation, a reluctance on Trotsky's part to "explain himself." Max clearly saw himself as being on a mission to make Trotsky speak and, failing that, to speak for him— as the more responsible spiritual son of Lenin, the strong, outspoken father he himself had never had.[103]

Scattered throughout the book were references to Lenin's "Testament," a document Lenin's wife had presented to the Party Congress, in which he advocated the removal of Stalin as secretary of the party and praised Trotsky as the outstanding member of the Central Committee. That letter had been locked away and, were it not for Max's efforts, would have been permanently lost to the world.[104]

As Max was wrestling with problems of paternal succession in Russian communism, his own father, after catching a cold during an automobile ride, fell ill. Samuel Eastman had left Elmira in December 1924 for Daytona, Florida, where he had built himself a small house. By February 7, 1925, the elder Eastman was dead. He was seventy-eight years old, and he slipped away as quietly as he had lived. Max's reaction is not reported. Years later, when he began writing the story of his family, Max found out how miserable his father's last years had been. His cousin Adra had, reluctantly and on many occasions, opened her home to "Uncle Sam," who was in love with her: "I've had many a difficult situation to handle with him," she told Max. "I doubt if anyone knows as much as I how sexually starved he was." For years, she had kept Sam's behavior a secret.[105]

Moscow's response to Max's new book came swiftly, in the form of a telegram sent by Georgy Chicherin ordering Eliena back to Moscow. She declined and promptly lost her job at the embassy, though she was allowed to keep her diplomatic passport. Max had hoped to force Trotsky into speaking up, and indeed he did, though hardly the way Max had expected. In various newspapers he denied that Max's book had any theoretical or political importance, denounced his absurd and subjective conclusions, disputed the existence of Lenin's "Testament," and accused him of aiding the enemies of communism. Pro-Stalinist Western papers quickly reprinted Trotsky's statements, solidifying Max's newly acquired reputation as a counterrevolutionary.[106] The fact that *L'Humanité* published two divergent versions of Trotsky's refutation (the later one was supposed to be "le texte définitive") suggested that Trotsky had agonized over this statement. But that was cold comfort to Max, who was busy defending himself in letters sent to publications in England, France, and the United States.[107] Max Eastman was a liar, exclaimed C. M. Roebuck in a review of Max's book for the *Workers Monthly*. Roebuck, who was in reality Andrew Rothstein, the press liaison of the Soviet embassy in London, took Max to task for his "distortions and untruths," which would do nothing but smooth the way for an eventual military attack by the West on Soviet Russia.

Chillingly, he added that a book like Max's should serve as a warning to Trotsky himself to "give up [his] futile policy and buckle to again." Max was a bourgeois coward. Unfortunately, there were many others like Max who, after having wandered into the Communist Party by mistake, suddenly discovered that its aim was to lead the workers to revolt against capitalism rather than providing an "opera stage where individual heroes hack at one another with paper swords." Would Max really want to be remembered as having inspired disagreement with the only party that really fought the battles of the workers?[108] Amid the barrage of negative criticism Max was able to take heart, however, from comments sent to him by Claude McKay, the only one of his former leftist friends in the States who seemed to have liked the book: "Whatever happens to Trotsky this little book of yours will live. . . . An electric thrill runs through it from beginning to end."[109]

Sam Eastman had left Max some money, which, along with Eliena's savings and Max's earnings from royalties, allowed them to move back to Juan-les-Pins and join the ranks of the cheerful exiles at the Château des Enfants. Since Max had nothing to lose, he redoubled his efforts to complete his wide-ranging assault on the foundations of dialectical materialism, a project he now felt more liberated to undertake. *Marx, Lenin, and the Science of Revolution,* the most scholarly book he had ever written, with over forty pages of "Notes and References," preoccupied him for the rest of the year. It required additional trips to Paris, where he was still grudgingly allowed to use the library of the Russian embassy, although the works of Lenin strangely always seemed to be locked up when Max came to consult them, and "nobody ever knows where the key is."[110]

Various trips enlivened Max's writing routine. On a trip to Corsica the small seaplane on which he was traveling crashed, and Max and the pilot had to wait for hours before they were rescued from where they were drifting in the Atlantic Ocean. The French destroyer that scooped them up had been alerted—by the pilot's carrier pigeon. Less exciting though more satisfying was Max's time in Munich, where, not normally given to drinking, he discovered the delights of German beer: "Such a thing I never tasted in my life.—It is indescribable—cooling and exciting, liquid and thick. I taste it yet, and it is an hour since I drank it."[111]

Max and Eliena also explored Austria, dropping in on a somewhat surprised Stefan Zweig in Salzburg. But the constant Austrian rain couldn't but discourage these devoted worshipers of the sun. Max was miserable. Remembering his long-standing desire to meet the idol of his Greenwich Village years, he wrote to Freud and asked for a meeting. Freud rebuffed him. "I know your name," he responded, in perfect, if formal English, on his stationery with "Prof. Dr. Freud" engraved in the upper left corner, "and I am very sorry that you turned up at a time especially unfavourable."[112] Ailing from the surgeries his jaw cancer had required, Freud had just endured the celebrations of his seventieth birthday and had been ordered to rest by his doctors. His lack of interest certainly didn't add to Max's comfort level in Austria. He escaped to France.

Left behind in St. Gilgen, Eliena wrote a letter to her "golden one," describing in a postscript written in Russian how she watched the fish in the Wolfgangsee fight for their survival: "The big fish waited until the little ones dragged a piece of bread under the water, and then it ripped it away from them—but it never went after the bread when it was floating on the water." A situation that, in its futility, was very much like Russian communism. She also used the time to sit down and read the manuscript of the novel Max had begun in Sochi: "I read your Jo Hancock last night and O I love it and it seems to me simply wonderful. It is beautifully written and it is alive and interesting and I want you to stop hanging around with all other things and go ahead. It is entirely different to read it without copying on the typewriter. I love it and I am sure it will be the great book."[113] Eliena struck up a friendship with Stefan Zweig's wife, Friderike, whose knowledge of music, French, and Freud impressed her. She tried to teach her the rudiments of the Russian language and picked up some German in exchange.[114]

Back in Antibes, which was hopping with famous and not-so-famous expatriates, F. Scott Fitzgerald was also reading Max's novel. Max wasn't a huge fan of *The Great Gatsby*, which he found too deliberately artsy and immersed in the problems of the past. Imagine Max's surprise, then, when Fitzgerald in turn called his manuscript a record of a bygone era of "liberal enthusiasm."[115] Max suddenly realized how long he had been gone from his own country, how much he, too, had become a relic of another time. When Eliena returned from Austria, Fitzgerald discovered he liked her much better than Max's book. "When you smile, everybody smiles," he told her. "When you come to the room, the room is lighted." Zelda, he added, thought so too. On which Eliena, with her characteristic dry wit, commented, "Too bad he was drunk."[116]

In his autobiography Max claimed he was present when Fitzgerald praised Eliena, but that wasn't true. He was in fact in Paris, where he was working with the well-known anti-Stalinist Boris Souvarine on the publication of the full text of Lenin's "Testament." A copy of the original, still in the possession of Lenin's wife, had been smuggled out to Paris so that Max, who now enjoyed some credibility as an expert on Russian affairs, could make it available and vouch for its authenticity. Most detective novels would pale in comparison with the conspiratorial effort that went into the publication of Lenin's text. Max was able to wangle $1,000 out of the *New York Times* for the exclusive right to print the document that would once and for all refute Trotsky's claim that he had made it all up. Souvarine, to whom Max had offered half of the payment, helped with the translation, and now they were both worried that the copy of the manuscript, which was headed to New York on the *Mauretania*, would not arrive on time. The full text appeared in the *New York Times* on October 18, 1926, with commentary by Max and a prophetic concluding state-ment: "If Stalin's policies ultimately and fully prevail, the landlords and the new bourgeoisie will prevail, the workers will be sold out once again, the Rus-sian revolution will have a 'bourgeois' revolution after all." Trotsky was the last hope of the international Left: "If the course indicated by Trotsky is adopted, the possibility still exists of creating in Russia the first Worker's Republic."[117]

But that was not all Max did in Paris. He was the life of the party wherever he went. At the house of some enticing *krasavitza* ("beauty") he created a new game that required each person to say, with absolute honesty, four things he or she thought about each of the other guests: their best and their worst phys-ical trait as well as their best and their worst trait of character. Max got, he admitted, "some pretty hard knocks" for his character but also "quite astonish-ing praise of my physique." Max left the party feeling "like a handsome but worthless worm."[118] Eliena hated the game, which she felt was not very nice. Why would anyone force people to say nasty things about one another? "You never can get over that afterwards, and you can not help disliking a person, or being self-conscious with a person afterwards, if she or he happened to say something bad about you, or good either." She, for one, was too "damn intel-legent [sic]" to say her real opinion to anyone's face." As far as the criticism was concerned, Max was perfect, no improvements needed: "Nothing can be changed in you, otherwise you will not be you, and you will be imperfect. That's what I think, and that's what I know. And who doesn't want to agree with me can be knocked out in four rounds." People had the most ridiculous impressions of Max's character but "seem to all agree with me about your physique." Precisely because of that, there was an easy solution: "Just go and kiss the girl that doesn't think nice things about you, and she will change her mind." In the same letter she told Max not to hurry back if he had found "a real krasavitza" over there.[119]

There is some evidence, however, that Max was more than a little worried about his character at the time. As he was putting the finishing touches on his novel he drafted a series of autobiographically tinged stories, at least one of which he shared with Hemingway, who was then living in Paris, too. One of the few American writers of note never to have been included in the pages of the Masses or the Liberator, Hemingway was already famous for his terse, tightly narrated collection In Our Time, a book that deeply impressed Max, who was thinking of asking Eliena to translate it into Russian. Heming-way's The Sun Also Rises followed in 1926, a "lean, hard, athletic" book, accord-ing to the New York Times.[120] In creating his wounded hero Jake Barnes, Hemingway had defined an entire generation. But Max didn't really seem to belong to it. An expatriate among expatriates—for he had come to France not from the United States but from Moscow, shaped not by the war but by his resistance to it—he was an instant outsider, and the characters he was fash-ioning in stories, clueless in ways that went beyond modernist disorientation, reflected that sense.

There was Paul, for example, the hapless American expatriate featured in Max's "Something French."[121] Paul's "narrow" conception of "personal excite-ment" nearly leads him to rape a young French girl who has reluctantly at-tached herself to him, since no one else has shown any interest in her. Taking the girl to Paris, Paul vacillates between vague feelings of paternal responsibil-ity and an equally undefined sexual urge to possess her. He pulls himself back from the brink, and the sobering moment of insight, when it comes to Paul, chilling in its clarity, shows priapic Max from a different side: "He realized now that outside of his imagination there had not been one mutual moment, one true communication of feeling between them." The characters in "Something French" are so forlorn, adrift in a world that obviously gets by just fine without them, that one finishes the story entirely without that sense of tragic dignity that distinguishes Hemingway's best characters.

It is not clear if Hemingway read "Something French," but he responded positively to another one of Max's stories, "The Sunrise Club," although the actual words of praise he offered, at least the way Max remembered them, seem somewhat less than fulsome: "I'm not saying I like it because I like you."[122] "The Sunrise Club" features a quack doctor of the kind Max had gotten to know only too well when he was seeking help for his back pain. The aptly named Dr. Bloodney of Bronxville, New York, is the proud progenitor of a book titled *Physical Culture and Hypnotism*, illustrated with photographs of mesmerized subjects so close to the state of nature that it cannot be sold publicly. Dreaming of becoming a famous scientist, Bloodney reinvents himself as the prophet of Nakedness and founds the Sunrise Club for the Better Understanding of Nakedness, a nudist club. His great insight is that modesty is a function of ugliness. Proof of his theory, which the narrator tells us is as momentous as Newton's discovery of gravity, rests mostly on freckled, slim-bodied, blue-eyed Pearl Minkowsky from Bronxville, a stenographer with luminous golden skin and golden hair and so beautiful she makes the other clothes-shedding members of the club look like "plants grown in a cellar." The complementary example is portly Mrs. James Gerbson Smith, a New Thought Healer who looks as if "she were carrying herself in a bag." When the inevitable happens and the police disrupt the first public meeting of the Sunrise Club, Mrs. Smith escapes, "crashing through the underwood like a great white moose," while Dr. Bloodney and Pearl Minkowsky are put in jail and tried for obscenity.

Dr. Bloodney, now widely known as "the supreme bestial pervert and prophet of whoredom in all history," sits through his trial sad-lipped and motionless, looking a bit, as Max tells us, "like a little church door that has been closed." He is sentenced to one year in prison, while freckled Pearl Minkowsky gets off with a lecture from the judge. *Physical Culture and Hypnotism*, however, with its risqué photographs, becomes an instant underground best seller. "The story Ernest Hemingway praised in Paris," Max wrote on his typescript. "It was written before 'nudist colonies' were heard of." Max's story is funny, sarcastic, and complex in the ways it subtly plays with the reader's expectations. Bloodney is a quack, to be sure, and his main supporter a ditzy stenographer at

Wanamaker's, but both rise to silent greatness at the end, martyrs to the cause of free self-expression—unlikely heroes to be sure, but sometimes that is all you have.

The more scholarly product of Max's Parisian endeavors, *Marx, Lenin, and the Science of Revolution,* had come out in a British edition in May. An American edition as well as French and Spanish translations followed later. Emboldened by his new, self-created status as the analyst of an entire political movement, Max mailed a copy of the book, a reminder of what he had to offer, to none other than Freud himself. His years in Russia had demonstrated to Max the shortcomings of dialectical materialism, which he still believed were the fault not of the Bolsheviks but of the Marxian system itself. History, Max had found, "is no one thing or process, except as it is made so by the interests of the historian; it has no one cause, either within or without the consciousness of men, which explains it all; it does not advance by a process of dialectic contradiction and the negation of the negation." Marxism conceals, whereas psychoanalysis reveals. What was needed was not a new metaphysics, but a scientific look at the behavior of those who only think they are acting scientifically, a "psychoanalysis of the social and political mind." Freud's theory could supply what materialism couldn't: a cold hard look at the motivations of human thought and behavior, which would be of great help in the grand project of "social engineering" that Lenin had initiated and that Stalin was threatening to undo: a true revolution devoid of party idolatry and other traces of religious thinking, a revolution that was a purpose and not a belief.[123]

Freud read the book and sent him a letter that was, by Freud's standards, appreciative, although he was also careful to remind him that he was, after all, *Professor* Freud. And he probably remembered, too, how Max had torn him apart in *The Sense of Humor.* Nevertheless, he had, he said, enjoyed *Marx, Lenin* much more than Max's previous books. He felt his analysis was important, perhaps even correct ("bedeutsam, vielleicht auch richtig"), though he also said his dislike for all philosophy and political parties prevented him from fully understanding Max's views. "I could not have tolerated your great Lenin for more than ten minutes."[124] Max was excited nevertheless and did what all authors do when they are praised by someone they admire: he asked for permission to quote from said letter. Freud shot back an ill-tempered note, in English: "I will thank you for *not* mentioning any of the remarks in my letter in public." And he added another sentence that attributed Max's lapse to his Americanness: "I seem thus far to have failed to accustom myself to the American life forms."[125]

In March 1927 the stars were finally aligning. Max was in Vienna again, staying with the radical poet Hugo Sonnenschein in the Josefstadt district. He had been feeling "very lonesome and not very conquering in my mood," but, as luck would have it, Freud now had time for his American admirer. "I can see you Friday at 3^h 30 pm," said Freud's postcard, treasured by Max in the decades afterward.[126] "See Freud tomorrow," Max telegraphed back to Eliena in Paris. "Happy Love—Max."[127] On Friday, March 25, Max made sure he arrived in time for his appointment. He was not a little nervous as he was walking past the massive old houses that lined the sloping street. He was finally going to see his "Father Confessor," the man who had been of such tremendous importance to his personal and intellectual life for so long.[128] When he had ascended the stairs to Professor Freud's book-filled practice on the mezzanine, he found a man who showed no sign of being diminished by the terrible illness that had, over the course of the past year, cost him half his jaw. It had made it necessary for him to wear a terrifying contraption—known as "the monster" to him and his daughter Anna—to fill the hole that multiple cancer surgeries had left at the back of his mouth.[129] It's fun to imagine the six-foot Eastman hulking over the thinner, shorter Freud. Freud was fully alert, at his caustic best. This was the "obscene Doctor Freud," "the cleanest man on two continents," as the cynical capitalist George Forbes calls him in Max's novel, *Venture*: "He digs under the talk. Digs under the mind. He puts words to a new use."[130]

Despite constant pain, Freud had remained relentlessly productive. Just the year before, he had published a book that some, including his biographer Ernest Jones, regard as one of his best, *The Question of Lay Analysis,* an accessibly written dialogue between himself and a so-called Impartial Person, which was intended to illustrate Freud's opinion that psychoanalysis, if it were to have widespread effect, would need to be embraced by people outside the medical field. Max, who had undertaken an exhaustive self-analysis in 1914, had the necessary credentials here. There was considerable urgency behind Freud's plea. He was overwhelmed by the grueling schedule he kept at Berggasse 19, where his day usually began at eight and ended at nine at night, with barely two hours for lunch.[131] Faced with the dramatic spread of neurosis in modern life, society was clamoring for a cure—a cure that should and could no longer be provided by doctors like Freud himself. Was he thinking of a "new kind of Salvation Army"? his interlocutor, the Impartial Person, asked. "Why not?" was Freud's reply.[132] Perhaps not unexpectedly, Freud's thoroughly democratic view of psychoanalysis was roundly rejected in the United States, where analysts were struggling to assert themselves against the hegemony of academic psychiatry and had no interest in diminishing their reputation by allowing nonmedical practitioners into the fold. In the fall of 1926 the American Medical Association, still small at the time but gaining in influence, issued a warning to American doctors not to cooperate with lay analysts.[133] That warning galled Freud, who, ever since his 1909 visit to Clark University in Worcester, had thought of American culture as disappointingly superficial. Max would find out later, from Jones's biography, that Freud referred to his chronic intestinal disorder as "my American indigestion."[134]

When Max visited him at Berggasse 19, Freud's feelings about America and the Americans were thus not particularly warm ones. Indeed, Freud wasted no time. "What do you want?" he asked. Max's answer, the way he remembered it later, was as lame as it was untruthful: "Not a thing."[135] For the main thing Max had wanted had already happened: he was finally here, walking across Freud's soft rugs and admiring the artwork on the walls. Freud was "smaller than I expected," Max scribbled in a small notebook, "slender-limbed and [with] something softer about him than you expect—tenderer, perhaps, or more feminine. . . . Greatness involves delicacy." He had a unique way of "moving about with his head and hands, oddly, looking up at the ceiling and closing his eyes, making funny little faces when he is trying to think of a word, or clarifying an idea, laughing a sudden and very sweet smiling laugh when something pleases him, and that with his head thrown back in an oddly childlike way."[136]

Max was so fascinated by Freud's appearance that his mind began to drift. But Freud was an excellent listener and would never let a conversation go astray. Max wasn't ready for such rigor. In a panic, he made the unfortunate decision to challenge Freud on his use of the phrase "the Unconscious," which to his mind still had remnants of metaphysical thinking stuck to it. Why didn't you say "brain states?" he asked. Freud, sensing he was being criticized, responded that the Unconscious was merely a concept, not a thing. Was Max a behaviorist? Referring to the work of the founding father of behaviorism, Freud added tartly, "According to your John B. Watson, even consciousness doesn't exist." But that was, continued Freud, nonsense: "Consciousness exists quite obviously and everywhere—except perhaps in America." Now there was that laugh again.[137]

Freud was surprisingly well informed about American psychology, even asking Max whether he had read William Bayard Hale's *The Story of a Style,* a psychoanalytically informed study of Woodrow Wilson's rhetoric. Max did know the book and started to talk about the reasons people like Wilson would simply stop thinking and support a war. "Why?" asked Freud. Now Max was prepared: "You know why people stop thinking. It's because their thoughts would lead them where they don't want to go." Freud laughed his little old man's laugh and immediately redirected the conversation to Max's support of the Russian communists. Max defended Bolshevism as the "trying out of an hypothesis," which satisfied Freud the scientist, if in a purely abstract way. For he was, said Freud, "nothing" politically and had no interest in a better future. Come to think of it, the present bothered him, too, and there was nothing that was at present more annoying than the United States. Why on earth did he hate America so much? Max demanded. Now Freud was on a roll. "I don't hate it," he said. "I regret it." He threw back his head and laughed uproariously.[138]

Freud had, Max discerned, made a joke, and one that fulfilled his own, higher definition of *wit*, the intellectual species of humor.[139] "Regret," according to the *Oxford English Dictionary*, implies "sorrow, remorse, or repentance due to reflection on something one has done or omitted to do." One can regret an action but not a country. Freud knew, of course, that he'd had nothing to do with making America into the ludicrous thing he thought it was now. He went on to offer another take on the subject: America was, he said, a "bad experiment conducted by Providence." Amused by his own cleverness, he added, "I think it must have been Providence. I at least should hate to be held responsible for it." When Max asked him "in what way" America had gone bad, Freud exclaimed, "Oh the prudery, hypocrisy, the national lack of independence, there is no independence of thought in America, is there?" And he encouraged Max to write a book about that "miscarriage" of civilization, the "Missgeburt" America. "This book would make you immortal." The meeting had ended.[140]

As Max stumbled down the well-worn stairs of Berggasse 19, he felt flattered and clobbered at the same time. In his mind Freud's previous, ambivalent praise of his book ("important, perhaps even correct") mixed uneasily with Freud's uncanny, satyrlike laugh. But he had not, he decided, come out a loser in this debate. Speaking with Max, Sigmund, with all his self-indulgent wit, had inadvertently unmasked himself. He was no longer an untouchable hero, an idol to be worshiped, the father no one needed. "For was it not to deliver mankind from just that kind of displaced emotion that this hero of self-knowledge was born into the world?" As his unorthodox disciple, the layman Max had reminded Dr. Freud of his original purpose in life. In the process, Max had rediscovered his own purpose. At least for now.[141]

7 · The Thinking Singer

Max's return to the United States was not a triumphant one. He was in his early forties now. Still dashingly handsome, he knew some of his youthful charm had rubbed off. He would still turn heads wherever he appeared, but now his body was beginning to catch up with his white hair. He had no position to come back to, no audiences eager for his thoughts. Most important, he had compromised some of his credibility with the American Left. His support for Lenin, vociferous opposition to Stalin, and endorsement of Trotsky (without receiving, as he had hoped he would, Trotsky's endorsement in turn) did not translate into an easily identifiable political position. Was he still a Bolshevik or not? That he was now married to Nikolai Krylenko's sister did not help clarify things.

Eliena, by contrast, was excited. To her, America was the land of boundless opportunity, even though it wasn't exactly a blank slate, filtered since childhood through the eyes of Huck Finn and, as she spelled his name, Tom Soyer: "I saw with my child's inner eyes America's countryside, its people, and joined the far-away American boys in their so fantastic . . . adventures. That story lived with me through my life, through two wars, revolution, famine." When Max and she later drove through Hannibal, Missouri, it was Eliena who showed Max where Judge Thatcher had lived and where McDougal's cave was. She was, she told Max, American before she had even come to America.[1]

Eliena eagerly embraced living in New York City, where they took apartments, first at 44 West Seventy-first Street, in the Lincoln Square neighborhood, and then in the Village at 501 Barrow Street and, finally, 39 Grove Street. And she loved the little house in Croton, where she enjoyed the company of artists like George Biddle, who hosted sketching parties at his house, and of

Max's old friends, including Ruth Pickering (now Pinchot). All by herself she attacked the weeds and clumps of high grass in the backyard—she was as strong as a bull, one of the neighbors said admiringly—and saw to it that the tennis court was repaired, this time with the help of the neighbors, each of whom contributed $10, in exchange for the right to use the court in perpetuity afterward. While Max himself struggled to fit in, it seems Eliena picked up Max's life where he had left it before he departed for Russia. She also made sure that Dan, Max's long-neglected son, had a good time when he came to visit for six weeks during her first American summer, "a beautiful and gay and very bright boy of 14," as she noted cheerfully. At the end of Dan's stay they all drove to Austerlitz, New York, where Edna St. Vincent Millay and Eugen Boissevain had recently bought Steepletop, a rambling estate close to the Massachusetts state line. Money was in short supply during those days, but the Croton grocer, Mr. Harmon, captivated by Eliena's charm, often went for months without getting paid. During her second summer in Croton Eliena oversaw the construction of an addition to the house known as the "yellow room." After years of living in hotels and rental rooms, she was taking ownership, of Max as well as of Max's house and his friends (fig. 35).[2]

Max had a much harder time getting used to his new old life. When he entered his barn he found that mice had eaten most of his papers. "It was very,

Figure 35. Eliena Eastman, left, and Marion Morehouse (later Cummings) in Croton. EMII.

very sad," noted Eliena. They bought a used convertible in Ossining, but Max had some difficulty readjusting to American traffic rules and soon found himself going the wrong way on one-way streets. No one, including Max himself, was sure what or who he was. A writer without readers whose last bona fide literary work had come out a decade ago, an editor without a magazine to edit, he was now known mostly as a self-taught political pundit. And while his bohemian friends were largely uninterested in politics, at least the way Eliena remembered it, his former political allies had moved on without him. Max's Trotsky biography had been published in an American version he disavowed, and the *Masses* was now the *New Masses*, a "free revolutionary magazine" edited by, among others, Mike Gold and Joseph ("Joe") Freeman.

Max couldn't very well complain. Maybe it wasn't true, as Freeman would claim later, that Max alone was responsible for turning over the *Liberator* "to the monsters of the Kremlin." But the way Freeman remembered it, Max had left written instructions that if the *Liberator* ran into trouble they should transfer the magazine, rather than letting it die, to the Communist Party.[3] No one could have predicted then that it would reemerge as the Communist Party's main theoretical mouthpiece. Nothing liberating was left: first retitled the *Workers Monthly*, Max's and Crystal's magazine was now known as, simply, the *Communist*. Freeman did try, valiantly, to create a new magazine that would fill the vacuum left by the old *Liberator*'s demise. The *New Masses* was supposed to carry on what the *Masses* and the *Liberator* had done so well, that is, present an interesting, provocative mix of politics and culture, without letting the former dominate the latter. It was going to be, as Freeman stated in a prospectus he wrote, a "medium of expression . . . for the new creative forces now taking shape in America."[4] He had secured financial support from the Garland Fund, also known as the American Fund for Public Service, a left-leaning philanthropic organization established in 1922 by Charles Garland, the son of a Wall Street stockbroker. With Freeman and Egmont ("Eggie") Arens as editors and some additional funding from the wealthy prolabor crime writer Rex Stout, who provided the office furniture, the new magazine was launched. All seemed well at first. Max's name appeared on the masthead as a "contributing editor," and he did indeed contribute a few items, among them translations of Alexander Pushkin and Isaac Babel, while he was still in Europe.[5] After his return he went to a few editorial meetings and even became a member of the executive editorial board. His impassioned response to the execution of Nicola Sacco and Bartolomeo Vanzetti appeared in the October issue of the *New Masses,* perhaps with more than a note of wistfulness resonating behind his admiration for two people whose lives had mattered: "Unlike many martyrdoms, the death of Sacco and Vanzetti was of very great use to the cause they loved."[6]

But it appears that Max was far from happy that he had been so effortlessly replaced. And his political affinity to Trotsky made him a welcome target among pro-Bolshevik intellectuals in America. When he published excerpts from *Marx, Lenin* (which was not yet available in the United States) in the *New Masses,* his ideological departure from the party line had become a matter of public record.[7] Dissatisfied with his marginal position but unwilling to commit more time and effort, Max resigned on January 7, 1928. Instead of the *New Masses,* the magazine should be called the *Yellow Masses,* charged Max, "to denote the lack of intellectual force and courage."[8]

There are different versions of what really brought about the rift. Perhaps it happened over the rejection of Max's plan to write an article on Trotsky's expulsion.[9] "I know of nobody who at one time did not have something rejected by NM," Freeman pointed out later. Even Mike and Floyd and Freeman himself had pieces turned down, and the editors had wanted to keep the new magazine free of political grandstanding. "Hell hath no fury like a vain author rejected," Freeman wrote to Dan Aaron.[10] But Max had a different explanation: the *New Masses* was pro-communist, plain and simple. Stout came to the same conclusion, incidentally, and withdrew, too.

The most hard-hitting response to Max's new theories came not from within the *New Masses* but from another student of John Dewey's, Sidney Hook. Widely considered Dewey's favorite student, Hook was twenty years younger than Max. He had just completed and, unlike Max, *submitted* his doctoral thesis. While not an orthodox communist, he took exception to Max's suggestion that Marx needed to be saved from his own philosophy. Hook's attacks on Max, which grew more intemperate as Max's responses, too, became sharper, began in a journal fittingly called *Open Court.* While Max had argued that Marx had anticipated Freud, Hook, who was not a fan of psychoanalysis, felt that Marx, as someone who had demonstrated the efficacy of ideas in the class struggle, should more properly be regarded as a precursor to Dewey. In Hook's reading, Marx saw ideas as *"instruments"* in the process of furthering class interests, a phrase that would have delighted the pragmatist.[11]

Predictably, Max wasn't happy with Hook's interpretation. The fact that Hook continued to regard him as a potential ally "in purifying Marxism of its deadly dogmatism and devitalizing orthodoxy" did not pacify him at all.[12] Hook repeated his charges in the *Journal of Philosophy,* and when Max, in a letter to the editor, vigorously protested, he reiterated them in a full-length review of *Marx, Lenin* for *Modern Quarterly,* in which he openly ridiculed Max, accusing him of having "bungled" a great subject, the magnitude of which had, apparently, "dwarfed" him.[13] "Marxism," Hook wrote, "is not so much a petrified set of bloodless abstractions as a fighting philosophy of the under-dog—a flexible method of organizational struggle in the bitter class warfare of industrial society." Max had not understood either Hegel's or Marx's depar-ture from Hegelian dialectic; his view of communism was clouded by his ob-session with Freud. Marxism was about social forces, not individual psychology. Hook mocked Max's "emasculated instrumentalism," his "child-like" fear of metaphysics, and his ignorance of Hegel, for which he should be punished by having to read the *Phänomenologie des Geistes.*[14]

There were more skirmishes after this essay, culminating in Max's asser-tion that Hook himself had wanted to write a book much like *Marx, Lenin* and must have felt "keen disappointment" when Max had beaten him to the finish line.[15] Hook responded mockingly by saying that if his views on Marx were as different from Max's as Max had claimed, why would he not welcome the publication of *Marx, Lenin* so that he could show how "false" Max's position was? In a way, though, Max was right. Both men essentially wanted the same thing, namely, to close the gap between philosophy and social action, Hook by redefining it, Max by eliminating it entirely.

There were many cheap shots in these exchanges, Max accusing Hook of vanity and unscholarly behavior as well as moral and intellectual libel, while Hook focused on Max's deception, lack of erudition, and failure to understand formal logic.[16] The controversy deeply scarred Max. When Hook, in 1933, pub-lished *his* book, *Towards the Understanding of Karl Marx,* Max ripped out many of the pages and littered the margins with scathing remarks: "again it means nothing" next to a passage explaining the dialectic as the interacting parts of a developing whole; "surprising that it should be discovered by S. Hook 70 years after his death" next to a sentence excoriating the "common failure to appreci-ate the nature of Marx's dialectical method"; and "Poor Marx!" scribbled on a page where Hook recommends that Marx's method be separated from specific results.[17] Max also wrote a formal review of Hook's book for the *Herald Tri-bune,* in which he called Hook's conflation of dialectical materialism with Dewey's version of pragmatism "as false and fantastic as it is historically im-probable." While the motives of the socialist and the pragmatist might be similar, the differences in terms of "concrete belief" were insurmountable. In the Marxian scheme the philosopher had to be convinced his program of action will be fulfilled. For the Deweyite, such a quest for certainty was the last remnant of a barbarous faith, the product of a bygone era. In his single-minded determination to turn Marx into a Deweyite, Hook had to tear down one of the central pillars of the temple of Marxism, the belief in "historic determinism." Max exclaimed, "He does this by mere arbitrary dictum—by telling you 'what Marx really means when he speaks of the historic inevitability of communism.' " And what Marx meant, in Sidney Hook's myopic reading, was *not* that communism was inevitable but that it was *possible,* an alternative worth striving for, one that one may help to "make true" just by believing in it. Communism optional? Max thought the very idea was risible. If Marx said *inevitable* when he meant *possible,* then everything was up for grabs. The snide subtitle of Max's review said it all: "Sidney Hook's Day-Dream of What Marx Might Have Said Had He Been a Pupil of John Dewey."[18]

Hook and Max later reconciled after Hook, too, turned against the Soviet version of communism. Nevertheless, the damage was done. When Max, as an old man, remembered that fight—for that's what it really was, a fight in which both men seemed determined to draw blood, a struggle no less lethal for being fought in the quarterlies and newspapers—the experience still seemed so close and painful to him that, in an autobiography otherwise rich with narrative tangents and irrelevant detail, he decided not to discuss it: "It struck me like a bolt—not from the blue, for there was no blue, but from the dead gray weight of fog that hung over my intellectual life in those lonely days."[19]

Some of Max's identity problems were reflected in the hero of Max's novel, *Venture,* a book left unfinished for years after he had first begun working on it in his dingy little room in Sochi. The novel's protagonist, the rather transparently named Jo Hancock, a college dropout and poet of modest ability, bore many features of Max himself, as Sinclair Lewis accurately perceived, mixed in with the muscularity and adventurousness of John Reed. And while Jo shared some features with other young men exposed to radical ideas—such as Hal Warner in Upton Sinclair's *King Coal* (1917) and Billy in Ernest Poole's *The Harbor* (1915)—Max's novel follows its own course by presenting Jo as really invested in two or perhaps three worlds: that of capitalist entrepreneurship, where he is quite successful, labor activism, and, last but not least, poetry. Jo's clever business idea—to deliver freshly roasted coffee via milk wagons to grocery stores all over New York, a "smooth-running New Yorker's utopia," a dream of a delightfully caffeinated city opening their wallets to him—is progressive enough to make it not entirely unbelievable that, in his other life, he would fall under the influence of the IWW organizer Bill Haywood and join and support the silk strikers of Paterson, New Jersey. Neither George Forbes, a Nietzschean businessman who encourages Jo's capitalist aspirations, nor the leaders of the strike know about the extent of Jo's double life. Rather than relieving the reader of the ambiguities the novel has created around Jo, its ending reinforces them. Jo's friends in Paterson discover that he is a bourgeois, his main investor pulls out, and his business fails before it even gets started. Jo's love interest in the novel is Vera, the daughter of one of the strike leaders, a proletarian, Russian version of Florence Deshon with a sprinkling of Eliena's wholesomeness and her gray eyes and prominent cheekbones. After Jo owns up to Forbes, Vera bestows a soft kiss upon him. But even that doesn't yet release Jo from the prison of indecision he has created for himself, as the novel's last sentence indicates: "He thought that perhaps real life can be lived after all—if you only make a few fundamental decisions."[20]

The Boni brothers published the book in November 1927, as bad luck would have it, the same month as Thornton Wilder's *The Bridge of San Luis Rey*, whose fame would eclipse *Venture*. Max's novel wasn't well served by the Bonis, who were equally lackluster in promoting *Marx, Lenin*, the other Eastman book they had taken on, under the title *Marx and Lenin: The Science of Revolution*. Max had expected so much more from them. After leaving Boni and Liveright, the firm he cofounded with Horace Liveright, Albert Boni had joined forces with his younger brother Charles to create an imprint that would publish innovative contemporary writers. Among their authors, apart from Wilder, were William Carlos Williams, Ford Madox Ford, and Marcel Proust in C. K. Moncrieff's translation; in 1925 they had published the iconic anthology *The New Negro*. Excellent company, to be sure. The Bonis had promised Max they would make *Venture* their "big book of the season," push it "as no big publisher would," and "get behind it with all [their] force." Yet, as Max pointed out in an angry letter to Albert that he ultimately didn't send, the book wasn't advertised anywhere until it had already come out. When, a few days after the official publication date, some friends of Max's asked for a copy at Brentano's in New York, no one there had even heard of it. Review copies weren't sent to the places Max had recommended. It seemed particularly ironic to Max that the *New Masses* never received a notice about a novel set in the times of the old *Masses* days, "a tragedy to me and a shame to you," he told the Boni brothers.

Not even lecture agents he was hoping to work with had received copies of either *Marx and Lenin* or *Venture*.[21]

Despite Max's fears, his novel, though it didn't become the best seller of the season, *was* noticed. The *New York Times* reviewer liked it and said it was well written. Maybe it wasn't startlingly original and maybe it was too patently autobiographical. But he also said it stood "well above the majority" of similar novels and praised its rich texture and firm handling of characterization.[22] From Delaware, where he and Zelda were renting Ellerslie, a thirty-room Greek Revival mansion, F. Scott Fitzgerald congratulated Max on his achievement, repeating some of his earlier reservations though packaged as praise: "It's so beautifully written and tells me so much about what are to me the dim days—1910–1917—that formed so many people of the liberal side in the generation just ahead of me and in mine." Max had made it all "real and vivid" again. "Nothing so sane on that terribly difficult subject—for it was after all a creed, a faith, in the surest and most helpless sense, has ever been written." Note that Fitzgerald was thinking of socialism as a historical fact—one that required study but not emulation—and of Max as its documentarian. At the time, he was trying to finish *Tender Is the Night,* a novel set so far removed from the environment of the New Jersey silk strikers that his reaction makes immediate sense.[23] Sinclair Lewis, however, didn't like it at all. *Venture* had "splendid things in it, fine scenes, spirited characters," but overall it was disappointing. Why hadn't Max written a novel about Bill Haywood, "including his last, rather futile, superbly tragic days in Moscow"? Now *there* was a protagonist! But Jo Hancock got on his nerves. He reminded Lewis of a type of protagonist he himself had championed, "young gent of good family and education who ambles into literary society, vaguely discovers there is such a thing as the Labor Movement, meets and sleeps with a hell of a lot of literary or smart women, and in the end feels vaguely that maybe, b' God, there's something *to* the Labor Movement, to socialism—and you know he'll only go on talking about it till the end of his life." Ironically, by castigating the inauthenticity of Max's book, Lewis had indirectly confirmed how authentic it was as a description of Max's own personal and political dilemmas.[24]

But no criticism of the book, public or private, descended to the level of the *Paterson Call,* which deemed *Venture* "one of the dullest and most bromidic books published in many a day" and, for good measure, "the sorriest stuff we ever read." The reviewer, who also said he wouldn't be wasting "valuable white space" on it were it not for the fact that his city was mentioned in the novel, concluded, "Now we understand why *The Masses* failed." One imagines that

Max, whose support of the silk strikers apparently had not been forgotten, would have been rather pleased with that review: once again he had managed to annoy the authorities of Paterson, New Jersey. He saved the newspaper clipping.[25]

Would Max have embarked on a serious career as a novelist, would he have written a second novel, if the Boni brothers had lived up to their promise and made his book into a big hit? *Venture* is a novel of ideas, capably written but, like other examples of the genre such as Aldous Huxley's *Point Counterpoint* (1928), it lumbers from one long dialogue to the next. Max's prose is driven less by finely imagined characters and intricate plotting than by the kind of epigrammatic succinctness he had perfected in his essays. "Selfishness is akin to candor, the natural attribute of an animal, but egotism is a special degenerate accomplishment of mankind, the mother of hypocrisy," the narrator tells us, for example, and "The shortest road to friendship is a mutual dislike." Predictably, given Max's authorship, the novel takes flight whenever Max imagines sexual desire. These are, indeed, some of the most memorable moments in the novel: Jo Hancock noticing, with evident pleasure, the half-bare shoulders and muscular arms of Mary Kittredge (a character based on Jack Reed's lover Mabel Dodge Luhan) or longing to touch the white skin, luminous "like china with lights under it," of another one of his lovers, Muriel Paxton-Kadner.[26]

If Jo Hancock couldn't make fundamental decisions, his creator wasn't doing much better in that department. For now, Max returned to what he knew best, giving speeches. He had spoken publicly in favor of women's suffrage, in favor of the Bolsheviks, and against the war. But women had gained the right to vote and the war was over and the Bolsheviks seemed busy self-destructing. Max's new subject was . . . himself and everything he had to offer. Through William Colston Leigh's agency in New York, Max began to market himself as a "poet, social philosopher, and psychologist," all rolled into one convenient package. Flyers featured a photograph of Max looking rugged but sophisticated, with just the hint of a tie hidden behind his leather jacket. Leigh's business was still new at the time, but his list of clients would later include such celebrities as Eleanor Roosevelt, Clement Attlee, and Will Durant.

As Max was trying to reinvent himself once again, Crystal was fighting for her survival, and she was losing the battle. Her life had been a series of disappointments. In April 1922 Walter Fuller, her second husband, had gone back to England to look for work. He started an occasionally successful literary agency before landing a position as managing editor for a weekly newspaper. Crystal joined him in October, her son Jeffrey and her one-year-old daughter Annis in tow. This was the second time she had followed Walter to England, and she found the experience draining. In June 1924 she returned to the United States but could not make ends meet there either, likely because her political activities had gotten her blacklisted.[27] By Christmas she was at Walter's side again. With no hope of permanent employment, she spent the summer of 1926 with Max and Eliena on the Côte d'Azur. But nothing could alleviate the periods of "real panic & despair" she suffered.[28] In August 1927 she and her children were en route back to the States. Crystal took up residence at her Croton house and began work for the *Nation,* where she had been promised a temporary job. A month after her departure Walter had a stroke and died, and the next summer, shockingly, Crystal, too, lay dying. Max probably never realized, during these final years of his sister's life, how troubled and then, finally, how sick she was. Her last hospital stay was at John Harvey Kellogg's Battle Creek Sanitarium in Battle Creek, Michigan, but Kellogg's enemas couldn't save her anymore. Crystal died on July 8, 1928, at her brother Anstice's house in Erie, Pennsylvania. She was buried in the Eastman family plot in Canandaigua, the site of happier times. She was only forty-eight years old. For the rest of his life the only birthday Max was ever able to remember, apart from his own, was Crystal's.[29]

Max was stunned by so much bad luck but not enough to want to burden himself with raising Crystal's two children, even though she had appointed him their guardian. His decision to let Crystal's friend Agnes Leach take care of them is not mentioned in his autobiography. Even the letters he sent Eliena from London, where he had gone in July 1929 to speak with the children as well as with Fuller's family, are extraordinarily reticent about his real motivation—apart from the personal and financial burden that parental responsibilities would have meant to a man who had, by some standards, already failed to be a father to his biological son. Admittedly, Crystal's daughter Annis did not seem to be too enthusiastic about returning to Croton with Max, threatening to "lock herself in the bath-room if I tried to take her back to America," though the prospect of staying didn't appeal to her either: "If I live in England, I'd have to go to Sunday School, and I don't mind going to school, but I don't want to go to Sunday School." Jeff Fuller, on the other hand, was "sweet and thoughtful" and more disposed to move back to the States, where there was "more to do," though not, as Max noted to his relief, necessarily with Max as his new foster father. Max, resting an appreciative eye on Cynthia,

Crystal's sister-in-law, "a soft golden-haired gracious princess," was distinctly out of his element, and the legal maneuvering that his "diplomatic mission" had produced inevitably bored and overwhelmed him. He did not sleep well at night, once dreaming that his house was surrounded by wild animals, with Eliena wanting to let them all in to play with. It was another warning to him not to agree to anything that would bring new responsibilities and thus new dangers with it.[30]

Was Max aware of the damage he did to Crystal's children? For years Jeffrey and Annis had lived messy lives, with no chance to grow real roots in either England or the United States. Her verbal commitments to parenting notwithstanding—in one of her last letters, addressed to her sister-in-law Cynthia, she said she wanted nothing more than to "make a happy childhood for Jeffrey and Annis"—Crystal always seemed ready to leave rather than to settle down with her family.[31] And now Max seamlessly continued the practice. "You all loved each other so much," wrote Annis to Max in 1965, remembering the adoration and love Max and Crystal had shown each other, "that Jeff and I feel a deeper loss than death. Almost as if we had not been *born* properly." Nearly forty years later, the pain had not subsided.[32]

To be sure, Crystal's death was an extremely traumatic event for Max. Gone was the person that, growing up, he had admired the most, "his angel of light," Anstice's "bunny girl," the fierce warrior for workers' and women's rights, the uncompromising advocate for peace, the only woman he had truly loved. Likely Max felt that anything that would have reminded him of Crystal's absence would have been too hard to bear. At least for a while, he became tongue-tied when he had to speak in public. Instead of the eloquent poet, audiences got a wooden reciter of canned sentiments from a script.

When Max was driving home to Croton the day after Crystal's death, he found himself passing through Canandaigua. He decided, with an aching heart, that he needed to go out to Seneca Lake and see Glenora, "our real home." On the way there he glimpsed the Pratts's farm, where his father had worked and Crystal and he had played when they were mere babies. It had been transformed into an inn. Max went in, took a room, and spent the night remembering specifically one incident, his earliest experience of anguish, of the fear that terrible things might and will happen to you in life. He remembered how so many decades ago he and Crystal had gone to the barn and climbed up to the corn crib to watch the pigs devour their grub below and how Crystal's beautiful straw hat, with all those lovely flowers arranged around the brim, had fallen down through a hole in the corn crib's floor and how the pigs then, grunting, squealing, snorting, had chewed on it and trampled it into the black mud, "until you could no longer see what it looked like."[33]

It took a while for Max to reemerge from where Crystal's death had hurled him, "way down in the oozy green depths under the sea."[34] The bad food and anonymous hotel rooms on his lecture tours didn't help, and, with his heart still noisily "buzzing" inside him, the speeches just wouldn't pour out of him as effortlessly as they once did. He had never been a natural orator, merely an "actor who knows how to act the part of an orator," and now he couldn't find his way back into that role. Had Crystal, in death, taken some part of his mind with her?[35] Max began to rely on sleeping pills and bromide, dutifully mailed by Eliena from Croton. The American landscape had changed since Max last toured it, and the stakes had become higher. Instead of random assortments of people in dance halls, abandoned warehouses, and school gymnasiums, Max now spoke at the invitation of clubs, foundations, and universities. He had vastly expanded his range of topics, offering everything from "The Art of Enjoying Poetry" to "The Russian Soul and the Bolsheviks." An Eastman lecture, announced the flyer with great confidence, was an event not to be missed: "Max Eastman takes lecturing seriously, and it is said of him that no lecturer before the public today so delightfully combines profound thinking with stimulation and entertainment." If earlier flyers declared that they didn't need to reprint tributes to Max the orator, later ones pulled out all the stops, quoting everyone from the State Teachers College in Milwaukee ("Mr. Eastman is a powerful platform lecturer and very stimulating and clear in presenting his particular philosophy") to Preserved Smith at Cornell ("You have made even Aristotle look unscientific"). Even when he was struggling for words Max cut an impressive figure at the lectern with his white hair, intense eyes, and ruddy, glowing skin.[36]

Not everyone was appreciative. In Des Moines he found himself surrounded by the "gloopy" women who listened to him with no discernible reaction on their faces. No one came up to him and said, "I like your books—where are you going from here?" No one even offered him a cup of tea. After the lecture he slunk out to eat his pimiento sandwich in a gray, dull hotel lobby, and he made sure he left that town for good.[37] But as the cities whizzed by— Kansas City, Fort Worth, Dallas, San Antonio, New Orleans, Oklahoma City— Max gradually regained some of his former confidence, and his affliction, which he described as his lips failing to "articulate words properly," vanished. Audiences glowed and smiled again. They asked him to read his poetry, and after he had finished in Dallas the organizer of the event came up to him and

said, "Max, I'm going to love you—I love you already." Away from the complications of the political scene of New York, Max was a big deal again: "That is
the way it used to be, a kind of glow after I spoke and people lingering around
in it." These people were genial, straight, direct, more like Russians.[38]

The return of his charisma made the smooth-talking Max endure even situations like the one in Oklahoma City, where he was babbling to a roomful of
"oil-soaked block-heads." The room was virtually dark because the organizers
had chosen to arrange big bunches of smilax all around the lights, "which were
dim as torches in a tunnel anyway, and the sad somber rays trickled out through
these half-withered leaves and made everybody feel that their last hour had
come." Nobody could see Max, who, despite the fact that he was talking about
humor, felt like a baker kneading with "fake energy" some hostile and inert
dough. "Cruel and unusual punishment" it was, he said, and yet one senses
from his letter that he also enjoyed the bizarre situation he found himself thrust
into. The next day, a trip to the oil fields in the company of several millionaires,
added to Max's merry sense of detachment from this absurd experience. The
highlight was the peek he got at a new well that had just begun to operate: "The
earth was black-wet and shiny for a quarter of a mile where this oozy geyser
puked and spit all over everybody and everything." In the evening, at dinner, a
girl made "brown eyes" at him, completing the color scheme.

The next stops on his itinerary were Salt Lake City, Pasadena, Charleston,
and Boston. Finally, like a kid in a crazy candy store, Max was having a grand
time: "It's a funny and fascinating country, America. I accept all invitations,
and just trot along and 'see' everything they have to offer." When he next gave
his humor speech in Tulsa, it was even funnier, so funny in fact that a girl sitting in the front row collapsed with laughter. Max began to fear for her health
and switched to a more serious mode for a bit until she got over it.[39]

On his trips through the American heartland Max never tired of observing
people, but none was more memorable than the sad, honest, blue-eyed little
man in Iowa City, looking like a "decaying Bobbie Burns," who had killed his
neighbor and "told exactly when where and how he did it," without dwelling
on any extenuating circumstance, as if he were the original pragmatist and his
life an experiment gone awry—no self-pity allowed. A reporter for the local
college paper had dragged Max along to the trial, and now he couldn't purge
the image from his mind.[40]

While Max was sweeping audiences in Oklahoma, Texas, and California off
their feet, Eliena struggled to reinvent herself as a painter, waking up at night—

as she reported in a letter to Max, who was lecturing in Fort Wayne, Indiana—
"sobbing and crying like malenkaia," like a little child, because "my pictures
are no good." Theodore Dreiser, one of her early sitters, seemed to agree. Peep-
ing" at his portrait, "he did not seem to like it too much." Eliena promised him
a second chance, when she would, she told Max, make him just as ugly as he
is."[41] Eliena was funny, and her capacity for finding humor in the most unlikely
places and frustrating situations helped both her and Max survive. When the
conductor on the train to New York chided her because she showed up late at
the Harmon station, she would just laugh, and "everybody in the car looked
startled as people do often when I laugh." When she wasn't taking the train
she drove her car to and from New York, and her letters were filled with self-
deprecating accounts of her driving mishaps. In February 1930 Eliena, fully at
home in her adopted country, submitted her application for citizenship.[42]

Max and Eliena were sleeping in separate beds by then, "wide apart," as
Charmion von Wiegand, one of Max's lovers at the time, asserted in an unpublished story. But Eliena's need for Max had not lessened, and even
Charmion couldn't but admire this energetic little Russian woman (called
Arga in her story), this fiercely determined nomad who had made Max, not
any particular country or place in the world, her home: "With Arga, her anxiety and inner fear at the remote possibility of his loss was like a wound that
never healed." Spinning a fine web of possession around him, Eliena was
holding Max bound to her as best she could.[43]

Max tried to break free at least once. In the summer of 1930, just having
returned from a lecture trip to California during which he had reconnected
with his old college friend Sid Wood (and perhaps even more so with Sid's
"two alluring daughters"), he sequestered himself in Gay Head near Chilmark
on Martha's Vineyard, where he hunkered down in an old sheep barn Eliena
and he had discovered the year before. There he engaged in some more self-
analysis, writing down his "inmost thoughts, dreams, and wishful emotions,"
as he had done earlier when he felt he was drifting away from Ida. This time
the result was more positive, even though he never touched, he felt afterward,
the real reason for his short-lived rebellion. Then and on many future occasions Eliena's fine web proved too resilient for him to escape.[44]

One of Eliena's early fans was the aspiring painter Ione Robinson (fig. 36),
a beautiful seventeen-year-old girl who had left her native Oregon and was
now working as an assistant to the artist and illustrator Rockwell Kent, helping him with his work on an edition of *Candide*. She also helped Eliena with
her painting. Eliena was a willing student, eager to soak up all the things Ione

Figure 36. Ione Robinson. EMIIA1.

had picked up in the desultory training she had had at the Academy of Arts in Philadelphia and the Student Art League. Ione was impressed. Writing to her mother from Croton, where she was staying with the Eastmans, Ione declared that Eliena had "so much enthusiasm, and such facility in her work, that I am positive she will accomplish something."[45]

In the mornings Ione and Eliena worked together; in the afternoons they swam in the Hudson or played tennis. Max, at the age of forty-five, took the opportunity to put into practice his free love philosophy again and began an affair with Ione, who was captivated, as so many women would be after her, by Max's "seize the day" philosophy of love: "Don't kiss anybody you don't want to—and kiss everybody you do want to (if you can)—this is the first and great commandment."[46] Max helped her extract herself from the clutches of Kent, who was a stern taskmaster and whose work as a painter, with its "cold, hard lines," she didn't even like all that much.[47] Finally, Max and Eliena drove her to Montreal, where she boarded the *S.S. Montrose* to France with a ticket Max had helped her obtain. "I love and I miss you," she wrote after Max had said good-bye to her, "so much of my thought is of you, of your gentleness and lovingness. I close my eyes and can see you near me."[48]

Distance made Ione's heart grow even fonder. Months later, after she had set up a studio in Cagnes-sur-Mer on the Côte d'Azur, she was longing for American bathrooms, American coffee, American toast—and Max Eastman: "Loving you when you are so far away makes you like my God, something beautiful that I saw and loved,—then it was taken away! Pooh!" Living alone in a strange country, with no real mastery of French, she felt that if Max only said the word, she would return home: "I have to see you! Or I'll jump in the *sea!*" And she appended a nude drawing of herself, arms extended, that gave voice to her feelings.[49]

Even if Max's and Ione's love didn't last, their friendship did. After her return a few months later Max introduced her to George Biddle, who then wrote a letter of introduction to the Mexican painter Diego Rivera. Two months later Robinson was living in the photographer Tina Modotti's house in Mexico City and helping Rivera with his National Palace frescoes. Yet another month later she found herself in a new relationship with a man who had come to Mexico to work for TASS, the Russian news agency, and who would turn into one of Max's archenemies, Joe Freeman. However much the circumstances of Ione's life changed, Max remained the friend she would turn to in times of need. As late as 1953 Ione, now the mother of a one-year-old son by a man she barely knew and living, once again, in Mexico, wrote to Max to ask for $200 since she couldn't feed herself or the child. Max wired her $50.[50]

Money was perennially in short supply in the Eastman household in those days, and it would remain so for the rest of Max's life. But in the 1930s Max actually had, perhaps for the first time in his life, some real income from his lecturing and writing. It helped that, in June 1930, he was able to sell his parents' cottage in Glenora (his share of the sale was $200).[51] Eliena, too, was doing what she could. She took up teaching Russian in Manhattan, to full classes, as she proudly informed Max.[52] In Russia she had studied with Mikhail Mordkin, the partner of Anna Pavlova, and in February 1930 she began to offer dancing lessons for couples. Later she would teach interpretive dance to children on Martha's Vineyard.[53] There was no limit to her creativity: at one point she even took on a job as a live-in minder of an alcoholic young man named Morgan Worthy at 400 East Fiftieth Street.[54]

Then there was the translation work. Together, Max and Eliena produced English versions of two Trotsky works: first, of *The Real Situation in Russia* and then, for the Boni brothers, the much more demanding nine-hundred-page *History of the Russian Revolution*. Trotsky, in his Turkish exile, was elated when he heard about *History*. Three previous translators had produced shoddy work. But Max was ideally fitted for the task since he combined knowledge of Russian with a deep familiarity with Russian history and literature. At first Trotsky couldn't believe his eyes when he saw Albert Boni's telegram: How could Max Eastman have decided to take upon himself such an enormous burden? "Evidently only so that you could save the book from complete death," he wrote. Max's commitment to "save his book from ruin" was evidence of his friendship, and Trotsky was worried only that Max wouldn't be paid enough.[55]

Under pressure from Trotsky, Boni, who had already kept half of a fee the *Saturday Evening Post* had paid to Trotsky for the serial rights, sold the translation rights to Simon and Schuster, and Max received one cent per word plus 10 percent of Trotsky's fees and royalties.[56] Max was relieved. Communicating with Boni had been like "signaling through a fog."[57]

Initially, Trotsky kept his distance. When the first installments of *History* were serialized in the *Saturday Evening Post,* he praised Max, writing, "I sense a fine translation," though in fact Max had mostly revised the work of his predecessors. It was only after the first volume came out in 1932 that he started to quibble. Here is a good example: in his often savagely funny chapter on the Executive Committee of the Soviet of Workers' Deputies Trotsky had described one of the members, Nikolai Avksentiev, as a teacher of "belles lettres" at a ladies' seminary. "That is really all you can say about him." Max, in his translation, called Avksentiev a "teacher of language," which ruined the joke and made him seem less pretentious than Trotsky needed him to be in order to reinforce his point that nothing good can come from a system in which the leaders separate themselves from the actual workers.[58]

While Max did not change this passage when *History* was reprinted, he made sure he consulted the author about nuances of meaning as he was plowing through volumes two and three of Trotsky's massive work. Trotsky responded chattily to Max's queries, with a dry wit that showed how comfortable he had become with Max's work.[59] He loved the fact that Eliena was an integral part of the work, too, and alluded to her "Ukrainian" roots—a joke, as Eliena well knew: although the ending "-*ko*," as in Krylen*ko*, is typical of surnames that are originally Ukrainian, Eliena's family was originally from Smolensk.[60] Eliena was always involved, from the first tentative drafts of Max's manuscript to the fair copy. She was Max's typist, native informant, copy editor, and proofreader. Before the second volume went off to the press, Albert Glotzer, who had served as Trotsky's guard in Turkey, Glotzer's wife, Bertha, and Eliena were sitting around Max's table reading "the thing," as Eliena reported, "till Bertha's eyes began to look in different directions and Glotzer thought he is again on the boat with Trotsky."[61]

Trotsky included a warm endorsement of Max's efforts in his introduction to volumes two and three. His American translator had, he said, "brought to his work not only a creative gift of style, but also the carefulness of a friend."[62] Such words were balm for Max's wounded political soul. Isolated from both the Bolsheviks in Russia and his old socialist buddies in the States, he found a sense of belonging in his new relationship with Trotsky. Maybe he was still a force to be reckoned with. Even the skeptical Joe Freeman, despite their political disagreements, seemed to believe the charismatic Max might yet again emerge as "the God Almighty . . . of all the thinking radical youth," in Eliena's no doubt somewhat exaggerated version of a conversation she had with Joe.[63]

In April 1931 Scribner's published Max's first collection of poetry since 1918, *Kinds of Love,* in which he combined works written during the previous decade with poems written and published earlier. The book's salmon-colored dust jacket characterized Max's ideal reader as "interested in the *liberal* thought of our time," an adjective that would come to haunt him over the next three decades. His poetry had assumed a new economy and clarity of expression that put him fully at odds with prevailing literary fashions, especially modernism. In "Egrets," collected in *Kinds of Love,* he recalled seeing photographs of these birds at the house of James Judson Carroll, a lumber industry executive, ornithologist, and organizer of the Houston Forum. Being Max, he found his mind wandering from the sinuous forms of the birds to the elegantly formed limbs of his host's daughter, forbidden fruit for Max since she was about to be married. After channeling his obvious longing into the more acceptable form of wedding advice, Max ended his tribute by encouraging the daughter (he sent her the poem!) to hold on to the primal wildness he had seen in her: "Give love which is the giving art, / But give the wild will never."[64]

Max's new poetry seems less eager to impress, more concentrated, more dependent on occasions or driven by definite purposes than ever before. In his sonnet "Modernist Poetry," for example, he sought to capture the challenge his old friend, natural science, had brought to literature. No more tunes, no more color in an age dominated by electricity and mathematical equations. But wait, thoughtfulness was not quite dead yet. Max certainly wanted to be perceived as a "thinking singer," as an intellectual not afraid to wear the colorful garments of the poet. He was a writer who got things done but done beautifully:

> Shall not some Goethe of a greater dawn
> Pick up this early bright cast coat of song
> And wear it strongly though his thought is strong,
> Confusing not the doing with the dress?[65]

The poem that perhaps best epitomizes the conflict between conventional form and less-than-ordinary subject matter was "Swamp Maple," a longish poem written in ballad stanzas, featuring the adulterer Abdiel, torn between the vow he made to one woman, his "dark love" (named Laura in a later version of the poem), and the desire he feels for another one, a mermaid-like, lithe-limbed, cheerful girl named Elaine. When Abdiel returns to Laura after a night spent with Elaine, Max evokes an image of betrayed domesticity with the guilty conscience of the experienced philanderer: "Her little house was sleeping like a picture / Of all that books had told him could be sweet. / Blue asters bobbed and nodded by her window; / Her gray soft cat came winding round his feet." He tries to make love to Laura but fails: "In his lips he tasted his dissembling. / He could not. He slid weakly from her bed." Much to his surprise, Laura not only knows what he has done but accepts him the way he is. The maple turns red in both spring and autumn, she says, and adds,

> "The kinds of love are many as the berries
> That autumn hangs like lanterns on each vine;
> Shall we not gather, while the winter tarries,
> Some sweet sharp-colored berries, yours and mine?"[66]

This was Max's philosophy of love pressed into the cramped space of four lines—not revolutionary as poetry but certainly provocative as a recipe for marital success (as least as far as the man's wishes are concerned). His ex-lover Genevieve Taggard, in reviewing *Kinds of Love,* was entranced. "Swamp Maple" was Max's best work so far, she wrote in a review for the *Herald Tribune.* The poem was "so fresh and natural that one rubs one's eyes" in wonder. It is easily the highlight in a volume that captures the changes in mood with such subtlety they seemed like light and shadow falling over grass.[67]

The companion volume to Max's *Kinds of Love* was *The Literary Mind: Its Place in an Age of Science,* published by Scribner's in October 1931. It offered a full-throated defense of Max the poet, who was writing sonnets and rhyming "song" and "strong" at a time when most poets around him had abandoned fixed forms and followed the seductions of free verse. It also took Max back to his early fascination with science. Max wanted to warn his literary friends that science was poised to assume all the importance—the right to speak about the world's problems—that had once been the prerogative of religion and more recently that of literature. Modernism was a retreat from the onslaught of science, helplessness cloaked in unintelligible language. People no longer wanted to know "the best that has been thought" but what had been "found out to be true." But the poets were unavailable to help: "Where our parents consulted the poets for direct guidance in the unmanageable crises of their lives, we consult the . . . psychoanalyst." Poetry, at its best, was more than mere talk, more than the chatter of fragments shored up against the poet's ruin. It was the enrichment, in vibrant, living colors, of that which is true, which for Max was another way of saying that in poetry substance mattered more than linguistic gimmickry.[68]

The Literary Mind was a crabby book, fueled by Max's contempt for literary experiment. He did not shy away from mockery, and he did not spare his friends either. One particularly convenient target was E. E. Cummings's poetry, specifically "Among / these / red / pieces of / day" from Cummings's volume *is 5* (1926). Resetting it first as prose, Max then reprinted the original version with the note that this is how the poem looked "after an attack of punctuation." Somewhat backhandedly, he also corrected an Italian error in Cummings's poem, changing "il trene" to "il treno," hoping it was "an orthographic mistake" and not part of the author's "lyrical inspiration." Max pointed out that the poem had no title—"It just jumps at you like a robber out of the brush and says, 'Listen or run!' "—and that one could not really say what it was about unless one had inside information, as Max, in fact, did: "I happen to be in a position to explain that it has to do with a ride on an Italian railroad train." He added a tongue-in-cheek paraphrase of the poem, taking Cummings's images as literally as possible: "It is evening, and the sun is just setting over the mountains— the day, that is, is breaking to pieces and the pieces are red. And the poet also is going to pieces in a manner of speaking." At the end of the poem, all was dark, or maybe "the poet is dead, or something." The poem was an experience alright but an expensive one "because you have to hire a couple of detectives and have the poet shadowed for a month or two until you catch him in a temporary fit of common sense and get him to admit what it is he is talking about." Punctuation and typography in Cummings's poem—all those hyphens between letters, the erratic commas and the blank spaces, the line breaks in the middle of words—served to make an obscure poem even more obscure.

Max then moved in for the kill when he quoted the critic Paul Rosenfeld's observation that Cummings's typographical idiosyncrasies had the purpose of marking the acceleration and deceleration of his melodic lines. Really? Just give the poem to two readers and lock them in separate soundproof chambers and have them recite the poem. Would they produce identical curves if recorded by a machine and transcribed on paper? Hardly. Rosenfeld's defense of Cummings's word salad was either bogus science or "literarious nonsense."[69]

However, *The Literary Mind* cannot simply be reduced to a visceral antimodern assault. Indeed, Max showed himself to be very au courant with recent developments in science. Invoking Werner Heisenberg's uncertainty principle, he saw science rapidly moving into all those fields hitherto reserved to literature. What was necessary, according to Max, was a theory of poetry that regarded it as a part of the flux of life itself. The prototype of the poet, he said provocatively, quoting from Herbert Spencer Jennings's *Behavior of the Lower Organisms,* was the flatworm, since he or she reacts, as the flatworm does, "to almost all mechanical stimuli, whether weak or strong . . . turning toward the point stimulated." At the end of *The Literary Mind,* Max advocated that all English Departments be closed and made into a branch of the Department of Psychology, since psychology alone could explain literature. But it was psychology regarded as a social science rather than as a science of the individual mind, since the social forces that shape a literary work were so much more important than the "motives of the individual which cause it." Max was straining after scientific terminology: works of literature are caused, not written.[70]

The Literary Mind revealed the extraordinary balancing acts Max was performing during those years. While his aesthetic taste gravitated to the tried and true, as a political thinker he was pushing boundaries, questioning orthodoxies. He faced the additional challenge of having to avoid the impression that his poetry was antimodernist the same way the Stalinists were antimodernists and sworn enemies of any literary experimentation that didn't deliver clear-cut messages. He was mightily pleased and relieved, then, when the British art critic Clive Bell, a great supporter of abstract, nonrepresentational art, loved his book, calling it "by far the best piece of literary criticism . . . that has appeared in English in my time."[71]

The Literary Mind angered even those of Max's readers who had so far accepted or even welcomed his turn against the Russian government. "I think Eastman has come out of the battle scarred and his vision gone blind," declared the *Brooklyn Citizen* mercilessly.[72] At a time when Max couldn't say for sure where his real audience was and why his books didn't sell, it was an enlightened decision on his part to agree to edit a selection of Karl Marx's writings, including excerpts from *Das Kapital,* for the publisher Bennett Cerf's Modern Library. For decades the small volume would pay him between $200 and $500 a year. A similar volume on Lenin, also promised to Modern

Library, never materialized, but Cerf generously allowed Max to keep his advance for that collection, too.[73]

In the first part of the Marx volume Max offered snippets from Marx's writings envisioning a future society, while the second part was dedicated to Marx's analysis of the past and the present situation and consisted mostly of sections from *Das Kapital*. A final section was called "The Method and the Call to Action" and included, among other texts, *The Communist Manifesto*. In his introduction Max rehearsed again some of his now-familiar arguments about Marxism, which was, he claimed, so alien to the Anglo-Saxon mind because of his indebtedness to German metaphysics. While Marx had done a service to science by insisting that the world was matter and not spirit, he had never let go of the arrogant philosopher's assumption that the world was sympathetic to his ideas: "He retained . . . the philosophic method and habit of thought," lamented Max. Enter Max's own and, of course, "non-philosophic" conception of Marxism, as a "system of social and political engineering." All one had to do was separate the engineer from the philosopher and la voilà! . . . a Marx for our time. The selections from *Das Kapital* showed Marx the engineer completing "the scientific task set by his apparently utopian aims—the task of finding out how the existing system of wealth production might be changed in such a way as to make these utopian aims possible of attainment." Note how Max avoids saying "necessary." No more reading one's own interests into the facts of history, a fallacy evident even in the first sentence of the *Manifesto*.[74]

To illustrate what he felt was the true Marxian method, stripped of the language of historic necessity, Max included a text he had translated himself: Marx's "Address of the Central Authority to the Communist League" from April 1850. In that speech Marx was talking to German workers in precisely the language of the engineer, discussing in very practical terms what the workers must do to prevent the republican petty bourgeoisie, whose ideal was a German federative republic, from permanently thwarting the fufillment of their class interests. "The workers," said Marx, "naturally cannot as yet, at the commencement of their movement, propose any directly communist measures." However, they could, for example, mount concerted attacks on private property by pushing for the concentration of factories as well as railroads and other means of transportation in the hands of the state.[75]

Max's edition brought Sidney Hook out of the woodwork again. His animosity toward Max undiminished, he now accused him of elitism, arguing that his science of revolution required a separation of the engineers from the common people. Max was advocating not the "dictatorship of the proletariat" but a "dictatorship over the proletariat."[76] After one more round of Eastman snapping at Hook and Hook hissing back at Eastman, V. F. Calverton, the editor of *Modern Quarterly*, officially ended the debate. Max did make an attempt to challenge Hook to a public debate, with Dewey on the panel as well, but the clever Dewey responded, with disarming frankness, that he did not know Marx well enough to feel up to the task. Word on the street was that Hook had killed the older, lazier Eastman. Max's self-characterization as a sensualist had worked almost too well: "Distracted from the strict practice of philosophy by poetry, travel, Freudianism, friendship, and other pleasures of the sense," Max didn't stand a chance against Hook, opined the literary critic Alfred Kazin.[77]

But Max was not done yet. A pamphlet, *The Last Stand of Dialectic Materialism: A Study of Sidney Hook's Marxism*, published through the imprint Polemic Publishers in 1934, reads in part like the *Last Stand of Max Eastman*.[78] Few people paid attention to it, but those who did would have encountered Max in full possession of his philosophical powers. Apart from a few personal gibes—Hook believed, said Max, that "Marx knew all that man can know" and was suffering from a "Talmudistic infatuation with the mind of Karl Marx"— Max proceeded carefully. He began by reasserting his belief that Marx himself had wanted to leave philosophy behind. Hadn't he said, in his *Theses on Feuerbach*, that, while philosophers had interpreted the world in various ways, "the thing is to change it"? Hook's defense of dialectical materialism works only by reducing the method's applicability to social history and by waiving the requirement that it follow the triad of thesis, antithesis, and synthesis. "Seeing that [dialectical materialism] in its crude nineteenth-century form will no longer stand up—you can no longer pretend that the world itself is with dialectic necessity achieving the aims of the revolution—he transforms it into a twentieth-century philosophy." But Dewey's instrumentalism had no fixed goals, no predetermined outcomes. In his philosophy, the truth and its working out in practice were one and the same thing: the process determined the result. In one aspect, though, Dewey's theory *was* painfully like Marx's. It, too, depended on some kind of "friendly cooperation between the objective world and the mind of man," which, in Max's understanding was animism, a "thin remnant," maybe, "wishing to vanish altogether," but nevertheless a reason for being cautious with Dewey, too. Ironically, what Dewey had preached, absolute skepticism regarding every idea "that lays claim to general truth," could be used to question his own philosophy, too.[79]

• • •

Max's aggressive disgust with Marxian dialectics spilled over also into his relationship with Trotsky. In June 1932 Max and Eliena took a boat to France, where they bought a car and made their way through the Mediterranean, spending a few days on Mallorca, where Max reconnected with his former lover and sometime nemesis Genevieve Taggard. In Milan they boarded the train for Istanbul. Within days they were on the deserted Prinkipo Island in the sea of Marmara, where they joined Trotsky and Natalia Ivanovna, who had found a temporary refuge from Stalin's persecutors in a crumbling villa that had once belonged to some pasha.[80] Max, who was working on the third volume of Trotsky's *History,* had high hopes for the visit. They stayed for almost two weeks, but things did not go well. Max found Trotsky unpredictable, childlike, and petty, especially in financial matters. Trotsky was not able to take lightly Max's philosophical differences. While Trotsky was not, in Max's estimation, vindictive, he appeared surprisingly vulnerable to Max, a combination that seemed more dangerous than simple vanity.[81]

What put Max off even more was Trotsky's lack of appreciation for anything beautiful. The house was dramatically situated. The island, Max noted, displaying his poetic talents, lay down beside the blue sea like some "prehistoric animal drinking," and yet there was no furniture on the balconies so that anyone could enjoy the view. Perhaps Max did not know that a year earlier there had been a fire in Trotsky's house that destroyed most of his library, a logical reason for the bareness he noticed. Things and people did not matter much to Trotsky, who lived in a world that consisted mostly of himself and who was unprepared to discuss, rather than merely restate, his ideas. Max repeated the argument he had been making since 1927 that dialectics was a form of animism, a "metaphysical contraption" and nothing more, theology, in other words, but not science. Trotsky turned beet red, and his throat was throbbing. Natalya became so worried she remained by Trotsky's side, "silent and austere," until Max gave up: "Well, let's lay aside this subject." But to Max this subject was of crucial and personal relevance, and Trotsky's intransigence bothered him deeply.

Trotsky's notebooks from those years prove that he understood Max's position only too well. Max had rejected Marx's statement that Hegel had turned philosophy "on its head," and in order to refute him Trotsky listed example after example of how science itself had worked dialectically, presumably in the hope that these instances would prove the scientific nature of the dialectic method itself. Galileo did not repudiate the "interdependence between the movements of the sun and the earth" but turned it on its head, just as Darwin did not reject the adaption of organs to environment earlier biologists had found but turned the concept on its head. Evolution and the translation of quantity into quality was Trotsky's master metaphor for social change, the process through which tensions, increasing slowly over decades, might erupt in a violent explosion, in the shape of class struggle and civil war.[82] Perhaps it would have been more effective for Trotsky to describe Max's repudiation of dialectics as yet another attempt to turn a concept on its head, but the truth is that Max agitated and angered him beyond measure, paralyzing his ability to argue: "He was almost hysterical—was actually gasping for breath—when he found himself unable to overpower me with the usual clichés within which the idea of dialectic evolution is defended," wrote Max eight days after he had left Prinkipo.[83]

But the real falling out between Max and Trotsky happened over something comparatively trivial. Trotsky's household, consisting not only of himself but also of a vast entourage of fans, aides, and secretaries, was expensive, costing him about $15,000 a year. Although his income from royalties was considerable—thanks to Max's services, for example, he had received over $20,000 for the serialization of his *History* in the *Saturday Evening Post*—Trotsky constantly worried about money.[84] Max had been acting as an unofficial liaison between Trotsky and the literary agent George Bye, who saw to it that Trotsky's articles were well placed and well compensated. Bye agreed to charge 10 percent for his services, while Max usually received 15 percent for his translations, an arrangement Max regarded as fair since he had done, as he put it, a "mountain of unpaid work" for Trotsky, too. But the system was not perfect. Once, when Max was traveling, his translation was delayed by a few weeks, so that the article Trotsky had written was no longer timely. In addition, Trotsky had given an interview about the subject of the piece, thus further reducing its value to the press. In the end the *New York Times* paid only $100 for it. Trotsky was furious and decided he would henceforward approach Bye directly, eliminating the apparently unreliable Max as middleman as well as translator but without telling him.

Max found out about the situation when he saw a letter from Bye on Trotsky's desk. He confronted Trotsky, who reacted angrily. Max claimed to be secretly relieved. The Trotsky articles had proved to be a constant interruption of his busy writing schedule. That he went on to describe the incident in such detail, however—in *Great Companions* as well as in the second volume of his autobiography—suggests he was more than a little hurt by Trotsky's cavalier dismissal of his services. Nonetheless, he continued to help, for example, by putting Trotsky in touch, a year later, with the well-connected agent Maxim Lieber.[85]

Another incident further complicated the situation. Sometime after their conversation about Bye, Trotsky pulled out a letter from a woman in Ohio who had inquired if he knew anything about her relatives in Russia. Trotsky asked Max if he knew who the woman was. Max said he did not, whereupon Trotsky announced, "I guess there is no use answering." Max agreed and crumpled up the letter and was about to throw it out when Trotsky stopped him. "Is *that* the way you treat your correspondence?" he asked. "What kind of a man are you?" The next day, when Max brought up the subject of Bye again and warned him that if he went with commercial translators the publication of his articles in the American press would likely take more time, Trotsky snapped at him: "I prefer not to send my articles to a man who grabs up his correspondence and throws it in the wastebasket!" A few years earlier, in 1925, Max had said Trotsky was a great man if not a great politician. When he left Prinkipo at the end of July 1932 he was no longer sure that even the "great man" designation still applied. He had come to dislike and distrust Trotsky, he told the French Trotskyist Alfred Romer.[86] It was a good thing he and Eliena were now headed for Palestine, where the "plump and healthy happiness" of the Jews at home in their own promised land, spending their days as if "just to be alive was a picnic," gave Max a feeling that not all dreams were destined to die.[87]

In retrospect it seems that two extremely vulnerable men had come together at a particularly bad time in each other's lives. Upset about not being given his due by the one man who still allowed him to retain his faith in a better world, Max was unable to understand Trotsky. And Trotsky, deprived of direct political power and fearful of being obliterated by his enemies and the forces of history, could not understand him. Instead, as Max saw it, he redirected his anger toward those who were in the best position to help him. Since Trotsky had not let him "finish a single phrase" when they discussed dialectical materialism in Prinkipo, Max took to letter writing to convince him he was mistaken—until Trotsky snapped and declared that philosophical arguments could not be carried on by mail. "I will not stand for such a thing: I have too great a volume of actual political correspondence."

As far as Trotsky was concerned, the gloves were off now, and he went on to berate Max for translation mistakes—"gaps" and "obvious misunderstandings"—he had found while casually paging through the

published volumes of his *History of the Russian Revolution*. One hilarious example occurs in volume 3, chapter 43, where Trotsky is describing the efforts
of the Menshevik Nikolai Sukhanov to persuade the workers at the Putilov
machine-building plant in St. Petersburg not to engage in revolutionary activities. The workers kept interrupting him, and as rain was drizzling down on
all of them Sukhanov finally gave up. Commented Trotsky, in Max's translation: "Under that impatient October sky the poor Left Democrats, even as described in their own writings, look like wet hens." Trotsky pointed out that
Max had inadvertently confused "neprivetlivyi" (неприветливый, or "bleak,"
"inhospitable") with "neterpelivyi" (нетерпеливый, or "impatient"). Acidly,
Trotsky added, "In what sense is it possible for the October sky to be 'impatient'?" That stung. And while Max rejected other Trotsky criticisms, scribbling "not a mistake" in the margins of Trotsky's letter, this one he fixed, at
least sort of. In 1957, when the University of Michigan Press reprinted all
three parts of Trotsky's *History* bound into one massive volume, Max exchanged "impatient" for "ungracious," retaining the personification Trotsky
had disliked while acknowledging what Trotsky had originally meant to indicate, namely, that something as trivial as bad weather had discouraged those
hapless Mensheviks.[88]

But Max wasn't ready to give up on Trotsky yet. In what was probably the
most passionate book he wrote during this decade, *Artists in Uniform: A Study
of Literature and Bureaucratism,* he characterized Trotsky as Russia's "greatest
living historian, essayist, and critic" and praised him for believing that "art
must make its own way and by its own means."[89] The title of the book, released by Scribner's in May 1934, a year after Hitler had assumed power in
Germany, was nothing if not inspired: it conjured a vision of columns of
mindless, marching soldiers, with any trace of individuality driven out of them
by the whip of totalitarianism.

Max's bête noir in the book was the Russian Association of Proletarian Writers, the organizing force behind the international congress of revolutionary
artists that had taken place in Kharkov, Ukraine, in November 1930. The program of art for communism's sake that was formulated in Kharkov had—that
much was certain!—a disastrous impact on artistic life in the Soviet Union,
and it seemed poised to have a similarly noxious effect on American literary
culture. A case in point was the fawning response of the editors of the *New
Masses* to the directives from Kharkov. Meekly, they had rushed to embrace a
verdict on their efforts that essentially told them they were incompetent. Wrote

Max, "I know of nothing in the sad history of the dwindling dignity of the literary mind to equal this sad picture of political (and financial) abjection parading as leadership in the creation of a new culture." While the roots of this wholesale oppression of the creative spirit lay in Marxian thought itself, there were some shining exceptions to the rule—Lenin and, of course, Trotsky. In an appendix Max included a lengthy exploration of Lenin's views on art and culture written by Vyacheslav Polonsky, the disgraced editor of the journal *Press and Revolution,* translated by Max himself. According to Polonsky, Lenin's pronouncements on communist art, or art for the Communist Party, applied only to art that aspired to carry on the work of the Communist Party. Everyone else was free to write and say everything they wanted, "without the slightest limitation." Case closed.[90]

Max's *Artists in Uniform* is so rich in extraneous detail, so saturated with Max's knowledge of Russian literary and political affairs, that it seems he had lost sight of its American target audience. In fact, the book's real strength lay not in Max's political commentary, as acute as it often was, but in his deeply moving portraits of writers who suffered under the Soviet regime. Perhaps the most heartbreaking of these is Max's chapter on Sergei Yesenin, who, from 1922 to 1923, was the husband of Isadora Duncan. To Duncan, everything was a dramatic gesture, wrote Max, and she was as helpful as a whirlwind after a hurricane to her wild poet-husband. In a society that expected him to follow the "bureaucratic boss rule," Yesenin, chanter of the sensual love and the beauties of the Russian landscape, was lost. Max imagined how Yesenin had sat down with a pile of monstrous textbooks, struggling in vain to grasp the principles of Hegelian–Marxist dialectics, and how he had sought oblivion in the beautifully shaped arms of the dramatic Duncan: "To Yesenin, the bewildered singer, wavering between those ponderous text-books from which he learned nothing but that he was useless in the new world being born, and the drunken Moscow tavern where all sorts of friendly and loose-thinking creatures, more like the old farm animals, loved him when he fed them with his songs—to him this glorious whirlwind seemed like a godsend." After one of Isadora's sublimely vapid gestures, Yesenin's Marxist tormentors suddenly looked small again. This was Max writing at the height of his powers. A single adjective like "loose-thinking" and the specter of Yesenin's inebriated fans mindlessly feeding on his songs in a dark taproom accomplish more than pages of dense analysis. Ultimately Duncan was not enough for Yesenin, just as she would soon prove to be not enough for herself anymore. Max's chapter ends with Yesenin's botched suicide in a Leningrad hotel, where he was found hanging from a steam pipe, his wrists slashed, for good measure. "He had had some trouble making himself die."[91]

Max's portrait of the flamboyant Vladimir Mayakovsky, "a great standing coarse-stemmed swamp-watered weed," was similarly effective. Loud, brash, "avid of the strong blows of life," Mayakovsky was singularly unsuited to doing what the party wanted him to do, which was to "get on the job and sing the right tune." Rather than sacrifice his independence, which he valiantly tried to do for a while, Mayakovsky ended up sacrificing himself, a "love boat / smashed against mores," as he characterized himself in the poem he left on the table before he died.[92] Max evoked other lives and careers touched by the foul breath of Soviet bureaucracy: Yevgeny Zamyatin pushed into exile; Isaac Babel threatened into silence; Valentin Katayev scared into becoming a supporter of the five-year plan. But the most humiliating, least heroic story was that of the novelist Boris Pilnyak, who had once said a writer ought to occupy himself only with his manuscripts and was now singing the praises of the Soviet system whenever possible, most recently on a tour through the United States, chaperoned by that "pure but diplomatic priest of Stalinism in the field of culture, Joseph Freeman."[93] Pilnyak answered Max's charges lamely and ineffectively in the pages of the newly founded *Partisan Review*. "Revolutions are not made with white gloves," he said. And he added, cryptically, "A man . . . standing on his head will see everything upside-down."[94] Pilnyak was shot, unceremoniously, four years later, after a trial that lasted fifteen minutes. His last words to the court: "I have so much work to do."[95]

Artists in Uniform, though not the book of a Trotskyist, is still very much an endorsement of Trotsky's ideas, and Max anticipated that orthodox Stalinists would find it to be counterrevolutionary. He was not disappointed. An old friend from Max's Moscow days, Karl Radek, who was himself fighting for his personal and political survival, denounced Max in *Izvestia* as a lackey of the bourgeoisie, precisely the same charge to which he would himself confess just a few years later before he was killed. Radek resorted to invective and irony, stating that the flippancy which Max had displayed toward "the greatest thinkers of mankind" (Marx and Stalin, one may assume) was "typical of a little dog to whom a piece of Michelangelo's sculpture is nothing but a stone to be used for certain needs." Max had pissed on Marxian theory, in other words. Somewhat contradictorily, though, Radek also wrote that the Soviets shouldn't underestimate people like Max, as garbage-filled as their heads might be.[96]

Those who actually read Max's book were confused by what, or rather whom, it had been intended for. What did the sad fate of Yesenin and the quirky habits of Mayakovsky matter to American readers? In the *Herald Tribune* the poet Babette Deutsch felt Max had missed a chance to articulate his message as clearly and relevantly as possible: "The fear is that he speaks either to those who will not listen or to the few who are in agreement with him, while some may overhear who are bound to misinterpret his message and turn it to purposes of their own. If the pen is indeed mightier than the sword, it should be handled in unambiguous fashion."[97]

Word to the wise. The problem was, of course, that Max himself was struggling to understand where he was headed. That was, certainly, the most charitable explanation Joe Freeman was able to come up with when he heard that Max had attacked him personally in his new book. Freeman was in bed when he got the news, his voice gone after he had spent the night arguing with Alexander Trachtenberg, the Communist Party's cultural commissar, about the need to leave the writers alone. Trachtenberg wouldn't have any of it and proceeded to call Freeman—the way Joe remembered it later—a "rotten liberal." And now Max was maligning him as Stalin's tool![98] If only Max had bothered to ask around, people would have told him that Joe Freeman was not a Communist hack. When working for TASS he had written an ironic jingle popular with his colleagues: "Never, never shall I moan a / Simple lyric from the heart. / I'll devote my new Corona / To the proletarian art."[99] It was hard for Freeman not to think the entire book was really about him. Thirty years later the wound was still fresh when Max became one of the main topics of a series of monstrously long and slightly paranoid letters Freeman wrote to Smith College professor Dan Aaron, who was collecting material for his magisterial account of American writers and communism, *Writers on the Left*. Freeman was still racking his brain as to what might have caused Max's evident hatred of him. Was it that oldest of reasons, a rivalry for women? Freeman's first wife was Ione Robinson, whom he left in 1932 to marry Charmion von Wiegand; both women had been Max's lovers.[100] Whatever the reason, the dazzling Max, who had once hovered over Freeman's own political coming-of-age, had become his enemy. Freeman was still telling himself and Dan Aaron, his new father confessor, he had never had anything but noble feelings for Max: "I am trying to save him from destroying the image of what he was when he was young, daring, magnanimous and wonderful."[101] Freeman's panicky soul searching shows how important Max had remained to a generation of leftist critics, even after he had unceremoniously left their fold.

Over the years, despite its historical density and Max's tendency to overgeneralize, *Artists in Uniform* has retained a measure of popularity. Fans of the book have included some unlikely folk, among them a son of Slovakian immigrants to the United States, Andrew Warhola, better known as Andy Warhol. Andy wore a uniform of sorts, courtesy of Brooks Brothers. But whoever saw him up close—tie permanently askew, the collar points of his shirt rolled up, his navy blazer glistening with use, his shoes scuffed and untied, the bizarre, ill-fitting toupee perched uneasily on his head—realized that he was in fact subverting the dress code: an artist on the cusp of shedding his uniform but holding on to it for now so that others might recognize the uniforms *they* are wearing (fig. 37).

Max's uncanny productivity during this decade was the direct result of the stability his relationship with Eliena gave him. The love she offered him was unequivocal, unquestioning, unaffected by his many absences when he was on the lecture circuit and likely also pursuing other women. Sometime during 1930, when Max was away on one of his trips, she penned a little note in which

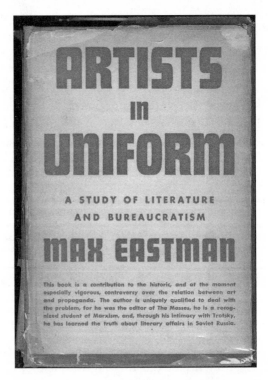

Figure 37. Andy Warhol's copy of *Artists
in Uniform*. Author's collection.

she described how she felt when she got one of Max's telegrams. She was trying to think of all the "beautiful words" that came to mind when she thought
of him, "all the words that mean joy, and life, and laughter," and she wanted
to write a poem for him, "a poem about a brook in the snow, cold and transparent and running swift and sure, dark and clear, with the snow white and silent
around it. Or about a pond in a moon light, when the woods are dark and quiet
and the ice is glistening and smooth." A telegram he sent her had made her
"incredibly happy," and it had also destroyed any aspirations to happiness the
telephone girl in Ossining might have harbored, Eliena mischievously suggested: "Oh, my beloved there are not many people in the world as happy as I
am. I know this girl in Ossining wished she would get your telegram and not
I. I know that her life is ruined because she will never find you, and there is
not one like you in the world . . . Ia tak strashno liubliu tebia [I love you so very
much]."[102] Then modest Eliena got a little naughty. In the mornings she
wanted to climb on top of Max and kiss his face, eyes, neck, and laugh and
smother (*zadushit*) him till he would throw her off. However, most of the time
she had nothing but a pillow to play with, "nobody to say moia maliutochka,
moia zolotaia" (my sweetheart, my treasure).[103]

Max responded in kind, sending fulsome declarations of love to the "loveli-
est laughing darling strong graceful clever devoted delightful friend anybody
ever had."[104] With Eliena at his side and audiences eager for his wisdom, Max
felt he was done with psychoanalysis: "I don't want to waste this summer waiting for Dr. Brill to restore my soul. I am going to try very hard with your help
to establish a little cult of myself."[105] When he was on the road Eliena willingly
listened to his tales of seedy hotel rooms, terrible food, train cars so shaky he
had trouble writing, and dreams so transparent no analyst was needed to in-
terpret them for her. In one of them Max saw himself lying on his back, snorting at T. S. Eliot.[106]

Max's salary for these appearances was not at all bad, given the circumstances. For a lecture on a "literary subject" ("The Art of Enjoying Poetry"),
given at the Norfolk Forum in Virginia, the oldest publicly subscribed speakers' series in the United States, he was to receive $200, about $3,600 in today's money.[107] More than once on these occasions Max felt out of place, but
his sense of humor and his desperate need for cash helped him through such
moments of potential crisis: "I wish you could have heard me explaining
Marxism and Lenin's party dictatorship to the regular weekly 'Convocation' of
the University of Minnesota. Nobody seems to understand how I got in there,
and I'm sure I don't."[108] But Max knew what he was doing on the podium, and

he especially enjoyed those events at which there was standing room only, which reminded him of his glory days as an itinerant agitator. He had been a grand success, he proudly informed Eliena about his lecture titled "The Future of Liberalism" in Houston. Seventeen or eighteen hundred people had come, and up to three hundred were standing in the back. "It is great fun to speak to a crowded hall, and the speech is really one of the best I've made." In Dallas, his next stop, they had to turn people away. What he called his "scared lamb" condition had now evaporated completely: "Well the great black SPEECH that hung over me like a cloud for weeks is over. I woke up this morning a poet and a person with leisure to look around—or rather I didn't wake up, for I hardly went to sleep at all, I was so excited." Lest he got overconfident, however, an old friend came for a visit during the night after the lecture:

> When I did go to sleep Sigmund Freud started chasing aeroplanes around the sky in a blimp. You and I were on a steamer in mid-ocean, and got off in a small boat to see better what Freud was going to do, for he was frightfully angry at these aeroplanes. He finally turned around and drove right across the deck of our steamer, taking off the smoke-stack and the mast, and as we soon realized breaking the whole ship squarely in two and turning it over. I woke up wondering whether we could pick up a passenger or two in our small boat before they all swamped us, wondering if we would have the nerve to row away and let them drown.[109]

Freud as a lethal force, and Max as the well-intentioned savior of humankind? The imagery is classically Freudian: consider the planes, the phallic smoke-stack, and the mast, broken by Freud flying kamikaze attacks in his equally phallic blimp. The ship, in Freudian dream analysis, as "a hollow space" capable of being filled, is associated with female genitals, whereas planes symbolize phallic penetration.[110] In Max's dream Freud's monstrous flying machine wreaks destruction on everything and threatens Max and Eliena in their makeshift boat, too small to save anybody but themselves from drowning. What a marvelous dream, opined Eliena, his main cheerleader and confidence restorer.[111]

But Max wasn't sure what he was doing. In his speeches he would still denounce America and religion "forty ways" and defend Russia and Lenin as "the only way out," and his audiences, consisting of the intellectual elite in whatever town he happened to be in, would applaud him "to the roof."[112] But what right did he really have to speak for communism in the first place?

"I represent the official or Stalin communists just about the way a bear represents a bee's nest," he joked in a speech in which he also said very clearly that the scientific communism he wanted was not found in the documents of any party or existing organization.[113] But he was still willing to take risks. For as long as he invoked the term "communism" in association with his views during his lectures, for as long as he blamed the government for the fact that twelve million people were out of work and even more were living like beggars on handouts, and for as long as he publicly advocated the transformation of capitalist society into another system not dependent on the fluctuations of the market, the authorities were taking notice. If the Depression and New Deal had made audiences more sympathetic to left-wing causes, communists and their alleged sympathizers nevertheless found themselves the targets of persecution all over the nation. The Fish committee, created in 1930 by the fervent anticommunist senator Hamilton Fish Jr., had begun its insidious work of investigating all groups and individuals suspected of advising or advocating the overthrow of the United States government by means of riots, strikes, or sabotage.[114] When Max was in Memphis in 1934 a man had just been jailed, he was told, merely for inquiring after the location of the communist headquarters in town. And now, since Max had said in interviews that he was a communist, the "poor little man" who had arranged his lecture at the Institute of Culture was shaking in his boots.[115]

As a lecturer Max was the consummate professional. He left nothing to chance: from the first draft to the written-out text he had memorized, from the smallest joke to the funny anecdote that had an audience of several hundred in stitches, all had been carefully prepared. Max's striking outward appearance helped: the white hair, the ruddy, young-looking face, his trim, fit physique. There was a barely veiled sexual undercurrent to his lecturing. That wasn't lost even on a sophomore at Wells College, Ruth LeSourd '39, where Max lectured in 1937. She gushed about her experience in the *Chronicle,* the college magazine. What stood out about Max first and foremost was the voice, which to her sounded like that of a minister reading the rolling cadences of a psalm. Just when she thought Max was merely putting on a show, albeit a very good one ("He has probably done it hundreds of times before, and can turn it on and off at will"), Max turned and seemed to smile right in her direction: "My doubts fled." He *meant* what he said, and, more important, he meant *her.* Under Max's steady hazel eyes, Ruth LeSourd's resistance melted. She became so enthralled with Max that "I often found myself losing track of what he was saying." Even Max's gestures were intoxicating, no mere add-ons but part of the complete Eastman Experience itself. For example, when Max explained that the function of poetry was to "cherish and communicate experience," he cupped his hands as if he were guarding a tiny glowing flame: "One could see that he did cherish experience, as a collector prizes a noble fire." Max had just been lecturing about how one should, yes, *cherish* the aesthetic possibilities of life; now he was modeling such an experience for them.[116]

But of course these events *were* performances, and the incessant speech making, with all the other efforts it required, wore Max out. His real mission in life was, he told Eliena, the writing of "great truth and poetry." Talking about communism and Russia and the future of the working class, and doing so not as an agitator but as a paid speaker before audiences that were distinctly not working class, felt "a little bit dirty and unpleasant."[117]

A distinct advantage of Max's new fame as a noncommunist communist was that he could help other people, preferably equally maladjusted ones. There was the novelist and anthropologist Zora Neale Hurston, for example, an unconventional thinker in her own right, who met Max in 1932 and thought he was simply brilliant.[118] Max repaid her admiration by writing a supportive letter for Hurston's 1934 application for a Guggenheim grant. Hurston's intention was to study indigenous religious practices in Nigeria and on the Gold Coast. But Max's recommendation was the only positive one coming from the all-white group of referees Hurston had listed, which also included Franz Boas, Ruth Benedict, and Carl Van Vechten. While Benedict bluntly said Hurston had "neither temperament nor the training" to succeed and Boas criticized his former student for having journalistic rather than scientific inclinations, Max unequivocally praised Hurston's "general intelligence, her social maturity and exquisite tact and good judgment." He, for one, found the scope of her project "captivating." Hurston did not get the grant.[119]

This was not the only occasion in Max's life when he stood by someone others had abandoned. On February 1, 1934, Claude McKay, after more than a decade in self-imposed exile, returned to New York on the SS *Magallanes* from Cádiz. Max had never lost touch with his friend. Over the years he had patiently listened to tales of Claude's medical woes and literary struggles. He had responded to desperate requests for money, dispatched, with alarming regularity, from France, Berlin, and, eventually, Morocco, where McKay had rented a house.[120] He sent money as well as the three "gorgeously bound" volumes of his translation of Trotsky's *History of the Russian Revolution*.[121] Gratefully, Claude kept a photograph of Max and Eliena close by, a reminder of Max's beautiful life—but apparently a nude one, surprising the Arabs, who didn't think the portrait was civilized.[122]

By 1933 McKay's financial situation had become dire. He had no warm clothes, was ill, and felt utterly lost, as he told Max. "No one has sent me a penny but *you*."[123] Max made some inquiries and had a hand in arranging a meeting with an American consul in Morocco, who laughingly observed that Max was not the best reference to have for a prospective immigrant but nevertheless arranged for a visa. Max wired funds for Claude's transatlantic passage.[124]

Destitute and without prospects, Claude was not looking forward to his renewed encounter with American racism. But Max stood ready to help. He continued to support his friend over the following months as Claude tried to scrape enough money together to survive in Harlem, a difficult undertaking for someone whose previous books hadn't sold. As Claude hatched and discarded a variety of plans, including launching a new magazine, Max continued to give him advice as well as money for new clothes.[125] Characteristically, Max's unwavering devotion to his friend in need did not keep him from beginning an affair with McKay's girlfriend, the gorgeous sculptor Selma Burke. When he retrieved one of his nude photographs of himself from Claude's apartment on West 63rd Street, tensions came to a boil: "It seems to me that if you had a sudden feeling of prudery and caution over a naked picture that you brought across the seas to present to me as a gift, all you needed to do was to ask me to remove it from the wall or return it to you." Claude was livid: "Think you that *I* would care to keep your picture or use it in any way that was objectionable to you? . . . Would you have liked anyone to go to your home in Croton and do this?"[126] But as they had done before, the friends reconciled quickly. By now a passionate anticommunist, Claude readily joined Max in denouncing Stalinism, surprising even the FBI with the vehemence of his opposition.[127]

Regardless of what Max was accomplishing in other areas of his life, much of the first half of the decade was overshadowed by his difficult collaboration with the director Herman Axelbank on the documentary that became *Tsar to Lenin*. The Russian-born Axelbank had come to him in 1929 with extraordinary film material that showed key moments in the Russian revolution. Max was captivated, signed a contract, and soon was doing more work for Axelbank than he had expected. He bought a Moviola, a film-editing device, and began splicing the film together in Croton. He supplied the narration as well as many of the additional images and film clips Axelbank incorporated into his documentary, with an estimated value of over $5,000. He also supported Axelbank during the protracted production process, ultimately paying him a total of $12,000, which he claimed he had to borrow from other sources.[128] And yet the movie seemed to be getting no closer to completion.

Axelbank was a colorful character, a man whose egotism matched Max's, and their collaboration soon became tense. After first considering him an idealistic moron, Max decided he was a crook: "I felt I was working with a mental cripple, but one who had at least seen a vision. I now think that Axelbank is a schemer, whose racket consists of playing the role of a crack-brained and irresponsible idealist."[129] The result of their struggles, one of the greatest political documentaries of the twentieth century, was released only after lengthy legal proceedings and then generated only more controversy. When *Tsar to Lenin* premiered at the New York Filmarte Theater on March 6, 1937, pro-Stalinists picketed the place.

Axelbank's and Eastman's film offers a stunning visual history of the Russian revolution, from the mounting anger over the pampered lives of the tsar's family and Russia's entry into the First World War to the tsar's abdication under pressure from the rebelling masses and the emergence of Lenin and Trotsky. *Tsar to Lenin* deftly fuses astonishing, unfamiliar visual material, much of which Max claimed he had assembled, into an unforgettable visual narrative about an event that changed the course of world history. One sequence shows a very small-looking tsarevich being served with lumps of sugar on a plate, which he then feeds to his horse, an unforgettable image of conspicuous consumption. Snippets of film taken with the tsar's own camera show the Russian ruler unsuccessfully encouraging members of his entourage to engage in a game of tag with him or swimming naked in a river and lifting himself up into a boat, providing viewers with a full and uncensored view of the royal butt. These clips are juxtaposed with images of the grinding poverty in which most of the Russian population lived while their clueless rulers were amusing themselves. But the most remarkable thing about *Tsar to Lenin* is Max's narration, delivered consistently at fever pitch, with a concentration that makes it clear that watching this film is no entertainment. Some of Max's comments have an epigrammatic, even poetic quality. For example, as viewers are being treated to a glimpse of the tall, handsome Grand Duke Nikolai Nikolayevich Romanov, Max remarks, "He would have been the tsar if this were a fairy story." After a cut to Nicholas II standing idly in a field, he adds, "Real tsars are not so imposing." The lethal consequences of the tsar's military incompetence are brought home dramatically when Max describes how the bodies of soldiers "were lying, like piles of rubbish outside the hospitals too crowded to contain them, wounded and dying with no clothes on their backs." As Max pronounces the words, spitting out the hard consonants—"*p*iles of ru*bb*ish," hos*p*ital," "*c*rowded," "*c*ontain," "*c*lothes," "ba*ck*s"—they seem to slam into each other, the violence of the images echoed by the aggressiveness of Max's enunciation. Max is capable of sweetness, too, though often with deeply ironical results. When he describes Alexander Kerensky's initial success, for example, Max's narration wraps itself around the images shown, subtly directing the audience to their proper understanding until we know that, indeed, nothing is well. Here is Max's softly alliterative comment when we see Kerensky being feted by the crowds: "Ladies of leisure pelted him with flowers." Contrast with that Max's admiration for Lenin's "sheer force of will, personality, and cold reason." Here is Max's original "social engineer" himself, fearlessly addressing the crowds, despite the fact that he is, as Max stresses, no longer well himself: a man who believed, as Max believed, too, that "facts are stubborn things." In a similar vein, Trotsky's military skill, freeing Soviet Russia from the stranglehold of multiple foreign nations as well as from counterrevolutionary interventions staged by Admiral Kolchak and General Yudenich, is dramatically illustrated in several sets of images that show soldiers advancing and then fleeing and then reuniting, not as enemies but as Russians or, more simply, as human beings.

In a memorable clip, Kolchak is shown not quite knowing what to do with a pair of geese handed to him as a gift by a local farmer, an amusing scene that seems less benign when juxtaposed with the executions of Red Army soldiers by Kolchak's men. Max shows one of the condemned laughing at his executioners, a laughter he keeps up through five rounds of executions until his turn arrives. "The Red soldier is still laughing," warns Max. The fearless man's laughter anticipates the happy ending of all these struggles, shouted into the microphone by Max: "All of Russia is now a Soviet Republic!" And a happy ending it would have been were it not for a brief appearance, just a few minutes before the film ends, of Comrade Stalin's dark profile. "Who could have known?" asks Max.

His political work did not prevent Max from pursuing his long-standing interest in the philosophy and psychology of laughter. His earlier book on the subject, *The Sense of Humor*, despite moments of levity, had been ponderous, cerebral, philosophical—in short, as Max now thought, not suited for making the subject accessible to a wider audience. His new book, *Enjoyment of Laughter*, published in October 1936, was a restatement of his theory but with much funnier examples. Freud shows up, too, as a "famous psychologist in Europe," and Max quotes his casual remark about the "Missgeburt" America, along with the common prejudice that America lacks depth. But Max's entire book is actually a polemic against the notion that such depth would or should be the hallmark of culture. Laughter, to Max, is "playful fun," even when it involves hostility (of the kind Max had felt during his visit to Freud in 1927). Three chapters explicitly deal with Freud, and in them Max represents himself as being on a mission to rescue sex jokes from a too-serious "theory that puts them in a false light." Jokes about sex are, says Max, about . . . sex: "They are easy to make and no special theory is needed to explain them." Freud himself was, Max recalled, "a jolly laugher" and capable of finding things funny the way children would, who, as a rule, do not require that "comic things should mask a serious thought, or tap a deeper reservoir of feeling." Max's alleged familiarity with the behaviors and needs of children is startling, given his own spotty parental record; yet the concept of the child at play is one of the foundations of his theory, which faults all previous efforts to understand humor with having taken it "too seriously."[130] The dust jacket of the volume featured Max, his white shirt unbuttoned, laughing uproariously, flashing two rows of perfect teeth at the reader.

Enjoyment of Laughter was a popular success. Not all readers were impressed, though. The philosopher George Santayana, for example, in thanking Max for his copy of the book, could not help mentioning he found the jokes ghastly: "I am not able to share the happy experience that inspires you to write it."[131] And Freud was not a fan either, although for a different reason. "Dear Mr. Eastman," wrote Freud and then immediately switched to German, as he went on to tell Max about something he had accidentally found on page 263 of his new book. Had he been less in awe of Freud, Max could have pointed out that in psychoanalytic theory there is no room for accidents; maybe Freud had looked himself up in the book's index? No matter, what Freud had found on page 263 was a joke attributed to him that he, in turn, had allegedly gotten from Heinrich Heine: "An unhappy man was advised by a friend to take a wife, and his reply was, whose?" But there was a problem with that quotation, and Freud addressed it head-on: "Now I don't know if the joke is Heine's—it's rather unlikely—but I am sure I have never and nowhere quoted it."[132] Freud was right: the joke was not Heine's but a version of a crack made by the father of the British playwright Richard Sheridan.[133]

Max hurried to have Simon and Schuster remove the error and sent Freud a copy of the revised edition. "Dear Dr. Freud," he wrote on December 27, 1936. "I have believed for so long that I got that story on page 263 out of your book that I can't say now where or how or why I made the mistake. Could it possibly be an English joke which Dr. Brill inserted in his translation of your book? At any rate, I have corrected the page." Max's hope was that such efficient damage control would positively affect Freud's image of America: "This will give you an example at least of the high speed of American culture, and I hope it will remove the obstacle to your saying something a little more profoundly critical of my book." Freud did not deliver. At the bottom of the carbon copy of that letter a disappointed Max left a note in pencil, "No answer!" With his note and subsequent silence Freud had thwarted Max's precarious attempt, begun more than a decade before, to best him.[134]

In retrospect, it seems Max never left out a chance to take issue with Freud's theory of sexual repression. He was protesting altogether too much against a view that, from the biographer's point of view at least, would indeed help make sense of Max's life. When Hemingway shared with him his guilt over ogling the girls in the dance halls of Paris, admitting that he always came home from his nights on Montmartre "disgusted with myself," and asked Max if he felt so too, Max snapped back, "No, I don't, Ernest. I enjoy lustful feelings, and what's more I don't think you're talking real." A sense of competitive masculinity, a question as to who was the better man and lover, had lurked in the background of Max's relationship with Hemingway ever since they spent time together in Genoa. At the time, Hemingway was, in Max's view, merely an "alert and vivid-minded journalist," a well-mannered but otherwise unremarkable man with a fine set of teeth.[135] Over the years, however, Hemingway had, unexpectedly, succeeded in what Max never accomplished: freed from the shackles of having to earn money as a hired hack, he had become an artist, someone who had succeeded in weaving his life experiences into his fiction. The tension Max felt whenever he read Hemingway erupted in a review he wrote of *Death in the Afternoon,* Hemingway's account of the tradition of Spanish bullfighting, a book that challenged the genre of journalism by making the brutal ritual a cipher for Hemingway's very personal search for meaning in life and nature.

"Bull in the Afternoon," published in June 1933 in the *New Republic,* is one of Max's masterpieces. Effortlessly, he mixes genuine admiration for Hemingway (his honesty, toughness, and, yes, courage, a "courage rarer than that of toreros") with a scathing critique of his male posturing, his adolescent idealizing of violence. Max offered some of his best writing in a passage in which he imagined the suffering of the bull, "this beautiful creature . . . gorgeously

equipped with power for wild life, trapped in a ring where his power is nothing." And he poured his contempt on the bullfighters, "these spryer and more
flexible monkeys," who hunt the bull till he sinks down, "leadlike into his
tracks, lacking the mere strength of muscle to lift his vast head, panting, gasping, gurgling, his mouth too little and the tiny black tongue hanging out too
far to give him breath, and faint falsetto cries of anguish, altogether lost baby-
like now and not bull-like, coming out of him." In a passage that would come
to haunt Max later, he likened writing that derived pleasure from such sense-
less bloodshed—writing like Hemingway's, in other words—to the "wearing
of false hair on the chest."[136] To Papa Hemingway's supporters this was blas-
phemy. "I don't know when I have written anything that I have heard more
about from various sources than that article," sighed Max.[137] Not bothering to
read Max's review carefully, Hemingway's defenders engaged in the kind of
public posturing and muscle flexing that ironically confirmed Max's concerns.
In a letter to the *New Republic,* for example, Archibald MacLeish rejected what
he saw as Max's psychoanalyzing of Hemingway—the suggestion that any
ostentatious display of virility in literature must be caused by a lack thereof in
life—as "scurrilous" and attested to having seen Hemingway behave courageously "once at sea, once in the mountains, and once on a Spanish street."
Hemingway chimed in from Cuba and challenged Max to put his speculations
in writing: "Here they would be read (aloud) with much enjoyment (our
amusements are simple)."[138] In response, Max emphatically denied he had
ever implied Hemingway was impotent, "although I have long been familiar
with the news that I am—and gymnastic enough to be syphilitic at the same
time," and reminisced about the time he had first laid eyes on him: "He had
just been blown out of a bathroom by an exploding gas-heater" and "arrived
half-way down the hall with a smile on his face like a man on a toboggan."
Somewhat less helpfully, Max, in his personal note of apology to Hemingway,
reiterated his criticism: "I suppose it is fresh to psycho-analyse a man by way
of literary criticism, especially one whom you esteem as a friend, but I think
there is plenty of cruelty in the world without your helping it along."[139]
Hemingway never forgave him.

The following year Max included the review in his collection *Art and the Life
of Action.* The book received generally positive reviews. Writing in the *Herald
Tribune,* Ernest Sutherland Bates loved it. If Max really believed art had no
tangible effects, his own style of writing—translucent, vigorous, trenchant,
and, yes, effective—disproved his theory. It was hard to imagine that a reader
with any appreciation for literary craftsmanship would *not* readily submit to

the persuasive magic of Max's language.[140] His former collaborator Floyd Dell, too, despite the fact that one of the chapters attacked his own book, *Love in the Machine Age*, felt Max had come into his own as a critic. Ignoring Max's attacks on his philosophy of normative heterosexuality, Floyd was pleased to see that his friend was no longer relegating art to the "function of a cocktail." The rest was subject for a later conversation. Incidentally, Floyd liked his "essay on Hemingway and bullfighting better—much better—than I like Hemingway on bull-fighting. In fact, I think you made literature out of the disgusting and embarrassing spectacle of Hemingway with his tongue hanging out as he watches the torture of a bull." Overall, Floyd was more sympathetic to Max's view of art than Max might have expected: "I quite agree with you about art needing to stand up on its hind legs and feel a self-respecting independence from political utility."[141]

The most forceful response to the book came three years later. On August 17, 1937, Max was visiting his editor Maxwell Perkins's office, discussing a new edition of *Enjoyment of Poetry*, when Hemingway sauntered in.[142] He was not in a particularly generous mood: his marriage with Pauline Pfeiffer was on the rocks, and he was about to return to Spain, where the civil war he had been covering had reinforced his contempt for literary refinement. Opening his shirt, he encouraged Max to assess the authenticity of his chest hair, while he mocked Max's chest, which was, remarked Perkins, as "bare as a bald man's head." Then everything went haywire. Seeing the well-fed, white-clad, good-looking Max, tanned from tennis and hours spent napping on the beach, Hemingway erupted. The way Max remembered it, Hemingway was crude and aggressive. "What did you say I was sexually impotent for?" he snarled. Conveniently, a copy of *Art and the Life of Action* was sitting on Perkins's desk. Max attempted to point out a passage—a positive one, we might imagine—that he thought would clarify that he had never wanted to trash Hemingway. But Hemingway, muttering and swearing, zeroed in on a different passage, and a particularly good one it was, too: "Some circumstance seems to have laid upon Hemingway a continual sense of the obligation to put forth evidences of red-blooded masculinity." This was Max at his best, the use of the plural "evidences" giving the line a rhythmic lilt: "évi / dénces of / réd-blooded/ máscu/línity."[143]

An altercation ensued, during which Max, as both parties agreed, got "socked" on the nose with his own book. Everything was happening very fast after that. Max charged at Hemingway. Books and other stuff from Perkins's desk went flying to the ground. Convinced that the much younger Hemingway was going to kill his friend, Perkins rushed in to help. By the time he had reached the two men they were both on the floor. Max was on top, although Perkins felt this was by accident only. But Max would later tell everyone who cared to listen that he had been the winner. Recognizing the disadvantage imposed on him by age and lack of physical fitness ("I would have kissed the carpet in a fist fight with Ernest Hemingway"), he claimed he had used a wrestling move to throw Hemingway on his back over Max Perkins's desk. Hemingway assured the *Times* no such thing had taken place, that Max instead had taken his slap "like a woman." He went on to challenge Max to meet him in a locked room and read to him his review in there, with "all legal rights waived"; the Hemingway equivalent to challenging his adversary to a duel. There is one detail, however, that does make Max's account credible: he did know how to wrestle. His work with the Lower Eastside boys' club had finally paid off.[144]

The literary "battle of the ages" was widely covered in the papers.[145] The *Herald Tribune* noted that while Max was older, both he and Hemingway were in the "heavyweight category." That said, Max would have been pleased to see he was trimmer than his younger antagonist:

Hemingway
Age: 39
Height: 6 feet
Weight: 197 pounds

Eastman
Age: 54
Height: 6 feet
Weight: 180 pounds[146]

The accounts of the fight differ, but there is independent confirmation of one other detail: the book Hemingway used, now kept at the Harry Ransom Center at the University of Texas, which features, on the flyleaf, a clumsy drawing of a paw with the resonantly poetic inscription, "This is the book I ruined on Max (the Prick) Eastman's nose, I severely hope that he rots forever in a hell of his own digging. Ernest Hemingway." It seems Hem had nicked the book from Perkins's office. His besmirched masculinity (when he talked to the *Times* he sported a bruise on his forehead that he claimed had *not* been caused by Max) required that he document his accomplishment for posterity.[147]

Max's friends and supporters rallied to his defense. In a telegram to him a group of ladies, the Ladies of Kings Beach on the Vineyard, felt the need to reassure Max that "you have got hair on your chest."[148] Millay and Boissevain told him he had seemed "dignified and lovely" throughout the entire unpleasant episode.[149] Some less generous observers thought the Hemingway–Eastman scuffle was a mere publicity stunt, hyped by Max to counteract his declining relevance in a changing world. One thing is sure: Max "the Prick" had gotten his point across. In September, the *New Yorker* ran a cartoon showing a rather unhappy-looking man at a physical being diagnosed as a writer merely because of the fluff on his chest.[150]

In the decades that followed, Max almost obsessively revisited the scene, seeking reassurances from others who had seen or heard what had happened—men who were now old, like Max, too—that Hemingway had not had the upper hand in their scuffle. What was at stake was more than literary criticism or Max's right to say what he wanted about a fellow writer. As Hemingway went from one well-publicized risky adventure to the next, Max continued to insist on his own version of masculinity that involved not loud displays of virility but a deliberate celebration of the human body and its infinite capacity for pleasure.

As it turned out, Max was not the only one with a grudge against Hem. Decades after the battle in Perkins's office a mutual friend of the two men, the painter Waldo Peirce, presented Max with a surprise gift. In the 1920s Peirce had been Hemingway's fishing buddy in Florida, and on one of those occasions Peirce persuaded Hemingway to pose for his camera wearing nothing but a kind of turtle shell or sponge on his head and the butt-rest of a fishing rod covering his privates (fig. 38). Waldo, despite his rough exterior, was a devoted family man, a "domesticated . . . cow," as Hemingway unkindly called him in a letter to John Dos Passos, and it's possible Peirce saw sharing the photograph with Max as an opportunity to get back at Hem.[151] He inscribed it on the back: "The great Pescador hiding his light under a but[sic]-rest." When he got the picture, Max, with evident satisfaction, noted the near-absence of chest fur. And he published it in the second volume of his autobiography, accompanied by the sarcastic caption, "Hemingway in the twenties." By then Hemingway had been dead for three years.

Whether Max or his publisher balked, we don't know. But in the published version of the photograph Hem is wearing a pair of dainty swimming trunks. No matter, Max had finally won the battle.[152]

When Max engaged in fisticuffs with Hemingway in Maxwell Perkins's office, he was actually in the middle of a profound personal as well as political crisis. He had staked a large part of his adult life on the supposition that there

Figure 38. *The Great Pescador.* Ernest
Hemingway on the Marquesas Keys, 1928.
Photograph by Waldo Peirce. EMII.

was something that art—which Max understood comprehensively as poetry,
writing, oratory—could accomplish or save and on the hope that thereby he
would be able to save himself, too. Through all the permutations of his political
views one hope had remained the same for Max: that the reforms he advocated
as a pragmatist, feminist, socialist, and defender of the Bolsheviks and then of
Trotsky would result in greater freedom for the individual to do exactly what he
or she wanted. As Stalin began to issue one decree after another, limiting the
rights of women, imposing a code of conduct for students in schools, and re-
placing internationalism with a jingoistic defense of the fatherland, Max became increasingly convinced the problem was inherent in Marxism itself and
could not simply be fixed by a different mode of interpretation, one that got rid
of the vestiges of Hegelian metaphysics. What had happened to the hope,
memorably expressed by Friedrich Engels, that as a result of the realization of
socialism "the interference of the state power in social relations" would become

utterly superfluous? Marx/Engels had been confident that the state, as a political entity, would not even have to be abolished but would simply "wither away" and become a museum artifact, like the spinning wheel and the prehistoric axe. It dawned on Max that any revolution involving some organized, collective effort to do away with state power would end up reestablishing something that would, in turn, look very much like yet another and perhaps even worse form of state power. And communist Russia had in fact, at least in Max's estimation, become worse than the tsar's regime. He had the personal experience to back this up. Under Stalin's rule Eliena's entire family, including her sisters Olga Drauden, Vera Krylenko, and Sophia Meyer, along with their children, and her other brother, the mining engineer Vladimir Krylenko, vanished. Olga was the last to be in touch with Eliena, in 1935. Since then, silence.[153]

In January 1937 Max published an article in *Harper's*, "The End of Socialism in Russia," which summarized his new thinking. Published as a small book just a month later, it confirmed that Max's issue with communism was no longer limited to Stalinism. Taking all those "liberal scholars and littérateurs" to task who were still defending Stalin, Max shifted his attention gradually away from what was happening in Russia—since there was nothing to be fixed there anyway—to what, under the influence of Stalin's propaganda machine, was happening at home in the United States. The Prince of the Village became the Cassandra of Gotham. In a letter to the receptive DeWitt Wallace, the editor of *Reader's Digest,* Max plaintively spoke of "the enormous circle of *Partial Dupes* and *Total Innocents*" surrounding the inner core of fellow travelers. "This circle includes many of the biggest men in the country," Max wrote, "capitalists, bankers, newspaper publishers, mayors, senators, congressmen, presidential candidates of two parties. It is practically interminable, and it extends the influence of Stalin's Holding Company, and its money-raising effectiveness, I should say, to some 25 or 30 million Americans." In Max's pessimistic view nearly one-fourth of Americans were under Stalin's influence, whether they knew it or not, and their institutions were, too, from the Consolidated Tribes of the North American Indians to the editorial staff of Ralph Ingersoll's *PM Magazine*.[154]

Stalin's "American power," Max lamented later that year in the *American Mercury,* extended to labor leaders, businessmen, movie actors, parsons, government officials, socialites, college professors, and publishers. Even First Lady Eleanor Roosevelt had been hoodwinked "into giving aid indirectly to a foreign dictator" when she welcomed former members of the Stalin-controlled American Youth Congress to a White House picnic.[155] Max singled out the

League of American Writers (which he said should be called the League of Writers for the Defense of the Soviet Union and the Substitution of Totalitarian Party Dictatorship for the American System of Government) and the APM (American Peace Mobilization, later the American People's Mobilization) as extensions of Stalin's propaganda machine. "These organizations have a rank and file membership of millions who are equally innocent of the real purposes behind them." Max believed he had identified a vast "communist conspiracy to destroy American democracy," fueled by people's manic conviction that there was a better system of government, a kind of superdemocracy, on the other side of the planet. And then he named names, in eerie anticipation of the witch hunts of the 1950s. Did he not realize his own name calling was the first step of the kind of paranoia Stalin wanted to induce in America? Watch out for any cause that had the names of known fellow travelers associated with it, he told his readers. Guilty by suspicion were, to name a few names that still resonate today, Franz Boas, Margaret Bourke-White, Erskine Caldwell, Theodore Dreiser, Lion Feuchtwanger, Dashiell Hammett, Rockwell Kent, Paul Robeson, and George Seldes. "It may be that none of these people belong to the Communist Party," Max warned, "but wherever their names are played up in a political 'cause,' you may suspect that a party nucleus is at work in the underground."[156]

While working on this essay Max began keeping lists, folders, and binders full of names. First, there were just handwritten notes regarding fellow travelers, but soon he was collecting entire portfolios from sources like the former TASS correspondent and fellow apostate Eugene Lyons and from information given to the House Un-American Activities Committee (HUAC). Everyone and everything was fair game, even the clarinetist Benny Goodman, whose Carnegie Hall concert with Paul Robeson in April 1941 had attracted Max's attention since it was funded by the American–Russian Institute.[157]

Deeply involved in his own game of name calling, Max had zero tolerance for those who called *him* names. In May 1938 he sued the *Daily Worker* as well as its editor, Clarence Hathaway, and Earl Browder, the general secretary of the Communist Party, for calling him a "spy for the British government" and an "agent of the German and Japanese secret services." (They had also called him a "bandit and notorious swindler.") Max claimed a ludicrous $250,000 in damages. "Browder is trying to assassinate my character because he cannot assassinate me," Max observed. But before the trial could take place Browder had been jailed for passport fraud, and Hathaway had gone into hiding. Max settled out of court for a paltry $1,500. But money had never been the issue.

Keeping in public view, by whatever means possible, was Max's ticket to survival. Stalin's killers would not go after someone who had been front-page news.[158]

As his stock as a political pundit was falling, Max became more successful as a kind of general purpose intellectual. In 1938 he hosted, for a period of five months, a weekly radio show called *Word Game* for CBS, which at least in part seems to have been intended as a plug for *Webster's Dictionary*. In his autobiography Max claimed his pay was $400, but a letter to Douglas Coulter at CBS in his papers reveals that he likely did not receive more than $100—not enough, as Max claimed, to compensate him for all he did and certainly not enough to cover his travel expenses. He had been hired, he pointed out, as "master of ceremonies, conductor, and coordinator of a variety program" but had instead become a "radio personality," expected to mix, during every live show, expert advice on linguistic questions with the ability to crack jokes at a moment's notice. *Word Game* required both extensive preparation and considerable improvisational skills, and the latter didn't come easily to someone who thought of himself as primarily a writer.[159]

A more intellectually challenging reinvention of the old-fashioned spelling bee, the program, broadcast each Wednesday at 9 p.m., brought together a team of five randomly chosen guests who were tested on their knowledge of the meaning, pronunciation, and finer nuances of the usage of words. "We all like to talk all the time—or at least as often as we can get anybody to listen," Max was quoted as saying. "Words are what we talk with. The contest is to see whether we know what we are talking about."[160] The show, conducted before a live audience of two hundred or more, started out with definitions and moved from there to spelling, grammar, and slang and, finally, to the popular parlor word game known as "Guggenheim," after which it ended with the announcement of the winner. Max was particularly creative in compiling lists of slang phrases—among my favorites are "caress the canvas" (get knocked down in a prize fight) and "lens louse," a motion picture actor who insists on getting into the foreground of a scene[161]—and he acquired a nearly endless supply of Guggenheim questions. Among the examples in the scripts are "Name a snake beginning with a G" and "Name a Russian composer beginning with an A," and the first to answer would be declared a winner (the answers to these two questions were "garter snake" and "Anton Arensky").

During the broadcast it was Max's task to keep things light and entertaining. He was a suave, self-deprecating, witty moderator, clearly enjoying the presence of a large audience without caring too much that they weren't there because of *him*. After each show he was on an emotional high for hours. This was his bailiwick. As a writer, he knew words intimately; in one segment of the show he joked that his main qualification for the job was that he had written several books, all of which contained words. And, as a proven expert on humor, he also knew how to be humorous.[162] Thus, he explained the origin of the verb "ham"—so called because of the preference of actors for acting the role of Hamlet and for acting it in a certain way—with the following epigrammatic definition: "The choice of term . . . was influenced by the fact that the front end of Hamlet happens to coincide with the rear end of a hog." And while he seemed to relish the role of the knowledgeable professor, he also had no problem admitting that some of his knowledge had been acquired only very recently. For example, here is Max's explanation, from the same show, of why "dictionary" should be pronounced "dictionĕry" and not "diction'ry" or "dictionãry": "You have to avoid saying it as though it rhymed with 'A long long way to Tipperary,' and yet also avoid saying it as though you were the British Prime minister." A very delicate matter, Max said, and he added, with a touch of self-mockery: "Now let's see how long it takes me to forget it."[163]

The ultimate authority on the show was *Webster's New International Dictionary,* second edition. Max had no intention of casting himself in the role of the English language tsar, and he pointed out with pleasure that his contestants were normal human beings, too: "I hope the contestants won't mind my calling them 'average.' Anyway, they're people. I can see that plainly." Since winning was not the point, all participants received a prize. The one with the highest score would get the large, unabridged *Webster's* and the runner-up a leather-bound regular edition, while the others would leave the studio with a copy of the collegiate version.[164]

As he had done with his lectures Max carefully wrote out his remarks in advance of each show. But there remained enough room, and need, for ad-libbing, especially when Max directly engaged with the contestants. And, inevitably, this is where sometimes things went wrong, as when Max once asked for a "more . . . firmer" answer and then had to defend himself against listeners who wrote in to criticize him: "I started to say a 'more firm' and changed it to 'firmer.' That was not a grammatical error but a slip for the brain."[165] But as Max became more comfortable, he responded more confidently to his listeners. When someone criticized him for his preferred pronunciation of "perémptory" over "péremptory," he retaliated, "Webster gives both and if he didn't I wouldn't say péremptory—I'd declare a boycott and decline to use the word until it came to reason. The same to those critics who want me to say poinant instead of poignant."[166] And listen to his apology for having slighted the Monongahela River: "In the game of Guggenheim last week, we hurt the feelings of the Monongahela River, which writes in to inform us that it not only *is* a river, but is the busiest river in the world, rivaled only by the Panama canal in the amount of tonnage carried." And he finished with a reference to situations in which people mistook him for the founder of the Eastman Kodak company: "I apologize to the Monongahela, whom I have known all my life, and I beg everybody to remember that in those last few seconds of our word game I am trying to think so fast that if you said Max Eastman, I wouldn't know whether it was a mountain chain or a camera."[167]

Max also included actual jokes, such as the one about the Italian who, during his immigration interview in Oklahoma City, was asked by the judge what he thought of polygamy. When it became obvious he didn't know what the word meant, the judge tried to help the hopeful immigrant: "Let me ask this question. Benito, what do you think of the idea of having two, or three, or perhaps four wives?" Responded Benito: "I think pretty good, Judge. What do you think?" The judge admitted Benito to American citizenship without any further questions since he so obviously had a sense of humor. Max offered the story after a listener had expressed doubts about Max's definition of "polygamy" as "having multiple wives and *husbands*," which Max insisted was technically correct.[168]

Why did Max spend so much time on *Word Game*, drafting or dictating scripts, collecting words and phrases, researching etymologies, answering a pile of inquiries from admiring or skeptical readers? He did get paid, of course, but what was more important to him than any financial incentive was the renewed sense of relevance the show bestowed upon him. The warm reception of *Enjoyment of Laughter* had given Max a taste of stardom, and *Word Game* allowed him to experience that feeling on a continuous basis. In July 1938 *Radio Guide* ran a full-page photo essay about him, celebrating Max the "genial ... radio star," under the enticing headline "You're as Young as You Think."[169] The photographs, taken by Bert Lawson, showed a white-clad, white-haired, smiling Max in Croton, consulting the dictionary and relaxing in his garden. Max mattered again, and he saved the letters in which people told him his show was one of the highlights of their week, even when those same people went on to tell him he had erred.

Word Game, a strenuously apolitical program in which democracy was less a concept than a word to be spelled, gave Max a sense of control over his life at a time when, politically and personally, he was at sea. It became a model of sorts for later shows, such as the BBC's *My Word* and *Says You* on National Public Radio. Unlike these programs, Max's show did not rely on a regular cast of qualified panelists, and it never aspired to their level of intellectual or even literary sophistication. The democratic nature of the program—the participants included a fireman, a mailman, a secretary, a dentist, a proofreader, a lawyer, a biology teacher, and a translator working for a bank—appealed to Max's own egalitarian sensibilities.[170] Max quickly adapted his voice to the needs of a radio broadcast and proved so adept as a host that he became the subject of several appreciative pages in a handbook on radio directing.[171] The show also made Max a popular culture icon, the recipient of fan letters such as the one sent to him, in the form of a poem, by a "Southern Gal." "I done seen yore picture in the Time Magazine," began the letter writer, affecting a redneck accent, and then offered the following observation:

> Dear Mr. Eastman:
>   I think you
> With such fine look, plus Glamour—,
> Are wasting scads of precious time
> In paying court to—GRAMMAR.

And in case Max didn't get it, the letter writer proposed the following paraphrase: "Doggonit! you're beautiful!"[172]

8 • A Test Case for the Kinsey Male

Word Game provided a respite from Max's political troubles. And brief it proved to be. On September 21, 1938, during a severe hurricane, Max gave his last performance as a game show host in an empty studio, with Eliena doing her best to supply the required laughs. As his show came to an end, the announcer interrupted the broadcast to inform listeners that Hitler had occupied Sudetenland, that the hurricane had wiped the village of Menemsha on the Vineyard off the face of the earth, and that Max Eastman would no longer be hosting *Word Game*, in that order.[1] From New Jersey to Florida Max's fans protested vigorously and inundated the network with angry letters. Reactions ranged from the plaintive ("I regret that you have taken off the air my favorite program") to the admonitory ("You can't disappoint your listeners that way").[2] One intrepid listener resorted to poetry to express her feelings—someone else's poetry, that is. Borrowing freely from the beginning of Longfellow's "Psalm of Life," she versified, "Tell me not in mournful numbers / Max Eastman will appear no more / He, of voice so suave and mellow / Must be held again, I Trow." Max's boss was unimpressed. In his autobiography Max revealed that he had failed to attract a sponsor.[3]

As Max watched his political identity, once so expansive he could think of himself both as a pleasure-seeking aesthete and the austere engineer for a better, socialist future, narrow down to a place where he often felt he had his back against a wall, he continued to anger the philistines by expanding the range of his erotic investments. A relentless, capable lover who awakened hitherto unknown feelings in women (not a few letters offer explicit comments on his erotic technique), Max rarely made any promises and even more rarely looked back. His political world shrunken to the size of his country cottage or to a sheet in his typewriter, Max's overactive erotic life took on dimensions that would have seemed unmanageable to lesser men.

Max now was the last one left of the outrageous Eastman children. Anstice died after suffering a heart attack on December 28, 1937, at the age of fifty-nine. A heavy smoker and a devotee of hard liquor, unlike his more careful brother, he had had warnings before, including two strokes, one in December 1934 and another in October 1935.[4] A respectable chief surgeon at Hamot Hospital in Erie, Pennsylvania, Anstice, or Peter, as family members usually called him, had publicly long officially gone by the name of Ford Eastman, M.D., as if he wanted to be liberated from his eccentric first name and therefore any reminders of his unusual mother.[5] Ford Eastman was the name, too, under which he was buried in Woodlawn Cemetery in Canandaigua—but in the same plot as his sister Crystal, his brother Morgan, and his parents, Annis and Samuel.[6]

It was up to Max now to carry the family flag, and he seemed determined to make the most of the decades he had left. A seemingly ageless Casanova of the No-Longer Left, Max had permanently said good-bye to his Greenwich Village hope that the political world would magically coalesce around his needs for individual self-realization. But he continued to insist on the right to do what he wanted with his body, and he almost felt obliged to dispense his zest for life as freely as possible. His correspondence files bulge with letters from women, some of whom have left only their first names to posterity, among them Marie, Lillian, Rada, Creigh, Martha, Amy, and, inevitably, a series of Florences. One of Max's heroes, the Russian poet Pushkin, had kept lists of the women in his life, those he had loved as well as those he had wanted to love. But Max was too classy for that: "I am too romantic ever to have 'kept count' of my love affairs, or listed the girls," Max wrote in a private note. "Love even in its lighter forms always seemed sacred to me—perhaps that is a reason for my success—and each one must have its isolated existence, integral and inviolate." To put it more unkindly, Max was a great compartmentalizer. One of Max's many girlfriends told him about a dream she'd had in which all the girls of the neighborhood were discussing Max's infidelities. She defended him. "No, it's not true," she said, "when he is making love to one of us he never thinks of the others." Mercurial Max himself had adopted a similar defense, which he articulated most succinctly in a poem, "The Swallow," collected in *Kinds of Love*. That bird was in the habit of merely dipping into the water of a river or pond without immersing itself in it, a perfect metaphor for Max's dealings with women: "I love the deeps but love not deeply." He would assure each of his lovers that she was unique even if only in the moment he loved her: "Be not sad because you've won me, / And we briefly intertwine, / For no other hand is on me / When your hand is warm in mine."[7]

Eliena had long accepted Max's unconquerable libidinal urges, taking comfort in the fact that he would always return to her. Cheered on by her relieved husband, she even engaged in some modest experimentation of her own, thus doing her part to turn the Eastman household into an entirely unscientific version of Alfred Kinsey's lab. As it happened, one of her extramarital partners was the poet Scudder Middleton, the perpetrator of such lines as "our hearts are music-makers in the clouds" and rumored to be one of the handsomest men in the Village.[8] To Max, he would have been more familiar as one of Florence Deshon's former lovers. Now shrunken into post-middle-age timidity, he was no threat to Max, who liked to imagine Eliena coming and going in Scudder's Waverly apartment. Eliena tried to joke about the time she spent with Scudder, but she sounded strained when she told Max that Scudder wanted to take her out for St. Patrick's Day ("as I have an Irish accent") while also worrying if he had enough money to pay for it.[9] Max was delighted when Scudder boasted that he enjoyed making love to Eliena "more than any other girl he had loved," and he eagerly assured Eliena he was fine with her affair: "My darling love," he wrote to her, "I haven't a single quiver of anything but joy in your feelings about Scudder and your being with him. It makes our love so much more four-square and perfect for me, and I hope you love him." As long as her feelings for him hadn't changed, whatever Eliena did was fine with him.[10] To encourage transparency Max sometimes even shared the letters of current girlfriends with her.

If the political Max had undergone a transformation, Max the lover still seemed stuck in his Greenwich Village days, inviting but ultimately avoiding confrontation with the authorities. "I'd always thought that you were . . . sort of in love with a lot of girls," wrote a girl named Lillian, who had just been unceremoniously dumped and wanted to know why: "You liked me more than ever until that detective came in—or was it that unsatisfactory session in the car that changed your feelings?" She would sure appreciate it if Max "could go into a little bit of self-analysis for me."[11] As Lillian must have already known, Max was emphatically not a family man. He freely acknowledged and made fun of his weakness for women, women younger than him, women his age, women conventionally considered beautiful and those who were not. Max liked them all. A joke he enjoyed so much that he wrote it down twice tells the story of the robin that built a nest and fixed it up with beautiful, colored ribbons and fancy feathers. When a blue jay came along and congratulated her on her taste, he noticed a hole in the middle of the nest. Asked the blue jay, "But why did you put the hole in the middle of the nest?" Answered the robin, "Well, you see, I don't like children, but I do enjoy the mating season."[12] Max was a bit like that lustful robin—an artist in the world of sexual gratification, equipped with libidinal energies that sometimes astonished himself. Even more amazing was the almost methodical nature of his pursuit—and his openness about it, both of which, in the late forties, regularly encouraged reviewers to invoke Alfred Kinsey's sex research as an appropriate context in which to view and understand Max's exploits.

While he might not have undertaken the kind of self-analysis Lillian wanted him to or at least not with the result she clearly wished for, Max knew that his sexual appetites transgressed the limits of ordinary bourgeois morality. In a personal note he once described himself as "afflicted with a desire to mate or devour the universe" and then, self-mockingly, pointed out there were limits, though perhaps not moral ones. His thirst for experience would, he admitted, even lead him to run after girls he did not particularly desire. "My penis, balking or behaving enigmatically, apprises me of the difference and shames me of my foully omnivorous thirst." So, there.[13]

There were potential legal problems, too. As Lillian's reference to the detective demonstrates, Max's extramarital experimentation was not risk free. In the thirties and forties the Mann Act, originally intended to prohibit the transport of women across state lines for "immoral purposes," was being used more broadly to police all kinds of morally unacceptable behavior. Despite such dangers, it seems women entered into affairs with Max willingly and knowingly. Some of them appreciated Max's fame, whereas others responded warmly to his capabilities as a lover, absent in their husbands and previous partners, or to his legendary beauty. Apart from the inevitable flashes of anger that would erupt when Max declared the end of a relationship, there were usually signs of genuine affection in the letters they sent to Max even after a relationship had ended.

In ways perhaps difficult to understand today, Max's lovers accepted his presence in their lives, however fleeting, as a gift. One woman, known only as Marie, clipped his name from newspapers, adding "Dear" before it and arranging the cutouts in such a way that they formed a pair of lips before she mailed her collage to him. Even the frustrated Lillian admitted she was surprised their relationship had lasted as long as it did. In 1942 one Florence Southard wrote about how "terribly appealing" Max, with his hair "all soft and wild over your forehead," seemed to her. And, overwhelmed by "so much physical beauty," she transitioned to describing, fairly explicitly, how sleeping with Max had liberated her, connecting her with her own "secret depths" and, afterward, rendering her "incoherent trying to tell you." Max had taught her to give up "a certain puritanical fear of bodies and the things bodies do." Ms. Southard was "more than certain that you will *have* to be the father of one of my children," a resolution she does not seem to have kept: the *Utica Daily Press,* on June 10, 1946, records her wedding to one William E. Richardson. But even if many of Max's lovers eventually receded into obscurity, it seems at least some of them carried their memory of him with them for the rest of their lives.[14]

These armies of other women notwithstanding, it was Eliena alone who offered Max the certainty and security he needed, and she took pleasure in her role. Max was "her lonely giant," she declared in a note penned in February 1938, when they were staying at Mrs. Gartz's vacation home in Palos Verdes, California. He was the rock on which her life rested. As her imagination took over and her language became lyrical, her image of Max assumed mythic proportions: "You stand alone, above and outside all that noisy swarm of self-deceived conceited patterned pigmeys [*sic*]—estranged from them, aloof, alone—doomed to aloneness by your size, your mind's magnificence, your courage, honesty, and even of truth relentless and unyielding."[15]

On a few occasions, however, Max's erotic economics got off-kilter, in ways he never expected. One of these was his affair with the much younger Creigh Collins (later, Creigh Stern). A recent high school graduate and excellent swimmer, Creigh, "hard and self-contained," found a way of conquering what Max called his "inner citadel."[16]

He met Creigh on a hot August day in 1938 on the beach in Martha's Vineyard. Lean, athletic, and self-confident, the blue-eyed eighteen-year-old made a big impression on Max, who, at age fifty-six, was just beginning to worry about the fading of his powers. "Because you dared divingly," began a poem he dedicated to her, right away, "I will make you a little poem." Max's tribute to the amazing Creigh, later published under the title "Unsheathed," goes on to describe the arrival of a special kind of flying fish on King's Beach:

> Bluer than ocean
> More than moon silver,
> Knife-blade blue and seen-through silver,
> Winged, finned,

Sheer through air and water,
Stark naked of the past and future,
Came to King's beach one day a flying fish.
Days after that cool swift-given unsheathed wonder,
Bathing on King's beach seemed
Hallowed more than by god
By Nature's bold free daring to be.[17]

Harriet Creigh Collins was not like other girls her age. A graduate of the progressive Francis Parker School in Chicago (which had merged with a school founded by Max's teacher Dewey), she had chosen to go by her unusual family name over her less exciting given name. Creigh had lost her father early, and one of her teachers at the Parker School, Sarah Greenebaum, had taken her under her wing and invited her to the Vineyard, where Sarah regularly spent her summers hobnobbing with other progressives.[18]

Eliena was instantly worried when she met the young girl, fearing that her radiant presence would put in jeopardy her and Max's open-marriage arrangement, in which confidences about extramarital affairs were normally shared like any other news. A poem she wrote a few months after Creigh had shown up in their lives describes her arrival in terms of sheer terror, as a home invasion rather than the beginning of a friendship: "We were silent as a frightened mouse / Who stays dead-still behind the pantry-shelves— / Afraid to let you into our perfect house, / Afraid that we might love you more than ourselves."[19] It is true Creigh didn't fit the mold of Max's previous lovers. Apart from the enormous age difference, she had nothing of the dark, mysterious aura of Ida or the intense vulnerability of Florence Deshon or the funny sturdiness of Eliena Krylenko. A high school yearbook from the year she met Max shows a determined-looking young woman with prominent eyebrows, a high forehead, her head slightly tilted back, as if in a deliberate attempt to avoid looking too pretty for the camera. The still somewhat adolescent roundness of the face is offset by the steely look of her eyes. But the surprisingly full lips offer a hint of the capacity for enjoyment that would have appealed to Max (fig. 39).

Liberated by her education, Creigh readily responded to Max's obvious desire for her: "I am there / I am there / Always there," she intoned in a poem she wrote for him at the beginning of their relationship.[20] The risk of discovery—the Mann Act was very much on their minds—added spice to their affair, especially after Creigh had quit Wheaton College, where she was a very indifferent student, and moved to Buffalo to join her sister's family "to try . . . to get back a decent perspective on life." Her mother's death a few weeks later

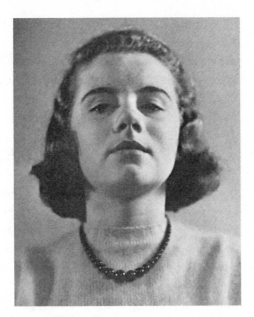

Figure 39. Creigh Collins, 1938. From the
Parker Record. Courtesy of The Francis Parker
School and the Chicago History Museum.

seems to have made her connection with Max even stronger. Max's longing for her was now so intense he couldn't sleep. Dreaming about her on his "little blue couch," presumably the place their love had been consummated, he completed a sonnet he had begun earlier: "It still has the form of a sentence in the 'future conditional,' but is filled up with astonishing fact."[21] The poem, originally titled "Prayer," appeared in his *Poems of Five Decades* under the title "Animal" but without any explanatory notes. And indeed no explanation seemed necessary for the wish the speaker directed at his lover, his "Diana down from heaven":

> Could you from this most envied poise descend,
> Moved by some force in me I know not of,
> To mix with me and be to me a woman,
> Diana down from heaven could not lend
> More ecstasy, or fill my faltering human
> Heart's hunger with a more celestial love.[22]

Max knew, of course, that the love he was hoping to extract from this earthy, insistently physical girl was hardly "celestial," a fact reflected in the excited enjambments linking the poem's last three lines.

In February 1939 Max and Eliena left Croton for their annual winter vacation in the sun. Creigh had taken Max's two cats to her sister's house in Buffalo, apparently without asking anyone for permission. Her sister's shock was outdone only by that of the Eastman cats: "Yesterday was spent following them around the house with a pail of water, scrub brush, and kitchen soap. I found that Peggy's most fragrant deoderant [sic] as a finishing touch was also helpful." In Florida Max was pining not for his cats but for Creigh, pelting her with notes in which he sent his "sun-warmed love" and worried that Creigh was forgetting him. Creigh responded to Max's anguished missives by threatening to "cut the wires" if he didn't relax. And she recommended what Max should do in order to properly think of her: "One of your days, Max, run, run, run down the beach until everything is out of sight then find the water and race the breakers. When you collapse on the sand think about me." But Max seemed on a quest to make a fool of himself, assuring Creigh he felt younger than ever and ready for another meeting with her. In reality, he was just a middle-aged male scribbling furtive notes on the window sill of a post office in Sarasota, Florida, to a girl one-third his age. Only a small part of him realized how silly this whole thing was.[23]

Their next clandestine encounter, elaborately planned, took place in a cabin somewhere outside of Albany, and while it felt magical as it was happening, in retrospect it failed to satisfy Max. All too soon he was back in Croton again, more lonely than ever. Eliena was preoccupied with her art and spending more and more time in New York, and even Biely the cat had "a girlfriend and begs so fervently to go out at night that I yield, although it means waking up at dawn to let him in."[24] His longing had become almost impossible to bear: "I love you," he wrote two days later, throwing caution to the wind. He wanted to start all over again, but this time without any residual panic about his undignified behavior: "I want to sit all day in the big arm chair with your head warm between my knees, and poetry, poetry, floating around me on your young voice as though thrushes carried its meaning to my ear." He had been valiantly fighting her power over him. To him, she was Keats's Lamia or the poet's Belle Dame sans Merci: "Was it your youth I feared, the suggestion of my death in it?" Love had almost killed him twice, and now memories of his agonized relationships with Ida Rauh and Florence Deshon came flooding back to him: "You are desirable to me beyond words, and mysterious, and I think you have genius, and your gift of love is as precious as though the stars had stooped down to make me young. . . . Come still a little nearer to me before you go away."[25]

Creigh succeeded marvelously in keeping her desirous lover at arm's length by reminding him how wonderful Eliena was. And she proceeded to give a more realistic version of the famous night in the Catskills that had assumed almost fantastic proportions in Max's overactive brain: "Max, a cube as small and square as ours was with two whole people in it has room for love and that is just about all." Max got the message, sort of. Maybe there was a lesson in his predicament, after all. He had always been afraid he had "too much brains" and not enough feeling, and loving Creigh had taught him otherwise: "That I could go out of my head over your lovely beauty of body and spirit is reassuring. It really is. I guess it is good for me . . . to have to play this role. I have played yours so many times!" But Creigh again summarized Max's lesson a little differently, with teenage nonchalance: "Max, will you relax for me and smile?" She had never wanted to hurt him, she said. "I love you Max and I slept with you because I love you not so I could say I love you."[26]

Delighted by her unexpected declaration of love, Max allowed himself to be gripped by new fits of adult ecstasy. Creigh did love him! He lost control of his feelings: "Your words flowed over and into and all through me like an *inundation* of bright clear water over a garden parched in early spring." She appeared transfigured to him, equipped with the wisdom of the ancients: "You speak almost like Plato sometimes, you sound so wise and mature and little like a school girl, much less a run-away-from-school girl." And, in recognition of her philosophical talents, he provided his teenage Plato with the draft preface to a new anthology for *Enjoyment of Poetry* he had been compiling.[27]

Unfortunately, Creigh's time in Buffalo had come to an abrupt end. Her sister was getting a divorce, and Creigh needed a place to stay. Now it was Max's turn to be offish, as he always would be when lovers came too close to the life he shared with Eliena. Creigh could certainly live with them, he said, but only if she agreed to work. Creigh was annoyed: "Your last letter was cold to a freezing point," she answered curtly. She went on to offer some shrewd criticism of his preface to the anthology: "I read your preface and enjoyed it." That's it—no clarifying "very much," "greatly" or "immensely" added. Perhaps her use of the verb "enjoy" was meant as a dig at the book's title, *Anthology for Enjoyment of Poetry*. And she did not hesitate to call Max out on his use of the hackneyed metaphor of the "symphony" of poems he had assembled. Did Max have to hide behind an "old" image to justify his choices?[28]

Once again the Vineyard community took Creigh in. On April 21, 1939, lying on the beach in Edgartown, Creigh wrote a long, involved letter to Max, a lyrical reflection on beauty and creativity inspired by his preface as well as the intense physical sensations caused by her reckless sunbathing: "The sun is so warm that my arm has some red splotches on it." The Vineyard heat made Creigh bold, and she proceeded to attack Max's philosophy head-on: "In your preface you said 'to increase enjoyment.' But what is enjoyment by it-self?" Shouldn't it always lead to something tangible, some action we want to take? Degas, for example, always made her want to dance.[29]

The final version of Max's preface directly responds to Creigh's criticism. "There are people in the world," wrote Max, "who cannot enjoy the vivid experience of an idea unless they believe in it, who cannot ride along with an action unless it goes toward their chosen ends, nor taste the flavor of a sunset or even a sandwich, unless it is linked by some specious or real wires of connection with what they adhere to or intend to do." One need not have lived through the specific event a poem describes in order to enjoy it, just as one need not be a warrior or warmonger to appreciate a battle song. Max had sorted his poems according to the themes and tonal qualities he had found in them, not in terms of the emotional resonances they engender in readers. But he had taken at least some of Creigh's advice. "Of course my book is not a symphony," asserted Max, "and it is too long to be so read."[30]

At the end of April Creigh reported that her period was late, perhaps a consequence of their "social racketeering." Her letter got Max's attention, and not just because of her phrasing, which he found offensive. "I suspect this child of being mental but we won't take any chances. Have you money enough for the fare here if necessary?"[31]

At just about the same time, with less than perfect timing, Creigh received a long letter in which Eliena (fig. 40) took her to task for being a "lazy weak-ling." It is unlikely Eliena didn't know what was going on between her husband and the liberated waif from King's Beach, and maybe that was why she didn't pull any punches. Creigh was, she said, "naturally or unnaturally lazy, and that is one of your big and unbearable faults." If Creigh didn't confront her problem "damn soon," there was no hope left for her: "you'll just disintegrate." Max would have loved her more had she decided to work for him instead of refusing to type his manuscripts because it would have made her—what a terrible prospect!—Max's secretary rather than his "poet-friend." Eliena, for one, had not hesitated when Max needed her: "I typed a whole book for Max when we were broke before I even understood the English words. And I typed it well."

Figure 40. Eliena Eastman, 1940. EMIIA1.

The further she got wrapped up in her dismay over Creigh's aloofness, the more venomous Eliena's comments became. For example, as a dance instructor she had noticed Creigh's awful posture: "Walk with your head up," she commanded, "instead of hanging your El Greco nose down to the ground like a chicken in a stupor." Rather than loping around with stooped shoulders, she should lift her head back, with her "laughing mouth" directed at the sky: "I saw you do it when you danced and that—more than anything else—made me like you." Eliena's final advice for her husband's young lover: "Stop fancying yourself as a listless weeping willow over an artificially irrigated pool and try hard and humbly to grow and be in real fact as much of a person as you can."[32]

Eliena's letter displays, in full force, the tigerlike fierceness Max had noticed in her virtually from the moment she had spotted him in the Imperial Palace hotel at Genoa. While Eliena was willing to share her wayward Max, there were invisible boundaries other women were not allowed to cross without waking that animal inside her. Creigh had done so, and one wonders what

would have happened had Eliena learned about Creigh's (fortunately unwar-
ranted) pregnancy fears.

By now Creigh's family had caught on and whisked her away to Illinois,
safely out of Max's noxious orbit. Pressured to make plans to attend college
again, she accused Max of having spoiled her for ordinary life: "Can you understand that you made me relax and love and now or soon I have to begin
reteaching myself all you have undone?" But in fact she had no regrets: "Even
if you had been an insurance salesman with your lovely body you would have
been aesthetic, too." And she added a coded description of Max in ecstasy, of
the moment the mouse turned into a woodchuck, as she wittily characterized
it: "Your eyes closed and your head went back half groaning, all of which for
some reason made my feeling so intense that even now I want to see and feel
you making a paralytic effort to stretch." In Creigh Max had found a fellow
devotee to the pleasures of the flesh. Using the tolerant Sarah Greenebaum as
a go-between, they continued to exchange letters.[33]

It wasn't as if Max didn't have other problems to deal with. On May 9, 1939,
Joseph Stalin, worried about the hesitancy of the Western nations to take on
Hitler, fired Maxim Litvinov, Eliena's former boss, and replaced him with Vyacheslav Mikhailovitch Molotov, the chairman of the Council of People's
Commissars and one of Stalin's staunchest supporters. Molotov immediately
began negotiations with his German counterpart, Joachim von Ribbentrop,
which led to the signing of the infamous nonaggression pact on August 23 the
same year. The Molotov–Ribbentrop Pact, as it became known, paved the way
for Hitler's invasion of Poland in the fall of 1939 as well as Stalin's own annexations of parts of Finland, Estonia, Latvia, Lithuania, Poland, and Bessara-
bia. Before the year had ended, Max's worst fears about Stalin's regime had
been realized. But he had seen it coming. He didn't need the proof offered by
the recent defectors, such as the former Soviet chief of European Intelligence,
Walter Krivitsky, who had left France for the United States at the end of 1938
and who had been writing a series of articles exposing Stalin's hypocrisies. He
was found dead a year later in a small Washington hotel, under suspicious
circumstances.

Max had been warning the world about Stalin since 1925; recent events
were just a matter of confirming his predictions. His former political allies
who hadn't seen the handwriting on the wall remained blind to the new reality
of Soviet hegemony. In an open letter published in the Nation the same
day the paper announced the Molotov–Ribbentrop pact, 400 of the most

distinguished intellectuals in the United States voiced their opposition to the "fantastic falsehood that the U.S.S.R. and the totalitarian states are basically alike," a fascist propaganda lie directed against the forces of progress and, more specifically, against a country that had proved to be a "bulwark against war and aggression." Only 165 signatories actually appeared under the letter, but they included the names of several people Max had regarded as friends, such as Louis Untermeyer and Jean Starr Untermeyer, along with those of well-known literary figures such as Hemingway, Klaus Mann, and William Carlos Williams.[34] In Santa Fe Ida Rauh was deeply worried about these dramatic developments, though she worried less for the world than for their son. She wrote to Max, "I can't know how seriously you are thinking or feeling about the imminence of war." Her nights were, she said, "made horrible" by the thought that Dan might get drafted and be "driven over there like cattle for foreign slaughter." Couldn't he write something "passionate and clear and intellectual" against the barbarity of war, as he had done so often before? American boys should not be sacrificed to European capitalism or whatever "supremacy" they were trying to save over there.[35]

But Max's head was still full of Creigh. On her first day in Highland Park, Illinois, Creigh had come across a copy of *The Sense of Humor* with its dedication to Florence Deshon and experienced "a sensation I never had before," feeling a kinship and spiritual sympathy with Max that carried her beyond the limits of their relationship. "I lived three complete lives in about five minutes. That queer sensation of knowing or thinking I understood every feeling & thought that Florence had ever had and then Eliena & then you. I can't possibly explain it or write it for it has no words." Powerfully touched by Creigh's vision, Max urged her to come see him as soon as possible and to not even think about postponing: "A week, it seems, is just the longest I can believe in your existence without a word from you. How do they manage to believe in God?"[36]

And they did meet. Eliena, of all people, invited Creigh to a ball game at the Heckscher Foundation on 104th Street and Fifth Avenue in New York because Max was playing on the Studs Lonigan Ball Team, a softball team headed by the novelist James T. Farrell, a good friend of Max's.[37] By then Max knew he had been permanently pushed to the sidelines. At ease among members of her own generation, where she was "so talkative and witty, so admired," Creigh had no real use for him. Max felt abject jealousy, imagining how she would cheat on him with other men, the "abstract crass male beast," as it were. He stayed up nights typing lengthy letters in which he lamented Creigh's coldness. Again, the possibility of a pregnancy—there were dark hints in their letters at "an errand" that was, or then finally didn't have to be, performed—sent him into a tailspin. And then Max found out he indeed wasn't the responsible party. The "awfulness" of his situation dawned on him: "While I was writing you these rapturous letters and lying nights long in anguish about your silence, you were going around full of highballs and being made ardent love to, all but persuaded to marriage, and actually persuaded to give your body." Max felt deceived and humiliated. "It brings everything so much lower than I thought it was." At his age, what was he to do with a broken heart?[38]

Creigh's confession ended their relationship. They would occasionally see each other, in New York, for example, where Creigh came to one of Eliena's exhibition openings. She sent Max Christmas cards as well as some of her poems. "Max, Max," she wrote to him in April 1940, after she had seen a positive review of Max's *Stalin's Russia* in the *New York Times,* "where are you? . . . I want to talk to you." In 1942 she spent time with Eliena at Max's new house on the Vineyard.[39] But Creigh's life post-Max was not a success story. A failed first marriage, to Alfred Stern, and an unhappy second marriage, to Frederick E. Wagner, and a protracted battle with her own demons, some of them, such as her penchant for alcohol, familiar to Max from their relationship, left little room for her to develop her considerable talents as a poet or thinker. While some would be inclined to view the story of her affair with Max as more sordid than poetic, the fact remains that to Creigh the year she shared with Max remained, as her daughter put it, the highlight of her life.[40] In a poem written long after her dealings with Max, titled "Half Fled," she imagines a visit to a dying person: "To find a shriveled, cradled form / That must have blood, but blood luke-warm / And blood that's thin and barely moves." Upon leaving that person's bedroom and before closing the door, she notices that "the bed / Has curved to fit the pattern of this one half fled." She signed the gruesome text simply "Creigh" and sent it to Max.[41] "Half fled" from his life as well as her own life, Creigh Collins, his "Diana down from heaven," his blue-eyed miracle diver from King's Beach, left no traces in the voluminous second installment of Max's autobiography. She was seventy-four when she died, on July 22, 1994, in Lyme, New Hampshire, at the home of one of her daughters.

By the beginning of the next year Max had reset his system and was deeply preoccupied with an aspiring but also very much married poet named Martha Ellis ("beautiful to my eyes"), originally from Mount Airy, Georgia, and now living in Atlanta.[42] Martha, a thirtysomething mother and alumna of Mount

Holyoke College, was, like many women before and after her, mesmerized by the white-haired, white-clad, mellow-voiced Max, whose abilities as a lover she freely evoked in letters and poems. He had transformed her world: "The mail box vibrates to my anxious tread," she rhapsodized in a sonnet dedicated to him.[43] But Max was profoundly affected, too, if for different reasons. Some of the triviality of his current existence was now painfully evident to him: "At your age," he told Martha in a letter from Mexico, "I was being tried in the United States courts for treason to my country! I was engaged in stopping a World War—so I guess you have me there." Life seemed to be moving past him so fast that nothing seemed so significant anymore, unless one was traveling anyway: "I just feel surprised. Experiences go by pretty rapidly for the most part like signs along the road—danger, dip, right curve, left curve, men working, village approaching. It all doesn't matter very much."[44]

The affairs with Creigh and Martha, separated by little more than a year, had shown Max that his athletic approach to extramarital sex had its pitfalls. He was not prepared for situations in which he would end up falling in love and, as a result, humiliate himself. With both Martha and Creigh his proud delight in sensual pleasure inadvertently yielded to furtive arrangements for trysts in Florida, Croton, and on the Vineyard, intended to keep his escapades secret from Eliena. "I want you to know that I felt utterly desolate," wrote Max to Martha after she had left him one night, "and I do still." Some little "owly creature" had given a cry outside, which had reminded him of that "immeasurable moment" when Martha was still in his arms, the moment "when our romance turned into love." As the ghost of Martha's absence was following him around the house, "going before me into every room, even the bathroom—which shows what an illogical being he is, for we were never there together," Max was suddenly afraid that in his love life he might have become irrelevant, too, as irrelevant as he feared he had become in the political arena: "Martha, don't sink back completely into the routine and forget me." And then he stopped himself. This was a letter he was writing to himself, he realized: "Oh, Martha, I forgot that I am not really writing to you! I cannot say these infinitely important things."[45] Martha had a family, and he did not—or had squandered every opportunity to have one, for the sake of an open marriage and an unconventional harem of girls as uncommitted to him as he was to them. The axis around which Martha's "no-matter-how free-going life" revolved was "you-and-your-children-in-their-home." If he had intended to mock Martha's priorities, this didn't work. He had tried to mail his letters but then couldn't, realizing how dangerous they were. "You possess my body and my thoughts." Maybe she should adopt an alias, such as Ellen Nellis, to whom he could mail his letters by general delivery? The full absurdity of his situation slowly sank in: "But what is the use suggesting this when I can't send the letter in which I suggest it?" There was something disarmingly undignified about these self-revelations of a now-fifty-seven-year-old man. Max worried about not being able to write "seemly" letters to Martha, but, as Max himself knew, just about the unseemliest thing about them was the naked despair displayed in them. There was no way he could send them.[46]

One wonders how Max found time to do any writing. But he did: in March 1940 Norton published his most ambitious political work to date, *Stalin's Russia and the Crisis in Socialism*. Running to roughly 270 pages, the book was too long to be an essay. Yet it had none of the dullness and long-windedness of the academic monograph. It was also deeply autobiographical. For the real theme of *Stalin's Russia* was not Stalin or Russia or what he called the Bolshevik fiasco (though Max had much to say about all these topics), but Max's realization—painful, torturous, gut-wrenching—that he was no longer a socialist. The crisis mentioned in the book's title was Max's own. After reasserting what he had already said elsewhere, namely, that Stalin had lost any right to call his politics socialist, he was left wondering whether or not the term "socialism" itself had survived its abuse at the hands of that "mountebank-Marxist." The answer was self-evident: thanks to Stalin, socialism had come to mean not the liberation of the working class but a "general surrender to some authoritative concept of the collective good." Max was done with Trotsky, too: "Those surrounding Trotsky accept the basic principles of totalitarian gang-rule, the one-party tyranny and immoralism in the cause of power, but promise that in a sufficiently advanced country, and provided the gang has the right leaders and a genuine proletarian policy, there will still emerge, even though like a rabbit out of a hat, the society of the free and equal." So much for dialectic materialism.[47] A few years before, he had gotten unexpected support for this view from his own son, Dan. A Cornell graduate, Dan had worked first as a science teacher and then as an investigator for the ACLU before, in Max's words, "becoming, being, and ceasing to be, a Trotskyist." In a statement coauthored with his then girlfriend Eleanora (Maya) Deren, later well known as a maker of experimental films, and presented to a gathering of American Trotskyists, Dan had argued that the USSR had reverted to a precapitalist economy and succumbed to a form of "industrial feudalism"—a view that, like Max's, contradicted Trotsky's prognosis of the transitional nature of Stalinism.[48]

Max felt that if one had to wait for a hat trick to see a truly classless society implemented, and even then only under the right circumstances, it was truly time to look elsewhere for a solution. And if the developments in Stalin's Russia, like the collectivization of property and government ownership of industry, could not be separated from the results they produced ("a nation of informers, spies, hypocrites, lickspittles and mass murderers"), then Max would have to find a new name for whatever dreams of an egalitarian society he had left.[49]

The specter of those brutally executed during Stalin's recent purges hovers behind every page of Max's book. His brother-in-law—and what a strange thing that connection must have been for Max—had been among those who died, murdered like an animal, the way he, in his heyday as Stalin's willing chief prosecutor, had had so many others killed. The inglorious end of the Bolshevik dream was Max's very personal nightmare, too: "The Russian revolution is perhaps the greatest tragedy in human history, terrible in the breadth of its impact, terrible in the depth of its significance, terrible in its personal details. Other revolutionary martyrs have been permitted a heroic death; the heroes of the Russian revolution have been shot like dogs in the cellar." The old feminist Max couldn't help but notice, too, what had happened to women under Stalin's rule. Was it a coincidence that totalitarian regimes were always run by men, leaving to women the business of breeding?[50]

With considerable bitterness Max on several occasions evoked Marx's promise, which seemed vapid to him now, that after the success of the revolution the state and all its organizations would simply fade away. Clearly that hadn't happened in Russia, where ordinary people were now worse off than under the tsar. Instead of Kingdom Come, Stalin, that mountebank Marxist, had given the Russian a monstrous, blood-smeared "Iron Heel of a thing," spawned in the inner circles of Hell. The Hitler–Stalin pact had confirmed the "vital union of two profoundly similar regimes." It had also removed any doubts Max might have had regarding the supposedly scientific nature of Marxism as a tool for social analysis. If Max had previously presented Stalinism as an ideological corruption of Lenin's hard-nosed, unmetaphysical version of social engineering, he now recognized that Lenin was part of the system. Whatever he was, Lenin was not a scientist. If he had conducted the revolution as an experiment, he would have realized that coercing the working class into cooperation destroyed the value of the experiment. Even Lenin's critics, such as the German socialist Rosa Luxemburg, who had faulted Lenin for not allowing sufficient room for the democracy of the masses in his system, were blind to the fatal flaw in Lenin's and, for that matter, Marx's thought. The expectation that the proletariat, once freed, would inevitably take "socialist measures" was nothing but a hypothesis. What if it didn't want to? Marx might have thought that the class struggle was a "dialectical tame beast" he could ride effortlessly into the Shangri-La of a cooperative commonwealth, but in fact he "had a wild leviathan by its tail."[51]

But Max wasn't willing to allow failure, his own, Marx's, Lenin's, or Trotsky's, to have the last word. The idea had been wrong, the methods had been mistaken, but the struggle itself, the struggle for some idea greater than the status quo, the struggle for the hope of a society better than the one we know, had not been wrong. "I find myself, in view of these facts, not only urging a more careful definition of the aims we have in view, but in my own mind falling back upon a thought with which, long before the Russian revolution gave such body to our hopes, I entered the socialist movement: that to participate in a struggle for those large aims, whether they be achieved or not, is to live a good life." There it was, Max's aim: living a life worth living. And if this uncharacteristically long, syntactically tortuous sentence hadn't yet done enough work for him, Max restated the basic idea in terms that blurred the political and personal: "To struggle toward aims that you know may or may not be realized, and find a part of your satisfaction in the superior keenness of a life edged and tempered by such struggle, seems a fair mixture of motives." Not just fair, perhaps even beautiful.[52]

In the final chapters of *Stalin's Russia* Max went on to sketch out his own dream for a better, reasonable, equal, humane society, one in which it would be possible, through cooperative effort, compromise, and common sense, to live a keen life. As incompatible as the desire for individual liberty and the needs of the collective might seem, Max in 1940 still hoped that some kind of adjustment or equilibrium between the two could be reached by all those who want to "join hands." What was necessary for such an adjustment was, above all, an unflinching willingness among all involved to face the facts of life, "a cool-purposed and relentlessly hard-visioned, but not bigoted, brutal or cynical condition of mind"—in short, a mind very much like that of Max Eastman. With considerable relief Max noted he was still a radical, if that term meant substituting "for an imported revolutionary metaphysics the attitude of experimental science." What the New Deal had achieved only in "desultory spasms" had to be transformed into a permanent adjustment suited for a society no longer based, as even the Bolshevik workers' paradise was, on the religious and, specifically, Christian model of the family as the basic unit of society. What was needed was "a movement of hard minds." Max imagined an army of clear-thinking, unsentimental activists working for a better future, people who would coolly dismiss, as the socialists once did, the obsolete moral and rationalistic creeds of the past but who were also fully aware, as the socialists had never been, of the fundamental errors in the Marxist faith. Here in the United States one could still find the ideal conditions for a truly democratic experiment—a radical one, in Max's opinion—and that was the most precious thing left to humankind.[53]

The hardness Max mentioned so frequently is, obviously, the firm, steely resolve he desired for himself. For, as he admitted in a moment of moving candor, it was difficult for a man to say that the cause for which he has given his life has failed. But there was one thing he was sure about. If the people around him had not gotten used to the emptiness of sky above them, he had. After he had rid himself of the Christian God of his childhood, and now of Marx, Lenin, and Trotsky, too, Max Eastman could confidently say about himself that he needed no clay gods.[54]

Max's book inspired a lively debate in the newspapers and magazines. The journalist Eugene Lyons, a recovering Marxist like Max, said that reading *Stalin's Russia* was like watching a devout Christian suddenly reexamining the basic tenets of his faith. He noted that Max wasn't a Trotskyist anymore either, if ever he had been one. *Stalin's Russia* left not "a shred of the amoralism common to all the totalitarians, from Lenin down to Stalin, Trotsky and Hitler."[55] Applause came also from John Chamberlain, a former member of the Dewey commission, officially the Committee of Inquiry into Charges Made Against Leon Trotsky in the Moscow Trials, which was chaired by John Dewey and in 1937 exonerated Trotsky of all the charges leveled against him by the Soviet regime. Chamberlain had just begun his own journey toward the political Right and said he was impressed by the scientific rigor Max had brought to his analysis: "Other intellectuals behave these days like bereft and inconsolable prophets: they wail and pound their breasts and cry to the firmament that Jehovah has deserted them." Max, however, instead of licking his spiritual wounds, had taken his defeat, the shattering of his ideals, as a man or, rather, a scientist, should, by immediately thinking about a way forward.[56]

The more critical voices, however, prevailed. The delicious irony of Max's new position dawned on Michael Florinsky, an economics professor at Columbia, who reviewed the book for the *New York Times*. Max was rejecting Trotsky—the same man he had made popular through his "admirable translations"! If you were a believer in Stalin, then the only possible reaction to books like Max's was wistfulness, the sad hope that "somewhere in the background angels hover over Stalin." Max's new proposal for a "scientific radical party" seemed as utopian to Florinsky as Marx's obsolete scheme: "But perhaps a utopian quality and an element of vagueness are essential ingredients of any comprehensive scheme for the salvation of mankind."[57]

The *Nation,* too, disagreed with Max's analysis of the shortcomings of Marxism: if socialism had failed, it was not due to Hegel and bad metaphysics. Marx simply had not understood the impact economic change has on human beings.[58] And the Labor politician Harold Laski complained that Max's critique of Stalinism had ignored the economic backwardness of Russia at the time of the revolution. Difficulties were bound to arise. According to Laski, Max's final call for equilibrium was an expression more of his temperamental longings than of sober political thinking.[59]

A few readers, while not accepting all of Max's analysis, agreed with its general tenor. Elias Tartak, in the *New Leader,* while he regretted that Max had paid no attention to the more "elastic" Marx to be found in the correspondence with Friedrich Engels, welcomed the book's general argument. *Stalin's Russia* was a much-needed, "bold and dexterously written call to men of liberal and Socialist good will to look at Russia, then at Marx, and think, think hard." It should be read and discussed.[60] And in the *Los Angeles Times* Max's friend from the old Hollywood days, Paul Jordan-Smith, supported his claim that Stalin was indeed worse than Hitler. The Moscow trials had driven everybody but the "lunatic fringe" away from the party. Max had reminded everyone it wasn't too late yet for a return to honest thinking and truth telling, a return, in a word, "to the integrities."[61]

Or was it? A few months after the publication of *Stalin's Russia,* on August 20, 1940, Stalin caught up with Leon Trotsky. The blow dealt to Trotsky's head—fittingly as he was reading—by Stalin's assassin Ramón Mercader was, in a sense, a blow also to all attempts to find anything salvageable in the tradition of revolutionary thought Max had worked so hard to keep alive. Max's friend Edmund Wilson, although he took note of Stalin's purges, still wasn't ready to dispatch the Bolsheviks, especially not Lenin, that "most selfless of great men." In September 1940 he published his response to the revolutionary tradition, which he called, evocatively, *To the Finland Station.* As the title suggested, communism still hadn't arrived. The book begins with one of the progenitors of bourgeois revolutionary thought, Jules Michelet, groping for the principles of a new science of history, and it ends with Lenin making history as he is arriving from Finland at that shabby little train station in St. Petersburg, ahead of the October Revolution, making speeches, filling his audience with "turmoil and terror." Wilson's final sentence, a quotation from Lenin's wife, Krupskaya, strikes the reader as ironic given that it comes at the end of a book that was almost five hundred pages long: "Everything was understood without words." Compared to Max's withering analysis of Russian communism, Wilson's still seemed upbeat, forward looking, eager to find meaning in a past that for Max now was nothing but misguided, built on shaky ground.[62]

Just a year later Wilson recanted somewhat, arguing in a short essay that Marxism had in fact reached a point of near eclipse. Marx and Engels, coming out of authoritarian Germany, naturally had imagined socialism in authoritarian terms, too, and Stalin and Trotsky, coming out of an autocracy, inevitably perpetuated what they, in turn, had known, a dictatorship. If this is a weaker argument than Max's, the conclusion of Wilson's piece was taken straight from the final pages of *Stalin's Russia*. Wilson claimed that in order to maintain what is laudable in Marxism—the need to get rid of class privilege based on the accident of birth and wealth—common sense and an "unsleeping exercise of reason and instinct" were needed. Marxist dogma, especially dialectical materialism, was passé, a creed like many others but not Holy Writ. But who wouldn't want to agree with the goal shared by all men and women of good hope, a goal all genuine Marxists had been striving for, "a society which will be homogeneous and cooperative as our commercial society is not, and directed, to the best of their ability, by the conscious and creative effort of its members"? Whether Wilson remembered this or not, these had been Max Eastman's concepts: cooperation, compromise, common sense. In 1950 Wilson reused this piece as the afterword for a new edition of *To the Finland Station*. Now the timing was right, and his book became a success. The year before, the Soviet Union, Bulgaria, Czechoslovakia, Hungary, Poland, and Romania had founded the Council for Mutual Economic Assistance, or Comecon, the most visible expression of Stalin's desire to achieve domination in Central Europe. The postwar divisions of Europe were in place, and Americans were taking notice, too. Max's book, however, was forgotten.[63]

Max's preoccupation with the topic of totalitarianism found its way also into a very different work, a long poem titled *Lot's Wife* on which he had been working since his visit to the Holy Land in the summer of 1932. In 1938, after Harper agreed to publish the poem, Max returned to it with renewed energy, and as he was putting the finishing touches on the manuscript he shared a set of proofs with Wilson, hoping for some additional encouragement.

Lot's Wife is an often bawdy retelling of Lot's escape from Sodom, delivered in a self-consciously folksy idiom Max had crafted for the occasion. Max had intended the work to be a turning point in his development as a poet, and he was dejected when neither his peers nor ordinary readers responded to it the way he had hoped. Praised by some friends and colleagues, among them E. E. Cummings ("your book delights me"), Granville Hicks ("a lot of fun to read"), and Edna St. Vincent Millay ("THE BEST THING YOU EVER DID"), the poem was roundly rejected by many others. To Max's great disappointment Wilson hated it and sent Max pages and pages of pedantic corrections. And Marianne Moore—to borrow a phrase from one of her most famous poems—"too, disliked" it. In a note to Max's publicist she offered to return her copy if the publisher felt its value had not been "impaired by" her reluctant handling of it.[64]

Max was willing to concede that as a poet he had some catching up to do. "My poetry has always been weak and too fluid because I divided myself into a poet and thinker," he admitted to Wilson. "I divided myself up as the Hebrews divide the week, with poetry the Sabbath." His mother had instilled the love of poetry in him, but she had also taught him to regard it as a special thing, "made out of pure feelings purified as though in prayer." Max always worried that this reverence for poetry, as manifested in his preference for fixed forms and meter, had made his forays into the genre sound stilted, removed from real life, self-consciously artsy rather than intuitive. And although he had theorized about humor, his poetry was mostly *not* funny. But in *Lot's Wife* he felt he had achieved the satirical fluidity that had eluded him previously. He had poured himself into these lines, he told Wilson, while also taking care to protect "the integrity and essential proportions of the stream."[65] Wilson, smarting perhaps from having had to play second fiddle to Max in all matters Russian for such a long time, was not convinced.

At first blush, the story Max had chosen for the poem, based on Genesis 13, 18, and 19 and set in the plains of ancient Jordan, was as remote as anything from Max's experience. The biblical Lot, Abraham's nephew and one of the ancestors of Jesus, was a wandering herdsman originally from Chaldea who had ended up in Sodom. Chosen by God's angels, he became the only one to survive a conflagration visited on Sodom by God himself after righteous men could not be found in the entire city. In Max's version, however, Lot is a religious terrorist and misogynist, an uncouth, scheming tyrant who abuses his wife and daughters and, by dint of force and the police, oppresses his fellow citizens. Max had wanted, he explained to his publicist at Harper's, Ramona Herdman, "to bring these old Biblical characters down out of their stained-glass window sanctity and velvety elegance and make them live the coarse rough life they actually lived." He added, "I grew up in a church, you know."[66]

In reimagining the story of Lot, Max took on not only his own religious upbringing but also the legacy of patriarchy he had battled since his adolescence. Yes, the circumstances of Lot's life were as different from his own or that of his contemporaries as one could only imagine:

> My friends who read your Bibles in Elmira,
> That ample valley, orchard-like, with trees
> All cloudy brimming, birds and bees
> And blossoms in the leafiness of these,
> Or you in still more ample Canandaigua—
> More Bible-reading too, there comes the thought,
> For there my father, not my mother, taught—
> You can not know what "city" meant to Lot.

Yet the point of Max's poem is precisely that Pastor Eastman's Canandaigua and Lot's Sodom are not so distant from each other, that when it comes to bigotry and zealousness the two are part of a continuum of intolerance. As much as the Bible-reading citizens of New York State might like to forget, theirs was a desert religion, born in the same unforgiving landscape where Lot ruled the citizens by "divine behest, / His judgments harsh, his proclamations loud, / His cowing down the crowd." Their God was Lot's, too, a "Hill Billy God," as Max acidly observed, come down to the valley to wreak havoc on human health and happiness.[67]

The Canadian humorist Stephen Leacock quipped—and Max proudly used the sentiment as a blurb for the book—that it was questionable whether Max's poem should be put in the hands of anyone under seventy. "But I am seventy-two," he added.[68] One thing was sure: Lot's Wife was not suitable reading material for minors. There is a lot of sex in the poem, though none of it joyful. Max had written a poem not just *about* the desert but *of* the desert, a place where men's and women's desires appear magnified by the stark landscape. In his poetic preface Max evoked his old master Whitman, who had wanted to write a poem as vibrant and candid as the earth itself yet had veiled it in a "slacking vapor." Max's approach was going to be very different. Formal innovation, to him, was not a goal in itself. His end rhymes and irregular iambic pentameters throw into bold relief a story that brims with illicit sex and violence. A hypocrite, Lot publicly condemns sinfulness but secretly relishes it: "Lot knew deep down in him that cities are sin; / He deeper knew them gorgeous to live in." Every night he mounts his thin, pale wife, her sagging, thickly blue-veined body worn down by his "faithfulness," as Max observes sarcastically. Lot possesses his wife, but he does not, as Max makes clear from the beginning, *own* her:

> A smell would waft against her, or a tune,
> And weakly like a weak rope she would give,
> And vow still, still before she died to live;
> But she would gasp and stagger from that sin,
> And drive it back and drive it down and in.
> She fed him forty years of help and hate;
> He wallowed in it blandly and all ate.[69]

Max accomplishes something quite difficult here: mimicking Lot's point of view, re-creating the predatory way he would look at a woman, he allows the woman's perspective to emerge from under the layers of male domination. Lot's daughters, for example, are described as "agate smooth and cool," one being golden and "all curves, gleamy and sleek" while the other one is "bronze down to her bones" and "slim and slender like a whip." Objects of men's desires—and, as Max scandalously suggests, their father's secret lust, too— the daughters don't get the chance to be agents of their own desires. "I would be clean if looking were a brook," one of his daughters observes. At the brutal climax of the poem Lot's wife turns away from him, metaphorically as well as literally. Fleeing from the burning Sodom, swollen with his importance as the chosen ambassador of God's wrath, Lot commands his wife not to look back. But she defies him and, in a powerful speech that sums up some of Max's own most cherished beliefs, delivers Max's version of the Sermon on the Mount: "Life's first commandment is that we should live it, / And life is jealous of all meaner gods." The real price one has to pay for not living one's life to the fullest is not biblical but one exacted by Life itself, the one God Max reveres. For that, Lot kills her, in front of their horrified daughters.[70]

Max's story ends with Lot's daughters, deprived of the right to live their lives the way they want, getting ready to take back what their father wrested from them, by the only means available to them. They drug him so he will be tempted to act out his secret fantasy and have sex with them because they know his guilt over the incest will kill him.

· · ·

In *Lot's Wife* Max's diction is not the smoothly flowing language of the classical epic, but that's his intention. His images are often exaggerated, and his rhymes numbingly predictable ("terror" / "error"), recherché ("this" / "parenthesis"), or cartoonish to the point of being humorous ("torture" / "orchard"). Sometimes they are almost painfully imperfect ("insectlike" / "oblique"). Commented Wilson, after he had taken a first look, "Your rhymes are not much alike at all." Max honestly thought *Lot's Wife* was the best poem he had ever written, and he was hurt when Wilson treated him as if he were a mere novice. When Wilson claimed he had found lots of "metrically impossible" lines and "stop-gap phrases," Max challenged him to make his objections more concrete, so Wilson penciled his comments (sometimes several a page) on the galleys. Wilson also asked a friend of his, the now-forgotten Harvard poet Theodore ("Ted") Spencer, for his views. The marked-up copy went back to Max and has survived: a record of exchanges often acerbic, with Wilson adopting a hectoring tone and Max responding defiantly. This was not Pound, "il miglior fabbro," offering advice to a brilliant peer, as had been the case with Eliot's *Waste Land*. Rather, it was Wilson the schoolmaster scolding a questionably talented student that he had no "ear for verse."[71]

On a single galley sheet, for example, Wilson marked several end rhymes, such as "Elmira," corresponding to "Canandaigua" a few lines down, and "body" / "lobby," and noted, in pencil, that they made him feel as if he had bitten into "lumps of solder in canned French peas."[72] Delayed rhymes, multiple rhymes, and off-rhymes were hard to handle in any poem, and if they were done at all, this had to happen consistently. "You don't seem to have paid any attention to what you were doing with them." On another page Wilson objected to the rhyme "cup" / "up" and called it banal (the "cup" was Max's metaphor for the concentrated excitement of city life, held in one place). Max lost his patience. "What does it mean to say a 'rhyme' is banal? All rhymes are banal," he wrote next to Wilson's comment. Somehow Wilson seemed to be on a personal crusade against him. In a few instances he was plain wrong and didn't really know how certain words were pronounced. The line "Our priest of Baal climbs an empty vat," for example, would seem metrically irregular only to those who thought "Baal" had just one syllable: "Bunny, you don't know how to pronounce Baal! With all your pedagogery!" However, because he feared other readers might have the same problem, Max changed the line anyway, to "Our priestly eagle climbs an empty vat."[73]

What irked Max more than anything was the squabbling about a sentence he regarded as one of the highlights of the poem. Spencer had asked that the second line of the verse "Lot's wife, who had for forty years been dead, / Here for one second lived, here turned her head" be changed to the lackluster "Here lived one second, having turned her head." The line was the inscription Lot's wife wanted to be carved on the pillar of salt that would commemorate her moment of rebellion; it was an evocation of the second for which Max's entire poem existed, a second made eternal through art. Lot's wife became a poet at that point, and it seemed crucially important to Max that her first and final act of rebellion not be veiled in a participle. "Ted Spencer's comments . . . I call quadrupedestrian," Max told Wilson. "You say he is a poet, but I judge him by his tracks to be a wingless one."[74]

Max found Wilson's and Spencer's criticisms harder to take than the predictable pans the poem received in the mainstream press. The *Nation* called it "a vulgar performance," suitable for inclusion in the pages of Hearst's *Sunday American*.[75] The *Washington Post* lamented that none of Max's characters seemed to be able to rise from the muck their author had placed them in, especially Lot's wife, who, despite bouts of rebellion, chose to become "an obelisk of sodium chloride on the forsaken desert of Palestine" rather than turning around her pigheaded husband.[76]

Yet some critics actually understood the poem. For example, Max was delighted by a review in the *New York Times* written by John Chamberlain, who attributed the provocative explicitness of the poem to Max's temperament, which was bound to rub certain readers, especially the ascetic radicals among them, the wrong way. Max's "mournful companions" had never been able to reconcile a "passionate interest in Lenin with an equally passionate delight in swimming at a Black Sea beach resort." Rebelling against a philosophy "which would put artists into uniform and banish simple pleasure in food, exercise and sun to the sky where you get pie when you die," Max had turned a crude biblical story into something more at home in the world of Hellenic paganism.[77] And Max's friends at the *Vineyard Gazette*, while admitting the "toxicity" of this material, compared the poem's cleansing effect on the reader to something that would have been instantly familiar to all Islanders, including, of course, Max himself: "It is a little like stepping gingerly into cold sea water, and then discovering the bracing qualities of a swim on a spring or autumn day."[78]

Confusingly, though, most reviewers seemed to express their view of Max's poem by *not* writing about it. In the *New Leader* Hendrik Willem van Loon named the elephant in the room. Van Loon, for one, had liked *Lot's Wife*, "one of the most outstanding works of literary perfection of our time," a poem he would not swap "for a dozen MacLeishes or Eliots." But other reviewers were apparently afraid readers would buy the book and then complain to their bosses about Max's immorality. And so they probably had said to themselves, "Suppose we put it aside and tell ourselves that we have not yet found anyone entirely suitable for this difficult job. As it is, the market is being flooded with new books. We can always claim that they come first. By and by, Max East-man's *Lot* will be old stuff and then we can tell him that it is too late now to do anything about his work." And thus one of the finest pieces of literary crafts-manship had been sunk, consigned to oblivion by souls too timid for their jobs.[79]

Neither Wilson nor the critics had understood the contemporary signifi-cance of Max's poem. Its chief character was the epitome of the tyrant, Hitler and Stalin rolled into one terrifying package. Lot exemplified Stalin's misog-yny, his treatment of women as machines producing cannon fodder, and his hillbilly roots—he is a mere "boarder" or "immigrant" in the city he sought to dominate—hinted at the modest origins of the Georgian-born Joseph Stalin and the Austrian-born Adolf Hitler. Even after the Hitler–Stalin alliance had collapsed and Germany had invaded Russia, Max held fast to his belief that Hitler and Stalin were two sides of the same coin, that defeating one meant containing the other one, too. The pact had reinforced his sense that the United States had a responsibility to stem the tide of totalitarianism, even if that meant violence. In July 1941 the Rand School Press, the printing outlet of the socialist Tamiment Institute, published, as a stapled little pamphlet, Max's *Letter to Americans,* in which Max was as unambiguous as anyone could have wanted him to be about the American need for intervention. The former anti-militarist had come a long way: "If Hitler wins this war totalitarianism will triumph over democracy throughout the world." Max saw the current political situation as a war between two ways of life, democracy and totalitarianism, a choice so stark it hadn't been seen before in history, not in the wars fought between Babylon and Judah, Egypt and Assyria, or Athens and Sparta. He supported his argument with a listing of twenty-one chief traits of totalitarian-ism. Condensing it into one sentence, the *New York Times* immediately picked up Max's message: "A study of this list should convince even the most con-firmed non-interventionist where our interest and our duty lie."[80]

At just about the same time, Max's official and final break with the Ameri-can Left occurred, too—as the result of an accident. Max had no money. And he had lost his following among American readers. Even though *Stalin's*

Russia had been translated into three languages, sales were sluggish, and his royalties barely exceeded the advance he had collected. Desperate about his lack of income, Max had sent, at the suggestion of his agent, an uncontroversial biographical essay about his mother to *Reader's Digest,* hoping it would qualify for their rubric "My Most Unforgettable Character." Max the linguist hated the label—how could anything be "*most* unforgettable"? Either you forget it or you don't—but he sent the piece anyway. Within two days DeWitt "Wally" Wallace, the founder and editor in chief of the *Digest,* called him up. He was impressed. They met, and Wally instantly asked him to write a series of essays to be called "The Art of Life." Max, remembering his literary beginnings, dug up his old piece "On the Folly of Growing Up," published long ago in the *Christian Register,* and sent it to the *Digest's* offices in Pleasantville, New York. Wally liked it but wanted something more practical. Max reworked it, made it worse, and it was rejected. Desperate for income, Max proposed a series about "Men with Ideas." That proposition appealed to Wally, and he offered him the position of "roving editor": an annual retainer or "pension" of $10,000 with an expense account in exchange for getting the first option on anything Max wrote, and separate payment for each article that was accepted. "I don't know what writer, who had been struggling along making his living with lectures and finding it harder and harder to do, would have turned down such a millennial offer," Max wrote later. And while the promised "pension" was, after Wally's initial burst of enthusiasm had subsided, quickly forgotten, Max's payment for articles could be substantial if Wally liked them, up to $5,000 apiece.[81]

The essay that ultimately cemented Max's association with Wally's magazine was not about great men and their good ideas. Instead, it dealt with what Max was now convinced had been a very bad idea from the beginning. Chatting with Wally, Max casually mentioned he had just written something expressing his new views on socialism. Wally, a dyed-in-the-wool anticommunist, jumped at the opportunity and accepted the piece, along with the article about Annis. In "Socialism and Human Nature," Max, relying on his reading of Freud, argued that visions of an earthly paradise ignored basic human drives— Freud's "id," which so appropriately resonated with the American pronoun "it." Wally made the rather clever editorial decision to publish both of Max's articles in the same issue, with Max's tribute to Annis immediately preceding his put-down of socialism. Thus, the earlier, softer piece set the stage for the attack that followed by presenting Max and, by implication, his political opinions as the product of his mother's sage counsel. "Be an individual," the reader learned Annis had taught her son. "Conformity with the crowd is beautiful until it involves sacrifice of a principle." And: "It is much more important to stand up straight than to understand Latin." There was only one problem. While Max had seen proofs of the socialism article, he had not been told about the new title the magazine had invented: "Socialism Doesn't Jibe with Human Nature." And he did not know about the endorsement they had solicited from Wendell Willkie, the presidential candidate of the Republican Party.[82] These editorial decisions, more than anything Max had said or written before, finalized his rupture with his former comrades. While many of them had long seen Max headed for the "imperialist war camp," Max's defection to *Reader's Digest* added a strange twist to that story. The devotee of the exhilarating freedom afforded by the enjoyment of poetry had become a hired hack. Agreeing to write for Wally meant making a pact with the devil, if an affable, immaculately dressed one, a preacher's kid, just as Max had been one.[83]

Wally, a hard drinker, was relentless, direct, crude. His *Reader's Digest* empire, which he ran jointly with his wife, Lila, was based on the simple idea that Americans mostly didn't like to read and that, if they did, they wanted to do so without being distracted by unnecessary detail, complicated arguments, or an author's idiosyncratic style. Wally's pocket-sized magazine mixed inspirational tales about the lives of the great with human interest stories, useful information on such topics as "Is Your Child's School Safe from Fire?," self-help articles, and conservative propaganda, all leavened with jokes, anecdotes, and uplifting quotations, the kinds of fillers that became a *Reader's Digest* trademark. If articles were drawn from other publications, Wally and his editors worked to simplify them; if the piece was produced in-house, the staff edited it. The result was, in the words of Richard Lingeman, "the magazine equivalent of Campbell's condensed tomato soup." Not all about *Reader's Digest* was bad news, though. The series "Life in These United States," a perhaps inadvertent Whitman echo, gave voice to heartwarming, funny, and strange stories from the lives of ordinary readers. Max would have liked Wally's somewhat relaxed approach to a topic of perennial interest to him, namely, human sexuality. *Reader's Digest* advocated birth control, though within the confines of marriage, and specialized in sometimes humorous advice on relationships and even what was decorously referred to as lovemaking.[84]

It didn't really matter, in the end, what kind of argument Max made publicly or privately to justify his servitude to Wally, whether it was the chance to reach an audience of more than seventy million readers, a forum to educate his readers about the evils of communism, or, simply, the money. One thing was certain: when he began to work for the *Digest* his writing life took a different turn. At least initially Max was the "king's favorite." Wally was, he felt, in love with him. In reality, this meant researching and writing about four articles a year in the "simplified and hastily-readable style," at once condensed and diluted, that had become Wally's hallmark. Mathematically, this didn't seem like much, but the psychological pressure, the sheer knowledge that Wally owned him, interfered with Max's sense of himself as a proud individualist. Cummings humorously called his friend a "demi-prostitute."[85] But Max himself, in a letter to Florence Norton, his longest-serving secretary, identified his *Digest* work as what he really thought it was—"slavery."[86] Unimpressed by Max's track record as a writer, Wally had no trouble rejecting articles Max was proud of, and he never hesitated to challenge him if he was overspending his expense account. Thus Max ultimately always complied with Wally's expectations.

In his capacity as roving editor Max, over the years, would write about every topic under the sun, from Robert Burns to microbes in the soil. He interviewed a zoo director, a former president of the Audubon Society, the queen of Greece, and the president of Mexico. And Max's "slavery" had many sweet aspects, too: besides giving him a modicum of financial security, working for the *Digest* allowed him to travel to Germany, France, Italy, Norway, Spain, and Ireland. And he did not entirely renounce his former interests. For example, after the opening fanfare of his socialism article, Max turned to a topic well familiar to him. "What We Laugh At—and Why," published in April 1943, gave Max a chance to advertise *Enjoyment of Laughter* while proving he had mastered the magazine's tone. Intended for the average reader, the article was almost entirely written in the second person ("A joke is not a thing, but a process, a trick you play on the listener's mind"). And while there was some theorizing, Max relied on accessible imagery to make his point: "Making a joke is like swinging the listener's mind out toward its natural home in a meaning, and just as it is about to arrive there, playfully yanking it back."[87]

There was a lot of such yanking back in Max's dealings with the *Digest*'s editorial staff, but none of it was playful. Writing for Wally was surprisingly hard work. It involved countless revisions, lengthy consultations with research assistants, and humiliating visits to Pleasantville.[88] At the end, more often than not, the article into which Max had put so much work was rejected anyway. It just wasn't right for the readers. But Max kept telling himself he was doing something really important.[89]

•   •   •

In the short term, the money he received from the *Digest* came in handy indeed. Beginning in 1928, the summer of Crystal's final illness, Max and Eliena had been spending more and more time on Martha's Vineyard, where they fell in love with one location especially, Scitha Hill in the Lobsterville area of Gay Head, or, as it is now known, after its old Wampanoag name, Aquinnah. Newly flush after his *Word Game* extravaganza, Max purchased the site for $4,300 (he paid $500, and the rest came from a banker who had heard him on the radio) and began building a new home there for Eliena and himself. Gay Head was a kind of seaside version of Croton, with the added advantage that it was even less accessible than any of Max's previous summer residences. To ensure this remained so and in order to "preserve the view," Max also acquired the lots around the house, amounting to ninety acres. He got the land "for a song," according to the Eastman family lawyer. It became one of the smartest investments Max ever made—in 2001, when the property, now down to twenty-three acres, was appraised, it was estimated to be worth close to nine million dollars.⁹⁰

Their new home, at 17 East Pasture Road, was in a section of the Vineyard that gave them what is still the best view on the island, shielded by scrubby trees, overlooking Menemsha Pond, and with access, albeit via a winding path and a now-crumbling boardwalk, to a private, pebbly beach. Even today the house can be reached only by a rough dirt road, made even bumpier by protruding gnarly roots, which would have kept everyone away who hadn't been invited to visit. Nailed to a tree was a hand-painted sign, still there today, pointing guests to "East Pasture." Max's new paradise, rural without the work a farm required, was a leisurely reincarnation—more perfect than the Croton house ever was, rendered rugged by the ocean air—of Glenora, the utopian refuge of Max's youth and early adulthood.

Eliena and Max replaced the original structure on the property with a house of their own design built by the local builder Roger Allen (fig. 41). The main house contained Max's study, a kitchen, a living room, a bedroom, and a bathroom on the ground floor with two additional bedrooms and ample storage space in the attic. When he sat at his desk, painted a rustic green, with a framed portrait of Annis on the wall and a large copy of *Webster's Dictionary* on a stand right underneath it, Max would have been able to see in the distance the old fishing village of Menemsha, now infamous for having served as the backdrop for the movie *Jaws*.

The house was simple but functional. The wood paneling throughout the interior made it more comfortable as well as rugged looking. The walls were

Figure 41. Eliena and Frosting in front of their Vineyard
house. From color transparency. 1950s. EMIIA1.

lined with books, some of them by friends and lovers of Max, such as Florence
Deshon, whose Keats editions sat on the shelves in the living room. Somewhat
incongruously for a house inhabited by two atheists, a copy of Giovanni Belli-
ni's *Madonna Adoring the Sleeping Child,* painted by Eliena at the Metropolitan
Museum, hung over the mantelpiece. In 1942 Max sold his beloved Croton
house to "old Doc Gross," a local orthodontist, and he did so knowing that
while he had given up one wonderful house "on top of the world" he had
found another.[91]

Aquinnah was one of the earliest whaling sites in the United States. Many
Wampanoag still lived there, and Max would come to befriend some of them.
The communist pastoral of Max's early years, his city upon a hill, had given
way to an ancient fisherman's paradise, an island reachable only by ferry and
inhabited by people who'd rather be left to their own devices. The Islander
mentality suited Max and Eliena just fine. Eliena continued to work as a

painter, raised chickens, planted vegetables, and, with increasing facility, typed her husband's manuscripts. Her animals were excited when Max's work was going well, too: she was beginning to be smothered under "personal eggs," reported Eliena, whose hens, especially the "shiny-feathered" Rhode Island Reds she had bought, enlivened the drab Vineyard landscape in unexpected ways, like "beautiful flowers."[92] A menagerie of pets took the place of the family Max had actively avoided having. When he was traveling Max would sometimes address his letters home to one of his cats or to his large white collie, Frosting. And on those rarer occasions when Eliena was away, he would send her letters pretending to be Frosting or, again, a cat. Max's marriage to Eliena, more or less accidentally begun and, at least by him, often only loosely adhered to, had become a success story of sorts. It gave comfort to them both.

The Eastmans built a studio for Eliena with two additional rooms, a large bedroom in the back and a smaller attic space on top, as well as a garage for their car. Eliena's warm, engaging manner and Max's large circle of friends ensured that she didn't run out of commissions. In a journal passage he shared with Max after Eliena's death, Cummings described what it was like to pose for Eliena in 1949. Sitting on a chair on the dais in her tiny studio while Eliena was painting his portrait, he would hear her muttering things, to herself as well as to him, "to make me less grim & more cheerful" and to "bring out of the posing effigy a myself." And what he could understand was extraordinary, a small little poem in the making: "Why don't you feel like a swallow, who comes s-woo-ping up into the sky, because she is so per-fectly happy because everything's wonderful & new, because it's spring & she has her babies." To Cummings, this was the essence of what it meant to be an artist. The artist feels "what IS": not an abstract concept such as "spring" but a bird and then "not merely a bird but a mother & therefore all joy & all mystery." She should have had children, observed Marion Cummings drily when he told her about Eliena's little act. Well, responded Cummings, he couldn't "say or gainsay." But as an artist didn't Eliena have children without having them? All experiences were available to her, as was apparent in her dancing, too, even in a drab structure like the Gay Head town hall. Etched in his memory was Eliena's impersonation of a faun coming to life after swooning, which she did "with a rapt solar psychic vitality" that affected everyone in the house. "Extraordinary human being!"[93]

As a painter Eliena was, no doubt, a traditionalist. As if modernism had never happened, her paintings were representational, marked by vigorous brushstrokes and splashes of color to indicate plasticity. Her landscapes were bathed in sunshine. Her light handling of the brush allowed her to achieve, in her best work, almost pastel-like effects. Perhaps because she so much enjoyed being with people, her portraits often sparkle with wit and insight. A good example is a beautiful oil painting of Max, which still hangs on the wall of her old Vineyard studio (fig. 42). It gives a vivid sense of the post-middle-age Max in one of his more contemplative moods. Max's gaze is turned inward, his head cocked at a slight angle that is echoed by his tie, creating the image of a mind in motion even when the body is at rest. Eliena's subtle modeling of Max's facial features with the help of dabs of color highlights the complexity of his character, one that simple outlines could never capture.

There was no inward turn for Max where American politics was concerned. From his island hill he was now launching ever more frequent attacks on what he saw as a gradual communist takeover of American media. If the Hitler–Stalin pact had presented him with an opportunity to ratchet up his campaign against totalitarianism abroad, the gradual rapprochement between Roosevelt and Stalin following the German invasion of Russia forced his attention back on what he had long criticized as the excessive American tolerance of communism. There was no detail of alleged communist infiltration that escaped his attention. And he fought back vehemently when he felt people were attacking *him*.

In public and private letters growing in length and often shrillness Max rejected what he regarded as the lies that had been spread about him by the "most efficient and unscrupulous propaganda machine except perhaps for Hitler's."[94] His misguided support of Hermann Krebs, aka Jan Valtin, a Gestapo agent posing as a refugee and the author of the fraudulent autobiography *Out of the Night*, didn't help his public image. Rather than defining leftist opinion, as he had once done, Max spent an extraordinary amount of time defining and defending his own position. He never tired of saying he was not anti-Russian. Rather, he was "anti-tyranny, anti-totalitarian, anti-lies, hypocrisy, assassination, and judicial murder." At the same time, he adamantly denied being an activist, as Crystal had been: "I am, alas, truly a writer." But he also insisted that Crystal, were she alive today, would be fighting the same fight he carried on through his writing. She would, he said, devote "every ounce of her energy" to making it known to the world that there were "upwards of 10 million slaves" dying in the concentration camps of the Soviet Union.[95]

Figure 42. Eliena Krylenko Eastman, *Max Eastman*. Oil on canvas. Eliena Eastman's studio, Martha's Vineyard.

Activist or not, Max was now more publicly visible than ever, doing Town Hall meetings for the radio in which he warned about the "Russian" danger. To Eliena and the other members of his little household he was a star, the knight in shining armor embarked on rescuing the world from totalitarian collapse. Dog, housekeeper plus baby, and Eliena huddled in the car to listen to Max on the radio taking on his former socialist brothers-in-arms, such as the "asinine" Dr. Laidler. Despite the nasty winds that rocked the car, the reception was good, and they could hear Max loud and clear, "almost without any static."[96] Eliena believed Max could do no wrong, and some of the people who listened to Max's anti-Stalinist rants agreed: "Your warnings should be re-broadcast on every station," wrote one C. E. Alamshah from Chicago.[97] But for every new friend he made Max was losing dozens of old ones. "I wish you would stop writing for the Reader's Digest and write for Max Eastman," complained the poet Carl Sandburg. Called a renegade, a reactionary, a fascist, Max felt increasingly frazzled, though he took comfort in the fact that, as he believed, he had always stayed true to his one goal, "a fight for liberty, and especially liberty for the working-classes." This was, he informed Sandburg, "exactly the same fight I was on the old Masses and the Liberator."[98] What used to be the Left had become a bunch of "muddle-heads and mush-heads," he told Joe O'Carroll when he reconnected with him in 1947. "It seemed inconceivable that you would support tyranny and slave labor in the name of liberty and the triumph of the working class." His increasing isolation had become inevitable: "So many that I trusted and believed in have made that torturous retroversion, twisting their mind, will and conscience without blanching or losing a pound of weight— indeed they are all on the plump side." Still as trim as he had been in his Village days, Max found himself alone, as the list of those that weren't his friends anymore kept growing: "Elizabeth Flynn, Bill Foster, Mike Gold, Bob Minor." His former colleagues had, Max felt, "betrayed—and, alas—even refuted the revolution," and they had done so for the comfort of clinging to something they could believe in. Being publicly denounced as a renegade was worse—and now Max was remembering the Masses trials—than "it was to be prosecuted as a traitor to my country in the old days."[99]

A note Max typed in September 1944 suggests how deeply his private despair and the loss of his political bearings were intertwined, how uncomfortable it was for the ex-socialist to find himself warning his fellow countrymen about the danger coming from what he had once himself embraced. He had spent a few hours looking over his old editorials in the Masses ("futile and diffuse"), and when he went to bed afterward he had a terrible nightmare. He found himself kneeling "before a statue of some great man like Milton, tight-lipped, dressed all in black, seated with arms outstretched as though at ease on a cross. I touched the rough back pediment of the statue. 'He even molded his own frames,' I said. I bowed my head down on the flagstone under him and wept." In his dream he saw Eliena coming to his rescue, as she always did in his waking life. "Malyutochka, what is it?" "I'm all right," Max smiled, still dreaming. "Don't worry. I'll get up and go on." But Eliena persisted, and so Max told her: "Eliena, I am sure I was meant to do something great. I am absolutely sure I was meant to do something great." When Max finally woke up he was bathed in tears, "for that is not only my deepest, but my most present sorrow: I have wasted my talents."[100]

9 • Max in Purgatory

While Max was clamoring for military intervention, his son Dan was washing dishes and cutting down trees at Civilian Public Service Camp #32 in West Compton, New Hampshire. As a conscientious objector, he was now sharing his life with a motley group of men that included Jehovah's Witnesses, lawyers from New York, Harvard professors, a violinist, and an insurance salesman, "the best man so far," as he wrote in a letter to Marion Morehouse Cummings. He felt like an "overactive member of an Eagle Scout troop." Hard labor, to be sure, was no "mental stimulant." He wanted to get out of camp desperately so that he might spend "every spare minute in some cozy bar or among congenial friends, or just lying on my back breathing my own air instead of gov't air."[1] Daniel Eastman, CPS worker 002431, was released on March 3, 1942, having served almost ten months.[2]

Max did not know what to make of his son's opposition to the war. As he saw it, Dan had returned home from camp with the distinct feeling that he was "superior in intelligence" to the rest of the world. Undoubtedly true, said his father in a letter to Dan's mother, Ida, but "so are you and I." Max was responding directly to an argument Ida had made previously that Dan was so pure that he should be given money just for the fact of his existence. Whenever he was angry Max's capacity for sarcasm got the better of him, and his prose soared. But Max's quip hid a deeper concern for a son who had never finished growing up, who was bouncing from idea to idea and from job to job and who now, in his thirties, found himself without all the things he kept saying he really wanted: a "place in the world," a steady source of income, children. Encouraged by Cummings, who Max said knew as much about thinking "as a nightingale knows about swimming," Dan had embarked on a quest for "literary truth" and now wanted to be a writer. The only problem: he wasn't writing anything. Not that there was anything wrong with just living one's life. That was indeed enough, but one had to do it well, do it greatly—which meant living it like Max did.[3]

The title of Max's autobiography-in-progress reflected precisely what Max felt his son obviously lacked, *Enjoyment of Living*. Ironically, Max the great life-enjoyer now needed Dan's help, since his editor at Harper's feared legal reprisals, especially from Ida. Dan obliged, read his father's manuscript, and, to Max's relief, saw "nothing that he thinks injurious to his mother in it."[4] What a convoluted situation this was: Max found himself relying on the opinion of the son in whose life he had played a marginal role as his justification for saying uncomfortable things about the wife he had abandoned. Max showed the manuscript to others and then wrote to Ida, reassuring her that "comparative strangers" also thought she was a "fine and noble character" in the book. Ida replied, caustically, that she wasn't a fine and noble character even in her own eyes: "Why not refer to our marriage, (if you feel you must refer to it) as an experiment which did not result in a permanent relationship? Is it necessary to justify yourself to the public or to justify me?" Ida remembered the terms of their original marriage contract better than Max did. The magnanimity of her letter is striking. Referring to Dan's struggles, for example, she did not place blame on Max entirely, as would have been easy for her to do: "He *has* problems, partly but not entirely due I think to certain elements in his childhood years, and also to the confusion in my own life. What more is there to say?"[5]

As he was working on his autobiography Max lumbered into a close, agonizingly intense relationship with his secretary, Florence Norton, a young, fresh-faced woman with dark, shoulder-length hair and beautiful white teeth, whom he had met during one of his lecture tours in Norfolk, Virginia, almost ten years earlier (fig. 43). The daughter of a minister who headed a large rescue mission in Norfolk, Florence was twenty-five when their paths crossed again, and almost painfully thin (her lack of appetite became a constant topic in their correspondence). Living in New York City, penniless and embroiled in a rocky relationship with a man from Switzerland, Florence one day showed up during a gathering at the house of Max's neighbor Doris Stevens and promptly fell for Max. He gave her some work to type and promised to help her get over her unreliable boyfriend, a task he seems to have taken so seriously that he got her pregnant. Norton's journal shows that Max didn't take the news well. When she asked for his help, Max provided a doctor's address

Figure 43. Max Eastman and
Florence Norton. From color
transparency, 1950s. EMIIA1.

but otherwise became "hysterical" and essentially abandoned her. Florence underwent a painful, nauseating abortion, without anesthesia, while Max kept out of sight in Croton.[6]

Five years later, however, she was working for Max once again, this time paid out of *Reader's Digest* funds. Now a student at Columbia, she typed Max's letters and manuscripts when she wasn't attending classes, helping him with his autobiography as well as *Reader's Digest* assignments. Typically, Max would dictate a first draft of an essay or a chapter and then revise Florence's typescript by hand, leaving it to her to produce the cleaned-up version. He set her up with a room in the same building on West Thirteenth Street, where he and Eliena had taken an apartment, as well as with a small house, The Brink, close to his own on the Vineyard.[7] During Florence's off-hours, when circumstances allowed and Max was able to slip away from Eliena's side, he went down to be, as Florence decorously put it in her journal, "friendly" with her. In addition to her secretarial duties Florence went shopping for the Eastmans, took care of their pets, gave them rides to the airport, and looked after their apartment when they were gone.

Florence's journals give us an intimate look at Max's unconventional and often vexed life during those years, a time when other men of similar age begin to settle down. Serenity would not have been a desirable state of mind for Max if he had been able to choose. But Florence's journals also reveal the terrible price Eliena, racked by feelings of humiliation and outbursts of jealousy, paid for continuing to stand by her husband. One of the chilliest entries in Florence's journal captures her view of Eliena entering the elevator in Max's building, headed for the airport and then on to DC, where she was going to help Max with some research at the Library of Congress. Her head wrapped in an unbecoming scarf, Eliena looked forlorn and pathetic like a child. "The tragedy is that she is not a child." While childlikeness was becoming in girls under twenty, observed Florence mercilessly, it was a bore in anyone older.[8]

In one form or another Max's relationship with Florence, which he kept carefully hidden from public view, lasted for more than two decades. It would be wrong to assume that Florence was merely the victim in this arrangement. Max provided her with much-needed income and a place to stay, and it was her association with him that later helped her get jobs as an assistant editor at *Reader's Digest* and as managing editor of the *Freeman* and the *American Mercury*.[9] She was powerfully attracted to him. Her journal entries from the 1940s evoke the fresh smell of his hair, his bronze skin, his tenderness, his timeless beauty. He was the "mountain whose beauty and majesty" she admired from the "valley" of her existence. "Max came down fragrant with sunshine and fresh wind-blown air," she noted after Max had just returned to New York from the Vineyard. After dropping him off at the airport for one of his frequent trips to the Vineyard, she gushed, "Max looked extremely beautiful when I left him." He was Apollo reincarnated, his body "exquisite in its proportions," "strong and delicate in its beauty," while his head, with its "wonderful defiant-free-casual tilt," looked resplendent against the blue sky.[10] Indeed, Max had a lot to offer Florence, apart from money, which was never lavish, and sex, which often left her sadder than she was before. There are touching entries in her diaries that describe the intellectual excitement he generated in her, descriptions of mornings in New York when she would sally forth to her Columbia classes with "glowing thoughts of Max." Max edited her term papers, engaged her in intellectual discussions, and appreciated her advice on his writing. He was the first person in her life to make her really care about thinking, she said, "and because thinking is the highest attainment and limitless in its potentialities, this seems to me a wondrous thing he has done for me. I felt—I do yet—that he has the priceless gift of the teacher in this esteem he has for thinking, and I wondered how great a teacher he might have been if he could have stayed as he is and remained a professor." Being with Max was not a one-way street, then: "I thought, too, how few people in my life have added something important like this to the development and growth of my self, and that he is the first man who gave me this something."[11]

Through Max she met interesting people, not only his new political allies but also musicians like Jascha Heifetz and Yehudi Menuhin, the latter a kind of younger version of Max, like him possessed of "beauty of body, intellect, curiosity, and love of health and physical vitality." She promptly fell in love with Menuhin. Her diary records magical moments on the Vineyard, "the shining quiet stretches of water all around us." During Heifetz's visit to the Vineyard, listening to records chosen by him while sitting outside under the stars, wrapped in a big blanket, Florence would sit with Max's head resting on her shoulder and felt transformed: "In the melodic darkness he seemed to me very young, a soft-haired boy, and I rather the older one, partly the parent."[12]

But such intimate moments were offset by others in which Florence insisted on her independence. Sexually active before she had met Max, she was ill-suited for the role of the compliant mistress. And while she realized and was often despondent about her dependent role in Max's life, she never lost her wit even if her other senses were clouded by the centripetal force of Max's beauty: "I love you and admire you and think you are a wonderful writer—especially on the subject of Max!" Sarcastically, she referred to Max's cottage on the Vineyard as the "Big House." Frequent fights, sometimes over trivialities, sometimes over money, were regularly followed by furtive lovemaking in the middle of the night, after which things seemed fine, until the next eruption. Add to that Eliena's frustration, which she would vent when Max was not around, and one gets a sense of the daily chaos surrounding Max. No serenity for him and really not much "enjoyment of living" either. Florence summarized the deadly triangle of the Eastman household and the options before them succinctly: "We three are full of passions; we can weed them or not, be animals or civilized." It seems, though, that instead they all opted for a state of permanent in-betweenness, in which bouts of anger and passion alternated with periods of pretending that all was fine. It would have been hard for outsiders to understand the emotional arrangements that had to be made, by everyone involved, so that Florence would be able to attend one of Eliena's popular dance classes in the morning and then sleep with Eliena's husband at night.[13]

Max himself was not sure how to account for his feelings toward Florence, finding himself gripped once again by the "throat-parching turmoils and agonies of adolescence." Weren't those hormonal bursts of longing supposed to die down "to a seemly calm at about the age of twenty-three or -four"? In a fragment that somehow ended up among Florence's papers, Max launched a frantic attempt at self-analysis, as he had done before when faced with a crisis that refused to go away. He began by offering a sobering assessment of his ridiculous situation: "I am sixty-five years old, and for five years I have been growing, with interludes of short duration, more and more in love with my secretary, Florence." Even more urgently than with Creigh he was looking for what he had lost or what he feared he was about to lose. Florence Norton was Florence Wyckoff, Crystal Eastman, and Florence Deshon all wrapped into one: "Florence is brown-eyed; her skin is rosey dark. She is the color of my sister, the color of my first Florence (no, it was my second!) whom I loved in utter rapture for the eternal span of a year and a half. Her hair is the same brown and grows so beautifully on her body that I think of those shaded parts of her as a worshipper of his shrine with the god's presence." Max's complicated desire for this new Florence made him, as he admitted, "insanely jealous," not only physically but also mentally: "I have never been able to, and I have since adolescence fervently determined not to, separate body and spirit in any experience, no matter how trivial or how sublime." Now he was facing the inevitable decline of his virility, and while he wanted Florence for himself, she obviously had no intention of restricting herself to Max.[14]

In that same document, hastily typed on yellow paper, with many passages crossed or x'ed out, he confronted his situation with both despair and self-irony: "The decline of my rather abnormal drive to make love to any and every attractive girl has been a dreadful thing to me, a loss of some sustained and sure value in life." A drive that had remained strong, Max went on, inadvertently switching to the present tense, "because I am attractive enough, and humble enough in my adoration of beauty, so that it is not very often frustrated if I set out to satisfy it." But satisfaction had never been the point of Max's quest. Rather, it had been the "continual upspringing lusty desire that kept me happy" when, for example, he would sit "in a café window, or at a little table on the sidewalk in Paris watching the girls go by," in ecstasy over the very fact that he was filled with such "powerful and never-failing" longing for physical contact. Now, in his beginning old age, just thinking about Florence was not enough; his desire needed her presence, "if not her touch," to be aroused: "I rarely awake in the night in my own lonely bed filled with erotic desire as I used to." Of all the things that had befallen him in life, this apparent loss of his libido was the worst, the one that was the most difficult to bear. Old men simply weren't explorers: "Don't you see the sadness in the eyes of all old men—even those who chirp 'It doesn't matter how old you are, you're as old as you think you are'—trying to cover with this sparrow song the symphony of gloom in their hearts"? Max did try to talk himself into believing that his ongoing affair with Florence, because of the professional advantages it had brought him ("No writer ever had a more perfect friend," he said), had left his love for Eliena, his "co-partner in everything I own," basically intact. But he knew that was not the case, and rather than confronting the problem he ended by attributing Eliena's hostility to menopausal depression, a passing phase, then.

But his relationship with Florence was not about to end. In September 1945 she was pregnant again. Aborting that child felt terrible this time. Max was being sweet to her now, not as callous as the last time. After her return from New York, where she had undergone the operation, Florence's nights were haunted by dreams. In a particularly memorable one Eliena had adopted a golden-haired, blue-eyed baby and allowed her to hold it in her arms, a "wonderful feeling." But the days weren't much easier to get through. On the Columbia campus Florence picked up a wounded pigeon, fussing over it as if it were a rare species, and even carried it to the zoology lab—all "because I need a baby so." Had it not been for "Eliena's opposition to me and to it," she would have never given up Max's child. Even Max admitted to having been "very sad thinking of the baby and how lovely it would have been." But he returned to Eliena again, playing the devoted husband and shunning Florence, "for he cannot be the knight in attendance upon more than one lady at a time." But maybe he was being nice to Eliena just so that he could keep Florence? Florence liked to think so, and yet she also keenly felt her "apartness" from him.[15]

Evidently Florence's portfolio encompassed so much more than typing for Max (and loving him, to boot). When Claude McKay suffered a stroke in the winter of 1943 it was Florence who went to visit him in Milford, Connecticut, where he was recuperating in a cabin Max and others had managed to secure for him. McKay was deeply grateful that Max had sent her, writing to him,

"You gave me a new lease of life."[16] Again through Florence, Max subsequently got him out of the YMCA in New York into an apartment on Long Island, but the room was too cold and the stove leaked. Now Claude turned around and declared that Miss Norton had "no understanding of the Negro world."[17]

Never easy to take care of, Claude was now severely depressed, and his mental state exacerbated his physical decline. A few years earlier the publisher Dutton had enlisted Max's help in whipping Claude's novel-in-progress, tentatively titled *God's Black Sheep*, into presentable form.[18] The story played among radical "Aframericans" (McKay's preferred term) and even involved a Comintern agent being hurled from a Harlem roof. Max had read the first few chapters and offered advice, but Claude chafed under the arrangement and simply went ahead and finished the book. John Macrae at Dutton was not amused: "You have failed to take advantage of Mr. Max Eastman's valuable and competent aid. I regret GOD'S BLACK SHEEP is so bad and so poor that I cannot offer you any hope of its being revised in a satisfactory way to meet what I believe a novel by you must be." Claude was crushed.[19]

"Battered, ready for the scrap heap," without a predictable income and effective medical care, McKay found it difficult to write.[20] Ultimately he sought relief in the arms of the Roman Catholic Church, a move that sincerely disappointed Max: if he had successfully resisted Stalin, why now warp his mind for the Catholics?[21] When, four years later, Selma Burke sent a telegram to tell Max that Claude had died of heart failure in a Chicago hospital, Eliena coldly observed that he had "stopped living years ago." But Max was still holding on to his earlier image of the shining Prince of the Revolution, the only black man among the Bolsheviks: "Poor Claude! It is hard to imagine him dying!"[22] For McKay's *Selected Poems*, published in 1953, Max provided a biographical note in which he praised his dead friend as "that rarest of earth's wonders, the true-born lyric poet." The selection ended with McKay's "Courage," a poem in which McKay described himself longing for "undisturbed and friendly rest," grasping the "understanding hands" of a friend, drinking his "share of ardent love and life."[23]

But Max himself felt his "beautiful life"—which is what Claude had so admired about him when they first met—slipping away from him. A trip to Cuba in early 1946 brought him face to face with his nemesis Hemingway again, who had also not been spared by the ravages of time. They had run into him by accident at the Bar Florida in Havana, where the Eastmans had gone to cash a check and had stuck around watching the delicate-handed barkeeper mix daiquiris. "Hello, Ernest," Max said when he recognized Hemingway and extended his hand. But he also quickly calculated what he would do if Hemingway decided to hit him: "He's in a perfect position to be tackled and thrown through the door on the sidewalk." Hemingway did not do him the favor: "Hello, Max," he responded quietly. The two men talked, cordially, and when Eliena joined them, Max said, as if they were at a cocktail party and nothing had ever happened between them, "You remember Eliena, Ernest?" Eliena couldn't believe this fussy, "top-heavy," soft-spoken man with eyes as brown and expressionless as a beetle's peering at her through small steel-rimmed glasses was the same "blood-lusty he-man" she had known in Paris. He looked like an overweight English professor on vacation; when someone tried to take his picture Papa fumbled with his glasses, took them off, and then smiled: "Now I look more like I used to."[24]

At the time, Hemingway was struggling to regain his footing in life and as a writer, scarred by his traumatic war experiences and a series of personal disasters, including a severe car accident. Max's life, by contrast, was proceeding as mundanely as possible. There seemed to be no end to the stream of words coming out of him, in long letters to friends and foes, political essays, and public talks, at the New School on Stalin's foreign policy, in Grand Rapids on laughter, and about himself at his parents' former Park Church in Elmira. His bank account was constantly overdrawn, while the writing he really wanted to do was frequently interrupted by *Reader's Digest* articles, which he could never be really sure would be accepted. He was afraid he was squandering his life. Officially, Florence was not sympathetic to his outbursts of self-pity. Max "worried me with his talk of it now being too late to do anything great," she wrote. Her spirit rose against such "negative and defeatist" talk. Max was speaking as if he had only ten years to live instead of looking forward to all the work he would still be able to do. He was in excellent health, and Florence seemed personally offended that he would "entertain so consistently this idea that his life is over. It *is* over if he has ceased to look forward to the next day and year as a chance to write better." Yet on other days she knew Max had a point: "Almost since his return from Cuba Max has had to devote his efforts to writing for Reader's Digest and to petty and troublesome, or depressing and time-consuming problems of one kind or another. . . . He is not happy this way, and the days go by with none of the writing he wants done—done."[25]

In a note Max penned on the anniversary of Crystal's birthday he caught himself asking his long-dead sister for advice: "Crystal . . . what do you think I should do?" He was "teeming" with things he wanted to write, he said, and yet financial necessity forced him constantly to do other stuff. Writing for Wally beat the alternative—growing old dully and drearily as a professional pundit on the lecture circuit. "But as time grows short and I see that I am not going to fulfill myself, it becomes harder and harder to do, thus taking more and more time, and giving me a feeling that I am trapped, I am beleaguered." How he wished he could consult with her![26]

Despite *Reader's Digest,* Max's life was a financial roller coaster, and Max and Eliena lived hand to mouth.[27] He was plunged into the deepest valley of despond whenever, "after all the work and sacrifice of time," *Reader's Digest* decided not to take an article.[28] Some of the most tedious work he did for the *Digest* consisted in condensing other people's books, such as Leopold Schwarz- schild's anti-Marxian diatribe *The Red Prussian* in early 1948. His visits to Wally's office were reminders of his serfdom, his dependence on the deci- sions of an editor whose views of what would interest the millions of *Digest* readers were sharply different from Max's. In a long response to Wally written in March 1948 Max, defending himself against the accusation that he wasn't devoting enough time to the magazine, listed some of the recent work he had done for the *Digest:* nine articles, paraphrases, and translations in 1944, all of them paid for, accepted, or published; eight in 1946, five of which were paid for or published; eleven articles or condensations in 1947, five of which had been accepted or published. "I don't really see," he wrote to Wally, "how I could put much more effort into my job than I did all of 1947 and so far in 1948."[29]

Max's volatile financial arrangements, which left him and Eliena subject to any "changes of tide," as Florence put it, contrasted oddly with their less-than- frugal lifestyle—the cook they kept, the two cars, the dinners and cocktail par- ties at West Thirteenth Street, the flights to the Vineyard, their annual vacations in the sun. Sometimes Florence had to drive them because their own car had no gas in the tank. On most days, the household seemed to be teetering on the brink of bankruptcy, with Max's charisma as the only guaran- tee of sorts that kept it from collapse. At a time when other people retired from work Max was running back and forth between two women, assuring his girl- friend of his love while also flaunting, when she was present, his continuing intimacy with his wife. Max had, as Florence accurately observed, not even begun to figure himself out: "Has he—a thinker, a student of philosophy—at 65 learned so little about himself?"[30] He seemed utterly lost.

 •   •   •

In March 1948 *Enjoyment of Living* appeared. One of the earliest reviews called Max's autobiography "iconoclastic" and "as outspoken and self-analytical as any I have ever read." But the reviewer also cautioned that a better title would have been *Prologue to Enjoyment of Living,* since—apart from Max's tremendous "lust for life and all it has to offer, in love, in work"—there was indeed little evidence offered that Max had in reality enjoyed what had been happening to him. That said, there was no better source of insights into left-wingish life in New York as it once was: "A tremendous tome, which will be avidly read by all who have been a part—or even on the fringe—of the world which was Eastman's."[31]

Enjoyment of Living was widely noticed; Max certainly couldn't complain. From the *Nashville Tennessean* to the *Lynchburg Advance* to the *Schenectady Union Star,* the critics weighed in. No doubt the rumored sexual explicitness of the book was an additional incentive. The time seemed ripe for a book like Max's that didn't aim for the shock value of pornography or obscure the author's intimate life behind the screen of fiction. In January 1948, just two months before Max's book came out, Alfred Kinsey and his team in Bloomington, Indiana, had published the first of two volumes on human sexuality, based on more than a decade's worth of collecting thousands of sexual histories, first of students and then of ordinary Americans. "There seems to be no question," Kinsey and his collaborators had written, "but that the human male would be promiscuous in his choice of sexual partners throughout the whole of his life if there were no social restrictions." Their work was meant to tear the veil of secrecy from activities that were only natural. "One may wonder what scientific knowledge we would have of digestive functions if the primary taboos in our society concerned food and feeding."[32] *Sexual Behavior in the Human Male* became a *New York Times* best seller.

The burly, bow-tie-wearing, good-looking midwestern college professor and the handsome, freewheeling, white-suited Max Eastman had a few things in common. Born in Hoboken, New Jersey, a decade after Max, Kinsey suffered through an intensely religious upbringing, the influence of which he was never quite able to shed. In the more traditional Kinsey household, the father wielded all the power, but both Kinsey and Max Eastman came to know firsthand what Kinsey's biographer called "the tremendous and terrible power of religion in human affairs."[33] Both experienced an agonizing, long period of sexual dormancy and celebrated the release from repression with a no-holds-barred celebration of sexual desire. Kinsey's two volumes on human sexuality (the sequel on female sexuality came out a few years later) were a paean to the uncontrollable, anarchic nature of sex, a power so massive it might, in orgasm, throw or toss one's body over a distance of several feet. No wonder society had imposed all sorts of rules, marriage among them, to restrict its anarchic impact, and no wonder, either, that reviewers of Max's autobiography turned to Kinsey to help them understand Max's impulse to confess all he had or hadn't done. Calling Max's book "perhaps the most outspoken autobiography since Rousseau's confessions," Sterling North said it bolstered the Kinsey report "concerning the early age at which a child may have his first erotic imaginings."[34] Mary McGrory, in the *Washington Sunday Star,* claimed Max's irrepressible "urge to tell all" reached its peak in the passages about his marriage to Ida—tediously pointless perhaps to everyday readers though pure gold to Dr. Kinsey. Not so, interjected Charles Lawrence, who predicted that the Kinsey Report would take care of all insinuations that Max had been guilty of bad taste in sharing so much about his desires.[35] In the *Saturday Review* Granville Hicks, the biographer of John Reed, invoked Kinsey without naming him when he called *Enjoyment of Living* "an interesting contribution to our knowledge of sexual behavior in the human male." Next to Hicks's review, in a sidebar, appeared the photograph of a bespectacled, bookish-looking man, a lawyer named Morris L. Ernst of Greenbaum, Wolff and Ernst and a former member of President Truman's Civil Rights Committee. Under the headline "My Current Reading," Counselor Ernst listed both Kinsey's *Sexual Behavior* and Max's *Enjoyment of Living.* Everyone was talking about Kinsey, but only Max talked like Kinsey.[36]

Max apparently never met Kinsey, though some of his friends, notably Edmund Wilson, did. After he had shed the straightjacket imposed on him by his upbringing and unsatisfying early relationships, Max's extraordinary defiance of the rules of sexual propriety in his personal life as well as in his writing can certainly be seen in the context of the sexual odyssey his biographer Jonathan Gathorne-Hardy found sketched out in Kinsey's two volumes, an episodic, picaresque journey toward guiltless gratification that shocked and mesmerized contemporary readers. One interesting issue addressed in Kinsey's report was the absence of "adequate" data about extramarital affairs, which had been especially hard to collect. Sex in marriage was the most extensive of all sexual activities of the human animal, but it was also, according to Kinsey, the most boring one: "So much of it is stereotyped and restricted to . . . age-old patterns," amounting to a severe diminishment of the variation of which we are capable.[37] Max had, for all we know, mostly heterosexual interests—men entered into the radius of his activities as colleagues and competitors but, apart from those early dreams during self-analysis, rarely as objects of sexual attraction. After his college friendship with Sidney Wood he seems not to have had very many close friendships with men. He continued to be most at ease with women, including those he hadn't slept with, such as his secretary and much-admired editor, Peggy Halsey. Kinsey mattered to Max not primarily because of the spectrum of sexual practices he had outlined but because he had, as Max put it in a note found among his papers, broken down the public's resistance to knowing, or admitting to, the facts of life. Kinsey was a scientist and almost comically exact and devoid of emotion when he reported his findings. He was the anti-Freud, the empiricist who had liberated sex from the stigma of pathology.[38]

It had taken Max considerable courage to disclose what one reviewer labeled his "30-Year Adolescence."[39] In the months before *Enjoyment of Living* was published he would lie awake at night, drenched in sweat, afraid of his daring in "putting down so exactly what my sexual experience had been."[40] Through the tell-all revelations in his book, Max had deflected attention away from his political views on to his personal life. Max the man had pushed aside Max the writer as well as Max the political commentator. But *Enjoyment of Living* did not appear on the best-seller lists, and reviews were somewhat mixed, a fact Florence, in her journal, attributed to the literary establishment's hostility toward Max: "Are they so unable to recognize—or admit—that there lives a man who can write rings around them?"[41]

But in other ways Max's strategy worked. If people weren't buying the book, they at least had become interested again in the man who had written it. When the journalist L. L. Stevenson went to see him, he had expected to find a "mama's boy" but instead encountered a physically fit, tanned man, an athlete in every respect, on the tennis court as well as at the writing desk. Max was still keeping a rigorous schedule, rising at the crack of dawn to share breakfast with his wife and, after a brisk walk, spending half his day working in a makeshift shack on his Vineyard property. "A man who gets a fat belly often gets a fat head," Max's wife summarized his philosophy to Stevenson, who was duly impressed with Max: "He watches his diet carefully and follows a physical regimen that would floor many another man in this age group—vigorous swimming, badminton, tennis and three daily walks." As an author, he was exacting, detail-oriented, making his "intellectual secretary" (Florence Norton) type and retype his manuscripts, adding numerous corrections, leaving each page of a draft "scrambled, scratched and rewritten until it looks like a henyard after a rainstorm" (fig. 44). *Enjoyment of Living* ran to one thousand pages in typescript, which the long-suffering Norton had to retype five times. Concluded Stevenson: "Probably not since Thomas Wolfe has there been a more determined re-writer of his own output." There was no mention of Florence's real role in Max's life.[42]

The *New York Post* magazine ran a full-page spread about him along with a large photograph featuring the white-haired Max stroking a white, somewhat crazed-looking cat by the name of Silver Leaf. The author, Mary Braggiotti, gushed about the "aura of perpetual youth" that emanated from Max, his beautiful, ruddy face and "dramatic eyes," offset by his shock of abundant white hair. With his attractive, also white-haired Russian wife and surrounded by white-furred animals, he was quite the sight. For her interview Braggiotti caught up with him and Silver Leaf at his West Thirteenth Street apartment, where she listened with fascination as Max assured her that, his affiliation with *Reader's Digest* notwithstanding, he had never written and would never

Figure 44. Max at work, with (likely) Florence Norton
holding the page, ca. 1948. EMIIA1.

think of writing a line he didn't like. Max was unstoppable and put on quite a show for the interviewer. About his departure from Columbia: " 'I satisfied my scorn for academic instruction,' smiled Eastman, stroking Silver Leaf and puffing on his cigaret [sic] through a holder, 'by never presenting my thesis in printed form.' " About his politics: he was never a member of the Communist Party (a half truth), though he had studied at the Marx–Engels Institute in Moscow (true only in a technical sense; he had consulted the library there), and he had not been a Trotskyite either. For now, he was a "radical democrat." And Russian he now spoke so well he was able to think in the language. And then there was his work ethic: the early rising, the constant tinkering with his manuscripts, the swimming at the beach, his natural asceticism. Sorrel soup, prepared by his Russian wife, was Max's favorite dish, and milk his drink of choice. Alcohol depressed him. His preferred reading was his dictionary, and he loved playing word games with his wife. He was fastidious about his hair- cuts, and while he didn't worry about his clothes he loved buying outfits for his wife. Asked why he liked white animals, the confirmed atheist gave a quizzical answer: "A white animal . . . is kind of a mystic in motion—silent, like God."[43]

Floyd Dell, Max's former comrade at arms, wasn't buying any of that. To him, the Maxian charm had run its course. Throughout his review of *Enjoy- ment of Living* in the *Herald Tribune,* Floyd deliberately used the past tense. "He had much missionary zeal," said Floyd, "but he was lazy and a poet." The obvious question was, of course, how poetic laziness could have produced a six-hundred-page book. Floyd regarded Max's success, especially as editor of the *Masses,* as being largely unearned, a function less of personality than of propitious circumstances and good looks: "The socialism of that time was be- coming less doctrinaire, the liberals were sympathetic to some socialist ideas, and a friendly relationship existed between various groups that might be called progressive. It was in this atmosphere that Max Eastman had political promi- nence and promise." In appearance Max was much like a member of the rul- ing class, an artistic version of Anthony Eden, the conservative British politician, and so he had an easy time extracting money from rich people. When it came to evaluating Max's book, Floyd avoided any commitment: "Its candor is extreme, and there will be no doubt two minds about it."[44]

Other reviewers were less circumspect. Orville Prescott, one of the main critics at the *New York Times,* had not enjoyed reading about Max's life, and he suspected Max had not enjoyed living it. Pointing out that most adults forget the erotic entanglements of their youth, Prescott complained that Max remembered his own love life "with an enthusiasm proper only to the psychiatrist's office." He found Max's book too detailed and too boring: " 'What of it?' one asks. 'Why do you insist on telling all this?' " Max could not have gotten a worse reviewer: Prescott, who would immortalize himself by finding Vladimir Nabokov's *Lolita* "dull, dull, dull," was widely known for his conservatism, especially in sexual matters.[45]

Such carping angered John Abbot Clark, a critic at the *Chicago Tribune,* who took it upon himself to respond to Max's critics in the form of a Whitmanesque poem: "Poetry-enjoyer for America," he addressed Max, reminding readers of the author's brilliant first book, still in print. Max was a "Laughmaker" (a reference to the two books on humor Max had written), a "Lover of Life, / Player with Metaphors and the Nation's Stalin-handler / Stormy, husky, brawling, / Critic of the Big-Shoulders." Clark's Max was the Max depicted on the dust jacket of *Enjoyment of Laughter,* baring his white teeth in merriment, as if Hemingway had never socked him with a book, laughing as if his and our survival depended upon it.[46] Another creative response, though differently slanted, came in the *New Yorker* in the form of a parody of Max's writing by Wolcott Gibbs. His re-creation of Max's panting persona captures Max's priapic confidence that an affair with him would leave any woman utterly transformed: "I was secretly and tremblingly desirous of observing her magnificent body in action, so one afternoon I took her down to the gymnasium in Cooperstown, where in those days men and women sometimes wrestled together. . . . Clare was insatiable when aroused and the experience in the gymnasium had taught her something she hadn't known about herself before."[47] Through the humor, however, one still gets glimpses of the liberating impact of Max's prose: a celebration of the beauty and desires of women in language that Kinsey's team—the volume on female sexuality had not yet come out—was still struggling to develop.

Inevitably, some readers finished the book believing Max was really a clinical case, if not a particularly unusual one. A popular advice columnist for the *Washington Post,* Mary Haworth, whose real name was Mary Elizabeth Reardon, invoked him when she tried to explain the male psyche to a female reader with the initials L. S. who was confused about her longtime boyfriend John's reluctance to propose to her. Misquoting the title of Max's new book as *Years of Enjoyment,* Haworth commended Max for having illuminated "the dual attitude of masculine nature to the opposite sex." Driven by both sexual desire and the need for romantic partnership, John had used L. S. to satisfy the former without deeming her a qualified candidate for the latter. "Man's Attitude Not Devotional," concluded Haworth.[48]

Yet Max's frankness had a restorative effect on others, who read *Enjoyment of Living* as the story of a man who successfully overcame debilitating personal timidity.[49] The many personal letters Max received from friends and strangers confirmed he was reaching people on a level other than the literary one. Even Floyd Dell was much more gracious off the record. He did tell Max he didn't like his present politics. Capitalism, he insisted, had failed much more spectacularly than communism ever could. But he liked what and how Max had written about his personal life: "Well, you were a queer fellow, much queerer than I knew—but what a delightful tale you make of it." Max was genuinely moved by Floyd's letter: "I have received more brickbats from the philistines than I can say I honestly enjoyed."[50] Upton Sinclair, too, liked the volume, although he said he was surprised to read about Max's many uncertainties, "for you always managed to impress me as an extraordinarily serene and well-balanced person." Max's honesty about his different states of mind he found heartening: "Personally, I always count that as a useful service—that is, of course, if I happen to be interested in the person who is telling me."[51]

And that is precisely what Max had always wanted to be—an interesting person, someone who had learned to be *himself,* a useful model for others learning how to be themselves, too, but not a character in a cautionary tale. Fifteen years after the publication of *Enjoyment of Living,* a California woman named Alfreda Lindholdt wrote to Max to thank him for allowing her to face her own difficult emotions "without fear or favor." She had recognized herself in Max's self-analysis, and his "incomparable sentences" had imprinted themselves forever on her mind.[52]

Larger than life on paper as well as in public, Max in private, to those who knew him intimately, seemed fearful, anxious, paralyzed by entanglements that had gone beyond anything he felt he could control. When Max and Florence took a trip to Florence's hometown, Norfolk, they stopped in Camden, New Jersey, and noted how spacious Walt Whitman's home was. "We had imagined it humbler and more cramped," remarked Florence.[53] Next to the good gray poet, Max's life seemed so little, so much more circumscribed. Harper's never recovered more than half of the advance it had extended to Max for *Enjoyment of Living,* and he now feared he had revealed entirely too much about himself for nothing and certainly without reaping the hoped-for financial benefits. Why on earth had he performed this "really wanton attack . . . on my quite glorious reputation as a great and all-conquering lover"? He had told the world he hadn't slept with a girl until pretty late in his young life, and the world didn't care enough to buy his book.[54]

Though noticeably frayed around the edges, the famous Eastman charisma still worked, pulling those who found themselves in Max's orbit ever closer toward him. Even the Eastmans' former housekeeper from the Croton days, an African American woman of great resilience and dignity, was not immune to it. In an undated note Eula Daniel talked about holding Max's picture to her heart and crying as she is imagining herself in his arms: "I do wish I didn't idolize you so but I guess it's not your fault. I think tho if you didn't care anymore and would not be my friend I'd die."[55]

Max added to the complications in his life by falling in love with a young woman named June Johnson, whom he met during an outing with Florence in the Shawangunk Ridge, "our young and altogether charming find," as Florence referred to her, with studied casualness, in her journal.[56] Still hurting from the lackluster reception of his book, Max was casting his net wider again, and June's unabashed admiration suited him well. "You are not . . . sixty-five," she wrote him. "You are my age which is ageless and timeless. We are as old as we wish to be, you and I, so we'll be sometimes adolescent, sometimes sixty-five, but most of the time we'll be either not yet born or millions of years old. You and I—we move in big strides and wide swings and are concerned with details only on occasion."[57] June was inviting him to be her "co-traveller in the empyrean," as Max delightedly noted, and he was willing to accept the invitation, at least momentarily forgetting his involvement with Florence.[58] His new lover was studying modern dance in the private residential dance program at the New Hampshire farm of the wealthy dance patron Barbara Mettler. Pride in one's body and physical fitness had always held tremendous appeal to Max, and with June he once again proved too weak to resist. In one of his letters to June he called himself a "many-willed, murky-souled craver of infinitudes."[59] This was an unanticipated twist: Florence now found herself competing not only with her lover's wife but also with a potentially expanding army of other possible lovers.

It was quite ironic, then, that Max was so wholly unprepared for Florence assuming similar rights for herself. When he discovered that she had taken a lover, too, Max was crushed. "You hold me in bondage but you will not cherish me," Max wrote upon hearing that Florence had invited her lover to the very room where they worked together. "You are a deadly danger to me." And: "You are destroying me and I can not save myself, for I love you. You are the only one I love." Try as he might, he could not do without her. Lying on the beach in Venice, Florida, where the Eastmans had gone in their annual quest for warmth, he reimagined the rays of the sun on his body, he told Florence, "as your warm lips kissing me." Florence's "genius for ecstasy" had transformed him, an experience he could describe but not understand: "Like the name of the living God," it had seemed too dangerous to him to even mention it. Arguably, Max was thinking not about religion but about sex.[60]

Early in 1949 Florence left for Europe, officially in order to work for *Reader's Digest* but really at Max's insistence. Almost immediately Max moved his study up to the eighth floor. But absence made his heart grow fonder—or, in Florence's case, it reinvigorated her desire for him. "I have no emotion whatsoever about the prospect of bearing any child but yours," she wrote to him. The paeans to Max's beauty Florence mailed from Paris and Rome are comical in their rhetorical excessiveness. Fanned by Mediterranean winds and fired up by the hot Italian sun, she imagined Max, a Greek god descended from the skies specifically to have his way with her, inseminating her between the pillars of the Acropolis. Such passionate billets-doux alternated with bizarre notes addressed from "Mamma Florence" to her cat Minkie, made even weirder by the replies Max composed in which he in turn posed as Florence's cat and his dog Frosting. "Maybe we should stay separated," Florence observed, "we love each other more that way."[61] At the end of April Max arrived in Rome, and together they took off for Greece. He stayed for a month. The God had become real "in that almost white Greek sun." Florence was even willing to overlook that Max didn't mean her but that other, more perfect Florence from his Village past when, admiring the pouting mouth of the Thyiad in the museum of Delphi, he remarked, "Her beauty is rather like my Florence's." Unlike Florence Deshon's love, hers was unconditional: "I have never known a companion, man or girl, that could anywhere near be what he is. He's always fun to go places with, to sit with, to ride, to talk, to swim, to picnic with. And besides I am always so proud because of his beauty. It's as though he shed an aura around him, and even I, who possess no beauty, shine forth a little in its wondrous light."[62]

Now that the *Reader's Digest* empire has crumbled it is hard to imagine the power that name commanded abroad during these postwar years. Max had access to the highest levels of government in Greece. He was excited to be back in the birthplace of philosophy, the country of Plato, the subject of his Columbia dissertation, but he did not have enough time to enjoy the experience. Wherever he went he was received like an ambassador of sorts. He had cocktails and lunch with the former prime minister Georgios Papandreou and, separately, lunch with the foreign minister and meetings with the current premier and the Greek queen, Frederica. Impressed by Frederica's beauty, he forgot all his democratic sympathies and described her gushingly as a lovely girl who knew her subjects better than anybody else and defended the homeless and hungry children of Greece against the communist bandits that still haunted the mountains.[63] He and Florence saw Delphi, Epidaurus, the ruins of Mycenae, and the plain of Marathon. At the prison in Ioannina he interviewed the members of the Greek communist party, the KKE, who had been arrested during the Greek civil war. When he arrived in Crete the mayor of Iraklion and the prefect of the province received him, and he got a personal tour of the palace of King Minos.[64]

Before she left for Europe Florence declared in her journal that Max had finally made a "definitive choice." But he hadn't. If anything, Max's month-long European visit confirmed that he didn't want to choose. June had receded into the past, and he loved Florence, but he wasn't ready to give up Eliena. Florence was frustrated. "He holds back what he thinks," she wrote, "then explodes with part of it at an inopportune moment." And that was how Eliena, who realized Florence wouldn't just vanish into thin air, behaved, too.[65]

And so the trio's unconventional, torturous life at West Thirteenth Street and at East Pasture Road continued, now punctuated by more frequent periods of travel, which sometimes involved the entire household. From January to July 1951 the Eastmans were in Europe, Max to gather material for more *Reader's Digest* articles, Eliena to pursue her painting. They bought a car they named Minxie and visited friends, among them Arthur Koestler in Paris and the race car driver and aspiring writer Hans Ruesch in Naples. While in Paris Max had dinner with George ("Yuri") Annenkov, who stared at him and then threw up his hands: "Why you haven't changed in a single line since I made your portrait twenty-five years ago!" After which Annenkov kept staring at Max as though he were made out of wax. Max was pleased.[66]

But there were more serious, introspective moments, too. In Rome, as Eliena and he were strolling through the garden of the Villa Borghese, a work by the contemporary sculptor Giovanni Nicolini impressed Max deeply. The *Fontana della famiglia dei satiri* made Max think of his relationship with Florence, minus the offspring, of course: a naked girl and a satyr stand laughing, with hands locked and pulling against each other, while their baby is sitting in the hands of its parents eating a bunch of grapes (fig. 45). "The whole thing is utterly joyous," he wrote to Florence, "the animal and the human, physical and spiritual, joining together—only pretending to struggle apart—in beautiful exuberant laughter." Max also liked the motto that was engraved, between the heads of four gargoyles, on the fountain's base: "Fons canit vitae laudem murmure suo," a line by the poet Raffaello Santarelli. "This fountain, with its murmuring, sings its hymn to life." Max might have given up writing poetry, as he said in the same letter ("I haven't the equilibrium"), but that didn't mean he'd lost his sense for it. Nicolini's sculpture of the frolicking satyrs suggested how he and Florence should live with each other: free, unencumbered, taking a pagan delight in sheer life in a world unrestricted by Eliena's demands and *Reader's Digest* deadlines. Coincidentally, the features of the lusty satyr uncannily resembled Max's own: the full head of hair, the strong nose and large ears. Did the grape-eating youngster remind him of his and Florence's unborn children? Here was the family he never had, through no one's fault but his own.[67]

Figure 45. Max and Eliena at the *Fontana
della famiglia dei satiri*, Rome, 1951. EMIIA1.

Leaving Eliena behind in Italy for two months, where she would sketch and paint, Max left for Switzerland and Germany. When he came back to the United States, Florence in turn had already departed for Europe, where the Eastmans' car was waiting for her. Back on the Vineyard after his "summer of much sunshine," Max had to grapple with his mounting debts.[68] He had Florence's cottage rebuilt and hired a local man to kill the poison ivy, for $16 an hour! Meanwhile he was staggering payments on electricity, plumbing, and carpentering. More and more he depended on Eliena's income, as she returned from her solo time in Italy with new pictures as well as new energy. She was keeping track of the rental income from the cottages on their property, "tending to leaks and things," taught dance lessons ("in succession, an hour each, twice a week") that would enroll as many as fifty-eight students, raised more chickens, and generated even more money from portrait painting ($5,000 for a recent commission). Every day or two she was bringing a check home, and he didn't even have to lift a finger, Max reported. He was chafing under the "slavery" imposed on him by Reader's Digest, but Eliena seemed excited about her life. She had found her place in life, whereas Max still had not.[69]

In a dream he had around that time, he was attending a Christmas party at the Reader's Digest, where he had been assigned the task of making a snowman in the image of Barclay Acheson, Wally's unimpressive brother-in-law. Max's snowman was not very good, and when he showed up with it for the planned holiday ride in a tally-ho coach, the other editors told him Wally had already asked someone else. Max threw his snowman down in anger, breaking it into pieces, and exclaimed, "To hell with you and your magazine!" If only he'd had the strength in real life to make such a move. As it was, Max, when writing for Wally, always had that "namby-pamby, Pollyannaish, Sunday School Herald flavor of the Digest" in his mouth. What he forced himself to produce for Wally was ephemeral, quick to evaporate, like snow.[70]

Florence was now working as a managing editor at the American Mercury, originally H. L. Mencken's creation, which was then beginning its fateful tilt to the right. But she hadn't given up on her wish to discuss "the more important matters of life," a coded reference to the future of their relationship, a conversation Max did not want to have. The future troubled him, too, he said, but he'd rather talk about it some other time. Or perhaps not at all. He clarified his evasiveness in a subsequent letter: "I was trying to say something that would make you feel free-moving, and not forced into anything even by expectation." Florence had said she didn't "dare think" where their love might lead them. Max's answer to the problem: don't think at all. "I must admit I don't think much about it. I just lie back waitingly in the flux of events, happy in the sureness and unfailingness of my love for you."[71]

Max's casual dismissal of Florence's concern was a recipe for trouble. And trouble did erupt the next year, when Max had moved his rocky ménage à trois to Europe again, and Eliena asked that her husband take her—and only her—to Spain. Florence was upset and threatened, after they had returned, she was going to seek "a new equilibrium." Max wailed that she was his "last love" and, the old paganism flaring up in him again, "my last deep absolute friendship to sanctify the earth with." He was sorry for his "brutish, ungallant and alto-gether uneducated folly."[72]

Nothing happened, of course, and things went on as before. During the summers at the Vineyard they enjoyed the "jewel-like days" close to the ocean and their sheltered access to the beach, which allowed—Max's abiding passion—nude bathing.[73] When it got too cold on the Vineyard the Eastmans returned to their apartment on West Thirteenth Street, often for only short periods of time, before taking off again, for Europe or to warmer regions, such as Mexico or the Caribbean.

Eliena continued to manage the rental income from their Vineyard proper-ties, keeping a watchful eye over all expenses. No tenant got away with any-thing; a letter survives in which she is instructing their local agent to "make sure that if the tenants order oil for the furnace, or electric bulbs, or to cut grass or fix the road, they pay cash."[74] Max in turn did what he could to further Eliena's artistic career. For example, in the summer of 1953 he helped pay for her trip to Paris, where she exhibited her work in a gallery. He missed her while she was gone but apparently not so badly that he wouldn't console him-self with Florence: "Florence came up for last week and we had a very sweet and happy time together, but when she was gone and I felt lonely, I was lonely for you. This is an experimental scientific verification of what I tried to tell you all winter."[75] Being with Florence was one of his "seizures," the code word he and Eliena used for his extramarital affairs, and Eliena had assured him that, despite his escapades, she would continue to love him as she had done from the very beginning.[76] Max liked his women strong, but he recoiled when they came on too strong, and that was the case especially when they threatened the one thing that kept him sane: his life with Eliena.

There had never been a sharp dividing line between Max's personal and political lives. To him, the Cold War was anything but cold. With the same red-hot passion he brought to his love affairs he excoriated the American tolerance of totalitarianism whenever he had an opportunity. Persuaded by James Burnham's argument in *Struggle for the World* (1947), Max was in disbelief about the attempts by American politicians to appease Soviet Russia, which would, as he saw it, cede more than half of the world to the Stalinists. All around him were organizations that acted as mere fronts for the takeover of American democracy plotted by the Russian "slave state": the National Council for the Arts, Sciences and Professions; the Joint Anti-Fascist Refugee Committee; the National Council of American–Soviet Friendship; the Voice of Freedom Committee; the Civil Rights Congress. American democracy seemed under attack wherever one looked. If his friends lent their names in support of any efforts Max had identified as fronts for Stalinist Russia, Max was unbending in his criticism. "You can't support Demosthenes and ally yourself with the Macedonian party," he lectured Louis Untermeyer in 1950.[77]

As he had done for several years now, Max insisted his basic values had never changed, merely the urgency with which he felt called upon to defend them. But that wasn't in fact true. The same man who in 1914 had railed against the anarchists because they would say no for the sake of saying no instead of working, with creative vision, toward some great end, now was cultivating mainly his own garden, vowing to inflict revenge on all those encroaching on his private property.[78] In an unpublished essay Max, who was registered to vote on the Vineyard, not in New York City, explained how reluctant he had become to vote at all. Democracy was the best of all forms of government, he conceded, but there was no guarantee that a majority would have better judgment than the minority. Government was a matter of chance, and in reality the choice one faced was not between different systems of government but between government and no government, between doing something and doing nothing. No one's vote makes a difference, and when faced with the question of waiting for election day on the Vineyard in the fall, when the winds were fiercely cold and there was "no little moisture in the leaves," Max thought there was no logical reason he shouldn't just close up his house early and go back to New York. There was, of course, Kant's categorical imperative, the injunction "to act that if your action were generalized the result would meet your approval," but then he was also categorically against anything categorical. He was, said Max, a "rank individualist," even an anarchist, "if it weren't so manifestly foolish to be one." He was someone to whom contact with any government was distasteful, even the one that, at least symbolically, would grant him the right to govern himself: "I don't like to vote! Maybe that's all I am saying."[79]

A traitor to some, Max was a hero to others, and writing for the *Digest* ensured that his opinions had a national and even international reach. As horri-
fying as it was, a letter from an East German reader, Werner Stecher, attests to
Max's growing fame as a "red baiter." Stecher had been sentenced to jail time
for distributing a typed translation of Max's *Reader's Digest* article "The Truth
about Russia's 14,000,000 Slaves" and had been released only after years of
abuse, with half his teeth missing.[80] The people to whom Max felt closest now
were a gallery of free-market advocates, right-wingers, and libertarians with
often widely divergent views. In a letter to Dell he mentioned Wilhelm Röpke,
William Henry Chamberlin, Friedrich Hayek, Henry Hazlitt, Ludwig von
Mises, F. A. Voigt, and the ex-communist Bertram Wolfe as his new models.
These were, he told a skeptical Dell, "the most poised and wisest writers on
current political questions in the world." Max diligently read the books and
articles his new conservative friends published, but, as he soon realized, he fit
somewhat uneasily into that new conservative mold. His trying out of many
different labels over the decades since *Stalin's Russia*, from radical to radical
conservative to libertarian conservative, was an indication of a basic discomfort he felt about defining his life as having gone from one extreme to another.
He didn't feel he was a turncoat, only that terms such as "left" and right" or,
for that matter, "liberal" and "conservative," had lost their meaning.[81]

In addition, his atheism made him an immediate outsider even among his
new allies. When William Buckley, barely twenty-six years old and on his way
to becoming the new wunderkind of American conservatism, published his
book *God and Man at Yale*, Max praised the young author's "arrant intellectual
courage" only to compare it to throwing a handful of chalk at a teacher who
had his back turned to the class. Buckley, a practicing Catholic, had dragged
God into a discussion that should have been an entirely secular one: "I fail to
see why God cannot take care of Himself at Yale." Max had no doubt that economics students at Yale were being indoctrinated. But the answer was not to
gather the alumni and put pressure on the faculty to "narrow the sphere of
academic freedom." Max didn't like to have his own opinions restricted, and
he wasn't going to propose limits on someone else's.[82]

To Max, the realization that a collective paradise was not attainable did not
mean we weren't each of us entitled to our own personal slice of heaven on
earth. It had taken him a long time to get to that particular insight, though, in
a letter to the poet Sara Bard Field, he asserted that, really, he had never, from
the beginning, wanted anything more than his freedom, the freedom to do

and think what he wanted to do and think.[83] The "state-ownership wagon" wasn't going his way; he had accepted that. But that was fine: "I care more about the freedom for the body and soul of man than I do about what is called 'social justice,' " he told Field. Like Diogenes, the Greek philosopher he celebrated in an early poem, all that the sun-loving Max desired for himself was that no one—"no God or King"—stand between himself and the light. And on the Vineyard Max had everything he had asked for in that poem, a "weedy meadow," a hill, and, most important, the sun.[84]

And yet he was no Diogenes, content to stay inside his barrel. His new political alliances made him more visible than he had been since his glory days as a male suffragette. More and more of Max's time was consumed with writing letters to those who challenged or misunderstood him. He was, he told Floyd in June 1954, "absolutely *afflicted* with the thought of all the things I want and need to write, and the decline in my small energy and the swift sliding away of time." Floyd, who had gone the opposite route, withdrawing "from political consideration into an ivory tower," thought Max's real problem was his "foolish and reprehensible" views. That stung. Max shot back: "It seems to me you can't properly descend from an ivory tower and pass out condescending epithets, as from a moral and intellectual mentor, to those who are working in the field with ardor and energy." He angrily called Floyd "a professional script-writer for the hypertrophied bureaucratic state," a remark aimed at Floyd's work for the U.S. Information Service since 1935. As far as Floyd's characterization of his conservatism as an aberration was concerned, Max caustically pointed out that these "are so precisely the words Gogol would put in the lips of a welfare state *chinovnik* retired on a pension, if he were satirizing him. . . . I wonder how you can utter them without at least a slight smile at yourself."[85] And he hurled back at Floyd an observation his friend himself had made long ago in reference to the old *Masses:* "It would remind you of something you seem to have forgotten. . . . 'No two of us thought quite alike. But none of us said exactly what the morning papers were saying.' " Whatever he had done in recent years was motivated by nothing else but "the terrible parody of civilization" into which Stalin and his henchmen had turned Russia. When Floyd implied there was something pathological behind his anti-communism, Max snapped back, "I am curious to know, however, what makes you think I am not 'now free to use my whole mind on the subject.' " But since Floyd insisted, fine: "If this refers to some presumed psychological inhibition, it's ok by me. Knowing that I am afflicted with all the neuroses, and all but one of two of the more extreme psychoses (about which I am only doubtful), I welcome and usually agree with all the different kinds of psycho-analysis that come my way. But I can't help wondering if you are so remote from the circles in which I move that you give any credit at all to the Communist myth that I have 'sold out' to the Reader's Digest."[86]

Floyd, of course, was not far off the mark. In his public pronouncements Max had become shriller, more unforgiving than ever. When he wrote about Stalinism all his humor was gone. In the same issue of the *Freeman* in which Henry Hazlitt, the editor, declared red-baiting to be necessary and redefined the frantic ferreting out of suspected communists by Joe McCarthy's Senate subcommittee as "permitting" communists to testify, Max declared American society to be infected by hordes of unrepentant communists and "their fringe of accomplices, dupes, and fellow-travelers." Not even "once-honest liberals" had proved to be immune to the power of Stalin's brainwashing. Now that Stalin was gone it was time to remember that the root of the evil he embodied was not the system he forged but the philosophy that had created it, a philosophy that had spawned "delinquent liberals in all lands." Max was not above repeating the old canard that communists are unmanly cowards who will dissemble and deceive when possible. Had he really forgotten the hundreds of people whose lives were permanently changed by their enforced testimony before McCarthy's tribunal or by governmental blacklisting? After all, those directly affected included former friends of Max's such as Charlie Chaplin and Louis Untermeyer.

According to Max, the one thing wrong with McCarthyism was McCarthy himself. The senator was, he told Floyd, "a misbehaved and sloppy-minded person functioning in a place where the prime demand was for a well-behaved and extremely accurate and exact mind." But Max's jaundiced view of McCarthy would not have seemed particularly perceptive or contrarian after Joseph Nye Welch had, on June 9, 1954, the thirtieth day of what would become known as the Army–McCarthy hearings, publicly accused him of having "no sense of decency." Indeed, Max went on to offer a kind of defense of McCarthy: "I think the idea that he is a 'menace' or that he has done any more harm to the prestige or reputation of innocent people than any through-going congressional investigation inevitably does is a myth." One of the reasons the "liberals" were so "hysterically" propagating that myth was that they were probably not so innocent after all.[87]

But the hysteria was partly Max's own. In September 1954 Harper and Brothers published an anthology of his poetry, five decades worth of it, everything he had written in a poetic vein that did not have some major flaw, as he explained in his foreword. Most people had forgotten Max was a poet, too. And yet poetry was the means by which he was able to communicate the need for "clear and distinct ideas" more effectively than in his political writing, where he often might have "failed to think things through." Max's volume contained the highlights of his poetic career, from the unabashedly Keatsian "To a Tawny Thrush" to his most recent work, the gloomy "Too Many People," which evokes an ecological wasteland caused by human exploitation:

> This hungry fungus, man, has spread his drab
> Compactions, and is spreading, till the space
> Made rich by nature for his ease and grace
> Is petrified as fruit is by a scab.[88]

In the *New York Times* the elderly Irish poet Oliver St. John Gogarty, a fixture in New York bars, called Max a "poet of very great stature" and compared him to Catullus. Yet Gogarty spent more time on Max's photograph on the jacket, in which he detected the ridges on the forehead that indicate genius, than on the actual poems. Max's decision to provide explanatory notes puzzled Gogarty, who felt them to be limiting ("it is like a personal photograph in which the universal is narrowed down to the particular").[89] By contrast, the reviewer for the *Los Angeles Times* liked the notes; they were, he thought, illuminating and amounted to something like a "history of ideas in America during the past 40 years."[90] No one seems to have looked at Max's foreword, where he explained whom he really had in mind when he composed his prose commentary: Dante, the author of the most touching of all love poems, the *Vita nuova*. And while Max hurried to assure his readers that his experience of love had been fundamentally different from that of Dante, who worshiped his Beatrice from a distance, they shared the same "impulse toward social communion."[91] The latter phrase, more than anything in Max's work in the fifties, explains what motivated him throughout his life: in all he did, Max's great fear was that he might be talking only to himself.

On February 28, 1955, Bill Buckley invited Max to join the new editorial board of *National Review,* the final seal of approval on his metamorphosis from Village radical to conservative pundit. But that appointment did little to alleviate his anxieties about his proper political place or about his search for "communion" with readers. He wasn't really a Buckleyan conservative, and the simplifications of Buckley's writers annoyed him. To Hamilton Long he complained that "the crude way in which the National Review uses the word 'liberal' to name everything they don't like distresses me and also seems to be unwise." After everything that had happened it still wasn't easy for Max to embrace the "coming defeat of communism," the title of a 1949 book by the ex-Trotskyite James Burnham, which Max was asked to condense for *Reader's Digest*. Burnham, a cofounder of *National Review*, would not have shared Max's worries. He was a former Catholic schoolboy, and although he had lost his faith, his thinking was still shaped by the theology he had imbibed during adolescence, including his dark view of the necessarily imperfect state of the world, in which all solutions could only be "temporary and partial."[92] While the Burnhamites might have seen the end of communism as a welcome opportunity to advance their own conservative agendas, Max's life was so intertwined with the history of the Soviet experiment that he couldn't much rejoice. As the ex-editor of the *Masses*, the only artsy socialist magazine the United States had ever had, and as the coeditor of the no-less-influential *Liberator*, he had not only had a front row seat from which to view the political developments that had now become discredited, he had helped shape them.

Max's small new book, *Reflections on the Failure of Socialism*, published by Devin-Adair in the spring of 1955, was intended to remind the American reading public of all Max had done and seen over his long career and to explain, to them and to himself, where he was now. The little volume was essentially a collection of stray pieces from *Reader's Digest*, the *Freeman*, and *American Mercury*, but combined they amounted to a ringing indictment of state interference. Socialists had, wrote Max, imposed their tastes and interests upon "the masses of mankind" out of a misguided, "soft-headed" (and ultimately religious) sense that there ought to be "peace in a brotherly society" so that all caste and class struggles may cease. "A false and undeliberated conception of what man is lies at the bottom of the whole bubble-castle of socialist theory." In reality, men, driven by the ownership instinct and by their need to acquire and exchange property, will always divide into groups with conflicting interests. All one could do was to keep them in a state of equilibrium. And the way to accomplish that was to make sure the government stayed out of people's affairs.[93]

One obvious problem with Max's theory: if humans long, by their very nature, for property and if, on top of that, they want nothing more than to be left alone, how can a political system—or, rather, the absence of a political system—guarantee the peaceful coexistence, in the same space, of such fully entitled individuals? The very idea of an instinctive drive for property seems to run counter to any hope for equilibrium. And if Max was no longer a socialist, what was he? Not a libertarian, to be sure. Libertarians were inclined to "lock themselves in a closet with the abstract truth." Not so Max, the scientific, hard-headed observer of human folly, capable of doing what he always had done since he had emerged from John Dewey's classroom at Columbia: facing the facts. Max felt he was now a radical conservative, a label he defended in an interview with the *New-York World Telegram and Sun*. Speaking to a reporter in a "big sun-lit room in his W. 13th St. apartment," Max also identified himself as a Malthusian, a believer in birth control as the route to a better future: "More Goods and Fewer People is the slogan I should like to see carried at the head of humanity's march into the future." But saying such things didn't mean he was a reactionary, he insisted: "To call me a rightist makes me sick." The problem was that those who believe in the basic freedoms of the individual were on the Right now, whatever that meant.[94] Predictably, reviewers on the Left didn't buy any of this. D. H., writing for the *American Socialist*, ridiculed what he thought was Max's bizarre defense of capitalism and pointed out that while Max seemed really concerned about political freedom in Soviet Russia, he had shown next to no sympathy for those on the American Left who were now suffering denial of their civil liberties. In that, he wasn't alone, unfortunately: "Not a single renegade from socialism who went over to the capitalists out of worries about freedom has yet been known to offer his services to those who are denied freedom in his own land."[95]

This is not to say Max was continually ranting about the sins of the Stalinist American Left. An extended trip to Europe in the spring of 1955, again on the payroll of *Reader's Digest*, allowed him to pay a visit to his former friend and rival Chaplin in his sumptuous château at Vevey: "He knows how to take care of himself, I must say, under the capitalist system!" Chaplin had lost his former good looks, as Max noted, perhaps with some satisfaction. His white hair and dark eyebrows and eyelashes made his eyes look smaller than they were. But the men were immeasurably pleased to see each other, and Max and Eliena promised another visit.[96] Seeing Chaplin again, after such a long time, inevitably reminded Max of his own mortality. He wasn't her Apollo anymore, he informed Florence. "I am not even my full self. My life, my chance for adventure, is in the past. It will soon be as though it had never been."[97] His plans for *Digest* articles included an article about Elba as well as a portrait of the collector and art historian Bernard Berenson, as well as a major piece about Norway, where he was headed in mid-June 1955. The Norwegians celebrated Max, and Max celebrated Norway, as a country where the dreaded "statism" seemed on the wane and individual freedom was still being respected.

Eliena was with him, but he missed Florence: "Sometimes the longing for you—to be with you at the Brink as it used to be when you wrote beautiful poems to me, or over on the beach naked in the hot sun with Frosting—in Athens climbing the steps to the Parthenon—is almost unbearable!"[98]

From Norway he went to Ireland, where he set himself up in the village of Enniskerry, County Wicklow, writing at a desk overlooking the ocean. He was using a Volkswagen, a horrible but reliable "short-nosed Nazi machine," to get around; his schedule included visits with the prime minister as well as the lord mayor of Dublin and Éamon de Valera, the controversial former leader of the Irish fight for independence. He liked Ireland and the Irish. Unlike the people of other nations he had visited, the Irish smiled for the sake of communication: they were the only people he had ever met who would use a smile as a form of speech. For a man of his sinful nature, the Irish girls had much to offer as they were passing him on their bicycles, showing one pretty calf after the other, "in a tantalizing brief and quick succession," their hair blowing back ravishingly in the wind. The landscape provided the appropriate setting for such encounters. Black and velvety, the mountains of Connemara seemed like a passageway into some supernatural realm, a world of ecstasy and mystery. The old faun wasn't done just yet.[99]

Back in the States on September 14—Eliena arrived a few weeks later by boat, along with the luggage—Max, his skin a "polished caramel color," was feeling on top of the world. Florence, however, was not doing well. Emaciated to the point of starvation, she seemed more troubled than ever. No doubt the situation with Max and Eliena and the responsibility she still had for his literary and financial affairs had taken its toll on her, so much so that even Max began to notice. He recommended that she monitor her calorie intake and write down the exact times, the nature of the food, the amount of her "feedings," until she had reached her daily total. No longer her lover, he was now her "brooding parent."[100]

At the beginning of the year Max and Eliena were off again, this time to Pacific Palisades, California, where they enjoyed the hospitality of the eccentric millionaire Huntington Hartford in the artist colony he had founded at Rustic Canyon. Hartford's conservative taste in art—he hated the abstract expressionists as well as T. S. Eliot—perfectly matched Max's own. A particular joy came in April 1956 when Max received word he had been included in a new edition of *American Men of Science*. He was proud of what he saw as his critique of I. A. Richards's psychological theories in *Enjoyment of Poetry*, his two books on the psychology of laughter, as well as his definitive refutation of Marxism as a scientific theory.[101] Finally, a corroboration of the quest on which he had embarked ever since his Columbia days!

That month, however, Eliena began to experience abdominal discomfort, and his nephew Peter Eastman, the newly appointed head surgeon at Kaiser Medical Center in Long Beach, California, ordered X-rays. A fibroid tumor was found.[102] They hastily returned to the Vineyard. Tom Filer, an aspiring writer from California, moved into Max's writing cabin to help take care of Eliena. Eula Daniel was called in to help with the housework.[103] Eliena bore the inevitable hospital stays with the mixture of toughness and optimism that had so often proved a source of strength. "Well, they got me here flat on my back again," she wrote to Tom Filer, from Beth David Hospital. "I guess for the time being it's a proper place for me—'let's face it!' " The room was cool and pleasant and sunny, and she liked watching the "plethora of types and faces that move in and out of the room in steady succession." They were her entertainment, comfort, and, occasionally, a welcome source of irritation.[104]

Max recalled that, in better days, when Eliena was sleeping soundly at night and he, unable to forget whatever worried him, lay awake next to her, he would occasionally see a flicker of sorrow travel across her sleeping face. Normally, Eliena approached sleep the same way she tackled everything else in her life, with fierce determination, as a "thing to be done." But in those slacker moments, which Max had come to fear, the corners of her mouth were pointing down, as if she wanted to communicate some "absolute and most bitter grief." Not knowing what to do, Max turned away.[105] Now, in the final weeks before her death, Max never left her side.

Of all the people he had known, Eliena was, he said in a note typed right after she had died, "the most perfectly equipped for living in this world" (fig. 46). And now he realized she was equipped for dying, too. Max marveled at the courage with which she bore, uncomplainingly, the devastation of her once so capable body, grown "misshapen almost beyond recognition" after she couldn't eat anymore and fluid had accumulated in her legs and feet: "Only once, when her arms and chest were bared, she looked down and said, laughing: 'I'm getting worse than Gandhi.' "[106]

As she had done before when healthy, Eliena once again managed to bring father and son together. In a smudged, perhaps tear-stained note written about a month before Eliena's death, Dan Eastman thanked Max for keeping him in the loop. "It makes me feel a part of a family with you and Eliena," Dan

Figure 46. Eliena with a tame bittern, on Martha's Vineyard,
ca. 1949. EMIIA1.

wrote. He was beginning to look more and more like his father as he was aging, too. Then he lamented his own helplessness: "It is a bitter thing to realize
that I cannot do more than send my love to you, and Eliena."[107] Incidentally,
Dan had just completed what his father had left unfinished. In 1956 he acquired his doctorate in psychology from Columbia, with a thesis titled "Self-
Acceptance and Marital Happiness."[108]

As Eliena got closer to the end, a professional nurse, Gertrude Kingsbury,
nicknamed Turk for unknown reasons, had to be brought in. Tactful as well as
skilled, she knew when to consult the doctor and when to stay away. Eliena
faced death the way she had faced life, without fear or apparent bitterness. Her
last worry was all about Max: "The fact of disappearing into a state of permanent unconsciousness never frightened or appalled me. What hurts is the
thought of playing such a dirty trick on Max." And indeed her death would leave
Max howling with loneliness, feeling "such anguish as I could never believe
existed in this world."[109] Now Max had to face life without the woman who,

despite his many "seizures," had, more than anyone, his own family included, given him the stability he needed. Max, the "murky-souled craver of infinitudes," suddenly found himself confronted with the finality of death—and with a renewed sense of admiration for his partner of more than thirty years, who embraced such finality without hesitation.

Eliena died on Tuesday, October 9, 1956, in Max's arms, after collapsing on her way to the bathroom. Max had managed to say good-bye to her first, though at the moment he hadn't realized that that was what he was doing: "I leaned down with my arm around Eliena and my lips against her cheek," he remembered. " 'I love you so very much,' I murmured, and she answered: 'I am so very glad you do.' " Those were Eliena's final words to Max.[110] It's hard to think of a sentence that would have better matched the way she lived her life. Her trademark mix of reserve and exuberance had sustained her as her life meandered its way from Lublin, Poland, to law school in Leningrad and then from Moscow, the domain of her fiery Bolshevik brother, to the vineyards of southern France and finally to the rocky beaches of Gay Head. As a final tribute to her, Max did something astonishingly Victorian: he cut off a strand of her white-blond hair and put it in an envelope. "Eliena's Hair when she died—," he wrote on it, his words trailing off on the paper.[111]

It was outside her Gay Head home that Eliena Krylenko Eastman was laid to rest. In a message for her "Gay Head Friends," printed after her death in the *Vineyard Gazette*, she had expressed her joy that she would be buried there: "I have felt happy and at peace ever since Max agreed that East Pasture is to be the place of my rest, and that he is not going to leave me and our home here. Now I can feel that I am just stepping aside on the shore, joining the others that landed ahead of me." From her perch on Scitha Hill she would be able to watch her neighbors go scalloping in winter on a bright sunny day.[112] A plaque installed there in her memory bears words written, in better days, by Max, lines as quick and to the point as Eliena had been too: "Nimble with laughter, loving to be, / Courage quick and as quick a skill, / Pride that contains humility, / Love that adoring is thinking still— / Most men love in a girl some star, / I love you for the things you are."[113] It seems characteristic—and at the same time fitting, given their unconventional relationship—that Max would take leave of Eliena with this understated declaration of love, a tribute to someone as complicated and multifaceted as he, someone who had enjoyed life to the fullest, perhaps more so than the author of *Enjoyment of Living*, despite his many protestations to the contrary, ever could. Left behind, Max was "in the shadows," as his old friend Ruth Pickering Pinchot observed, who also asked him, mercilessly, if "feelings of guilt or inadequacy in your relation with Eliena" were at least part of the cause for the pain that would just not go away.[114] Years later, in the summer of 1962, Max happened to come across a sheet torn from Eliena's desk calendar. On Wednesday, May 9, 1945, she had written, "I left Max in Florence's care, resentful of course." And she continued her thoughts in the form of a poem, trying to capture her sense of abandonment: "A sparkling laughing stream whose rapid course / Has been impeded by a fallen tree / Will swell its waters to its lowest shore / And seek another channel for its force; / And so do I in my despondency / Look for new gods to worship and adore." But if she did go looking for new gods, it seems she never found one to replace Max. Flooded with guilt, Max left a brief note on Eliena's old journal page: "How this cuts my heart today . . . I never dreamed I could suffer such remorse."[115]

10 · Realtor and Realist

For the first time in almost half a century Max, at the age of seventy-four, was without anyone to keep him company. Florence had become tired of waiting for Max and was now married to Guy Ponce de Leon, a shady descendant of the famous Spanish explorer and a self-declared writer. Her marriage naturally limited her availability to Max, who felt he could no longer talk freely to her even in his letters. "I am going to be bereaved all over again," he wailed.[1] It turned out that Guy was no good, either as a husband or as an author. But Max could not have known that during the long, awful winter of 1956–57, when he found himself utterly alone. It was at that time that Yvette Szekely— vivacious, funny, free-spirited, with a gift for words that matched his and a slim, flexible body that would have reminded him of Florence Deshon— reentered Max's life. And she did so with full force.

Born on October 12, 1912, in Budapest, the outgoing, cosmopolitan Yvette was the daughter of the Hungarian politician and intellectual Artur Székely and a Swiss-French woman named Marthe Meylan, whom her father quickly abandoned (he asked Marthe to relinquish her child to him). Later, when her marriage to Artur was falling apart, her stepmother, Margaret, took Yvette and her half sister Suzanne to New York, where she supported herself as a designer of ladies' underwear and by writing for magazines back in Hungary. Among the writers Margaret interviewed was Theodore Dreiser, who seduced the then seventeen-year-old Yvette, the beginning of a long relationship Yvette recalled in her memoir *Dearest Wilding*. At one of her mother's dinner parties in early January 1931, she met Max, who was deeply impressed with the "lithe and dark-haired," "dark-eyelashed" girl with the interesting cosmopolitan background.[2] A pen he left behind in Yvette's room brought her to where Max probably wanted her—his apartment at 39 Grove Street, where Max followed Dreiser's example and became Yvette's lover, too. They stayed in touch over the next two decades, as friends and occasional lovers, exchanging notes that reveled in the possibilities of a fuller relationship.[3] Max continued to inhabit Yvette's dreams: "Two weeks ago I dreamed that you had 'just arrived from Europe'—and thought in my dream—'oh *that's* why I haven't seen him in so long!' Which is to say in waking that I'd like to—very much." Come for dinner, Max, or for tea or a drink, she said, and "let me look at your beautiful head."[4]

By February 1957 Yvette was in Max's dreams, too. He had gone back to Rustic Canyon, the last place Eliena and he had enjoyed a few months of undisturbed happiness. And it was there that Eliena came back to him, if only in a dream, of the kind that continues to haunt one's waking life. Max dreamed he was having a nightmare when, still in his dream, he heard Eliena calling out his name. Gasping and squirming, he wanted to alert Yvette, who was— still in the same dream—lying next to him. Max was puzzled by what he had dreamed, and he shared his confusion about Yvette's appearance in his dream with Florence: "I've known her off and on for so long. I suppose that's how she got into the dream."[5]

But Yvette ultimately also got into Max's life. She had been working for the New York Department of Welfare on Fifty-seventh Street, most recently as the director of a very successful Senior Citizen Center in Brooklyn, and among the perks of her job were regular paychecks, salary increases, and a pension, due to her when she turned fifty. She had a boyfriend in Woodstock, the painter Bernard Steffen.[6] And she seemed ready to put all that aside for the privilege of helping Max get back on his feet. "She wanted to come absolutely, and never made me feel it was a sacrifice," Max explained to Florence, who was, of course, upset.[7]

Financially, Max had very little to offer Yvette. Things had looked promising for a while: he was able to sell Rosebank, one of his Vineyard properties, and, in the spring of 1957, an unexpected opportunity arose when David Randall, who had been appointed head of the Department of Rare Books and Special Collections at Indiana University, asked him if he was interested in selling his papers. Randall had just been negotiating with Upton Sinclair about his papers, "with high hopes of success," and Sinclair had recommended he approach Max, too. Randall wanted the Lilly Library, as Indiana University's Special Collections would be named, to be the "finest collection of literary and source material—in first editions, manuscripts, etc.—of any library between the coasts." He offered Max $15,000 for his archives, a large sum that, accounting for inflation, would be the equivalent of $127,000 in today's money, with $4,500 due at signing and the rest to be paid in two equal installments in July 1958 and July 1959. This loose arrangement would give Max enough time to sort his papers, an important provision given that he was still working on the second volume of his autobiography. Randall assured him he had no intention of enforcing timely delivery of what he had paid for.[8]

But by April 1958 much of Max's money was gone again.[9] To make matters worse, his island citadel was under siege. Nude bathing, Max's abiding passion (he would regularly encourage his visitors to shed their clothes, too),[10] had become more difficult even in Max's little corner of the Vineyard. A new paved road had come within just a hundred yards of Max's private jungle, and when he had people over for swimming parties he felt as if they were holding "obsequies for a dying paradise." The Gay Head selectmen drove the knife in even further when they put ads in a Boston newspaper to "advertise the wonderful 'seclusion' to be found out there." Max felt that was "a case of killing by slow torture the goose that lays the golden egg."[11]

He tried to evoke some of the glorious Vineyard past by writing down a story told by his Wampanoag friend Amos Peters Smalley. A former whaler born in Gay Head, Smalley in 1902 had killed a ninety-foot white whale—possibly Melville's Moby-Dick—as he was sailing south of the Azores. To Max, Amos Smalley was a modern embodiment of Melville's Tashtego, the "unmixed Indian from Gay Head, the most westerly promontory of Martha's Vineyard," a symbol of Islander perseverance.[12] The notion that someone from Gay Head had such a direct link to Melville's great novel pleased Max immensely. He was even more ecstatic when the *Digest* awarded a prize to Amos and agreed to publish Max's story in its June 1957 issue. But joy gave way to embarrassment when Max learned that Amos was expected to share the $2,500 prize money with him. Max's hatred of the "Prisonville" machinery of the *Digest* was instantly revived. The "infantile fribble" Wally was promoting bothered him more than ever, as did the religious undertones of much of what Wally published, about the effectiveness of prayer, divine intervention, and so forth. When Max had asked Wally to read the manuscript of *Enjoyment of Living*, the only concern he had was about Max's use of the phrase "by God"; he obliged his boss and replaced it with the less instantly blasphemous "by heck."[13]

In addition, Max found he was having trouble staying at the East Pasture house. Eliena's presence was felt everywhere. Walking around his property, revisiting "all the things and places we made and loved together," he thought it would be nearly impossible for him to go on living there: "A glance at the rose-garden, the studio, the little garden along the wall, those old chicken-houses, anything and everything in the house—one glance, one lifting of my eyes, destroys my wish to be myself to continue my life. If I'm not in tears all the time, it's only because my eyelids are tired and my soul is tired of sorrow." He wasn't sure what to do. Maybe he would have to remain holed up in his little room at 8 West Thirteenth Street, though the only reason he had been able to manage there over the winter was that he was looking forward to being back up at Gay Head again. Maybe he should share the Vineyard house. His friend Charles Neider, a Twain scholar nearly forty years younger than Max and newly married, came to mind, and Max was thinking of asking the couple to move into Florence's vacant home, The Brink: "Maybe that would make it new and different enough and make me feel not so totally alone with the awful, awful fact of Eliena's non-existence."[14]

Max returned to New York, dragging with him two suitcases full of Eliena's clothes and other things from her bureau, which he simply passed on to Yvette when she came for dinner—a "kind of treason," to be sure, but one that Eliena herself would not have hesitated to commit: "I have to remind myself how re-alistically firm and brave Eliena was about things like that." He threw a party for the Neiders, the Cummingses, Yvette, and Eula at his house, went to din-ner with Yvette, and forced himself to look ahead. But his thoughts kept going back to the "awful nothingness" into which Eliena, "with all her vigorous gaiety and boundless interest in life," had stepped so suddenly, so abruptly, so fi-nally.[15] Normally not one given to self-medication, Max was now preparing cocktails at home, not for guests but for himself: "I was sitting here wishing that I had company for dinner . . . and suddenly I said to myself, 'Well it doesn't take ten to drink an old-fashioned,' and there I was in the kitchen conversing with Satan while I prepared it." Physically, he was as well as ever in his life. Apart from an old hernia, his body—heart, lungs, joints, nerves, prostate—was in fine shape. His doctor told him he had ten or fifteen more years to live—news that both elated and depressed him. It seemed that only yesterday he'd had his entire life ahead of him. But now? "Dreadfully, desperately lonesome," he found himself staring at a void, trying to regain his balance, the serenity that people had once attributed to his father. Or maybe, knowing what he now did about Sam's loneliness, that serenity had just been "a power of insensibility"?[16]

By February 1958 Yvette Szekely would show up every morning at Max's apartment to make breakfast for him. "She does so with a joy that is completely contagious," noted Max, surprised not only by her dedication but also by his own eager responsiveness to it. After breakfast, Yvette would make his bed and straighten everything else in the apartment. Like him, Yvette, who had just given up smoking (as Max noted with pleasure), was full of vigor. "I enjoy her companionship more, not less, than I thought I would." Four times a week the faithful Eula Daniel, now one of Max's closest friends, came by to cook him dinner and do his laundry. Max paid her $35 a week. On Mondays, Tuesdays, and Sundays, he dined out with friends.[17] Life was going on.

What helped, too, was that another specter from his past came back and paid him a not altogether unwelcome visit, and it looked very much like his old antagonist Sidney Hook. Max had, of course, long divested himself of all his ties with Karl Marx, attributing the failure of communism no longer to its flawed practitioners but to its ideological progenitor. But he had never confronted, at least not in any fundamental way, his own debt to John Dewey, the pragmatist father he shared with Hook. An essay by Hook in the *New Leader* reignited the competition between Dewey's two favorite students that had lain dormant since the 1930s.[18] The essay's ostensible subject was Lincoln, but Hook had grander ambitions. Lincoln was a pragmatist, Hook declared, finding in Lincoln's preference for action over interpretation an anticipation of Dewey's instrumentalism, in much the same way that Marx had anticipated Dewey. The latter was well-trodden ground for Hook, but he was now returning to it with a new perspective, that of the anti-Stalinist. It irked Max to no end that Hook's Marxism had emerged from all their earlier squabbles relatively intact, as if Max had never exposed it as the ersatz religion it was, and that he was now acting all scientific about it. Max responded angrily in the September issue of the *New Leader,* ridiculing Hook's Lincoln analysis but then moving on to weightier issues. For, as Max had now realized, he himself was no longer a pragmatist. Max insisted he was still Dewey's true intellectual son, but a son who had seen his father without his clothes. In his definitions of pragmatism, Dewey had invariably confused the true method with the truth itself, the thinking with the purpose of the thought. A successful experiment yields not the truth but merely evidence of it—to mistake one for the other is ideology.

Of course, Hook wasn't going to take Max's counteroffensive sitting down, and a tit for tat unfolded that finally exasperated also the editors of the *New Leader.* "Here we present," sighed the editors, in a comment box preceding

Max's answer to Hook's answer to Max's critique, "what is positively the last installment of a controversy which nearly led us to change our name to *The Epistemological Leader.*"[19]

But Max now had a new problem. In his dealings with Hook he was eager to shed the label of the pragmatist, as pragmatism itself was yet another pseudoscientific method—like Marx's—that suggested practicality whereas in reality it was based on acts of faith, too. But among his new conservative friends, Dewey was anathema, and Max, for reasons that weren't just emotional ones, felt he had to defend his former teacher. A few months after his skirmishes with Hook, Max published an article in *National Review* in which he lauded rather than rejected Dewey: "I find myself now in the company of a group who call themselves libertarian conservatives. Many of them cherish religious notions which I regard as primitive mythology, and which I think diminish their influence." The commitment of Max's new friends to "limited government, individualism, and a free market as the basis of other freedoms" made Max's association with them well-nigh inevitable. If only they didn't dislike Dewey so much: "He is regarded as the fountain-source of every horror from teenage delinquency to the confiscatory taxes of the Welfare State. Indeed I wouldn't be surprised if a good proportion of the younger recruits to this banner think of John Dewey as the man who introduced socialism into the United States."

Max's John Dewey was different—the Walt Whitman of philosophy, a poet in anything but his writing style, a benevolent father who would give his due to all the members of his intellectual family. Dewey's thought lacked "keen edges," Max admitted, and his theory of "progressive education," the idea that kids can and should have fun in school, might have produced some spoiled brats unworthy of the confidence placed in their innate desires to free themselves from the shackles of their teacher's expectations. But that didn't mean Dewey was being ridiculous when he said that disciplining a child was justified only when the experience of punishment taught him or her to do things *deliberately* rather than merely as the result of a stern command issued by an "irrelevant ogre" of a pedagogue. When Max saw himself confronted with the authoritarian hard-liners among his new allies, Dewey's softness suddenly seemed appealing: "Those who imagine they are dancing at the funeral of another wild radical, will be surprised, if they open a book and read a few lines actually written by him, to see how moderate he was, how cautious, how bent on conserving as well as multiplying the finest values of life in a free society."[20]

Dewey was Max Eastman as Max Eastman would have very much wanted to be—but in a world where humans were humans and not, as Max now knew them to be, *animals*.[21] Max lived in the real world, and therefore he now felt closer to men like Jim Burnham, who saw the redemption of Western society in Machiavellian realism rather than in some soft ideal of human perfectibility. There was yet another option, and that one became more and more attractive to Max as he was entering his twilight years: like Voltaire's Candide he would cultivate his own garden, even as the world around him was going to shreds. And Max's garden was on Martha's Vineyard, a rocky, pebbly, windswept paradise.

On March 23, 1958, Max and Yvette were married—in the casual manner that had by then virtually become routine for Max (fig. 47). There was no public announcement and no celebration. In fact, there was barely even a ceremony. External circumstances had dictated that the move be made, Max explained, somewhat sheepishly, to Florence—so much so that "my inner resistance to committing myself to any woman doesn't get much free play in my mind." He picked as unromantic a place for the wedding as he could think of, the village of Wappingers Falls near Poughkeepsie, in part because of its unappealing name. It was, he declared proudly, "one of the ugliest towns I ever passed through." Eula drove them there, after meeting them at the train station in Harmon. The town clerk was sick, replaced by a young woman enveloped in massive blobs of fat. She had to call her boss all the time for instructions because she did not know how to complete the license. The next day an elderly judge indifferently pronounced Max and Yvette husband and wife. When the ceremony was over, Yvette, Eula, and Max went for daiquiris and dinner and drove over to Hyde Park to take a look at the Roosevelt estate. Max ended his day by falling asleep in the back seat of the car.

When he told Florence, she was aghast. Max could not understand why. There was nothing sudden about his marriage. He pointed out that he had been living with Yvette for two months now: "I'm perfectly serene and unquestioning about it—a state I've rarely been in about anything but intellectual problems before." Maybe his age and the realization that there was no time left for any "alternative enticements" had something to do with that serenity. "But I also love Yvette; everybody does who knows her." She was devoted and generous, and with Eula about to leave him—she needed better-paying work for the fall and winter—Yvette stood ready to take charge of his life.[22]

Figure 47. Max and Yvette in Max's Impala convertible, 1958. From color
transparency. EMIIA1.

Otherwise, Max carried on the way he had before his marriage. A delightful
surprise was a visit from his actress-lover-friend Rosalinde Fuller, "vivacious
and full of zeal for life's adventure" as ever—and without the need for a companion that had, once again, led Max into matrimony. She spent the evening
with Max, and one can assume they picked up right where they had left off the
last time. They had dinner at Longchamps with Crystal's daughter Annis and
her husband, Charles Young, and Rosalinde gave a well-received performance
of her one-woman show. The "impresarios" in the audience were impressed
and Rosalinde got what she wanted, an invitation to return next year for a tour.
Rosalinde was "amazingly young looking," a living example of how one could
defy biology. "Too bad you and I weren't built that way, as the whole animal
kingdom and the vegetables, too, would have been if I had been the Creator,"
Max said to Florence, a somewhat backhanded remark which nevertheless af-
fords a glimpse of Max's utopia: a place of continued sexual pleasure in which
all living things are equal, all wishes are gratified, nothing decays, the resources are infinite, and no one needs to feel guilty about anything at all.[23]

If Rosalinde carried herself with the utmost confidence, Max was having a
hard time accepting that he was not similarly ageless. He continued to fuss
about his weight and tried out various ways to get it under control, including

the antidepressant Dexamyl. At one point he had the entire household—himself, Yvette, and their maid—dieting on Metrecal, a kind of flavored shake made from powder that had become popular in the 1960s and, Max believed, helped him bring down his weight from 203 to 190 pounds.[24] He simply could not bear to think of himself as old. The very idea, he said, seemed incongruous to him.[25] People told him he was still good-looking, he proudly told Florence Norton a few weeks after his seventy-sixth birthday. He wryly added, "By not looking at the glass at the wrong time of day I try to believe it."[26]

At times Max found it hard to believe he had gotten married again. His "gamophobia"—yes, there was a word for it!—was almost like a religion to him: something that belonged to the better, more interesting part of him. He hated the barbaric custom of applying the man's name to the woman: "Against that, my revolt is absolute and fanatical," he said in a conversation over coffee at his house with Yvette, Ruth Pinchot, and another couple just a few weeks after his marriage. "Why should a man who loves a woman as herself want to express it by pasting *his* name on her—an act of childish egotism, indifference to poetry, and execrable bad taste!" He cringed when he heard Yvette introduced as Mrs. Eastman. Of course, he had married Yvette for not entirely unselfish reasons: he knew she would take care of him for the remainder of his life. At the same time, marriage had not entirely been a business transaction for either Max or Yvette. In fact, Yvette's income, had she continued to work, would have significantly improved Max's perennially precarious financial situation. And, depending on one's point of view, Yvette's decision to reject the stability her job had offered for the semibohemian uncertainties of life with an elderly writer who had successfully avoided permanent employment all his life, was either stupid or heroic.[27]

Max was grateful to her, so grateful, in fact, that he did something he'd rarely done before—he began to plan for the future and, even more astonishingly, for a future in which he knew he'd play no part. Now that Eliena was gone, his own death had become more real to him than ever before. "Yvette is so good to me, so utterly given to caring for me and keeping me happy so long as I live, that I want to make her as happy afterward as I can."[28] One way in which he could make that happen, he felt, was by requesting that Florence Norton end her quasi-ownership of The Brink so that he could again directly profit from renting it. Florence reacted angrily. But Max felt he was entitled to do with The Brink as he saw fit, since he had been taking care of the repairs and dealt with the tenants. The situation was complicated by the fact that

Yvette was just as jealous of their "loving friendship" as Eliena had been, "more humbly perhaps, but just as implacably."[29]

Jealousy or not, Yvette was indeed good for Max. It helped that, in her mid-forties, she still had a stunningly beautiful body, a fact Max celebrated in a series of nude photographs, taken with a rented Yashica, photographs their lab on the Vineyard did not want to develop.[30] Lying on the sand, her face turned away from the viewer, arms crossed behind her head, one leg raised and slightly drawn back, Yvette, in Max's photographs, seems like a chthonic goddess, the ripples of her body replicating the patterns in the sand around her. Compositionally, even the crumpled clothes under Yvette's head make sense, as does the little towel on which her body rests. Yvette was Max's demotic Venus, an old man's fantasy made manifest—just watch the sunlight dancing on the sand and playing over Yvette's body in the photograph (fig. 48).

And Max, too, was good for Yvette (fig. 49). On a note he kept in his wallet, Yvette rhapsodized about their relationship: "Loving you and being involved with things that are yours, I feel alive and shining, and since I feel that way I look that way and act that way and the change givers in subway stations smile when they hand me tokens. Like Whitman I find myself celebrating myself and they all cheer."[31] Since she had herself been one of Max's occasional lovers, Yvette knew about the power of his erotic instincts. But she also knew that time was on her side. In his late seventies and contained, for at least half the year, on their remote Vineyard property, Max would find it harder to play the

Figure 48. *Y* [Yvette]. Photograph by Max Eastman, September 1958. EMII.

Figure 49. Max on the beach, ca. 1958. EMII.

part of the Lothario. Not that he gave up on this side of his life entirely. While the "Norton woman," as Yvette angrily called her, was fading into the background, others, notably Rosalinde Fuller, remained, if only as indistinct shadows in the wings. Yvette was worried about them, and not knowing where else to turn she occasionally shared her "tortured jealousy" with her half sister Suzanne Sekey, who advised her not to think too much of it.[32]

The book Max was working on then, *Great Companions,* slated for publication by Farrar, Straus, and Cudahy in spring 1959, was based on previously published biographical portraits of the "greatest people of his time," from Leon Trotsky to Pablo Casals. It ended, touchingly, with a tribute to Annis Ford, previously published, like two of the other articles, in *Reader's Digest.* Max thought Wally would be excited about the exposure the *Digest* was getting and couldn't believe his eyes when Wally sent him a note in which he threatened to cut his salary because Max seemed to be more interested in publishing books than in putting his nose to the grindstone at the *Digest.*[33] Max struck back, defending his record: "The simple truth, Wally, is that I've been working more continuously for RD this last year than ever before—although most people who have passed their 76th birthday have retired on a pension and are not working at all." Max complained that his pieces got turned down too often, which had given Wally the misleading impression that he wasn't writing enough for him. He pointed out that he had already reduced his expense account after a similar complaint the year before. Max ended the letter by almost begging Wally to give him another chance: "Couldn't we let it ride as it is for a couple of years more, and check the results together at that time?"[34] Wallace relented: "Please pardon me for having written too impulsively." He also ordered that Max's pending essays on Socrates and Alexander the Great be printed.[35]

Max hated writing for Wally's magazine. He disliked "jamming" complex thoughts into "a too small can of mixed sweets," and he was embarrassed by the way he'd had to beg him for another chance. Maybe, he said to Florence, he should just call it quits. He could rent out the big house on the Vineyard and move into a hut on the property with a sign over it: "*Max Eastman, Realtor and Idealist*"? But Max was, in fact, a *realist,* too realistic to give up a job that allowed him to travel whenever and wherever he wanted. He knew he needed Wally's money.[36]

But his troubles with the *Digest* were far from over. In August 1960 Wally sent back his beautifully crafted essay on the city of Florence because he wanted Max to focus precisely on what Max had chosen to omit, extensive discussion of the history of the Renaissance. Wally also sent $500 as a "guaranty payment" on the fee Max hadn't yet earned, but that did not appease Max at all.[37] In its original form Max's essay was a beautiful reverie on *le temps perdu,* but without any sign of wistfulness. What Max had tried to do was capture the almost erotic experience of lounging on a square in modern Florence, say, the Piazza della Signoria, and letting the present fade into a vision of the past, when life moved more slowly and there was time for friendship, for, in a Maxian phrase, the enjoyment of living: "You can substitute the pretty red-painted wheels of mule-drawn carts for the fat black super-tires of sightseeing buses; the jewel colored velvets and glistening furs of the rich merchants for the sport-shirted, camera-laden shoulders of tired tourists. You can blot out the roaring vespas and the girl in the drip-dry dress sitting at a café table wiring a postcard to her family in Kansas." Instead of the boisterous youth-hostelers snapping pictures of each other while sitting astride the nymphs and satyrs of the *Fontana del Nettuno,* close your eyes and imagine a different scene (and, as you are doing this, listen to Max's prose caressing the bodies of those ancient Florentines as they walk again before his enchanted inner eye). Imagine "two dignified maidens stepping along in long slim-flowing satin gowns. A jewel-studded silken braid outlines their bosoms, which are lifted high and cradle a jeweled crucifix,—or perhaps it is only a pagan medallion or some precious stone. Their elaborate coiffures, dyed blonde, are strung up and tied and anchored with ropes of pearls." Behind them, in the lingering trail of their sweet, heavy perfume, trudge brown-hooded monks with shaven heads and bare feet and, behind those, boys in leather aprons "horse-playing and swearing" as they make their way to the dyers' or carpenters' or stonecutters' shops where they are apprenticed. But perhaps they were not walking anywhere; perhaps they had spent the day amid paintings, panels, inlaid tables, and other treasures, at the studio of Raphael's friend Ridolfo Ghirlandaio. And look closely, there walks Master Raphael himself, "a warm-eyed young man with sweet shapely features, who will look almost feminine to you as he passes clad in a rich purple tunic with auburn hair hanging down, so neatly combed, to his shoulders." Or, for that matter, you would see Lorenzo de' Medici, Lorenzo the Magnificent, dark and angular, chanting his own ballads at the head of a procession of excited citizens. The Florentines were lovers of beauty and devotees of violence—just look at Donatello's statue of Judith right ahead of you: clutching the stringy hair of Holofernes, she is aiming her sword for the fatal blow.

This was Max, the novelist manqué, at his best, writing at a fever pitch, his every word evoking the ecstasy of immediate experience. These weren't idle ruminations either: no one familiar with the glorious Florentine past would have trouble understanding their courageous resistance against the Fascists and the Nazis.[38]

Not much of Max's draft was left when the essay eventually was published, several years later, in *Reader's Digest*.[39] Instead of Max's sinuous sentences, readers found dry lists, the paratactic banalities of the guidebook prose: "Here Dante lived, the great poet of the Middle Ages, who stands beside Homer and Shakespeare in the praise of posterity. . . . Here Boccaccio lived. . . . Still another immortal Florentine was Giotto." And the anticlimactic conclusion: "A final and very practical thing to be said of the beauties to be seen in Florence is that they are all near together." This wasn't even good writing—just note the piling on of passive constructions or that bête noir of copy editors, the use of "thing" as the subject of a sentence. If Max believed that his desire to earn a living had never really interfered with his more literary pursuits, he was telling himself what he *wanted* to believe.

In an unusually strained metaphor he compared the different tracks of his writing to a "troika" of horses, with the challenge of keeping the two darker horses (his political writing in the service of the "cause of freedom" and his writing for money) from interfering with the "white stallion" of his creative life. Writing for money was his "roan horse," and Wally had never put him in a situation, he said unconvincingly, where the "craft of writing timely articles for an average of some sixty million readers" had corrupted "my art of writing as I think writing should be done." That confident assertion, contained in a draft of the final chapter of his autobiography-in-progress, was scrapped from the printed version, where Max did concede he had found "signs of pressure" on his style, if perhaps not on his thought, in the articles he had written for the *Digest*.[40]

But the lusty lion of the Left hadn't lost all of his teeth yet. In the introduction to a new edition of *Reflections on the Failure of Socialism,* Max now proudly called himself a "libertarian conservative," revising his earlier skepticism about that label. Just being "conservative" seemed unacceptable, since it suggested that "one's whole program is to 'sit tight' on what we happen to have." He now liked the activist sound of "libertarian"—an improvement over the wishy-washy "liberal"—and the suggestion that one would take such action boldly and not through "tight-knit secret societies and rabid crackpot organizations whose super-patriotism suggests the beginning of a counter-tyranny rather than an effort to defend and enlarge the freedoms that we have." Additionally, libertarianism was a thoroughly secular concept. Being a libertarian conservative meant that one wasn't a "reactionary obscurantist" but a defender of hard-won freedoms, among them the freedom not only to worship but also *not* to worship, a right enjoyed by all those "who can find no evidence on human events of the reign of a benign Deity." That is what the preacher's son still cared about: "I must make clear that it is downright liberty of individual thought and action in this world, and not some community of belief about another world, that in calling my views conservative I mean to defend."[41] The source of such liberty was not God, as Barry Goldwater had said in his "Statement of American Principles," a text that annoyed Max to no end, but life itself—the only God at whose altar Max would worship.[42] Recall his 1918 preface to *Colors of Life:* "Life is older than liberty. . . . And life is what I love."[43]

For Max was not an agnostic, as John P. Diggins has asserted, perhaps in an attempt to still be able to claim him for the *National Review* camp, but an unabashed atheist, and what he saw as Buckley's persistent conflation of anti-communism and Christianity angered him as much as Goldwater's vision of the divine purpose of free-market economy.[44] Some aspects of Buckley certainly appealed to Max, the ocean-yacht racing, for example, or the easy way he had with words: Buckley once said that "the socialized state" was to "justice, order, freedom what the Marquis de Sade is to love" and announced that he

would rather be governed by the first two thousand people in the Boston telephone book than by the faculty of Harvard University. And he was a milk
drinker. But this was also the man who believed that there were limits to the
free exchange of ideas and that the ultimate meaning of the human experience
resided in God.[45]

In 1962 Max sent Buckley an essay titled "A Question to the National Review," in which he seized the bull by the horns. "Whether or not this has any
relation to its vastly increased circulation or not, it seems to me that the National Review is becoming more and more explicitly a religious magazine."
Max went on to clarify: "I mean a magazine devoted to the defense and propa-
gation of religion in general, and the Christian religion in particular." As examples of the rhetoric he found objectionable Max cited several passages from
recent *National Review* articles, notably senior editor Frank S. Meyer's conten-
tion, in the January 30, 1962, issue, that it was the main task of the conservative to defend the "Christian understanding of the nature and destiny of man,
which is the foundation of Western civilization."[46] He was similarly put off by
L. Brent Bozell's statement, in the April 24, 1962, issue, that it was "our commission . . . to plant in history the ideals and the standard contained in Christian truth—and to build institutions and foster mores that will help sustain
these ideals: in short to build a Christian civilization."[47] To Max, this was sheer
hubris. The struggle against communism and a controlling superstate here at
home was a worldwide effort, not one carried out by a handful of Catholics in
America. "To regard it as a Christian struggle seems to me parochial and self-
defeating." Buddha and Confucius, in his modest opinion, had been wiser
than Jesus "in their attempt to work out a guiding set of precepts for a good
life in this world without the concept of God, or the appeal to any super-natu-
ral authority." Freedom must be defended but not "with the bigotry instinctive
in those who believe themselves backed by an inside knowledge of the will
of God."[48]

Buckley did not want to print Max's note. Somewhat lamely, he defended
himself by pointing out that signed articles did not represent the views of the
magazine and that therefore Max's critique had missed its target.[49] But that
only delayed Max's departure from *National Review*, which finally took place in
January 1964, when Buckley did publish a sort of farewell from Max, in which
he asked, "Am I a Conservative?"[50] The answer: if being a conservative required turning the clock back to the Middle Ages, well, then he wasn't one. A
note among Max's drafts related to his problems with *National Review* yields
what is perhaps a more appropriate self-description, though it would seem

deeply ironic to anyone for whom HUAC was still a vivid memory. He was, reflected Max, "a fellow traveler of the conservatives," but one who had found "the going a little rough at times."[51] Add to Max's atheism his continuing—if now severely qualified—admiration for Lenin, and one understands how difficult it would be simply to put Max into the *National Review* camp. In February 1965 Max was in Honolulu, en route to Japan (his first trip to the Far East), where he gave an interview to KNDI radio as part of their series "Personality of the Week."[52] The interviewer asked him how he felt about Stalin's body being removed from Lenin's tomb, and Max replied that Stalin's condemnation of him as a "crook and gangster of the pen" had been the "chief honor" and the "high point" of his life. But Lenin he still defended. "Ruthless" Lenin was and a zealot, but he had integrity: "He would do anything which he was sure would lead to the liberation of the working class."[53]

The hankering for a world outside the political zoo of human life led Max to become more seriously interested in animals (fig. 50). He had always been a keen birdwatcher and had devoured C. Lloyd Morgan's *Animal Life and Intelligence* (1891) while still in college, but now he was undertaking a systematic study of the subject, stacking his desk with popular books on zoology and the behavior of wild animals.[54] The more disenchanted Max became with human society and the forms of collective organization that ideologues, from the Far Left to the Far Right, had tried to impose on it in order to make it more than a random accumulation of individuals with different incomes, different interests, and different ideals, the more he felt drawn to animals. As Whitman had said, they don't lie awake at night and "weep for their sins," and they do not make you sick "discussing their duty to God."[55]

There is evidence in his papers that Max was planning to do a book about animal behavior, comprising several of his *Digest* pieces as well as some new essays. One of those, on the "father instinct" among animals, hit close to home. "So much has been said about the mother instinct as the model of altruism and the foundation of all morality in the evolution of man that it seems fair to say a few mild words about the father instinct." Drawing on his experiences with pigeons he had kept as a boy, Max pointed out that nature was full of examples of "share and share-alike arrangements." Among pigeons, the father's devotion to his children seemed "quite as mysteriously generous as the mother's." With certain species of marine animals, too, the father was the main provider. An extreme example was the seahorse, where the male of the species carries a pouch in which the female deposits her eggs. Once they are

Figure 50. Max and Brandy. EMIIA1.

hatched, the father takes care of them full time. Max cited copious other ex-amples to reinforce the case he wants to make for male parental "gentleness": the male ostrich sits on the eggs to protect them; the male beaver lives in a separate burrow where he can monitor the dam and thus the safety of his fam-ily; the gorilla father decides when it's bedtime for his little ones and builds his nest nearest the ground so he can best protect them; the Emperor King penguin is solely responsible for keeping "his" egg warm in subzero tempera-tures and never eats a thing while he is doing that.

Was Max indeed so oblivious to his own near-absence in his son's life? Or was he reliving—through the lens of animal psychology—his own days as a male suffragette?[56] Max wanted to call his new book *How Human Are Ani-mals?*, after an essay he had written for the *Saturday Review* about courtship rituals in the animal world, which Max had found to be every bit as passionate as those of humans, without the element of sinfulness injected into them. Swans are monogamous, but in a book by the ethologist Konrad Lorenz he had read the tale of a male swan that rejected the advances of a determined female when she approached him close to the nest where his mate was sitting. Later that same day the male was seen on the other side of the lake making love to precisely the female he had rejected earlier, "without more ado." If social conventions and gender roles were fluid among animals, they nevertheless had a well-developed sense of property, marking their territory with songs, special scents, or, if need be, violent action. "It was nature, not man, who invented the delight of owning a little piece of this planet we camp on."[57]

Animals are driven by pleasure, not by the categorical imperative, and in "Love Among the Insects," first published in *Audubon Magazine* in May 1963 and then in condensed form in Wally's magazine, Max gently pushed the boundaries of propriety at the *Digest* by describing, with relish, the mating rituals among crickets. Seduced by the male's energetic scraping, the female climbs on the male's back, where she feeds on the secretions of a special gland, which, Max explains, may be the animal equivalent of the "gift of a box of chocolates" in the world of human dating. The final union, a vigorous exchange of "singing and nudging, giving and receiving," goes on for quite a while. The reason for that, apart from the obvious purpose of procreation: to make things as pleasurable as possible for both parties. Max approved. Even when the male gets eaten in the process, as happens with the praying mantis, this is, as Max sees it, but a noble sacrifice in the service of sensual delight: "He surrenders his life to love and posterity without a quiver of hesitation." The grayling butterfly sprays perfume on the sensitive antennae of his inamorata, and the female moth attracts suitors, sometimes as many as fifty at a time, by dispersing, weather conditions permitting, her scent in all directions. And the dance of the male mayflies has but one purpose—getting the females to join them so they can fly away together, in pairs, to mate. Bowing, curtsying, kissing, snuggling, fondling, embracing, giving presents, seducing with perfume, serenading, dancing, and rubbing noses, animals make and mate their way through their brief lives. Concluded Max: "It remains a mystery why the slender demoiselle dragonflies link themselves together and fly around in tandem for hours before mating, and why they continue in this position long afterward, the male bringing the female along behind him as though on a flying bicycle-built-for-two, until she has laid her eggs on the leaf or stem of some plant growing in the water."[58]

Love and Revolution, the second volume of Max's autobiography, appeared on January 4, 1965, Max's eighty-second birthday, under the imprint of Random House. It had taken much effort to get a publisher interested in the book, and the final form of the manuscript owed much to the advice of Max's friend Dan Aaron.[59] The unabashed delight Max took in his own life, including his sexual escapades, spread out over almost seven hundred pages, was bound to alienate as well as intrigue. But nothing could have prepared Max for the demolition job performed by George Lichtheim in the *New York Review of Books*. A German-born historian of Marxism, Lichtheim was known for his wit as well as his intellectual arrogance, both of which were on full display in his review. He wasn't put off by Max's tales of sexual conquest. What bothered him was the "staggering banality" of Max's political and philosophical views and the "insipidity of his poetic tastes." As Lichtheim saw it, Max simply wasn't smart enough. He was "the Frank Harris of Socialism," Lichtheim quipped, in a backhanded reference to the author of the semipornographic *My Love and Lives* (1922–27). Max's ideological commitments had never been serious ones. He became an "indoor Marxman" only after his girlfriend Ida Rauh had explained communism to him in three easy steps: "There is no evidence, despite his professions to the contrary and an enthusiastic endorsement from Edmund Wilson, that he ever went deeper into the subject." Paired with Lichtheim's condescension came his obvious anti-Americanism. Max had been able to speak so freely about subjects he knew nothing about because Americans didn't suffer from the same inhibitions as their more refined European counterparts. And, to be sure, Max Eastman was "one of the least inhibited specimens ever to make an appearance between two hard covers."[60]

One wonders why the editors of the *New York Review of Books* had allowed such a blatant ad hominem attack—ironically shaped by the same lack of deeper engagement with the subject of its critique that the reviewer had identified in Max's writing—to be published in their pages. Max wondered, too. Sensing he would feel hurt, the editor Barbara Epstein sent Max a note: "I was terribly upset. But it will probably sell a lot of copies of your book. It *does* give it a lot of attention." She would happily print his letter if Max wanted to respond. A deeply disappointed Max wrote back to say that, no, he didn't want to respond to those "five long columns of sneers and insults." What Mr. Lichtheim had delivered was not a review "but a spitting on the author." If Epstein, who apparently had no respect for him either, really felt that this character assassination posing as a book review would sell any copies of *Love and Revolution*, she was mistaken. "I am sad to see you do this, not only because it concerns me and my book, but because in a civilized society such unrestrained effluvia of political and personal hate posing as intellectual and literary criticism ought not to be published at all."[61] Clearly, Max had forgotten some of his own gloves-off polemics against Eliot, James Joyce, and even his friend Cummings.

Norman Podhoretz, the newly minted editor of *Commentary* and not yet the conservative polemicist he is remembered as today, hadn't forgotten. In *Book News* he wondered why, after reading so much about Max, he felt so little respect for him. In many ways Max's was the quintessential American story: "The beautiful son of two Congregational ministers, the brilliant protégé of John Dewey, the famous young poet and polemicist and orator (and lover), the center of that rollicking upsurge in the Greenwich Village of the 'teens against bourgeois morals and capitalist values, the early supporter of Trotsky against Stalin—could such a person in any other country in the world end his years in the masthead of such a publication as *Reader's Digest?*" The problem, for Podhoretz, was the "streak of vulgarity" in Max, as manifested especially in his stubborn rejection of modernism in literature. This resistance had made him, curiously, very much like the Stalinists he opposed. In a period when Wilson and other leftists were defending Eliot and Joyce against the charge of "unintelligibility" leveled by American middlebrow critics and when the label of "bourgeois decadence" was freely applied to the modernists by Communist Party hacks, Max had unaccountably joined that assault. In Podhoretz's eyes, the result of Max's confused allegiances was plainly evident in *Love and Revolution:* self-indulgence and a fondness for cliché, in terms of both substance and style. Ironically, Podhoretz was complaining about some of the same flaws in Max that, three decades earlier, had bothered Max about Trotsky: Max was a boor.[62]

Fortunately for Max other reviewers were more excited. Alan Pryce-Jones, writing in the *Herald Tribune,* noted some of the book's faults—"too ardent a romanticism, too nervy a self-importance, too little discipline, too little confidence"—but then pointed out that Max himself had freely confessed to all of them. To Pryce-Jones, the total picture was an "endearing" one. He was especially touched by Max's account of his marriage: "Although quite a hopeless lover, Eastman was a better husband than most."[63] In a similar vein Jessie Kitching, the reviewer for the *New York Post,* while conceding that the book was perhaps "over-wordy," basked in Max's "flashes of wit, wisdom and revelation."[64] But the critic who probably best understood Max's intentions was Joseph Slater, a professor at Colgate University. In the *Saturday Review* he recalled Max's earlier autobiographical volume, *Enjoyment of Living,* and offered collective words of praise for both books. They were, he said, the great novel he never wrote: a "rich and dramatic" bildungsroman but also a Rabelaisian romp, "discursive, gossipy, unbuttoned," an entertaining account of a wild life, not invalidated by its conventional, *Reader's Digest*-y ending.[65] Wasn't that how a good bildungsroman was supposed to end—with the hero's self inevitably diminished, taken down a few notches by life's circumstances, but replaced by the narrator's superior insight and ability to recall all that led to the present moment?

Yet, as especially the negative reviews of his new book showed, Max's life had in some ways always resisted all such attempts to fit it into a neat story line. For what the reviewers really objected to wasn't the book itself but the life that it was about. A former socialist wasn't supposed to end up on DeWitt Wallace's payroll. And if he did, he had to be shallow, vulgar, confused. Thus, in a sense the dénouement of Max's life wasn't a conventional one at all: the male suffragette, the leftist critic of modernist experimentation, the erudite intellectual writing articles for magazines typically found in podiatrists' waiting rooms had not lost his ability to puzzle the critics.

Max's final book, or at least the last to appear in his lifetime, was *Seven Kinds of Goodness,* published in 1967 by Horizon Press, an exploration of what it means to live the good life. Again, some of the essays had first appeared, in shorter form, in *Reader's Digest.* But collected in a book, they assumed new significance, opening yet another window into Max's life. Once again he was grappling with the idea that morality and religion were necessarily connected. As prayer and religious ritual were losing their importance in public life, the time had come to revive the idea of individual morality, the code by which Max had organized his own life. The communists had thrown their half of the world into utter confusion by substituting historic necessity for any concept of morality: "Apparently it has not occurred to any of them that, on those grounds, once the proletarian society is achieved, . . . no standards of honorable and good conduct, will have any validity at all." But in the modern world those who had been brought up to believe that moral standards had been set up by God were similarly disoriented. Hence Max's descent into what the great moral lawgivers in history had thought about the matter of the good life.

Max's quick portraits of Buddha, Confucius, Moses, Mohammed, Socrates, Plato, and Jesus show he was still a master of the caustic epigram and witty aperçu: "It is said of Socrates that he stood thinking in a portico all of one night. The same thing is reported of Gotama except that he had the forethought to sit down." Buddha would have, he observed, made a "good bookkeeper, for he loved to arrange things in neat little lists, with numbers attached to it: the four noble truths, the eight-fold path to salvation," and so forth. And Plato "went so far as to say that the idea of beauty is more fun to be with . . . than a beautiful person." An admirer of athletic prowess and perhaps a former athlete himself, Plato "would not have known what to make of the long, frail, languid, ineffectual saints that populate most of our church windows."[66]

For all that he had learned from them, Max found his seven teachers wanting in different ways. They were, he concluded, internally divided, self-contradictory, given to savage fits of violence—and all because they could not entirely let go of the supernatural. Among the seven, Buddha, who had told his disciples to accept as truth only what their experience and "thorough investigation" had told them they could (was Max remembering his old pragmatist days?), and Confucius, who thought the ills of the world could be cured without crying to the gods for help, came closest to Max's own vision of goodness. Moses, while he was mindful of God, presided over mass terror and massacres; only when he had nearly forgotten about God did he find himself capable of offering useful moral advice. Socrates went nowhere without his little private God, like a dove, sitting on his shoulder and, despite his insistence on the everyday logical use of the mind, could not let go of his belief in the immortality of the soul. And Jesus and Mohammed alike shrank from the delights of sex.

Max's own stakes in the book are clearest in the chapter on Jesus, where he remembers his religious upbringing and being forced to learn the beatitudes by heart: "Even now those vividly arresting words lie beaten down like a racetrack through my mind." That was not his mother's fault: "My mother, who was not responsible for this Sabbath-day exercise, loved Jesus with an unorthodox yet fervent love; and I loved my mother. I learned from her to think of Jesus as in all respects, though not a divine, yet an ultimate teacher of the wisdom of life." He found it hard to forgive Jesus for his condemnation of "the least flicker of extramarital desire in a man" (that one spoke to Max personally) but praised him for having given a new poetic expression to the idea of "humbleness about oneself."[67]

Max ended his book—did he know it was going to be his last one?—with a moving tribute to his past: "Coming from a tribe of Christian ministers, I have always felt the temptation to compose a sermon." But his was a different kind of sermon, based not on a biblical verse but on Robert Herrick's very secular encouragement to "gather ye rosebuds while ye may."[68] Max the renegade preacher felt compelled to dispense with faith as well as with hope, that "heavenly decoy." Instead, he offered his readers something less spiritual in their place: growth. "To grow continually without growing old—that is affirmative, dramatic, difficult." This was the old Max Eastman, resisting his own inevitable decline, tending, as his father once did, too, his garden to the end, but free of the sexual guilt that had paralyzed Sam Eastman. "A man who knows himself and knows the world, whatever his attitude to the mystery of the universal, needs no God and no Sunday-school-teacher to tell him to be good. If he preserves, together with mindfulness, courage, sympathy, temperance, justice, and the art of inquiry, the gift nature gave him of growth, he will live well, and with good luck will live happily; and when his time comes to fall to the ground with the sparrow, he will know that he has made a jewel of the accident of his being." Note the biblical language, a reference to the fall of the sparrow that does not happen without God's will (Matthew 10:29), that slips into Max's rejection of religion. Max had remained a minister's son—or, rather, the son of two ministers!—to the end.[69]

When the Poetry Society of America asked Max to speak at their annual dinner in July 1966 he readily accepted and impressed everyone. "That great throbbing sweetheart of a bygone Greenwich Village" hadn't lost his touch, exulted Pat Smith, who covered the event for the *World Telegram*. Guests in the Versailles Suite at New York's Astor Hotel had been fidgeting on the edge of their chairs after having to endure a lecture by Professor John Gassner called "The Lack of Poetry in Modern Drama." Salvador Dalí, wearing a flowing necktie and scarf, was in attendance and read one of his poems in Spanish, which sounded like Morse code to the audience. They couldn't wait for Max to begin: "Nearly all the 300 members . . . were old enough to recall when Eastman was considered by the New York literati of the '20s as the handsomest man in the world."

And Max didn't disappoint: "The big, good-looking man rose to his full height of 6 feet 3 inches, took the podium and ran his fingers through a heavy head of flowing white hair." (The infatuated reporter had grown Max by a full three inches!) A young actress named Scottie MacGregor, later known for her work in *Little House on the Prairie*, whispered, "Good heavens. They say he must be 80, but it can't be." Max was eighty-three. "They asked me to speak on 20th century poetry," declared Max. "But, my feelings on 20th century poetry are not the kindest." Applause burst through the crowd. Max continued to explain, in "a quavering, but lusty voice," that good poetry had died with the French symbolist movement, in the aftermath of which poems became "puzzles, things to decipher." They had stopped being enjoyable. The room rocked with agreement. Many might have remembered plowing through the notes accompanying *The Waste Land*. "I trust," intoned Max, that "within the next generation, poetry will change back to art, and away from the metered blur that it is today." He ended his talk, timed to be no longer than ten minutes, by "reviewing several episodes in his well-chronicled romantic years, drawing laughter with nearly every phrase." The poet-critic-lover was done.[70]

A close friend and protégé of Max's during these last years was the young novelist Nicholas ("Nick") Delbanco. He was Carly Simon's boyfriend, and while Max was certainly receptive to Carly's extraordinary beauty, he took a more than casual interest in Delbanco, whose talents he recognized. Max's sense of craftsmanship was still impeccable. When Nick read, or rather chanted, to him passages from his novel-in-progress—lavishly resonant lines composed in a fine frenzy, smoldering with the "ecstasy of self-congratulation"—Max, who hadn't forgotten his reservations about literary hermeticism, gently brought him back to the ground. What does it all mean? he asked. And after Nick volunteered a more mundane paraphrase of what he had just read, Max suggested, "Why don't you write it down"?

Nick would occasionally stay with Max at East Pasture Road, remembering later, with lyrical precision, the rather magical atmosphere of the place: "The morning would be glorious: that crystalline light, those sizable skies, the pine trees somehow greener against the sere scrub oak." As Nick, after a morning of working on his novel, would dash toward the pond, Max would already be in the water, beckoning to him, his white hair fluttering in the wind like the feathers of a snowy egret. Nicholas Delbanco went on to become a distinguished novelist and widely admired teacher of a new generation of writers. But in his memory that scene on the Vineyard beach repeats itself again and again, even decades later, "in perfect clarity": the young man on the shore, the old man in the water, waving at him, a kind of reversal of the final moments in Thomas Mann's *Death in Venice*, with Max calling his friend to embrace life, a beginning, not an end.[71]

But in reality time *was* running out for Max. In January 1967, during a winter vacation in sunny Barbados, the famous swimmer almost drowned. Despite the rough sea, Max had gone for a swim when Yvette realized he "wasn't making it." The current was too strong, and Yvette had to call for help.[72] A few months later, however, Max and Yvette were en route to Paris again and then on to Nice and London. On the inside at least, Max was as restless as he had always been. And he was still living from day to day. When his nephew Samuel Ewer Eastman, Anstice's son, asked him for a loan, Max explained that he couldn't really help him: "I'm 84, almost 85, years old, and I have no securities and no life insurance, nothing to leave Yvette but a lot of vacant land and a very small sum of money in the savings bank." Yvette would need whatever he had, and *what* he had was close to nothing. He was as short of cash as he had been in his old Village days.[73]

His son Dan, now a practicing psychologist, had become a part of Max's life more than he had ever been before (fig. 51). "There must be a lot of conflicting emotions towards such an inadequate parent as I have been," admitted Max. But he was now ready to treat Dan as an equal: "I vastly enjoy your wit and charm and speculative intelligence and rich stores of knowledge, and so does Yvette." Dan's new wife, Marie Jo, was so lovely that Max instantly wanted to see more of his son: "But the fact that you never respond by calling us or coming of your own accord makes me feel that you don't inwardly like being with us."[74] But Dan was keeping busy, though not only with his work. His mother, Ida, had just broken her hip, "the fourth major medical crisis in the last eight years." Since Dan was the one who was ultimately responsible for everything that was done for her, "you can imagine that I am just about as fed up with it as she is." Ironically, Dan had been working on creating a life that at least outwardly resembled his father's. He was building a house for Marie Jo that was, "like yours," on a hill. In Warwick, New York, there was no ocean in sight, but one had magnificent views of the mountains wherever one looked. "No more New York City! I tried it for thirty years!" He was also trying his hand at being an author, without much immediate success.[75] Max read Dan's manuscript "with excited admiration," especially a chapter on determinism in science. He returned the manuscript to Dan with suggestions for revision. Any traces of Dan's book, like the tracks of the author himself, have faded.[76]

Max was now experiencing a medical crisis of his own. "Max depressed," Yvette noted in her journal: "I don't quite know how to help and do everything else."[77] He was struggling with the beginnings of Parkinson's disease, a diagnosis he seems to have shared with only a few close friends. One sign of Max's newly fragile self was that it didn't take much to move him to tears. When, at the end of April 1968, he saw the new Katharine Hepburn and Spencer Tracy movie about interracial dating *Guess Who's Coming to Dinner?*, his sobs of "joyous pain" interrupted the movie. Known as the pseudobulbar affect, such outbursts are often associated with Parkinson's. Not that Max wasn't genuinely moved. He said he hadn't been so affected by a public performance since as a child he had heard his mother pray. In the movie the white-haired Tracy, who

Figure 51. *Father and Son* (Max and Daniel Eastman). Photograph by Charles Neider, 1957. Inscription by Max Eastman. EMIIA1. By permission of Susan Neider.

was dead within two weeks after the filming was completed, looks like a shorter, chubbier, more professorial version of Max. Marked by death—Hepburn was said to have cried real tears during her lover's final speech—Tracy would have reminded Max of himself, with the exception of the intense paternal feelings expressed by Tracy's character.[78]

Max was also having panic attacks that made it difficult for him to sleep comfortably. He would wake up in the middle of the night terrified by the idea that he would not "wake up as Max tomorrow morning." Sue Sekey and Yvette did their best to comfort him when this happened, but Max's anxiety was so profound that nothing seemed to help. It was, wrote Sue in her journal, "saddening, nearly unbearable." Max was failing, there could be no doubt. And what a sad sight he was at the breakfast table, wearing a sweater over his pajamas, unshaven, his hands, mouth, and voice trembling. Suddenly he had become an old man. But at least occasionally, inadequately buoyed by the antidepressant Tofranil, "for moral and good feeling," he could be found working fitfully at his desk.[79]

There was indeed some unfinished business Max felt he had to attend to. In the 1930s he had almost completed a translation of a dozen chapters written by the exiled Trotsky on the life of the young Lenin, a fragment of a full-scale, ultimately abandoned biography Trotsky had undertaken in an attempt to rescue his former idol from the clutches of the Stalinists. But then Max's copy of the manuscript suddenly vanished from his barn-study at Croton. "It had been stolen and destroyed," Max wrote, suspecting some kind of Stalinist foul play.[80] Mysteriously, it showed up some twenty years later at Harvard's Houghton Library. Houghton sent him a copy; like the return of the repressed, it was now back on his desk. Florence Crowther, Max's agent, discovered that there was a decades-old contract between Doubleday and Trotsky and that Max had already been paid $600 for work he had never finished. It seemed appropriate that he was now returning to it. His career as a critic of Marxism had begun with a biography of the young Trotsky, and it was now to end with Trotsky's biography of the young Lenin.[81]

It was nearly too late, though. After a hospital stay Max had trouble walking and wasn't getting far even on crutches or with a walker.[82] The famous Maxian charisma lingered on despite the mounting physical impediments. To Rosalinde Fuller, he was as attractive as ever. "Darling First Love," she wrote, celebrating the arrival of his letter: "I tore it open and held it against my body—It was part of you and now it looks rumpled like people after making love . . . that sweet exciting disorder." It transported her back to nights lying naked in the sand dunes with Max beside her, hearing the seagulls pass over her with the "sighing feathery sounds their wings make." Carried away by the memory, she imagined herself putting her arms all the way around his wheelchair so that she could "hold you and kiss your lovely mouth." With Max in it, any wheelchair would look like a throne, asserted Margarita Dobert, another infatuated friend. Dobert, a travel writer who had undertaken a "one-woman safari" through Egypt, Sudan, Chad, Nigeria, Niger, Cameroon, and Mali equipped with nothing but a map, an air mattress, and three dresses, quoted one of Max's poems back to him: "Give the wild will never."[83]

And Max didn't, not yet at least (fig. 52). Undeterred by his physical impairments, he again felt the pull of warmer climates. In February 1969 Yvette and Max left New York, as they had done several times before, for his beloved Barbados, to rest and bask in the sun. He was scheduled to start a new, experimental treatment for Parkinson's after his return.[84] Sue arrived on March 5 to keep Yvette company and, presumably, also help her take care of Max. A successful interior designer in New York, she was also a passionate writer of journals, and she left a detailed, atmospherically rich account of what became the last month of Max's life. Once again Max had surrounded himself with beautiful things. Enjoying the ride from the airport to Max's rented

Figure 52. Max Eastman, undated. EMIIA1.

summer home, Sue took in, with appreciation, the bursts of red and white hibiscus, bougainvillea, and poinsettia in the gardens all around her, and she loved the shimmering ocean directly behind the house. Max was using a wheelchair, but he and Yvette were tanned and looked much younger than their years. Yet Sue noticed the constant, low-level bickering that was going on between the two, and Yvette complained to her that she was starved for meaningful conversation.[85]

On March 18, what turned out to be the last day of his conscious life, Max watched some television and then lamented that he had wasted his life. Yvette and Sue vehemently disagreed and asked him why on earth he would think that. Max replied that he should not have spent "those many years in politics." He refused his routine nighttime snack and said he just wanted to go to bed, even though nights were usually far from comfortable for him then and he would often wake up feeling cold and in pain.

The next morning Yvette couldn't rouse him. Sue rushed in to help and was devastated by what she saw: oblivious to the world, Max was lying in bed, making strange gurgling sounds. He had lost control of his bodily functions. In desperation Yvette and Sue hoisted his big body into the wheelchair and fastened him with a bed sheet only to be told by the doctor, who had meanwhile arrived, that they should put him back in bed again. Like his mother, he had suffered a massive brain hemorrhage. And like Annis, too, Max fought against death with all he had left. What Max had feared the most—that one day he wouldn't wake up as Max—had happened. Max was admitted to St. Joseph's Hospital in Bridgetown, where the nurses scrupulously avoided saying prayers over him. It was only then that Yvette broke down: "How terrible not to even say goodbye." She called Dan in New York, who did not offer to come down, and Max's nephew Peter in California, who arrived a day later.

For eleven years Yvette and Max had never really been apart, and it seemed impossible that Max had now abandoned her, leaving behind nothing but this massive body pointlessly struggling to survive on its own, inert except for the labored breathing that sounded more and more like a bellows as the days went by. Ironically, Max was still beautiful. His legs were thin again, like those of a young man, freed from their burden of carrying his ailing body.

To Yvette, it seemed as if Max, in death, had allowed himself to be drawn into the script he had first described in his poem "Epitaph," written some three decades earlier:

> Now life has had her fill of me,
> Death, less cruel, has me in her bed.
> Yet think not I came lustingly,
> Or by her mother-tender touches led.
>
> She dragged me to her bosom drugged,
> She forced her peace like gas into my face.
> I lie, torn fainting from the pains I hugged,
> Frigid forever in her kind embrace.[86]

Death was the lover to end all lovers, Max's terrible, final mistress—a dealer in drugs and sedatives, not the mother of beauty. Characteristically, Max had imagined it, or rather *her*, as the end of his famous capacity of giving and receiving pleasure.

Max had seen Florence, Crystal, and Eliena die, but when his own death finally came, on March 26, 1969, at 1 a.m. in room 108 of St. Joseph's Hospital, he was alone. He had asked that his body be cremated. Dan brutally suggested Yvette simply get the body burned in Trinidad. But she would hear none of that. *Reader's Digest* sent $2,500. There was no word from Dan or his nephew Jeff or his niece Annis. What goes around comes around.

On April 2, when Max's body was to be transferred to the States for cremation and burial, their flight was delayed—as if Max wasn't ready to leave just yet: "My fantasy is," wrote Sue, "that Max is not conceding to death and that this flight delay is a further ruse." But then Sue, seated on the plane, was looking out the window, and she saw the great, long, raw wooden box traveling up the belt. It was a shock to realize that Max, or something that had once belonged to Max, was in there. It seems likely Max, deeply antimetaphysical as he was, would have enjoyed the manner of his departure from the only world be believed in, and likely, too, he would have relished even what happened to his ashes. Due to some bureaucratic mix-up they were delivered to Yvette by regular mail, with additional postage due and signature required. Sue became overwhelmed by "the thought of Max, the person reduced to a box of ashes and the horror of the delivery by ordinary, everyday mail." Cremation might be the sanest way to dispose of a body but seeing this residue was another matter, "the most brutal expression of the end," she felt. "I recall Max of bones and blood and muscle and nerves and mind, a moving, thinking, talkative person now DUST." What Max once was now lived on only "in print and the minds of friends." For the next few months what was left of the Max of bones and blood and muscle—and there was more of him even now than of most other people, since he had been so big in life—remained locked in a file cabinet at 8 West Thirteenth Street.

In a lighter moment Yvette told Sue that the next time she married it would be for money. Did Onassis have a brother? But the truth was that Max had left her well provided for—so well, in fact, that Max's son, who was now drinking heavily, found it difficult to be around "the bitch," as he would refer to Yvette. Dan did inherit some of Max's property on the Vineyard, about ten acres, and Yvette suspected he had been nice to his father only for the sake of the land. Now that he didn't have to pretend anymore Dan felt free to announce that he "hated Max's guts" and wasn't even going to attend the memorial. Ironically, the few surviving photographs show that Dan, as he was aging, too, was beginning to look more and more like a younger, stockier version of his father.[87]

In the end Dan did show up for the memorial. Standing next to Jeff Fuller, he did not make a scene, and he did not embarrass Yvette, who sat through the proceedings clutching a small spray of lily of the valley. The ceremony took place on May 19 at the Williams Club, a private club at 24 East Thirty-ninth Street in Manhattan open to the alumni of Williams College. There was standing room only. Dick Green, the Eastmans' lawyer, acted as master of ceremonies. Roger Baldwin spoke, a neighbor on the Vineyard and one of Max's and Crystal's allies when they were still on the Left, a cofounder, with Crystal and others, of what later became the ACLU. Baldwin, clearly moved and speaking partly extemporaneously, recalled his long friendship with Max, untroubled by their later political disagreements, buoyed by a common delight in life and the pleasures it had offered them. He evoked the many causes to which Max had contributed, from women's suffrage to antimilitarism, and graciously honored Dan Eastman as well as Fuller and their work for the ACLU. From the other end of the spectrum, there was Hobart ("Hobe") Lewis from the *Reader's Digest,* who had taken the reins of the magazine after Wally's retirement in 1965. Perhaps nervous to be speaking to an audience he suspected to be rather on the highbrow side, he'd cobbled together excerpts from Max's articles for the *Digest* and, at least according to Sue, went on for far too long. Marie Bullock, the president of the American Academy of Poets, paid tribute to Max the poet. Then the actress and theater director Margaret Webster, the first woman to direct at the Met and another neighbor of Max's on the Vineyard, and the poet and editor John Hall Wheelock read a dozen of Max's poems, among them "Epitaph," "Lisa in Summer," and the obligatory "At the Aquarium." Despite the fact that Webster, who had spent a significant part of her career in England, lent an unexpected Shakespearean lilt to Max's lines, making them sound even more formal than they were, Sue thought these poems had never sounded so thrilling. Wheelock closed with Max's version of the Ten Commandments, as delivered by Lot's wife: "To yourself for life's sake, speak the truth," a commandment Max had, for all his flaws, always honored. The ceremony ended with the reading of a fond note that Leon Edel, the acclaimed biographer of Henry James, had sent from Hawaii. Afterward, a small group went to have dinner at Del Pezzo's restaurant on Forty-seventh Street. Dan did not join them.

By all accounts addicted to alcohol, Daniel Eastman died within six months of his father after suffering a heart attack while talking on the phone, long distance, with his mother.[88] That is one version. Current family members continue to believe that Dan, who had been in a "bad way psychologically" after Max's death, in fact committed suicide.[89] In his will he left his father's land to a barmaid he had spent time with in the Village: a final gesture of anger directed against Max and, presumably, also Yvette. Frantic about this unexpected development, Yvette invited the woman out to the Vineyard. She arrived wearing high heels and a tight, sexy dress and was entirely unprepared for how rural things were out there. Obviously, Dan had wanted to alienate the family, but it's hard not to imagine how pleased Max would have been with such a lovely looking visitor, never mind why she had come. Yvette offered the woman some cash, and the new would-be resident readily relinquished her claim and made a hasty exit back to more familiar territory.[90]

• • •

On August 3, 1969, Max's ashes were interred at East Pasture Road. Again, Roger Baldwin spoke. Again, poems were read, and each person in attendance shoveled a scoop of earth into the hole.[91] And there Max still lies, a rocky ledge behind him, his grave overlooking the improbably blue, improbably still waters of Menemsha Pond. It was Yvette who selected the inscription for the plaque that was laid into the rock: "Max Eastman / Poet-Philosopher / For whom life was / a celebration / and a joyous affirmation of freedom." He was the last of the outrageous Eastman children to die, more than four decades after Crystal and three after Anstice, who had seemed so much stronger than everybody else.

Writing to express his condolences to Yvette, Max's former editor William Buckley, who, like others of his conservative friends, was never entirely comfortable with Max's atheism, expressed the hope that dear old Max, "notwithstanding his stubbornness," was now "off enjoying the Elysian fields."[92] It is tempting to imagine Max dancing there in the buff, or insisting that he be allowed to. Jungle Beach, the place on Martha's Vineyard where he did so in life (when he wasn't sunbathing on his own pebbly lot), eventually stopped being a haven for nudists. It enjoyed a brief boom period after Max's death, with, by one account, hundreds of nudists hiking a mile to shed their clothes there, long-haired hippies as well as respectable families. But then a syndicate headed by the former defense secretary and president of the World Bank Robert McNamara bought the land, cordoned off private areas, and eventually instituted patrols to curb such excesses.[93] They weren't able to eliminate them entirely, but today Jungle Beach seems a shadow of what it once was. Characteristically, Max didn't like being called a nudist—this was a word only philistines would use, since it implied there was something wrong with being naked.[94] But regardless of the terminology, among those on the Vineyard who like to shed their clothes Max is still remembered, without any equivocation, as a great hero, a god during a time when the island wasn't yet the playground of the rich and people still loved their bodies. "He was a rascal and a rake," remembers one longtime Vineyard resident, now in his late seventies. Not only was he always naked, he always had three or four naked women with him. "He was a great believer in life. How can you believe in life if you're all clothed?"[95] And thus Max Eastman lives on, in the memory of some, a modern God Pan, though more handsome and with soft hands, parting the bushes, stepping out onto the warm sand and into the glowing sun.[96]

NOTE ON SOURCES

This book relies on rich archival and, in most cases, unpublished sources. Since most of the Eastman papers at the Lilly Library are not processed and still in the original folders, with titles provided by Max or Yvette Eastman, my citations refer to sources by the name of the collection only. Readers desiring more guidance to specific materials are welcome to get in touch with me at www.christophirmscher.com. My transcriptions scrupulously follow the original manuscripts, except for obvious mistakes and idiosyncrasies that disrupt the flow of reading. Additions I have made for clarity are indicated by square brackets. Where available, I have silently substituted postmarks for missing dates on letters. Carbon copies are indicated by "cc"; copies made by Max or others are listed as "copy."

Max Eastman was prodigiously productive, and no bibliography can hope to do full justice to his output. Archie Henderson has been maintaining a bibliography of Eastman-related archival collections, which is available on my home page.

For their generosity and cooperation I am grateful to the following estates and their representatives: Carol Leadenham, Hoover Institution Archives, for permission to quote from Joseph Freeman's letters (copyright Stanford University); Diana Lachatanere as the Representative of the Works of Claude McKay, for permission to quote from the poems and letters of Claude McKay; Chris Hyman and Catherine Stern for allowing me use of the letters and poems of Creigh Collins Stern; and Breon Mitchell, literary executor for the Yvette and Max Eastman Estate, for permission to quote from the published and unpublished works, letters, and journals of Max Eastman, Eliena Eastman, and Yvette Eastman. Material from the papers of Max, Eliena, and Yvette Eastman also appears courtesy of the Lilly Library, Indiana University Bloomington. W. W. Norton has given me permission to quote from Max Eastman's *Stalin's Russia*.

All translations from the Russian are by Anna Arays. ALA-LC Romanization has been used for Russian words throughout the text, with the exception of proper names with standardized spellings.

Notes

The following abbreviations appear in the notes. All books, articles (other than those published in newspapers), and poems listed without an author are by Max Eastman.

Persons

AE	Anstice Eastman
AFE	Annis Ford Eastman
CC	Creigh Collins
CE	Crystal Eastman
DA	Daniel Aaron
DE	Daniel Eastman
EE	Eliena Eastman
FD	Florence Deshon
FN	Florence Norton
IR	Ida Rauh
JF	Joseph Freeman
ME	Max Eastman
SEE	Samuel Elijah Eastman
YE	Yvette Eastman

Collections

AEM	Anstice Eastman Mss. (Lilly Library, Indiana University Bloomington)
CEP	Crystal Eastman Papers (Schlesinger Library, Harvard University)
DAP	Daniel Aaron Papers (Houghton Library, Harvard University)

DM	Deshon Mss. (Lilly Library, Indiana University Bloomington)
EEM	Eliena Eastman Mss. (Lilly Library, Indiana University Bloomington)
EM	Eastman Mss. (Lilly Library, Indiana University Bloomington)
EMII	Eastman Mss. II (Lilly Library, Indiana University Bloomington)
EMIIA1	Eastman Mss. II, Addition 1: Vineyard Collection (Lilly Library, Indiana University, Bloomington)
EMIIA2	Eastman Mss. II, Addition 2: New York Collection (Lilly Library, Indiana University Bloomington)
Houghton	Houghton Library, Harvard University
Lilly	Lilly Library, Indiana University Bloomington
MM	Claude McKay Mss. (Lilly Library, Indiana University Bloomington)
Schlesinger	Schlesinger Library, Radcliffe Institute, Harvard University
TM	Trotsky Mss. (Lilly Library, Indiana University Bloomington)

Books

| EL | Max Eastman, *Enjoyment of Living* |
| LR | Max Eastman, *Love and Revolution* |

Major Works by Max Eastman Cited in the Notes

Enjoyment of Poetry. New York: Scribner's, 1913. Expanded edition (with *Other Essays in Aesthetics*), 1939.

Child of the Amazons and Other Poems. New York: Mitchell Kennerley, 1913.

Journalism Versus Art. New York: Knopf, 1916.

Colors of Life: Poems and Songs and Sonnets. New York: Knopf, 1918.

The Sense of Humor. New York: Scribner's, 1922.

Leon Trotsky: The Portrait of a Youth. New York: Greenberg, 1925 (American edition); London: Faber and Gwyer, 1926 (British edition).

Since Lenin Died. New York: Boni and Liveright, 1925.

Marx, Lenin: The Science of Revolution. London: Allen and Unwin, 1926 (British edition). New York: Albert and Charles Boni, 1927 (American edition).

Venture. New York: Albert and Charles Boni, 1927.

Trotsky, Leon. *The Real Situation in Russia*. Translated by Max Eastman. New York: Harcourt, Brace, 1928.

Kinds of Love: Poems by Max Eastman. New York: Scribner's, 1931.

The Literary Mind: Its Place in an Age of Science. New York: Scribner's, 1931.

Capital, The Communist Manifesto, and Other Writings by Karl Marx. Edited, with an introduction, by Max Eastman. New York: Modern Library, 1932.

Trotsky, Leon. *The History of the Russian Revolution*. New York: Simon and Schuster, 1932 (vol. 1); 1933 (vols. 2 and 3). Later published by the University of Michigan Press in one volume (1935).

Artists in Uniform: A Study of Literature and Bureaucratism. New York: Knopf, 1934.

Art and the Life of Action with Other Essays. New York: Knopf, 1934.

The Last Stand of Dialectic Materialism: A Study of Sidney Hook's Marxism. New York: Polemic Publishers, 1934.

Enjoyment of Laughter. New York: Simon and Schuster, 1936.

The End of Socialism in Russia. Boston: Little, Brown, 1937.

Anthology for Enjoyment of Poetry. New York: Scribner's Sons, 1939.

Stalin's Russia and the Crisis in Socialism. New York: Norton, 1940.

Marxism: Is It Science? New York: Norton, 1940.

Heroes I Have Known: Twelve Who Lived Great Lives. New York: Simon and Schuster, 1942.

Lot's Wife. New York: Harper & Brothers, 1942.

Enjoyment of Living. New York: Harper & Brothers, 1948.

Poems of Five Decades. New York: Harper & Brothers, 1954.

Reflections on the Failure of Socialism. New York: Devin-Adair, 1955.

Great Companions: Critical Memoirs of Some Famous Friends. New York: Farrar, Straus, and Cudahy, 1959.

Love and Revolution: My Journey through an Epoch. New York: Random, 1964.

Seven Kinds of Goodness. New York: Horizon, 1967.

Trotsky, Leon. *The Young Lenin.* Translated from the Russian by Max Eastman. Garden City: Doubleday, 1972.

Introduction

1. Daniel Aaron, *Writers on the Left* (1961; rpt. Oxford: Oxford University Press, 1977), 315; FN, Journal, September 9, 1945, NM.

2. Carly Simon, personal communication, February 7, 2016.

3. Max's typing is fondly evoked by Nicholas Delbanco, *Lastingness: The Art of Old Age* (New York: Grand Central, 2011), 187.

4. *Reader's Digest Student Guide. Close-up of a Digest Writer: "Max Eastman Recalls . . ."* (Pleasantville, NY: September, 1961), S-3.

5. "What will trouble me most," July 2, 1954, EMII.

6. Charmion von Wiegand, "Arrows of the Sun," EMII. The title was inspired by Max's poem "Coming Spring": "Arrows of the sun are flying!" (*Child of the Amazons*, 29).

7. "I Have the Gift of Leisure and of Life," "Poems and Sketches" [1913–15], EMII; *Time* (April 4, 1969): 90.

8. On April 19, 1938, Max declined, for the second time, an invitation to supply biographical material for inclusion in *Who's Who in American Jewry*. "I explained before that much as I appreciate the compliment to my intellectual ability, I am not a Jew, and have no Jews among my ancestors so far as they are known." ME to ?, April 19, 1938, EM.

9. Ted Daniel, personal communication, March 4, 2014.

10. ME to Frank Lieber, June 21, 1967, cc, EM.

11. ME to FN, January 25, 1956, NMII.

12. William L. O'Neill, *The Last Romantic: A Life of Max Eastman* (1978; rpt. New York: Transaction, 1991), xi, 295.

13. "Myself," "Poems and Sketches" [1916], EMII.

14. *Venture*, 57.

15. ME to EE, June 27, 1953, EEM; Louis Menand, "Stand by Your Man," *New Yorker*, September 26, 2005.

16. Edmund Wilson, "Max Eastman in 1941" (1941), in Wilson, *Classics and Commercials: A Literary Chronicle of the Forties* (New York: Vintage, 1962), 57–69.

17. Conversation with Daniel Aaron, January 30, 2015.

18. ME to Granville Hicks, November 23, 1935, Granville Hicks Papers, University of Syracuse Special Collections.

19. Michael Kazin, *American Dreamers: How the Left Changed a Nation* (New York: Knopf, 2011).

20. *Venture*, 42.

21. "I always cry when people are very happy," June 19, 1958, EM.

Chapter 1. The Devil at Park Church

1. *EL*, xiii; AFE to ME, April 27, 1899, EMII.

2. AFE to Grace Bill, February 11, 1879, EMII.

3. AFE to ME, [April 24], 1909, EM.

4. "Rev. Dr. Eastman, Pastor Emeritus of The Park Church, Succumbs to Illness Developed While in South," *Elmira Star-Gazette*, February 7, 1925. George and Sam Eastman had a "common great-great-great grandfather" (*EL*, 4).

5. SEE to AFE, September 23, 1874, EMII; AFE to SEE, October 21, 1874, EMII.

6. SEE to AFE, September 23, 1874, EMII; *EL* 40.

7. AFE to Grace Bill, February 1, 1876, EMII.

8. AFE to Grace Bill, February 24, 1876, EMII.

9. AFE to SE, November 8, 1891, EMII.

10. *EL*, 79.

11. "Mark Twain's Elmira," *Harper's Monthly Magazine* 176 (December 1, 1937): 620–32.

12. Marion S. Bryan to ME, November 6, 1936, EMII.

13. AFE to ME, March 16, April 17, 1900, EM.

14. SEE, "Pretty little aster!" November 5, 1901, *Cherith-Log*, 1901–1904, EMII.

15. ME to AFE, February 16, 1909, EM.

16. "To My Father," *Colors of Life*, 78.

17. "From notebook marked *Recollections at Glenora*," EMII.

18. AFE to ME, March 21, 1906, EM. Annis describes how, after she had forced down a quart of milk at bedtime, hoping it would relieve her troubles, all the milk came up again, "as if my soul rose up and said . . . 'Enough.' "

19. AFE to ME, March 27, 1906, EM.

20. AFE to SEE, n.d., EMII.

21. AFE to CE, "Saturday evening alone by the fire," n.d., EMII; AFE to ME, May 27, October 27, 1907, EM.

22. AFE to ME, March 23, 1908, EM.

23. AFE to CE, February 13, 1905 (letter separated into different folders).

24. AFE to ME, September 24, 1898, EM.

25. See http://www.theparkchurch.org/history.

26. ME to AFE, March 19, 1907, EM.

27. ME to AFE, February 1, 1907, EM.

28. AFE, "Man's Place in Nature," n.d., CEP.

29. AFE to ME, February 21, 1909, EM.

30. AFE, "Men and Reform," n.d., CEP; *EL*, 114.

31. "When I knew I should speak here tonight," EMII.

32. *Compendium of the Eleventh Census: 1890, Part III* (Washington, DC: Government Printing Office, 1897), 13.

33. "Some people will think I violate the sacredness," EMII.

34. ME, "We were all," EMII; *EL*, 62, 86.

35. *EL*, 66.

36. ME to CE, October 2, 1897, EM.

37. ME to CE, October 17, 1897, EM.

38. ME to CE, October 17, 1897, EM.

39. *EL*, 94; folder "My Character," EM.

40. AFE, "Men and Reform," undated, CEP.

41. *Cherith-Log*, 1901–1904, September 1, 4, 1901, EMIIA2.

42. *Cherith-Log*, 1901–1904, July 7, 1901, EMIIA2.

43. AFE to ME, February 21, March 11, 1899; AFE to AE, January 19, 1910; AFE to ME, January 21, 1899, EM.

44. ME to CE, May 28, 1899, EM.

45. *EL*, 116.

46. AFE to ME, undated note, with Max's addition: "found and read on September 23 [1898]," EM.

47. AFE to ME, September 17, September 16, 1898, EM.

48. AFE to ME, September [?], 1898; February 7, February 18, 1899; January 6, 1899; all EM. The "no-breakfast plan" was a new fad in Annis's repertoire of self-healing techniques, and she had already convinced Samuel and Max's cousin Adra to adopt it; AFE to ME, January 12, February 21, 1899, EM.

49. Annis, characteristically, encouraged Max to have sympathy for them: "They are probably beginners and doing their best. I think young people are apt to be very cruel and thoughtless"; AFE to ME, September 24, 1898, EM.

50. AFE to ME, February 21, February 26, 1900; AFE to ME, April 2, 1899, EM.

51. Max initially thought not. Annis told him he was wrong and should start reading a good weekly newspaper; AFE to ME, January 12, 1899, EM.

52. AFE to ME, January 21, 1899, EM; *EL*, 122.

53. AFE to ME, October 26, October 10, 1898; January 6, 1899; EM.

54. CE to ME, December 18, 1899, CEP.

55. AFE to ME, May 14, 1900, EM.

Chapter 2. Dearest of All Lovers

1. CE to AFE, July 2, 1899, CEP.

2. CE to ME, October 2, 1899, CEP.

3. CE to ME, October 2, 1899, CEP.

4. CE to ME, January 20, 1900, CEP.

5. CE to ME, February 4, 1900, CEP.

6. CE to ME, February 24, 1900, CEP.

7. ME to CE, September 27, 1900, CEP.

8. ME to CE, October 1, 1901, EM.

9. ME to CE, October 28, 1900, EM.

10. ME to CE, October 4, 1900, CEP.

11. Williams College Freshman Year "Experience Book" ("Autumn of 1900 to February 1901"), EMII.

12. *Venture*, 11–15.

13. ME to CE, February 19, 1901, CEP.

14. "Experience Book," EMII.

15. ME to CE, October 28, 1900, CEP.

16. "Experience Book," EMII.

17. CE to ME, January 17, 1901, CEP; ME to CE, February 8, 1901, EM.

18. "Experience Book," EMII; ME to CE, February 8, 1901, EM.

19. ME to CE, February 7, 1901, EM.

20. CE to ME, September 29, 1901, CEP.

21. Ralph Erskine to ME, May 9, 1938, copy, EMII.

22. ME to CE, October 6, 1901, EM.

23. ME to CE, November 18, 1901, EM.

24. ME to CE, November 22, 1901, EM.

25. ME to CE, December 3, 1901, EM.

26. ME to CE, January 19, 1902, EM.

27. ME to CE, March 16, 1902, EM.

28. AFE to ME, April 22, 1902, EM.

29. CE, Journal ("Catherine Crystal Eastman Her Book"), June 2, 1902, EMIIA2.

30. For this and the following quotations see ME's "My Western Trip," 1902, EMII.

31. Frederick William "Fritz" Updegraff or Up de Graff (1871–1927) later managed to get himself lost, for no less than seven years, in the Amazonian jungle, an experience he recounted in *Head Hunters of the Amazon* (1923).

32. CE to ME, August 13, 1902, CEP.

33. ME to CE, September 26, 1902, EM.

34. ME to CE, October 5, 1902, EM.

35. CE to ME, October 14, 1902, CEP.

36. ME to CE, October 14, 1902, EM.

37. ME to CE, October 26, 1902, EM.

38. ME to CE, December 7, 1902, EM.

39. ME to CE, January 14, 1903, EM.

40. ME to CE, October 26, 1902, EM.

41. ME to CE, January 14, 1903, EM.

42. CE to ME, January 19, 1903, CEP.

43. ME to CE, September 26, 1902, EM.

44. ME to CE, February 1, February 3, 1903, EM.

45. ME to CE, February 8, February 18, 1903, EM.

46. AE to CE, September 22, October 12, 1901, AEM.

47. CE to ME, June 12, 1903, CEP.

48. AFE to AE, July 24, 1903, CEP.

49. AFE to ME, October 19, 1898, AEM.

50. CE to ME, February 13, 1904, CEP.

51. *EL,* 212. Margaret ("Gretchen") Fassett, born 1881 in Elmira, whom Max "liked . . . better than any other girl in Elmira" (*LR,* 103), would later marry Frederick Grady Hodgson. Her daughter, the poet Martha Hodgson Ellis, became Max's lover in the early 1940s. Gretchen responded to Max's admiration more ambivalently than Martha would, offering him her friendship but nothing else (Gretchen Fassett to ME, March 16, July 24, 1904, EM).

52. Ralph Erskine to ME, May 9, 1938, copy, EMII.

53. CE to ME, February 18, 1905, CEP.

54. CE to ME, March 9, 1905, CEP.

55. *Decennial Record of the Class of 1905, Williams College,* ed. Herbert Barber Howe (Waterbury, CT: Tuttle, Morehouse and Taylor, 1915), 51. Max did not participate in the reunion but contributed his poem "At the Aquarium" to the volume.

Chapter 3. A Village Apollo

1. "On the Folly of Growing Up," *Christian Register* 8 (October 22, 1908): 1139–40.

2. "The Poet's Mind," *North American Review* 187 (March 1908): 417–25.

3. See Lyn Burnstine, *Anita Trueman Pickett: New Thought Preacher* (Boston: Skinner, 1991), 63.

4. ME to AFE, April 28, 1906, EM.

5. ME to Henry Loomis Nelson, draft, May 15, 1906, EM.

6. ME to AFE, May 15, 1906; ME to AFE, [June 1906]; insert and envelope [June 1906]; EM.

7. CE to AFE, September 30, 1906, CEP.

8. *EL,* 258.

9. ME to CE, November 11, 1906, EM.

10. CE to AFE, November 14, 1906, CEP.

11. CE to ME, November 15, 1906, CEP.

12. ME to CE, November 29, 1906, EM.

13. *EL,* 268–69; Anna Carlson to ME, January 20, 1907, EM.

14. Anna Carlson to ME, January 14, 1907, EM.

15. Anna Carlson to ME, January 11, 1907, EM.

16. Anna Carlson to ME, January 26, May 7, 1907, EM.

17. ME to CE, December 20, 1906, EM.

18. CE to ME, December [?], 1906, CEP.

19. CE to AFE, January 5, 1907, CEP.

20. CE to AFE, January 6, 1907, CEP.

21. ME to AFE, January 14, 1907, EM.

22. ME to CE, February 12, 1907, EM.

23. CE to AFE, January 18, 1907, CEP.

24. *Report of the New York City Commission on Congestion of Population: Transmitted to the Mayor and the Board of Aldermen,* February 28, 1911 (New York: Lecouver, 1911), 6, 11; ME to AFE and SEE, January 6, 1907, EM.

25. CE to AFE, September 30, 1906, CEP; ME to AFE, March 6, 1907, EM.

26. CE to AFE, January 24, 1907, CEP.

27. CE to AFE, May 8, 1907, CEP.

28. *EL,* 268.

29. *Great Companions,* 283.

30. ME to AFE, March 14, April 26, 1907, EM. Publishing under the name R. E. Hobart, Miller later caused a stir in the field with his views on determinism and free will.

31. ME to CE, March 11, 1907, EM.

32. CE to ME, March 6, 1907, CEP.

33. CE to ME, January 21, January 15, 1907, CEP.

34. CE to ME, March 13, 1907, CEP.

35. CE to AFE, February 26, 1907, CEP.

36. CE to ME, March 13, 1907, CEP.

37. CE to ME, March 9, March 28, April 12, April 29, May 4, 1907, CEP.

38. AFE to ME, February 1, 1907, EM.

39. ME to AFE, March 19, 1907, EM.

40. ME to AFE, April 10, 1907, EM.

41. See Max's explanation in his show *Word Game*, CBS, May 4, 1938, EM.

42. ME to AFE, May 6, 1907, EM.

43. *Great Companions*, 250–52.

44. "The New Art of Healing," *Atlantic Monthly* 101 (May 1908): 644–50.

45. *EL*, 279.

46. AFE to ME, November 6, 1907, EM.

47. September 1, 1907, *Cherith-Log*, 1904–1908, EMIIA2.

48. June 26, 1909, *Cherith-Log*, 1909, EMIIA2.

49. Annette Kellerman (1886–1975), a pioneer of synchronized swimming and the right of women to wear one-piece bathing suits; July 24, 1909, Cherith Log, 1909, EMIIA2.

50. F. J. Brunner, "Diving as a Fine Art: Hints for the Competitor in this Fascinating Sport," *Outing* 68.5 (August 1916): 543–54; 552.

51. June 26, 1909, *Cherith-Log*, 1909; June 29, 1908, *Cherith-Log*, 1904–1908; July 24, 1909, July 24, September 10, *Cherith-Log*, 1909, EMIIA2.

52. August 5, 1907; July 8, 1908, *Cherith-Log*, 1904–1908, EMIIA2.

53. August 4, August 14, 1908, *Cherith-Log*, 1904–1908, EMIIA2.

54. Whitman, "Song of Myself," 48; AFE to ME, March 23, 1908, EM.

55. *The Wound-Dresser: A Series of Letters Written from Hospitals in Washington During the War of the Rebellion*, ed. Richard Maurice Bucke (Boston: Small, Maynard, 1898), 42 (author's collection).

56. "Walt Whitman's Art," EMII.

57. "Whitman's Morals," EMII.

58. AFE to ME, September 17, 1898, EM.

59. *EL*, 301.

60. Whitman, "Song of the Open Road," 6.

61. CE to ME, October 6, 19, 1907, CEP.

62. CE to ME, October 6, 19, 1907, CEP.

63. CE to ME, January 14, 1908; CE to AFE, June 8, 1908, CEP.

64. CE to ME, July 4, July 10, 1908, CEP.

65. ME to AFE, February 10, 1909, EM.

66. ME to CE, [1908], EM.

67. ME to AFE, October 7, 1908, EM.

68. ME to AFE, September 23, 1908, EM.

69. ME to AFE, September 26, 1908, EM.

70. *EL*, 296.

71. *EL*, 303.

72. ME to AFE, November 29, 1908, EM.

73. ME to AFE, December 7, December 13, 1908, EM. The praise had come from Dudley Sargent, the director of the Hemenway Gymnasium at Harvard. Kellerman was also known for offering a correspondence course intended to help women acquire "health and a beautiful figure."

74. ME to AFE, May 5, 1909, December 19, 1908, EM.

75. ME to CE, June 8, 1909, EM.

76. ME to AFE, October 11, 1909, EM.

77. As mentioned in ME to AFE, May 12, 1909, EM.

78. ME to AFE, September 28, 1909, EM.

79. "Notes of Phil. A. Lectures," EMII.

80. "The Meaning of Pragmatism," n.d., EMII.

81. ME to AFE, November 19, 1908, EM.

82. ME to AFE, October 9, 1908, EM.

83. Annis is listed as a member of the Harvard Summer School of Theology in the *Harvard University Catalogue* for the years 1899 / 1900, 1901 / 1902, 1903 / 1904, 1905 / 1906, and 1909 / 1910.

84. "Attitude to Nature," EMII.

85. CE, *Work-Accidents and the Law* (New York: Charities Publication, 1910), 5.

86. *EL*, 306.

87. *EL*, 317–18.

88. ME to AFE, December 3, 1909, EM.

89. *Men's League for Woman Suffrage: Constitution and Charter Members* (New York: n.p., 1910), Miller Scrapbooks Collection, Library of Congress.

90. "Someone Will Be Killed While Suffrage Battle Is On," *Buffalo Courier*, November 13, 1909.

91. "There is a class of people in this world" [1910?], EMII.

92. *EL*, 310.

93. "When I knew I should speak here tonight," EMII.

94. "Woman Suffrage as a Man Sees It," *Rochester Democrat and Chronicle*, January 14, 1911.

95. According to Patterson, the bill, apart from weakening the men, would distract women from their "true and heavenly mission," which was to "bless the home and teach truth, honor and courage to their children"; "Governor Patterson's Veto of the State-Wide Prohibition Bill of Tennessee," January 19, 1909, in *Prohibition: Its Relation to Temperance, Good Morals, and Sound Government* (Cincinnati: n.p., 1910), 231–36; see 235.

96. ME to AFE, January 23, 1910, EM.

97. *EL*, 315.

98. "Men Suffragists Dine Mrs. Snowden," *New York Times*, December 14, 1910.

99. *EL*, 298; ME to AFE, January 28, 1910, EM.

100. ME to AFE, January 16, 1910, EM. The event took place on January 12, 1910; Eva Boice, "Woman Suffrage, Vassar College, and Laura Johnson Wylie," *Hudson River Valley Review* 20.2 (2004): 37–50.

101. "No Need Here of Militant Tactics by Woman Suffragists, Says Prof. Eastman," *Baltimore American,* February 28, 1910.

102. "Women in Industry: Max Eastman Discusses Need of Ballot for Them," *Pittsburgh Gazette-Times,* April 5, 1911.

103. Paula Jakobi to ME, [1912?], EM. In 1917 Jakobi collaborated with Marie Jenney Howe on *Telling the Truth at the White House,* a play documenting the trial of suffragettes who had picketed the White House.

104. "Is Woman Suffrage Important?" *North American Review* 193, no. 662 (January 1911): 60–71.

105. "I used to think there was nothing like the heroines of the Early Martyrs," EMII.

106. "Inez Milholland," *Masses* 9.5 (March 1917): 22.

107. ME to AFE, January 16, 1910, EM.

108. ME to AFE, February 25, 1910, EM; "Someone Will Be Killed While Suffrage Battle Is On," *Buffalo Courier,* November 13, 1909.

109. "Man Suffragette to Speak," *New York Daily Tribune,* October 11, 1910; ME to AFE, March 9, 1910, EM.

110. ME to AFE, March 31, 1910, EM.

111. ME to AFE, January 21, 1910, EM.

112. ME to AFE, May 19, 1910, EM.

113. "I passed all the requirements for a Ph.D., and satisfied my millennial and rebel yearnings by not going up to get it" ("Part I. My Political History," EMII).

114. "The Paradox of Plato," front matter, 9, 11, EMII.

115. "Paradox," 15, 64, 52, 53, 62.

116. "Paradox," 54.

117. AFE to ME, October 6, 1910, EM.

118. AFE to ME, May 5, 1909, EM.

119. AFE to ME, January 18, 1910, EM.

120. AFE to AE, January 21, 1910, EM.

121. "Mark Twain at Rest. Buried Beside Wife," *New York Times,* April 24, 1910.

122. ME to AFE, April 26, 1910, EM.

123. AFE to ME, October 1, 1910, EM.

124. See Crystal's letter to Max, written around the anniversary of Annis's death; CE to ME, October 17, 1911, CEP.

125. *EL,* 344.

126. AFE to ME, February 21, 1909, EM.

127. CE to ME, April 3, 1911, CEP.

128. CE to ME, February 11, 1911, CEP.

Chapter 4. The Flea from Tangier

1. CE to ME, June 29, 1911, CEP; ME to SEE, May 6, 1911, EM.

2. Mabel Dodge Luhan, *Movers and Shakers* (New York: Harcourt Brace, 1936), 484.

3. Bob Brown, "Them Asses," *American Mercury* (December 1933): 403–11; 409.

4. "Part I. My Political History," EMII.

5. No man would ever publicly admit doubts he had regarding his virility, wrote Max in an autobiographical fragment. The barrier against such confessions was "stronger than a religious tabu" and probably the reason the subject had been kept out of literature; "A Vital Subject That Is Tabu," EMII.

6. As their marriage was collapsing, Ida wrote to Max, "I don't suppose any boy or man with your sexual make-up has ever really gone through his whole youth as you did before you met me without actual sexual and complete experience" ("Auto-Analysis," vol. III, August 17, 1914, EMIIA2).

7. *EL*, 360.

8. ME to SEE, May 6, 1911, EM; CE to ME, May 20, 1911, CEP.

9. ME to SEE, May 15, 1911, EM.

10. ME to SEE, May 19, 1911, EM.

11. CE to ME, June 29, 1911, CEP.

12. ME to SEE, May 23, 1911, EM.

13. ME to SEE, June 19, 1911, EM.

14. John Donne, "The Flea" (1633).

15. *Child of the Amazons*, 59; see note in *Poems of Five Decades*, 25–26.

16. ME to SEE, July 31, 1911, EM.

17. September 6, 1911, *Cherith-Log*, 1911. EMIIA2.

18. CE to ME, June 29, 1911, CEP.

19. CE to ME, October 14, 1911, CEP.

20. CE to ME, November 6, 1911, CEP.

21. September 22, *Cherith-Log*, 1911, EMIIA2.

22. "Another Severely Attacks Eastman's View of Marriage," *Elmira Star-Gazette*, December 4, 1911; "Not Advocate of Free Love. Divorce Laws Are Not Fair," *Elmira Star-Gazette*, January 2, 1912; "Rev. Eastman's Views on Marriage," *Elmira Morning Telegram*, January 7, 1912.

23. "Legally She is Mme. Eastman but Maiden Name of Ida Rauh is Still Used by Her," *New York World*, November 29, 1911.

24. CE to ME, July 25, 1911, CEP.

25. SEE in *Cherith-Log*, 1911, July 1912, EMIIA2.

26. *EL*, 391–92.

27. IR, "Young as the Dawn," EMII.

28. *Journalism versus Art*, 26.

29. "New Masses for Old," *Modern Monthly* 8 (June 1934): 292–300; 292.

30. "Part I: My Political History," EMII.

31. "Editorial Comment," *Masses* 4.3 (December 1912): 3.

32. "Editorial Notice," *Masses* 4.4 (January 1913): 2.

33. *Journalism versus Art*, 32–33, 68, 85, 79.

34. E. W. Scripps to Kate Crane Gartz, October 8, 1916, EM.

35. Floyd Dell, "Pagan Missionary on the Left: Dual Personality of Max Eastman Revealed in His Autobiography," *New York Herald Tribune Weekly Book Review*, April 11, 1948.

36. John Reed, "The Worst Thing in Europe," *Masses* 6.6 (March 1915): 17–18.

37. "One of the Ism-ists," *Masses* 4.6 (March 1913): [5].

38. "Paterson Strikers (25,000 of 'em!)," May 23, 1913, EMII.

39. "Feminism—Cooper Union," EMII. The event, which took place on February 14, 1914, was organized by the People's Institute, originally founded by Charles Sprague Smith to teach political philosophy to workers and immigrants in New York City.

40. "Procreation," "Poems and Sketches" [1913–15], EMII.

41. Whitman, "Out of the Cradle Endlessly Rocking" (1859).

42. Philip Larkin, "Dockery and Son" (1964).

43. *Enjoyment of Poetry*, 61, 83, 133, 152.

44. *Enjoyment of Poetry*, 197–98; Whitman, *Leaves of Grass*, section 32.

45. CE to ME, August 1913, CEP.

46. Jack London to ME, May 31, 1931, EM.

47. *Close-up of a Digest Writer: Max Eastman Recalls*, S-4.

48. IR to ME, June 28, 1913, EMII.

49. IR to ME, June 30, 1913, EMII.

50. IR to ME, July 1, 1913, EMII.

51. *Child of the Amazons*, 23.

52. *Child of the Amazons*, 60, 69, 59.

53. Vida M. Scudder, "The Muse and the 'Causes,'" *The Survey* (July 5, 1913): 489–90.

54. "Feminism Poeticized," *Minneapolis Journal*, June 8, 1913.

55. *LR*, 434.

56. "A Visitor," "Poems and Sketches" [1916], EMII; *Colors of Life*, 56–57.

57. "The timid morn," "Poems and Sketches" [1913–15], EMII.

58. "To My Maltine with Cod-Liver-Oil," "Poems and Sketches" [1913–15], EMII.

59. "Exploring the Soul and Healing the Body," *Everybody's Magazine* (June 1915): 741–55; "Mr.-Er-Er Oh! What's His Name? Ever Say That?" *Everybody's Magazine* (July 1915): 90–103.

60. "Mr.-Er-Er," 96.

61. "Mr.-Er-Er," 96.

62. "Mr.-Er-Er," 98.

63. "Mr.-Er-Er," 99. See Freud's *Psychopathology of Everyday Life:* "In former years I observed that of a great number of professional calls I only forgot those that I was to make on patients whom I treated gratis or on colleagues" (trans. A. A. Brill) (New York: Macmillan, 1915, 167).

64. *EL,* 491.

65. "Summer of 1914: Auto-Analysis," vol. I, July 30, July 31, EMIIA2. ME's notes are only incompletely rendered in *EL,* chapter 59.

66. "Summer of 1914," vol. I, July 30, EMIIA2.

67. Freud, *Three Contributions to the Sexual Theory,* trans. A. A. Brill (New York: Journal of Nervous and Mental Disease, 1910), 20–21.

68. "Summer of 1914: Auto-Analysis," vol. I, July 30, July 28, 1014; vol. II, August 1, 1914.

69. "Summer of 1914," vol. II, August 5, 1914.

70. Adra Ash Mann to ME, undated, EMII.

71. "Summer of 1914," vol. II, August 2, 1914.

72. "Ida Rauh, Helped Create Theatre," *New York Times,* March 12, 1970.

73. Robert Károly Sarlós, *Jig Cook and the Provincetown Players: Theatre in Ferment* (Oxford: University of Mississippi Press, 1982), 18–19.

74. "Provincetown," "Poems and Sketches" (1913–15), EMII.

75. *EL,* 271–72.

76. *EL,* 5.

77. Joseph Freeman, *An American Testament: A Narrative of Rebels and Romantics* (New York: Farrar & Rinehart, 1936), 246; "Eliena's Memories of Our Homecoming (1927) and the Ensuing Years," EMII.

78. Clare Sheridan, *My American Diary* (New York: Boni and Liveright, 1922), 130.

79. *EL,* 385–87; "The Masses at the White House," *Masses* 8.9 (July 1916): 16–17.

80. "To the People of Chicago," *Chicago Tribune,* February 5, 1917, EMII.

81. "Excerpt from My Speech in Detroit on the Eve of the Declaration of War," April 1, 1917, EMII.

82. "Conscription for What?" *Masses* 9.9 (July 1917): 8.

83. ME to Local Board, 153, New York City, October 31, 1918; War Department, Local Board 153 to ME, October 15, 1918; War Department Local Board 153, October 16, 1918, EMII.

84. "To the Editors of the Masses," March 27, 1916, EMII.

85. "To the Editors of the Masses," March 27, 1916, EMII.

86. "Annual Meeting of the Stockholders of The Masses Publishing Company," April 6, 1916, EMII.

87. "Editorial Split Mars Harmony on the Masses," *New York World,* April 7, 1916.

88. Floyd Dell, *Homecoming: An Autobiography* (New York: Farrar & Rinehart, 1933), 251.

89. "Bunk about Bohemia," *Modern Monthly* 8 (May 1934): 200–208.

90. IR to ME, n.d. ("I am writing this on the train"), EMII.

91. IR to ME, n.d. ("O Max"), EMII. In the absence of dates on most of these notes, I have reconstructed their likely sequence.

92. ME to IR, n.d. ("Dear Ida, I have tried"), EMII.

93. "The Wife of Mr. Eastman Again," *Elmira Morning Telegram*, June 11, 1916; "Eastman and Young Indicted a Second Time for Wounding Delicate Feelings of Poor A.P.," *New York Evening Call*, January 1, 1914; "Not Guilty of Libel," *New York-Herald*, January 1, 1916; "Birth Control Urged Publicly," *New York Evening Call*, May 21, 1916; "Mrs. Ida Rauh Eastman Soon to Be Put on Trial," *Elmira Star-Gazette*, January 7, 1917.

94. ME to IR, n.d. ("Dear Ida, I have tried"), EMII.

95. IR to ME, February 11, 1918, EMII.

96. ME to IR, February 12, 1918, EMII.

97. IR to ME, n.d. ("I am writing this on the train"), EMII.

Chapter 5. We Were Beautiful Gods

1. *LR*, 9–11.

2. See Washington Births, Pierce County Register, 1883–1935. Florence called her mother by what was likely her middle name, Caroline. Florence Spitzer's death certificate, provided by Florence Deshon's great-nephew Philip Danks, reveals that she was the daughter of Morris (Moritz?) Spitzer and Regina Stein (both from Austria). Certificate of death, May 11, 1944, Department of Health of the City of New York.

3. Twelfth Census of the United States, 1900, Enumeration District 266, sheet 17 (Borough of Manhattan); Thirteenth Census of the United States, 1910, Enumeration District 151 (Bloomfield Town, NJ), Sheet 19. Flora "Danks" is listed as a widow in the 1917 New York City Directory. Personal communication from Philip Danks, June 6, 2015.

4. Max became fond of comparing Florence to a gypsy, a characterization she encouraged, perhaps to obfuscate her Jewish descent. See, for example, "Secrets of the Movies Revealed," *Aberdeen Daily American*, June 4, 1920 ("Perhaps you have already suspected that there is something of the gypsy in Florence's dark-eyed beauty"), and Florence's own comment: "I am gypsy, partly by blood, mostly by instinct. My mother was a Hungarian gypsy, my father English" (Gordon Brooke, "The Lady of the Square Room," *Picture-Play Magazine* 12.2 [April 1920]: [48–49]).

5. *LR*, 11.

6. ME to FD, February 7, 1917, DM.

7. FD to ME, February 14, 1917, DM.

8. ME to FD, February 16, 1917, DM.

9. ME to FD, May 25, 1917, DM.

10. Geoffrey R. Stone, "Judge Learned Hand and the Espionage Act of 1917: A Mystery Unraveled," *University of Chicago Law Review* 70 (2003): 335–58; *LR*, 61.

11. ME to FD, August 13, 1917, DM.

12. ME to FD, August [?], 1917, DM.

13. ME to FD, August 19, 1917, DM; "5,000 at Pacifist Rally: 'American Kaisers' Denounced by Eastman and Others at Chicago," *New York Times*, August 20, 1917.

14. ME to FD, August 19, 1917, DM.

15. ME to FD, August 26, August 23, 1917, DM. Leila Faye Secor, the cofounder of the People's Council, had arranged Max's 1917 tour (*LR*, 49).

16. ME to FD, August 23, 1917, DM.

17. ME to FD, August 25, 1917, DM.

18. ME to FD, August 26, 1917, DM.

19. ME to FD, August 28, 1917, DM.

20. ME to FD, August 28, 1917, DM.

21. FD to ME, August 29, 1917, DM.

22. ME to FD, August 29, 1917, DM.

23. "Sweet Lonely Night," EMII.

24. ME to FD, November 7, 1917, DM.

25. Stone, "Judge Learned Hand"; FD to ME, November 7, 1917, DM.

26. "Indicts the Masses and 7 of Its Staff: Federal Jury Grand Jury Charges Writers and Artists of Socialist Magazine with Conspiracy," *New York Times*, November 20, 1917; FD to ME, April 1918 [?], DM.

27. "Editorial," *The Liberator* 1.1 (March 1918): 3.

28. *LR*, 88.

29. Art Young, "Art Young on Trial for His Life," *The Liberator* 1.4 (June 1918).

30. Floyd Dell, *Homecoming: An Autobiography* (New York: Farrar and Rinehart, 1933), 316–17; *LR*, 96.

31. "To the Twelfth Juror," *Kinds of Love*, 6.

32. *LR*, 122; Art Young, *Art Young: His Life and Times* (New York: Sheridan House, 1939), 351; Robert Rosenstone, *Romantic Revolutionary: A Biography of John Reed* (New York: Vintage, 1975), 333.

33. *Max Eastman's Address to the Jury in the Second Masses Trial: In Defense of the Socialist Position and the Right of Free Speech* (New York: The Liberator [1918]), 18, 15; *LR*, 122.

34. ME to FD, December 15, 1918, DM.

35. *Colors of Life*, 65, 75.

36. *Colors of Life*, 74, 67–68.

37. "To My Love," EMII.

38. *Colors of Life*, 1–2, 26–27, 35.

39. Harriet Monroe, "Comment: A Radical Conservative," *Poetry* 13.6 (March 1919): 322–26; Floyd Dell, "Colors of Life," *The Liberator* 1.10 (December 1918): 44–50.

40. *Colors of Life,* inscribed "To my friend Edward Weston. Max Eastman" (author's collection).

41. FD to ME, February 17, 1919, DM.

42. ME to FD, March 4, 1919, DM. Starring Lillian Gish, *Hearts of the World,* the story of a romance between an American boy and a French girl who both find themselves faced with the need to kill a German soldier, was made at the request of the British government. The hope was that it might sway Americans in favor of the war. The book Max promised to Griffith was Ward C. Osborne's *The Ancient Lowly: A History of the Ancient Working People from the Earliest Known Period to the Adoption of Christianity by Constantine* (Chicago: Kerr, 1907). If Max ever sent the book, it didn't convert Griffith to socialism.

43. *LR,* 146–49; *Heroes,* 185.

44. ME to FD, May 11, 1919, DM.

45. FD to ME, May 12, 1919, DM.

46. FD to ME, May 21, 1919, DM.

47. FD to ME, May 22, 1919, DM.

48. ME to FD, May 16, 1919, DM.

49. *LR,* 430.

50. ME to FD, May 23, 1919, DM.

51. John Reed and ME, "Two Letters," *The Liberator* 1.7 (September 1918): 34.

52. ME to FD, May 26, 1919, DM.

53. ME to FD, May 26, 1919, DM.

54. ME to FD, May 26, 1919, DM.

55. *The Sense of Humor,* 38, 40.

56. FD to ME, May 27, 1919, DM.

57. ME to FD, May 29, 1919, DM.

58. "Reds in Garden Urge Revolution and Bolsheviks Here," *New York Times,* June 21, 1919; "Shows New Theft of State Message," *New York Times,* July 19, 1919.

59. ME to FD, July 10, July 14, 1919, DM.

60. FD to ME, July 10, 1919, DM.

61. FD to ME, July 22, 1919, DM.

62. Diana Serra Cary, *Jackie Coogan: The World's Boy King* (Lanham, MD: Scarecrow, 2003), 33–36.

63. FD to ME, July 16, August 31, 1919, DM.

64. ME to FD, July 22, 1919, DM. In *The Auction Block* (1917), a Rex Beach Corporation film directed by Laurence Trimble, Florence played the role of the villainess.

65. FD to ME, July 16, 1919, DM.

66. Thanks to Public Access Coordinator Cassie Blake and Nitrate Curator Melissa Levesque for allowing me to watch *The Loves of Letty* at the Academy of Motion Pictures Arts and Sciences Film Archive in June 2014.

67. FD to ME, September 4, 1919, DM.

68. FD to ME, August 3, 1919, DM.

69. FD to ME, July 25, 1919, DM.

70. Rob Wagner (1872–1942) was the author of *Film Folk* (1918) and a fountain of information on the Hollywood industry.

71. "I have such a strange—almost passionate—feeling sometimes when you give me money"; ME to FD, August 13, 1919, DM.

72. FD to ME, July 25, 1919, DM.

73. FD to ME, August 17, 1919, DM. In *The Cup of Fury,* released in 1920 and now lost, Florence played the role of Polly Widdicombe, the heroine's friend and "one of the best-dressed women in the world" (according to Rupert Hughes's novel).

74. FD to ME, September 19, 1919, DM.

75. ME to FD, July [?], 1919, DM.

76. ME to FD, July [?], 1919, DM. George Andreytchine confirmed that "Max saved the life of a little boy and we nearly paid a high price for it" and that, a day later, Max, "being our sailor," saved *their* lives during a hurricane (Andreytchine to FD, August 1, 1919, DM).

77. "Editorials," *The Liberator* 2.18 (August 1918): 28–30.

78. FD to ME, August 5, 1919, DM.

79. ME to FD, August 9, 1919, DM.

80. Claude McKay to ME, July 28, 1919, MM.

81. "Editorials: Claude McKay"; Claude McKay, "If We Must Die," *The Liberator* 2.7 (July 1919): 7, 22; Tyrone Tillery, *Claude McKay: A Black Poet's Struggle for Identity* (Amherst: University of Massachusetts Press, 1992), 41–42.

82. ME to FD, August 23, 1919, DM.

83. *Heroes I Have Known,* 161, 193.

84. FD to ME, December 15, 1919, DM.

85. The admiration did not last. In 1928 Taggard edited an anthology of poetry from the *Masses* and the *Liberator* called *May Days;* her alleged misrepresentation, in that volume, of Max's testimony at the second *Masses* trial led to a massive falling out between the former lovers. Taggard, who remained loyal to Stalin, later sold her well-worn, inscribed copy of Max's poems. When Max saw the volume advertised by a secondhand bookstore at a steep price, he bought it and tore out the dedication page (ME to FD, [December 21, 1919], DM; ME to Taggard, cc, September 25, 1925, EM; *LR,* 179).

86. Vera Zaliasnik to ME, January 9, 1920, EM.

87. FD to ME, July 22, September 19, August 31, 1919, DM.

88. ME to FD, January 19, 1920, DM.

89. FD to ME, December 15, 1919, DM.

90. FD to ME, January 7, 1920, DM.

91. FD to ME, January 7, 1920, DM.

92. *LR,* 172; ME to FD, December 21, 1919, DM. On Mather, see Beth Gates Warren, *Margrethe Mather and Edward Weston: A Passionate Collaboration* (Santa Barbara: Santa Barbara Museum of Art, 2001).

93. Chaplin seems to have cut this scene. The only existing version of *A Day's Pleasure* is the one Chaplin produced in 1963, adding musical accompaniment so that copyright could be extended. Communication from Nicola Mazzanti, Conservator, Cinémathèque Royale de Belgique, September 17, 2012.

94. FD to ME, January 11, 1920, DM. Chaplin was not the only one vying for Florence's favors. The eccentric British actor Reginald Pole camped out in her apartment, declaiming poetry and vowing his love. When Florence apprised him of Pole's efforts, Max was "shaking from hand to foot" (ME to FD, January 17, 1920, DM).

95. FD to ME, January 23, 1920, DM.

96. ME to FD, February 2, 1920, DM.

97. *Heroes*, 165.

98. FD to ME, January 12, 1920, DM. Gabriel-Maximilien Leuvielle, better known by his stage name, Max Linder, was a French comedian known simply as Max. His routine was to impersonate a well-dressed, befuddled character perennially in trouble because of his fondness for beautiful women. American audiences did not cotton to Max; Linder and his wife committed suicide in 1925.

99. FD to ME, February 20, 1920, DM.

100. FD to ME, March 9, 1920, DM.

101. FD to ME, [March 1920], DM.

102. FD to ME, March 16, 1920, DM.

103. Max was alluding to Wordsworth's much-anthologized poem, "I Wandered Lonely as a Cloud," published in 1807. ME to FD, March 16, 1920, DM.

104. Born Elisabeth Milker in 1898, "Lisa Duncan" had received training in Isadora's dance school from the age of six. Jacqueline Robinson, *Modern Dance in France: An Adventure, 1920–1970* (London: Routledge, 1998), 55.

105. ME to FD, March 22, 1920; FD to ME, March 29, 1920, DM.

106. Lisa Duncan to ME, April 24, 1920, EM. Although mentioned only peripherally in Arnold Genthe's autobiography, Lisa, according to the index, was the model for Genthe's *Modern Torso* (the nude photograph facing p. 178; Genthe, *As I Remember* [New York: Reynal & Hitchcock, 1936]).

107. Lisa Duncan to ME, June 23, June 26, 1920, EM.

108. Lisa Duncan to ME, July 9, 1920, August 18, 1920, EM.

109. Lisa Duncan to ME, January 18, 1921, EM.

110. Lisa Duncan to ME, August 30, 1920, EM.

111. Lisa Duncan to ME, November 20, 1920, EM.

112. *Kinds of Love*, 35.

113. Lisa Duncan to ME, October 9, 1962, EMIIA1; June 1, 1962, EM. Cut from the same cloth as Max, Lisa at the age of seventy took a young lover awestruck by her glorious past. Irma (Duncan) Erich-Grimme to ME, December 27, 1968, EMIIA1.

114. ME to FD, April 9, 1920, DM.

115. ME to FD, April 15, 1920, DM.

116. FD to ME. April 26, 1920, DM.

117. ME to FD, May 10, 1920, DM.

118. FD to ME, August 7, 1920; ME to FD, August 9, August 14, August 17, 1920, DM; *LR,* 206–7.

119. ME to FD, October 19, 1920, DM. The western *The Twins of Suffering Creek,* directed by Scott R. Dunlap, was a Fox Studios production. Partnered with William Russell, who appeared in more than two hundred silent films, Florence played the part of Jess Jones.

120. ME to FD, October 21, 1920, DM.

121. ME to FD, November 5, 1920, DM.

122. ME to FD, November 5, 1920, DM. See, for example, *Florence Deshon with Rose,* 1919, in Warren, *Margrethe Mather and Edward Weston,* 59.

123. FD to ME, November 30, 1920, DM.

124. ME to FD, May / June 1921, DM.

125. ME to FD, June 8, 1921, DM.

126. ME to FD, June 18, 1921, DM.

127. FD to ME, June 21, 1921, DM.

128. ME to FD, June 27, July 2, 1921, DM.

129. The portraits were signed by Mather and Weston, but Max states that Mather had in fact taken them; see *LR,* 172.

130. FD to ME, July 20, 1921, DM.

131. ME to FD, December 6, 1921, DM.

132. Marie Howe to ME, February 6, 1922, EMII.

133. FD to ME, November 21, 1921, DM.

134. "Actress Dies of Gas Poison," *New York Times,* February 5, 1922.

135. See certificate no. 3448, Department of Health of the City of New York.

136. "Eastman Denies Rift with Miss Deshon," *New York Times,* February 6, 1922. Several newspaper accounts suggested Florence had accidentally overdosed on veronal, which "she was in the habit of taking as a sleeping potion"; "New Movie Sensation in Death of Actress," *Brooklyn Standard Union,* February 5, 1922.

137. McKay to ME, [1935?], MM.

138. FD's mother, Caroline Danks, signed the "Medical Examiners Returns" certificate, Department of Health of the City of New York.

139. *LR,* 279.

140. Correspondence with Karen Grego, Mount Zion Cemetery, September 18, 2014.

141. Marie Alamo Thomas to ME, February 6, 1922, DM.

142. Marie Alamo Thomas, "To Florence Deshon," Thomas to FD, September 7, 1920, EMII.

143. Marie Alamo Thomas to ME, February 6, 1922, DM.

144. Now in EMII.

145. "To One Who Died," EM. For a slightly different version, see *LR*, 282.

146. *Sense of Humor*, 6. A note in ME's papers attributes the smile to Florence (ME, note "From *The Sense of Humor*, chapter I," EMII).

147. Richard Le Gallienne, "Science Probes the Mystery of Laughter," *New York Times*, February 19, 1922.

148. *Sense of Humor*, 48.

149. *Sense of Humor*, 25.

150. FD to ME, [November 1921], DM.

Chapter 6. Malyutochka

1. *Great Companions*, 43.

2. ME to Special Agent Carpenter, Office Memorandum, Federal Bureau of Investigation, August 18, 1953. An informant told the FBI that ME's name was dropped from the membership ledger of the New York branch of the Workers Party as early as December 2, 1922. See the FBI document "Max Eastman," dated September 15, 1952. Documents obtained through author's FOIA request; FOIA CASE RD 42256.

3. Draft for chapter 43 of *LR*, in EMII.

4. *LR*, 301.

5. Eliena's birth date appears on the temporary passport issued by the French consulate in London, July 26, 1924, EMII.

6. EE, "Gone with the Revolution," EMIIA1. This and the following sources are fragments from EE's unfinished autobiography.

7. EE, "Eliena About Her Father," EMIIA1.

8. EE, untitled sketch, EMIIA1.

9. EE, "I have been driving a cab for ten years now . . .," EMIIA1.

10. Lillian T. Mowrer, *Journalist's Wife* (New York: Morrow, 1937), 121.

11. Ione Robinson, *A Wall to Paint On* (New York: Dutton, 1946), 15, 34–35.

12. Max saved the rose and kept it together with a "carpe diem" poem titled "At Santa Marguerita" [*sic*], in which he imagines the waves of the Ligurian sea casting their "momentary foamy jewels" at her and Max's feet (EMIIA2; *LR*, 304–5; *Poems of Five Decades*, 77).

13. ME, "More congenial to my nature," EEM; *LR*, 304.

14. For more on Nikolai Krylenko's long, blood-soaked career, see Daniel Johnson's *White King and Red Queen: How the Cold War Was Fought on the Chess-Board* (Boston: Houghton Mifflin, 2008), 27–38; Donald Barry, "Nikolai Vasil'Evich Krylenko: A Re-Evaluation," *Review of Socialist Law* 15.2 (1989): 131–48.

15. EE, "To My Brother," EMII.

16. ME, "In Russia," Journal 1922–23, EMII.

17. ME, "In Russia," August 22, 1922, EMII.

18. *Kinds of Love*, 68.

19. "In Russia," August 22, 1922, EMII.

20. "In Russia," August 26, 1922, EMII.

21. "In Russia," August 28, 1922, EMII.

22. *LR,* 319; "In Russia," August 29, 1922, EMII.

23. "In Russia," August 29, September 4, September 7, 1922, EMII.

24. "In Russia," August 29, 1922, EMII.

25. Likely a reference to Lloyd George's characterization of Russia, in a speech to the House of Commons on May 25, 1922, as mired in a "pit of squalid misery," "Commons Approves Premier's Policy by 235 Votes to 26," *New York Times,* August 26, 1922.

26. "In Russia," August 29, 1922, EMII.

27. "In Russia," August 30, September 5, 1922, EMII.

28. "In Russia," August 31, 1922, EMII.

29. O. E. Cesare, "Lenin and His Moscow," *New York Times,* December 24, 1922; Walter Duranty, "Artist Finds Lenin at Work and Fit," *New York Times,* October 16, 1922.

30. "In Russia," August 31, 1922, EMII. Paxton Hibben, "Lenin's Little Father Substitute: Pictures by Cesare," *New York Times Magazine,* November 22, 1922.

31. "In Russia," September 1, 1922, EMII.

32. "In Russia," September 1, 1922, EMII.

33. "In Russia," September 3, September 8, 1922, EMII.

34. "In Russia," September 11, September 12, 1922, EMII.

35. "In Russia," September 14, 1922, EMII; "The Sail," *Kinds of Love,* 71.

36. "In Russia," September 16, September 17, 1922, EMII. On language learning and sex, see *Art and the Life of Action,* 161–73.

37. "In Russia," September 21, 1922, EMII; Nina Smirnova to ME, October 15, 1922 (in Russian), EM; *LR,* 325.

38. "In Russia," September 24, 25, 1922, EMII. The incident is reported differently in ME's postcommunist autobiography: "The [guard] glared at us ferociously, and then shouldered his rifle and marched away long enough to let us fill our hands full and go down over the bluff to the sea" (*LR,* 325).

39. "In Russia," September 26, September 27, 1922, EMII.

40. "In Russia," September 28, 1922; Nina Smirnova to ME, October 15, 1922 (in Russian), EM.

41. "In Russia," September 30, October 1, 1922; Nina Smirnova to ME, November 15, 1922 (in Russian), EM.

42. "In Russia," n.d., EM.

43. "In Russia," n.d., EM.

44. Nina Smirnova to ME, November 15, 1922, EM.

45. Nina Smirnova to ME, n.d., EM.

46. "In Russia," n.d.; McKay, "Report on the Negro Question," *International Press Correspondence* 3 (January 5, 1923): 16–17.

47. "Moscow's Answer," *The Liberator* 6.7 (July 1923): 23–34.

48. Draft from "In Russia," EMII, retyped as "A Statement of the Problem in America and the First Step Toward its Solution," n.d., EMII.

49. ME to McKay, March [?], 1923, cc; McKay to ME, April 3, 1923, MM.

50. McKay to ME, April 3, 1923; McKay to ME, May 18, 1923, MM.

51. McKay to ME, May 18, 1923, MM.

52. See McKay, *The Negroes in America,* trans. Robert J. Winter, ed. Alan L. McLeod (Port Washington, NY: Kennikat, 1979).

53. *LR,* 334.

54. George Grosz, "Russlandreise 1922," *Der Monat* 56 (1953): 153–52; see 147.

55. *LR,* 340–41.

56. *LR,* 357.

57. See Johanna Conteiro, "Taking the Waters at Sochi," Birkbeck College Project on "Reluctant Internationalists," http://www.bbk.ac.uk/reluctantinternationalists/blog/sochi/.

58. "In Russia," n.d., EMII.

59. "In Russia," n.d., EMII.

60. "In Russia," n.d., EMII; *LR,* 384.

61. ME to EE, August 14, 1923, EEM; *LR,* 385–86.

62. ME to EE, August 14, 1923, EEM.

63. ME to EE, August [?], 1923 (in Russian), EEM.

64. ME to EE, August?, 1923 (in Russian and English), EEM.

65. ME to EE, August 23, 1923, EEM.

66. ME to EE, August [?], 1923, EEM.

67. ME to EE, August [?], 1923 (in Russian), EEM.

68. ME to EE, October 3, 1923, EEM.

69. ME to EE, September 19, 1923 (in Russian), EEM.

70. ME to EE, Thanksgiving Day 1923 [November 22, 1923] (mostly in Russian), EEM.

71. ME to EE, September 1, 1923, EEM.

72. ME to EE, September 1, 1923; September–October [?], 1923, EEM.

73. ME to EE, September 1, 1923, EEM.

74. ME to EK, October 1, October 3, 1923, EEM.

75. ME to EE, January 23, 1924 (in Russian), EEM.

76. *LR,* 399.

77. ME to Harry Schwartz, August 11, 1963, EM.

78. ME to EE, February 6, 1924 (in Russian), EEM; Bertrand M. Patenaude, *Trotsky: Downfall of a Revolutionary* (New York: HarperCollins, 2009), 193–94.

79. ME to EE, February 6, 1924 (in Russian), EEM.

80. ME to EE, December 20, 1924 (in Russian), EEM.

81. ME to EE, February 13, 1924 (in English and Russian), EEM; *LR,* 402.

82. ME to EE, February 5, 1924, EEM.

83. *LR*, 417.

84. *Trotsky*, 1, 2, 3, 25.

85. *Trotsky*, 26, 43n, 63, 142.

86. *Trotsky*, 110, 126.

87. *Trotsky*, 48, 154, 166.

88. *Trotsky*, 169, 171. Max deemed the Greenberg edition an "ungroomed and blotchy monster" (*LR*, 497). However, the edits Max made in the later edition seem to be motivated less by aesthetics than by politics, i.e., his desire to make the now-beleaguered Trotsky appear more respectably masculine than a mention of a "sleepy-eyed" childhood pet would seem to allow. Some of the changes in the Faber edition can be attributed to his wish to appeal to a British audience ("us Americans," for example, became "us Anglo-Saxons"); others are the results of a stylistic makeover, which does make the book more appropriate as a biography but less interesting as a work of literature. The most important addition is a passage in the letter to Trotsky from Lenin's wife, in which she describes how Lenin listened very attentively when she read to him Trotsky's "characterization of Marx and Lenin." And whereas the previous book concluded with Lenin's death, Max ended the new edition by praising Trotsky, who was by then Max's only hope: "It is surprising that a mind so brilliant can be so wise" (*Leon Trotsky: The Portrait of a Youth* [London: Faber and Gwyer, 1926], 194–95, 197).

89. See the marriage certificate, issued by the Moscow Civil Registry Office, EMII; *LR*, 436.

90. EE to ME, November 17, 1924, EEM.

91. EE to ME, "There is a letter from you," November 23, November 26, November 27, 1924, EEM.

92. ME to EE, November [?], 1924, EEM.

93. ME to EE, December 20, 1924, EEM.

94. ME to EE, December 24, 1924, EEM.

95. EE to ME, December 24, 1924, EEM.

96. ME to EE, December 27, 1924, EEM.

97. EE to ME, December [?], 1924; ME to EE, December [?], 1924, EEM.

98. EE to ME, December 31, 1928, EEM.

99. EE to ME, March 19, 1926, EEM.

100. EE to ME, "But in the morning I wake up . . .," EEM.

101. *Since Lenin Died*, 9.

102. *Since Lenin Died*, 52, 89–90, 97n.

103. *Since Lenin Died*, 97n, 100, 106, 94, 95.

104. *Since Lenin Died*, 29–31.

105. Adra Ash Mann to ME, n.d., EMII.

106. "À Propos du livre d'Eastman 'Depuis que Lénine est mort': Réponse du camarade Trotsky à ce livre," *L'Humanité*, July 16, 1925.

107. *LR*, 449–51.

108. C. M. Roebuck [Andrew Rothstein], "Since Eastman Lied," *Workers Monthly* 4.8 (June 1925): 369–72.

109. McKay to ME, May 1925 [?], MM.

110. ME to EE, January [?], 1926, EEM.

111. ME to EE, March 28, 1925, EEM.

112. Sigmund Freud to ME, May 11, 1926, EM.

113. EK to ME, May 31, 1926, EEM.

114. EE to ME, June 7, 1926, EEM.

115. *LR*, 466.

116. EE to ME, October 4, 1926, EEM.

117. "Lenin Testament at Last Revealed," *New York Times*, October 18, 1926; see also ME to EE, October 9, 1926, EEM; ME to Trotsky's biographer Isaac Deutscher, April 20, 1956, EM.

118. ME to EE, October 2, 1926, EEM.

119. EE to ME, October [?], 1926, EEM.

120. "Marital Tragedy," *New York Times*, October 31, 1926.

121. "Something French," EMII.

122. *Great Companions*, 49; "The Sunrise Club," EMII. ME's stories were part of a projected collection titled *Venus Bolshevik and Other Stories*, which would have also included "An American Virgin," "Venus Bolshevik," "Shy," and "The Red Maple" (none of them located) as well as the previously published "The Animal Lover" (*Masses*, April 1917).

123. *Marx, Lenin*, 50, 81, 215.

124. Freud to ME, December 4, 1926, EM. Freud expressed his misgivings about communism in *Civilization and Its Discontents* (1929): "In abolishing private property we deprive the human love of aggression of one of its instruments" (trans. James Strachey) (New York: Norton, 1961), 67.

125. Freud to ME, December 14, 1926, EM.

126. ME to EE, March 23, 1927, EEM; Freud to ME, March 23, 1927, ME.

127. ME to EE, March 24, 1927, EEM.

128. *Heroes*, 263.

129. See Ernest Jones, *The Life and Work of Sigmund Freud*, 3 vols. (New York: Basic, 1953–57), 3: 95.

130. *Venture*, 147.

131. Jones, *Life and Work*, 2: 382–83.

132. Freud, *Die Frage der Laienanalyse: Unterredungen mit einem Unparteiischen* (Leipzig: Internationaler Psychoanalytischer Verlag, 1926), 123.

133. Robert S. Wallerstein, *Lay Analysis: Inside the Controversy* (New York: Routledge, 2013), 27–29.

134. *Great Companions*, 181; Jones, *Life and Work*, 2: 59–60.

135. "Talk with Freud," EMII; "Visit in Vienna: The Crotchety Greatness of Sigmund Freud," *Heroes*, 261–73; "Differing with Sigmund Freud," *Great Companions*, 171–90, which reprints Max's review of vol. 1 of Jones's Freud biography, "Was Freud Scientific?" *The Freeman* 4.9 (January 25, 1954): 315–17.

136. "Talk with Freud," EMII.

137. *Heroes*, 266.

138. *Heroes*, 270. In 1930 Freud and the American diplomat William C. Bullitt would collaborate on an analysis of Woodrow Wilson, arguing that the man who wanted to make the world "safe for democracy" was controlled by a paralyzing fixation on his father and Jesus Christ (*Thomas Woodrow Wilson: A Psychological Study* [Boston: Houghton Mifflin, 1966]). The extent of Freud's influence on the final version of the text is unclear.

139. Freud, *Wit and Its Relation to the Unconscious*, trans. A. A. Brill (New York: Moffat, Yard, 1916).

140. "Talk with Freud," EMII.

141. *Heroes*, 273. Not everyone agreed that Max had in fact figured Freud out. Thanking him for a copy of *Heroes I Have Known*, Freud's sister Anna Freud Bernays added that the book should have been called *Heroes I Have Met*, for "as far as my brother is concerned . . . you never *knew* him"; Anna Bernays to ME, April 5, 1942, EMII (my emphasis).

Chapter 7. The Thinking Singer

1. EE, "My first introduction to this country," EEM.

2. "Eliena's Memories of our Homecoming," EEM. Dates in this chapter rely on Max's "Chronology in Europe, 1924–1927," EEM.

3. JF to DA, September 20, September 21, 1958, DAP.

4. JF to DA, September 26, 1960, DAP.

5. Pushkin, "Message to Siberia" (translated by ME), *New Masses* 1.5 (1926): 9. Babel, "Crossing the Zbruch" (translated by ME), *New Masses* 2.1 (November 1926): 14; Babel, "After the Battle" (translated by ME), *New Masses* 2.4 (February 1927): 14.

6. "Sacco and Vanzetti: Anarchists and the Revolutionary Science," *New Masses* 3 (October 1927): 4–7.

7. "Karl Marx Anticipated Freud," *New Masses* 3.3 (July 1927): 10–11; "Lenin Was an Engineer," *New Masses* 3.7 (November 1927): 14.

8. ME to *New Masses*, January 27, 1928, cc, EMII.

9. Aaron, *Writers on the Left*, 317.

10. JF to DA, September 25, 1960, DAP.

11. "Karl Marx Anticipated Freud"; Hook, "Marx and Freud: Oil and Water," *Open Court* 41 (January 1928): 10–25.

12. Hook to ME, August 4, 1927, EMII.

13. Hook, "The Philosophy of Dialectical Materialism, Parts I and II," Review of Vladimir Lenin, *Materialism and Empiro-Criticism, Journal of Philosophy* 25 (March 1, 1928): 413–26, and 25 (March 15, 1928): 141–55. For Max's reply, see *Journal of Philosophy* 25 (August 16, 1928): 475–76.

14. Hook, "Marxism, Metaphysics, and Modern Science," *Modern Quarterly* 4.4 (May 1928): 388–94.

15. "As to Sidney Hook's Morals," *Modern Quarterly* 5 (November 1928–February 1929): 85–87.

16. Hook, "As to Max Eastman's Mentality," *Modern Quarterly* 5 (November 1928–February 1929): 88–91.

17. ME, annotated pages 363, 354, 356, 327 from Hook, *Towards the Understanding of Karl Marx: A Revolutionary Approach* (New York: John Day, 1933), EMII.

18. "An Interpretation of Marx: Sidney Hook's Day-Dream of What Marx Might Have Said Had He Been a Pupil of John Dewey," *Herald Tribune, Books, Sunday,* April 16, 1933.

19. *LR*, 499.

20. *Venture*, 398.

21. ME to Albert and Charles Boni, February 21, 1928 ("not sent"), EMII.

22. "Venture, by Max Eastman," *New York Times*, December 11, 1927.

23. F. Scott Fitzgerald to ME, 1928 [?], EM.

24. Sinclair Lewis to ME, January 2, 1928, EM.

25. Review of *Venture, Paterson Call,* January 7, 1928.

26. *Venture*, 67, 86, 61, 81.

27. G. Peter Winnington, *Walter Fuller: The Man Who Had Ideas* ([Mauborget, Switzerland]: Letterworth Press, 2014), 334.

28. CE to ME, 1928 [?], CEP.

29. ME to FN, June 25, 1957, NMII.

30. ME to EE, September 21, September 22, 1929, EEM.

31. CE to Cynthia Fuller Dehn, December 31, 1924, quoted in Winnington, *Fuller,* 369.

32. Annis Young to ME, January 5, 1965, EMIIA1.

33. *EL*, 57.

34. ME to EE, February 6, 1930, EEM.

35. *EL*, 508; ME to EE, February 11, 1930, EEM.

36. See Max's publicity flyers in EMII.

37. ME to EE, February [?], 1930, EEM.

38. ME to EE, February 11, 1930, EEM.

39. ME to EE, February 24, 1930, EEM.

40. ME to EE, February 29, 1931, EEM.

41. EE to ME, December 31, 1928, January 1, 1929, EEM.

42. EE to ME, February 13, 1930, EEM. Eliena was naturalized on January 19, 1931; certificate in EMII.

43. Charmion von Wiegand, "Arrows of the Sun," EMII.

44. See *LR,* 552, and "Chronology [1927–31]," EMII.

45. Ione Robinson, *A Wall to Paint On* (New York: E. P. Dutton, 1946), 34.

46. ME to EE, September 20, 1929, EEM.

47. Robinson, *Wall,* 33–34.

48. See Robinson, *Wall,* 37; Ione Robinson to ME, August 22, 1928, EM.

49. Ione Robinson to ME, February 5, 1929, EM.

50. Ione Robinson to ME, February 5, 1953, EM.

51. ME to EE, June 18, 1930, EEM.

52. EE to ME, February 8, 1929, EEM.

53. "Eliena Krylenko Dies at Hilltop Home at Gay Head," *Vineyard Gazette,* October 12, 1956.

54. See ME to EE, January 27, 1934, EEM.

55. Leon Trotsky to ME (in Russian), March 11, 1931, TM.

56. *LR,* 554. Boni had received $45,000 from the *Post* (ME to Trotsky, March [?], 1933, TM). See also Trotsky to ME, May 7, 1931, TM. Max was paid $1,928 for translating volume 1 of *History;* Simon and Schuster paid half that sum to Boni and covered Max's taxes. See ME, "Chronology," EMII, as well as Albert Boni to Simon & Schuster, Inc., November 11, 1931, cc, EMII.

57. ME to Herbert [Solow], May 18, 1931, cc, EMII.

58. See Trotsky, *History of the Russian Revolution,* trans. ME (1932, 1933; rpt. New York: Pathfinder, 1980), 248, and Trotsky to ME, March 22 (to ME and EE), 1932, TM. Max did suggest "polite letters" as an alternative; ME to Trotsky, April 15, 1932, cc, TM.

59. Trotsky to ME, May 2, 1932, TM. See Trotsky, *History,* 248, 739.

60. Possibly the Ukrainian-born Trotsky used the occasion to establish, playfully, his own complex connectedness to a country and culture Eliena had left behind years before him. Communication from Anna Arays, May 31, 2015.

61. January 25, 1932, EEM. The second volume of *History* was due at the publisher January 15, 1932; Leon Shimkin to ME, November 17, 1931, EMII. In 1930 Eliena had helped Scribner's with the translation of another Trotsky book, perhaps his autobiography; see EE to ME, February 1930, EEM.

62. Trotsky, *History,* 498.

63. EE to ME, February 8, 1929, EEM.

64. *Kinds of Love,* 49; explanatory note in *Poems of Five Decades,* 101–2.

65. *Kinds of Love,* 4.

66. *Kinds of Love,* 19, 21, 23.

67. Genevieve Taggard, "Soft-Phrased Webs of Verse," *Herald Tribune,* May 3, 1931.

68. *Literary Mind,* 157.

69. *Literary Mind,* 59–62.

70. *Literary Mind*, 212–13, 194, 288.

71. Clive Bell to ME, August 25, 1932, EM.

72. Michael March, "Page after Page," *Brooklyn Citizen*, November 28, 1931.

73. *LR*, 547.

74. "Introduction," in Marx, *Capital*, ed. ME, ix, x, xv.

75. Marx, *Capital*, 366.

76. Hook, review of *Capital and Other Writings*, edited by Max Eastman, *Modern Quarterly* 7 (May 1933): 248–50.

77. *Alfred Kazin's America*, ed. Ted Soltaroff (New York: HarperCollins, 2003), 46.

78. According to O'Neill, "Polemic Publishers" was Max's own jocular creation (*The Last Romantic*, 145). But the series was in fact sponsored by S. L. Solon of the *Modern Quarterly*; see Gary Roth, *Marxism in a Lost Century: A Biography of Paul Mattick* (Leiden: Brill, 2015), 146.

79. *The Last Stand of Dialectic Materialism: A Study of Sidney Hook's Marxism* (New York: Polemic Publishers, 1934), 9, 16, 20, 42, 44, 46, 47. For more on the Eastman–Hook controversy, see Christopher Phelps, *Young Sidney Hook: Marxist and Pragmatist* (Ithaca: Cornell University Press, 1997), 38–44, 96–100.

80. Isaac Deutscher, *The Prophet Outcast: Trotsky, 1929–1940* (London: Verso, 1963), 11.

81. Max reworked his notes from the visit for the chapter "Problems of Friendship with Trotsky," in *Great Companions*, 151–69.

82. *Trotsky's Notebooks, 1933–35: Writings on Lenin, Dialectics, and Evolutionism*, ed. Philip Pomper (New York: Columbia University Press, 1986), 112–13.

83. "Two Impressions after Living Three Days in Trotsky's House," July 10, 1932, TM.

84. Deutscher, *Prophet Outcast*, 21. Trotsky biographies (including Deutscher's) assert that Trotsky had received $45,000 from the *Post*, forgetting that Boni had already claimed half of the fee.

85. See ME to Trotsky, July 3, 1933, cc, TM.

86. ME to Alfred Rosmer, November 25, 1940, cc, TM.

87. *LR*, 570.

88. Trotsky to ME, March 15, 1933, TM. See Trotsky, *History of the Russian Revolution*, vol. 3: *The Triumph of the Soviets* (New York: Simon and Schuster, 1932), 181, and Trotsky, *The History of the Russian Revolution* (Ann Arbor: University of Michigan Press, 1957), 3 vols. in 1, 3: 181.

89. *Artists*, 170, 129.

90. *Artists*, 24, 251.

91. *Artists*, 55, 59.

92. *Artists*, 63, 64, 68, 71.

93. *Artists*, 124.

94. Boris Pilnyak, "Max Eastman: The Man under the Table. In Reference to Myself," *Partisan Review* 1.3 (1934): 17–21.

95. Rosa Mora, "The History of Hell," *The Independent*, January 8, 1995.

96. See "Lackey without a Uniform: Appraisal of Max Eastman by Famous Russian Critic," *Daily Worker*, August 25, 1934.

97. Babette Deutsch, "Dictatorship and the Artist: Max Eastman Attacks the Soviet Bureaucracy for Its Effort to Keep Literature in Communist Channels," *Herald Tribune*, June 3, 1934.

98. JF to DA, July 3, 1958, DAP. Since Trachtenberg was still alive then, Freeman used a pseudonym (Peter Leonov).

99. JF to DA, April 7, 1960, DAP.

100. JF to Josephine Herbst, June 13, 1960, copy, DAP.

101. JF to DA, September 25, 1960, DAP.

102. EE to ME, "Oh my darling, my beloved" [1930], EEM.

103. EE to ME, January 25, 1932, EEM.

104. ME to EE, [1930?], EEM.

105. ME to EE, June 24, 1930, EEM.

106. ME to EE, "Darling, It is four o'clock," n.d.; Eliena answered, "Too bad you dreamt about T. S. Elliot [*sic*]. Next time give him po zadnitze," i.e., "a slap on the ass" (January 25, 1932, EEM).

107. Contract between W. Colston Leigh and the Norfolk Forum, February 27, 1934, EMII. Max met Florence Norton, his future secretary and lover, at this event, an experience that "overwhelmed" her (note by Norton on envelope).

108. ME to EE, February 13, 1932, EEM.

109. ME to EE, January 27, 1932, EEM.

110. Freud, *Introductory Lectures on Psychoanalysis* (1917), trans. James Strachey (New York: Norton, 1966), 155–56.

111. ME to EE, January 13, 1933, EEM; EE to ME, January 30, 1932, EEM.

112. ME to EE, February 2, 1932, EMII.

113. "In a way it is highly improper," 1932, EMII.

114. Robert Justin Goldstein, *Political Repression in Modern America from 1870 to the Present* (Cambridge, MA: Schenkman, 1978), 200–201.

115. ME to EE, January 24, 1934, EMII.

116. Ruth LeSourd '39, "The Lecturer," *Chronicle* (Wells College) (December 1937): 50–51.

117. ME to EE, February 2, 1932, EM.

118. Hurston to Charlotte Osgood Mason, April 16, 1932; *Zora Neale Hurston: A Life in Letters*, ed. Carla Kaplan (New York: Random, 2007), 251.

119. Valerie Boyd, *Wrapped in Rainbows: The Life of Zora Neale Hurston* (New York: Simon and Schuster, 2997), 252. Hurston did win a Guggenheim for 1935 / 1936 and used it to study folklife in the West Indies. As late as 1955 Hurston would write to Max for advice regarding her projected biography of Herod the Great (Hurston to ME, August 2, 1955, EM).

120. McKay to ME, December 1, 1931, MM.

121. McKay to ME, April 21, 1933, MM.

122. McKay to ME, September 7, 1933, MM.

123. McKay to ME, October 5, 1933, MM.

124. McKay to ME, October 20, October 30, 1933, MM.

125. Wayne F. Cooper, *Claude McKay: Rebel Sojourner in the Harlem Renaissance* (Baton Rouge: Louisiana State University Press, 1987), 300–301.

126. McKay to ME, undated, MM. Max kept Burke's nude photos; see the collection of photographs in EMIIAI.

127. Tillery, *McKay*, 162.

128. "New York Supreme Court, Appellate Division, Second Department, Max Eastman, Plaintiff Against Herman Axelbank, Defendant-Appellant, and Samuel A. Malitz, Defendant," November 1935, 10, EMII.

129. "My Dealings with Axelbank," EMII.

130. *Enjoyment of Laughter*, 163, 248, 31.

131. George Santayana to ME, November 20, 1936, EM.

132. Freud to ME, November 14, 1936, EM. My translation.

133. Walter Jerrold, ed., *Bon-mots of Sydney Smith and R. Brinsley Sheridan* (London: Dent, 1893), 191.

134. Freud to ME, November 14, 1936; ME to Freud, December 27, 1936, cc, EM.

135. *Great Companions*, 50, 46.

136. "Bull in the Afternoon," *Artists*, 91–92, 98, 95.

137. ME to Archibald MacLeish, July 3, 1933, cc, EM.

138. Archibald MacLeish to *New Republic*, copy, June 7, 1933; Hemingway to *New Republic*, copy, June 12, 1933, EM.

139. ME to Ernest Hemingway, June 15, 1933, cc, EM.

140. Ernest Sutherland Bates, "A Magician with Language: Max Eastman's Essays Are Brilliant and Zestful, Though His Theories Are Open to Debate," *Herald Tribune Books*, December 16, 1934.

141. Floyd Dell to ME, [1935?], EMII.

142. Maxwell Perkins to F. Scott Fitzgerald, May 24, 1937, copy provided to Max by Fitzgerald's biographer, Andrew Turnbull, August 24, 1937, EMII.

143. "Pair of Authors Go to Mat Over Hair on Chest," *Herald Tribune*, August 14, 1937.

144. "Hemingway Slaps Eastman in Face," *New York Times*, August 14, 1937.

145. *Great Companions*, 68.

146. "Pair of Authors." Hemingway was in fact thirty-eight.

147. Michael Gilmore, "Book Annotations Document Scuffle between Ernest Hemingway and Max Eastman," *Cultural Compass*, August 22, 2013. http://www.utexas.edu/opa/blogs/culturalcompass/2013/08/22/hemingway-eastman-feud/.

148. Telegram to ME, August 14, 1937, EM.

149. Edna St. Vincent Millay and Eugen Boissevain to ME, August 18, 1937, EM.

150. "Alain" (Daniel Brustlein), "Writer?" *New Yorker*, September 4, 1937.

151. Ernest Hemingway to John Dos Passos, April 12, 1936, Hemingway, *Selected Letters*, ed. Carlos Baker (New York: Scribner, 1981), 445.

152. *LR*, 592. The photograph also appears in Waldo Peirce's scrapbook of the 1928 Key West Visit at Colby College, Maine. The same scrapbook contains a photograph of Peirce in a similar pose wearing a fig leaf, an indication that these images were part of some joke. Information provided by Erin Rhodes, Special Collections, Colby College.

153. EE to Nikolai Bulganin (Prime Minister of the U.S.S.R.), September 3, 1956, copy, EEM.

154. ME to DeWitt Wallace, May 26, 1941, EM.

155. Eleanor Roosevelt, "Why I Still Believe in the Youth Congress," *Liberty* 17 (April 1940): 30–32.

156. "Stalin's American Power," *American Mercury* 53, no. 216 (December 1941): 671–80.

157. See the folders titled "Stalin's American Power" in EMII.

158. "Max Eastman Sues the Daily Worker," *Socialist Appeal*, May 14, 1938; "Leftist Libel," *Time*, May 23, 1938; *LR*, 627.

159. ME to Douglas Coulter, CBS, June 24, 1938, cc, EMII.

160. "New Word Game," *Free Lance-Star*, April 27, 1938.

161. "Word Game," June 1, 1938, EMII.

162. "Word Game," May 18, 1938, EMII.

163. "Word Game," September 27, 1937, EMII.

164. "Word Game," April 27, 1938, EMII.

165. "Word Game," May 11, 1938, EMII.

166. "Word Game," May 18, 1938, EMII.

167. "Word Game," May 28, 1938, EMII.

168. "Word Game," June 8, 1938, EMII.

169. "You're as Young as You Think," *Radio Guide* 7.38 (July 9, 1938): 19.

170. Participants' occupations: "Notes and Records of 'AdLibbing,' " EMII.

171. Earle McGill, *Radio Directing* (New York: McGraw-Hill, 1940), 203–14.

172. [?] to ME, "Saturday, 1938," EM. Max responded in his show on July 6, 1938, claiming he was "too modest" to quote the letter. He then pointed out that "glamour" and "grammar" had the same origin and were once used to designate the same thing— a "magic spell or enchantment that was supposed to be exercised by speaking words in a certain order" ("Word Game," July 6, 1938, EMII).

Chapter 8. A Test Case for the Kinsey Male

1. *LR*, 620.

2. Edna Wilson (West Palm Beach, Florida) to Columbia Broadcasting System, October 9, 1938; Marion K. Chadwick (Detroit, Michigan) to ME, October 6, 1938, EMII.

3. Rachel Edgard (Bayonne, NJ) to Station WJZ, September 22, 1935, EMII.

4. AE to ME, 1931 [?], AEM ("I smoke a hell of a lot"). Anstice describes symptoms of a stroke to ME, January 10, 1935, as does his wife, Lois to ME, October 3, 1935, AEM.

5. *Michigan Alumnus* 44, no. 14 (February 12, 1938): 262.

6. Canandaigua Cemetery Association to Lois Eastman, October 14, 1943, AEM.

7. "What will trouble me most," July 2, 1954, EMII; *Kinds of Love,* 33. Pushkin's "Don Juan" lists were published by P. K. Gruber in 1923.

8. Scudder Middleton, "Romance," from "A Group of Poems," *Yale Review* 8 (1919): 610.

9. "I haven't a flicker," EMIIA1; EE to ME, January 30, 1932, EEM.

10. ME to EE, February 13, 1932, EEM.

11. Lillian [?] to ME, September 4, 1937, EM.

12. In folder marked "Funny," EM.

13. "Afflicted with a desire," note in folder "My Character," EM.

14. Marie [?] to ME, [1932?]; Florence Southard to ME, 1942 [?], EM.

15. EE to ME, February 16, 1938, EEM.

16. ME to CC, March 26, 1939, EM.

17. "Because you dared divingly . . . For Creigh, August 1938," typescript, collection of Catherine Stern, VT; *Poems of Five Decades,* 121.

18. Creigh Collins was born on May 6, 1920, in Chicago, the daughter of Harriet Oliphant Collins and John Joseph Collins, an engineer. Biographical information from her daughters Catherine Stern and Chris Stern Hyman as well as from her obituary, *Journal Opinion,* Bradford, Vermont, July 27, 1994.

19. EE, "For Creigh" (January 1939), from the papers of Creigh Collins Stern, New York.

20. CC, "Song," January 6, 1939, EM.

21. CC to ME, January 12, 1939; ME to CC, January 14, 1939, EM.

22. *Poems of Five Decades,* 122.

23. CC to ME, February [?], 1939; ME to CC, February 11, February 16, February 19, 1939, EM.

24. ME to CC, March 20, 1939, EM.

25. ME to CC, March 22, 1939, EM.

26. CC to ME, March 24, 1939; ME to CC, March 29, 1939; CC to ME, March 29, 1939.

27. ME to CC, April 2, 1939, EM.

28. ME to CC, April 15, 1939; CC to ME, April 20, 1939, EM.

29. CC to ME, April 21, 1939, EM.

30. *Anthology for Enjoyment of Poetry,* vii–viii, xi.

31. CC to ME, April 25, 1939; ME to CC, April 27, 1939, EM.

32. EE to CC, April 27, 1939, EM.

33. CC to ME, May 28, 1939, EM.

34. "To All Active Supporters of Democracy and Peace," *Nation* 148 (August 26, 1939): 228.

35. IR to ME, March 23, 1939, EM.

36. CC to ME, [May 1939]; ME to CC, June 4, 1939, EM.

37. EE to CC, June 7, 1939, telegram, EM. The "Studs Lonigan Athletic Club," captained by Farrell, was to meet the Marxist Maulers, captained by "Snorky" Jim Cannon, on June 10 in a benefit for German, Austrian, and Czech fighters against fascism. "American Fund to Benefit by Baseball Game," *Socialist Appeal* (May 30, 1939): 2.

38. ME to CC, June 22, June 23, July 1, 1939, EM.

39. CC to ME, April 1940 [?], EM; ME to EE, April 29, April 30, 1942, EEM.

40. Chris Stern Hyman, personal conversation, August 23, 2013.

41. CC, "Half Fled," n.d., EM.

42. ME to Martha Ellis, January 18, 1940, EM. For more on Martha Ellis, see her biographical sketch and poems included in *An Atlanta Argosy: An Anthology of Atlanta Poetry* (Atlanta: Franklin, 1938).

43. Martha Ellis, "To Max, Loquacious at 2 A.M.," EM.

44. ME to Martha Ellis, April 4, 1940, EM.

45. ME to Martha Ellis, January 18, 1940, EM.

46. ME to Martha Ellis, January 20, January 21, 1940, EM.

47. *Stalin's Russia*, 63, 144, 155.

48. Dan Eastman and Eleanora Deren, "No Workers State without Workers Control," *Internal Bulletin of the Organizing Committee for the Socialist Party Convention* 2 (1937): 36–37; ME to Vladimir Simkhovitch, draft, undated, EMIIA2. Max was so impressed with Dan's essay that he suggested he use it as a writing sample in his application for graduate study at Columbia.

49. *Stalin's Russia*, 181, 159–60.

50. *Stalin's Russia*, 161, 89–90.

51. *Stalin's Russia*, 170, 181, 104, 157, 220–23, 241.

52. *Stalin's Russia*, 213.

53. *Stalin's Russia*, 205, 202, 245, 253, 255, 256.

54. *Stalin's Russia*, 69, 81.

55. Eugene Lyons, "The Light that Failed," *Saturday Review*, March 16, 1940.

56. John R. Chamberlain, "Up from Marxism," *Common Sense* (April 1940): 25–26.

57. Michael T. Florinsky, "Max Eastman's Critical Examination of Stalin's Russia," *New York Times Book Review*, March 17, 1940.

58. Abram L. Harris, "The Crisis in Marxism," *Nation*, June 8, 1940.

59. Harold J. Laski, "Critic of Stalin," *New Statesman and Nation*, September 14, 1940.

60. Elias L. Tartak, "Books and Writers: Max Eastman, Stalin and Marx," *New Leader* 23, no. 12 (March 23, 1940): 2.

61. Paul Jordan-Smith, "What I Liked Last Week," *Los Angeles Times*, March 31, 1940.

62. Edmund Wilson, *To the Finland Station: A Study in the Writing and Acting of History* (Garden City: Doubleday, 1940), 392, 472, 474.

63. Edmund Wilson, "Marxism at the End of the Thirties," in *The Shores of Light: A Literary Chronicle of the 1920s and 1930s* (New York: Farrar Straus Giroux, 1952), 732–43. Wilson later admitted that some of his main concepts had come straight from Max's books (Wilson to ME, January 2, 1960, EMIIA1).

64. E. E. Cummings to ME, September 27, 1942; Edna St. Vincent Millay to ME, telegram, October 12, 1942; Marianne Moore to Ramona Herdman, September 28, 1942, all EM. The allusion is to Moore's poem "Poetry" (1919), which begins, "I, too, dislike it." Granville Hicks's comment was solicited by the publisher and appears on a sheet of blurbs in EM.

65. ME to Edmund Wilson, August 31, 1942, cc, EM.

66. ME to Ramona Herdman, 1942 [?], EM.

67. *Lot's Wife*, 4, 3, 12.

68. Sheet of blurbs for *Lot's Wife*, EM.

69. *Lot's Wife*, vii, 3, 1–2.

70. *Lot's Wife*, 7, 38, 27.

71. Edmund Wilson to ME, September 26, 1942, EM.

72. All subsequent quotations are from Wilson's copy of the galleys in EM.

73. *Lot's Wife*, 2, 12, 19.

74. *Lot's Wife*, 29.

75. "*Lot's Wife*, by Max Eastman," *Nation*, May 16, 1943.

76. Paul H. Oehser, "Sal O'Sodom," *Washington Post*, October 25, 1942.

77. John Chamberlain, "Books of the Times," *New York Times*, December 15, 1942.

78. "The Vineyard Bookshelf: Lot's Wife," *Vineyard Gazette*, November 20, 1942.

79. "Van Loon's Diary," *New Leader*, March 13, 1943.

80. *Letter to Americans*, 13; "Books and Authors," *New York Times,* July 27, 1941.

81. The sum Max received for "The Fate of the World Is at Stake in China," *Reader's Digest* (May 1944); ME to DeWitt Wallace, March 19, 1948, cc, EMII; "How I Got My Job on the Reader's Digest," July 9, 1952, EMII.

82. "The Most Unforgettable Character I've Met"; "Socialism Doesn't Jibe with Human Nature," *Reader's Digest* 38 (June 1941): 37–40; 41–49.

83. J. R. Johnson, "Max Eastman Dives into Jingo Waters. So Perish All Traitors!" *Labor Action* 5.21 (May 26, 1941): 4.

84. Richard Lingeman, "Produced in Pleasantville," *New York Times*, August 22, 1993.

85. "It is hard reasonably to complain," June 25, 1954, EMII.

86. ME to FN, August 18, 1951, NMII.

87. "What We Laugh At—and Why," *Reader's Digest* 42 (April 1943).

88. DeWitt Wallace had moved the *Digest*'s offices to nearby Chappaqua in 1939, but he had retained the familiar postal address.

89. ME to EE, May 14, May 18, 1943, EEM.

90. "It is Crystal's birthday," June 25, 1954, EMII. Conversation with Stephen Lindsay, October 12, 2014, Martha's Vineyard; Neal Balboni to Stephen Lindsay, November 15, 2001, EMIIA1.

91. EE to ME, ["Monday"], 1941 [?], EEM; ME to EE, April 30, 1942, EEM.

92. EE to ME, ["Saturday"], 1942 [?], EEM.

93. E. E. Cummings to ME, September 19, 1956, EM.

94. ME to Ernest A. Moore, November 5, 1945, draft, EM.

95. ME to Ernest A. Moore, November 5, 1945, EM.

96. EE to ME, ["Sunday"], 1941, EEM. Harry Laidler, the executive director of the League for Industrial Democracy, and Max appeared on *Wake up, America* on WJZ, June 7, 1942.

97. C. E. Alamshah to ME, October 8, 1946, EM.

98. ME to Carl Sandburg, January 30, 1946, cc, EM.

99. Joe O'Carroll to ME, n.d. [1947], EM; ME to O'Carroll, [1947], draft, EM.

100. "I spent the last evening," fragment, September 11, 1944, EM.

Chapter 9. Max in Purgatory

1. Dan Eastman to Marion Morehouse Cummings, June 12, 1942, June [?], 1942, Houghton, bmS Am 1823.2 (70).

2. See the website "The Civilian Public Service Story," http://civilianpublicservice.org/workers/2431.

3. ME to IR, July 19, 1943, cc, EM.

4. ME to Edward C. Aswell, June 19, 1947, cc, EM.

5. ME to IR, October 2, 1947, cc; IR to ME, October [?], 1947, EMII.

6. FN, Journal, February 14, 1940, NMII.

7. Florence was in apartment 4RE at West Thirteenth Street, and Max and Eliena lived four floors up, in 8RE.

8. FN, Journal, April 2, 1948, NMII.

9. That said, money remained a continuing source of friction between Max and Florence; see, for example, FN, Journal, March 18, 1948, NMII; ME to FN, September 9, 1958, NM.

10. FN, Journal, January 13, March 24, 1945; May 19, 1946; April 3, 1949, NMII.

11. FN, Journal, January 15, 1945, NMII.

12. FN, Journal, March 24, 1945; April 27, 1945; July 10, 1945, NMII.

13. FN to ME, June 11, 1948, NM; FN, Journal, July 17, July 25, August 30, 1945, NMII.

14. "If I could summon the energy," July 3, July 4, 1948, NM.

15. FN, Journal, October 30, November 19, 1945, NMII.

16. McKay to ME, December 7, 1943, MM.

17. McKay to ME, January 13, 1944, EMIIA2.

18. Likely an earlier version of the recently discovered McKay manuscript "Amiable with Big Teeth: A Novel of the Love Affair between the Communists and the Poor Black Sheep of Harlem"; see Nick Obourn, "Detective Work Authenticates Novel by Harlem Renaissance Writer Claude McKay," *Columbia News,* October 19, 2012.

19. McKay to John Macrae, August 8, 1941, cc; Macrae to McKay, August 7, 1941; McKay to ME, August 6, 1941, EMIIA1.

20. McKay to ME, November 26, 1943, EMIIA1.

21. ME to McKay, June 7, 1944, MM.

22. ME to EE, May 24, 1948; EE to ME, May 25, 1948, EEM.

23. *Selected Poems of Claude McKay* (New York: Bookman, 1953), 8, 110.

24. "Page for a Diary (Max's version)," Havana, Cuba, February 16, 1946; "Eliena's Version," Havana, Cuba, February 16, 1946, EMII.

25. FN, Journal, October 30, 1945; April 28, 1946, NMII.

26. "It is Crystal's birthday," June 25, 1954, EMII.

27. ME to Boris Souvarine, July 26, 1946, Houghton, bMS FR 375 (370).

28. FN, Journal, April 29, 1946, NMII.

29. ME to DeWitt Wallace, March 19, 1948, cc, EMII.

30. FN, Journal, June 18, August 7, 1946; March 25, March 10, 1948, NMII.

31. "*Enjoyment of Living,* by Max Eastman," *Kirkus Reviews,* March 31, 1948.

32. Alfred C. Kinsey, Wardell B. Pomeroy, and Clyde E. Martin, *Sexual Behavior in the Human Male* (Philadelphia: W. B. Saunders, 1949), 4, 589.

33. Jonathan Gathorne-Hardy, *Kinsey: A Biography* (1998; rpt. London: Pimlico, 2005), 31.

34. Sterling North, "Eastman Bolsters Kinsey Report," *Washington Post,* April 4, 1948.

35. Mary McGrory, "Contrasting Memoirs from Two Authors: A Troubled Christian; a Resolute Pagan," *Washington Sunday Star,* April 11, 1948; Charles W. Lawrence, "The Breakfast Commentator Has a Fine Time Reading a Book Before It Is Panned," *Cleveland Plain Dealer,* April 7, 1948.

36. Granville Hicks, "Sorrows of Eastman," *Saturday Review* (April 17, 1948).

37. Gathorne-Hardy, *Kinsey: A Biography, 313;* Kinsey et al., *Sexual Behavior,* 585, 582.

38. "Contrary to expectations" [1954], EMII.

39. North, "Eastman Bolsters Kinsey Report."

40. "What will trouble me most . . .," autobiographical fragment, July 2, 1954, EMII.

41. FN, Journal, April 16, 1948, NMII.

42. L. L. Stevenson, "Max Eastman Follows a Stern Physical Regimen," *Bluefield W. Va. Telegraph,* June 15, 1948.

43. Mary Braggiotti, "Lively, Snowcapped Non-Communist Radical," *New York Post Magazine,* July 1, 1948.

44. Floyd Dell, "Pagan Missionary on the Left: Dual Personality of Max Eastman Revealed in His Autobiography," *Herald Tribune Weekly Book Review*, April 11, 1948.

45. Orville Prescott, "Books of the Times," *New York Times*, April 2, 1948. For his notorious Nabokov review, see "Books of the Times," *New York Times*, August 18, 1958.

46. John Abbot Clark, "A Paean to the Laughing Max Eastman," *Chicago Tribune*, April 11, 1948.

47. Wolcott Gibbs, "Clare (A Fragment of Autobiography to the Tune of Max Eastman's 'Enjoyment of Living')," *New Yorker*, May 8, 1948.

48. "Mary Haworth's Mail," *Washington Post*, May 16, 1948.

49. Lawrence, "The Breakfast Commentator."

50. Floyd Dell to ME, [1948], EM. On a transcript of Dell's letter Max noted that he had received it on April 16, 1948; ME to Floyd Dell, transcript, EM.

51. Upton Sinclair to ME, April 19, 1948, EM.

52. Alfreda Lindholdt to ME, August 2, 1963, EM.

53. FN, Journal, May 21, 1948, NMII.

54. "What will trouble me most," July 2, 1954, EMII.

55. Eula Daniel to ME, [1947], EM.

56. FN, Journal, April 17, 1948, NMII.

57. June Johnson to ME, June 29, 1948, transcribed by Max ("From June's letters"), EM.

58. ME to June Johnson, July 20, 1948, EM.

59. ME to June Johnson, June 18, 1948, EM.

60. ME to FN, July 30, 1948, NMII; ME to FN, January 31, 1949; FN, Journal, January 2, 31, 1949, NMII.

61. FN, Journal, December 22, 1948; FN to ME, March 5, April 13, 1949, NM.

62. FN, Journal, April 30, 1949, NMII.

63. "Conversation with a Queen," *Reader's Digest* (September 1949): 124–28.

64. ME to EE, May 19, 1949, EEM.

65. FN, Journal, October 4, 1948; May 18, 1949, NMII.

66. ME to FN, January 11, 1951, NMII.

67. ME to FN, February 2, 1951, NMII.

68. ME to FN, August 6, August 1, August 12, 1951, NMII.

69. ME to FN, August 12, August 18, 1951, NMII.

70. "A Dream and an Interpretation," December 28, 1952, EMII.

71. ME to FN, August 25, September 1, 1951, NMII.

72. ME to FN, October 17, October 19, 1952, NMII.

73. ME to EE, September 10, 1953, EEM.

74. EK to Nell [Howell], cc, August 23, 1955, EEM.

75. EE to ME, June 27, 1953, EEM.

76. EE to ME, September 23, 1953, EEM. See also ME to EE, June 27, 1953: "Yes, let's be happy and adventurous and have no more seizures—or, as you say, not many!" EEM.

77. ME to Louis Untermeyer, July 24, 1950, cc, EMII.

78. "The Anarchist Almanac," *Masses* 5.6 (March 1914): 10.

79. "October Twenty-Fifth: An Illogical Duty" and "October twenty-sixth: The Only System of Government," fragments of a book to be called "Summer Days," EMII.

80. Werner Stecher to ME, June 20, 1954, EM. The article in question was "The Truth about Soviet Russia's 14,000,000 Slaves," *Reader's Digest* (April 1947): 140–46. Max, touched by Stecher's trials, sent $50 (ME to Werner Stecher, November 15, 1954, cc, EM).

81. ME to Floyd Dell, May 14, 1954, cc, EM; *Reflections,* 71.

82. "Buckley Versus Yale: A Seasoned Iconoclast Considers a Young Campus Rebel," *American Mercury* (December 1951): 22–29.

83. ME to Sara Bard Field, January 21, 1955, EM.

84. *Child of the Amazons,* 34.

85. For the figure of the *chinovnik,* see Nikolai Gogol's "Leaving the Theatre after the Presentation of a New Comedy" (1842).

86. ME to Floyd Dell, May 14, 1954, cc, June 27, 1954, cc, EM.

87. Editorial, "The Necessity of Red-Baiting," *The Freeman* (June 1, 1953): 619; ME, "The Religion of Immoralism," *The Freeman* (June 1, 1953): 622–24, 624; ME to Floyd Dell, September 16, 1954, EM.

88. "Foreword," "Too Many People," *Poems of Five Decades,* xv, 154.

89. Oliver St. John Gogarty, "A Poet in Love with Nature," *New York Times,* October 17, 1954.

90. "Max Eastman's Life Seen in 'Poems of Five Decades,'" *Los Angeles Times,* October 3, 1954.

91. *Poems of Five Decades,* xv.

92. Daniel Kelly, *James Burnham and the Struggle for the World* (Wilmington, DE: ISI Books, 2002), 128. Debilitated by a stroke, Burnham eventually returned to the fold of the Only Holy Roman Catholic Church.

93. *Reflections,* 51, 37, 29, 40.

94. Nelson Frank, "Socialism Chains Liberty, Max Eastman Contends," *New York World-Telegram and Sun,* April 5, 1955.

95. D. H. [likely David Herreshoff], "From Marx to Hoover," *American Socialist* 2.7 (July 1955): 29–30.

96. ME to FN, May 8, 1955, NMII.

97. ME to FN, June 1, 1955, NMII.

98. ME to FN, July 1, 1955, NMII.

99. ME to FN, August 17, 1955, NMII.

100. ME to FN, September 28, 1955, NMII.

101. ME to Jacques Cattell, April 16, 1956, cc, EM.

102. ME to Edmund N. Goodman, April 20, 1956, cc, EM.

103. Eula Daniel to EE, 1956 [?], EM.

104. EE to Tom Filer, August 25, 1956, EEM.

105. "Note about Eliena," October 22, 1956, EMII.

106. "More congenial to my nature"; "Though she had to watch her beautiful body," EEM.

107. DE to ME, September 22, 1956, EM.

108. Dan's finding that "marital happiness is related to self-acceptance, acceptance of others, and psychological status in both subjects and their mates" was the result of interviews with fifty couples. An abstract of his 1956 thesis appeared in the *Journal of Consulting Psychology* 22.2 (April 1958): 95–99.

109. EE to Ruth Pickering Pinchot, July 9, 1956; ME to Diana Lewis, October 21, 1956, EM.

110. "The nurse was having her afternoon off," EMII.

111. In folder "Manuscripts, Poetry," EMIIA2.

112. "Eliena Krylenko's Message to Gay Head Friends, 'A Word of Greeting and Best Wishes,' " *Vineyard Gazette*, October 12, 1956.

113. "Eliena," *Kinds of Love*, 45. Max had written this poem on December 2, 1929, "on the train from Croton" (note on the autograph; EMII).

114. Ruth Pickering Pinchot to ME, [1956], EM.

115. EE, "A sparkling laughing stream," EMIIA1.

Chapter 10.   Realtor and Realist

1. ME to FN, February 27, 1957, cc, NMII.

2. *LR*, 538.

3. YE, *Dearest Wilding: A Memoir* (Philadelphia: University of Pennsylvania Press, 1995), 59.

4. YE to ME, January 26, 1955, EM.

5. ME to FN, February 7, 1957, NMII.

6. YE's correspondence with Bernard Steffen ("Steff") is in EMIIA2.

7. ME to FN, September 9, 1958, NMII. See also YE's unpublished memoir, pp. 398, 420, EMIIA2.

8. David Randall to ME, March 20, April 26, 1957, EMIIA1. Max requested an additional $500 upon signing his agreement with Indiana University in January 1957 (YE, unpublished memoir, p. 426, EMIIA2) as well as two more payments of $5,250 each for 1958 and in 1959; ME to Randall, August 12, 1958; invoice for the final payment, June 30, 1959 (Lilly Administrative Files, David Randall, box 3).

9. ME to FN, September 9, 1958, NMII.

10. Daniel Aaron, personal communication, February 5, 2013.

11. ME to FN, August 24, 1957, NMII.

12. Melville, "Knights and Squires," *Moby-Dick*, chapter 27; Amos Smalley, "I Killed 'Moby Dick,' " *Reader's Digest* (June 1957): 172–80.

13. "Re Wally and the *Readers Digest*," November 2, 1957, EM; *EL,* 554.

14. ME to FN, March 13, May 2, 1957, NMII.

15. ME to FN, May 7, May 18, May 8, May 28, June 25, 1957, NMII.

16. ME to FN, April 20, June 2, 1957, NMII.

17. ME to FN, February 8, 1958, NMII.

18. Sidney Hook, "Abraham Lincoln, American Pragmatist," *New Leader* (March 18, 1957): 16–18.

19. "Marx, Dewey and Hook," *New Leader* (February 10, 1958): 16–17; 16.

20. "The Reaction against John Dewey," *National Review* 6.1 (June 21, 1958): 9–11.

21. "Reaction against Dewey," 10.

22. ME to FN, March 20, March 23, March 28, August 12, 1958, NMII.

23. ME to FN, March 29, 1958, NMII. Max states that Rosalinde's show was at the "McDougall [*sic*] Street Theatre," but the *New York Times*, March 11, 1958, advertises it as taking place at the Sullivan Street Playhouse, also in the Village.

24. ME to FN, May 16, 1958; October 22, 1960, NMII.

25. ME to FN, October 22, 1960, NMII.

26. ME to FN, January 14, 1959, NMII.

27. "My Feelings about Marriage," May 18, 1958, EMII; ME to FN, May 21, 1958, NMII.

28. ME to FN, May 16, July 15, 1958, NMII.

29. ME to FN, July 5, 1959, NMII.

30. EE to Marion Morehouse Cummings, September 26, 1958, Houghton, bMS Am 1823.2 (73).

31. YE, "Loving you and being involved with you," EMII.

32. Suzanne Sekey, Journal, April 10–June 6, entry for May 17, 1964, EMII2A. Reinventing herself as a designer of ladies' underwear, Margaret Szekely dropped the "z" and the "l" from her last name. While Suzanne adopted the new name, Margaret's stepdaughter Yvette preferred the original spelling (YE, *Dearest Wilding,* 14).

33. ME to DeWitt Wallace, January 29, 1959, EM.

34. ME to DeWitt Wallace, February 2, 1959, cc, EM.

35. DeWitt Wallace to ME, February 16, April 6, 1959, EM.

36. ME to FN, March 31, 1959, NMII.

37. ME to FN, August 5, 1960, NMII.

38. "Florence: The City of Renaissance," draft, cc, September 14, 1960, EMII.

39. "The Immortal Treasures of Florence," *Reader's Digest* (September 1964): 154–51.

40. "My Self and the *Reader's Digest*," EMII; *LR,* 643.

41. "Reflections on the Failure of Socialism: Introduction to the Paperback Edition," EMII. In the paperback these passages appear as a postscript to chapter 6 ("What to Call Yourself"), minus Max's antireligious comments; *Reflections on the Failure of Socialism* (New York: Grosset and Dunlap, 1962), 79–80.

42. Senator Barry Goldwater, "A Statement of American Principles," *Human Events* 18.49 (December 8, 1961): 839.

43. *Colors of Life*, 13.

44. John P. Diggins, *Up from Communism: Conservative Odysseys in American Intellectual Histories* (1975; rpt. New York: Harper Torchbook, 1977), 344.

45. William Buckley, *Rumbles Left and Right: A Book About Troublesome People and Ideas* (New York: Putnam, 1963), 86, 134, 86.

46. Frank S. Meyer, "The Separation of Powers," *National Review* 12 (January 30, 1962): 59. Meyer was responding to an essay by Morton Auerbach in the same issue, "Do-It-Yourself Conservatism?" (57–58).

47. L. Brent Bozell, "To Magnify the West," *National Review* 12 (April 24, 1962): 285–87. A radical Catholic conservative and editor at the *National Review*, Bozell was also Buckley's brother-in-law.

48. "A Question to the National Review," EMII.

49. On Eastman and Buckley, see O'Neill, *The Last Romantic*, 241–44.

50. "Am I a Conservative?" *National Review* 16 (January 28, 1964): 57–58. Max was alluding to an essay by one of his free-market icons, the Austrian economist Friedrich Hayek, "Why I Am Not a Conservative" in Hayek's *The Constitution of Liberty* (Chicago: University of Chicago Press, 1959), 397–411, 529–31.

51. ME, undated draft note, EMII.

52. "Who's News with Cobey Black: Life and Loves of a Living Legend," *Honolulu Star-Bulletin*, February 20, 1965.

53. "Personality of the Week," KNDI Honolulu, February 1965, EMII.

54. "Foreword" to "How Human Are Animals," EMII.

55. Whitman, "Song of Myself," 32.

56. "The Father Instinct," EMII.

57. "How Human Are Animals?" *Saturday Review*, June 22, 1957; rpt. *Reader's Digest* (August 1957): 112–16.

58. "Love Among the Insects," *Reader's Digest* (June 1963): 163–69.

59. Pascal Covici to ME, January 28, 1957; Seymour Lawrence to ME, June 15, 1960; ME to Jason Epstein, December 5, 1960, cc, as well as multiple undated notes by Daniel Aaron, all in EMIIA1; ME to FN, October 22, 1960, NMII.

60. George Lichtheim, "The Romance of Max Eastman," *New York Review of Books* 3.11 (January 14, 1965).

61. Barbara Epstein to ME, undated [December 1964]; ME to Barbara Epstein, cc, December 23, 1964, EMII.

62. Norman Podhoretz, "Out of the Brambles into the Cornfield," *Book Week*, January 24, 1965.

63. Alan Pryce-Jones, "Love and Revolution: Max Eastman's Story," *Herald Tribune*, January 7, 1965.

64. Jessie Kitching, "Capsules: Non-Fiction," *New York Post*, January 3, 1965.

65. Joseph Slater, "On Coming Home to Poetry," *Saturday Review*, February 6, 1965, EMII.

66. *Seven Kinds of Goodness*, 19, 22, 87, 95.

67. *Seven Kinds*, 119, 120, 134.

68. From "To the Virgins, to Make Much of Time" by Robert Herrick (1591–1674).

69. *Seven Kinds*, 149.

70. Pat Smith, "Max Eastman at 83 Still Is Life of Party," *New York World-Telegram*, January 21, 1966.

71. Nicholas Delbanco, *Lastingness*, 185–87; Delbanco, personal communication, April 3, 2015.

72. YE, Journal for 1967, January 8, 1967, EMIIA2.

73. Samuel Ewer Eastman to ME, September 29, 1967, EM; ME to Samuel Ewer Eastman, October 1967 [?], draft, EM.

74. ME to DE, December 21, 1962, copy, EMIIA1.

75. DE to ME, July 12, 1965, EMIIA1.

76. DE to ME, July 12, 1965; ME to DE, September 5, 1965, copy; DE to ME, October 26, 1965, EMIIA1.

77. YE, July 11, 1967, Journal for 1967, EMIIA2.

78. "Last night Yvette and I went to see . . .," EMII.

79. Suzanne Sekey, August 9, 1968, in Sekey, Journal, May 31–August 21, 1968, EMIIA2.

80. Typescript of introduction to *The Life of Lenin* (later: *The Young Lenin*), EMIIA2. W. H. Bond, Librarian of Houghton Library, believed the translation might have come to Houghton via Harvard University Press, a supposition not confirmed by the publisher; W. H. Bond to ME, August 5, 1968; Mark Carroll to ME, August 16, 1968. Correspondence with Doubleday does show that, in late 1937, they saw and had in hand both the original and a copy of Max's translation; H. E. Maule to ME, December 3, 1937; all in EMIIA2. The book was published in 1972 with an introduction that combined Max's draft (which Doubleday's Sam Vaughan found wearing "a bit heavily" in a letter of August 8, 1968) with notes provided by the prominent Slavicist Maurice Friedberg. Examination of the typescript ("The Young Lenin," bMS Russ 90, Houghton) gives credence to Max's theory that it was somehow taken from him. It is a patchwork at best: original typescript pages alternate with carbons, and polished chapters finally yield, with chapter 9, to drafts heavily annotated by Max. A comparison between the Harvard typescript and the published book reveals that the mostly light revisions of Max's translation—made, presumably, by Friedberg—sacrifice literary adventurousness for blandness: for example, the "eager and life-loving atmosphere prevailing" in the Ulyanovs' dining room has been toned down to the level of a "cheerful mood" (Trotsky, *The Young Lenin*, 1, 13).

81. Suzanne Sekey, Journal, May 31–August 21, 1968, entries for August 9 and August 6, EMIIA2.

82. He was suffering from an "arthritic condition of the spine," ME to William Buckley, September 19, 1968, cc, EMIIA2.

83. Rosalinde Fuller to ME, October 25, 1968, EMIIA2; Margarita Dobert to ME, December 16, 1968, EMIIA1; "Egrets," *Poems of Five Decades*, 101. See also Patricia Sullivan, "Margarita Dobert, Cosmopolitan Travel Writer, Dies," *Washington Post*, June 27, 2004.

84. Likely Max was considering L-dopa, which had just entered clinical practice; Peter Eastman to ME, February 22, 1960, EMIIA1.

85. The account of Max's last weeks is based on Suzanne Sekey's journal, March 5 to May 16, 1969 (see especially the entries for March 5, March 18–April 2, May 10) and a typescript of Yvette's "Journal entries during Max's last days," EMIIA2.

86. First published as "Epitaph for a Masochist," *Kinds of Love*, 46.

87. Dan was to get Lot 451 and Lot 428, with a right-of-way to the beach. Codicil to ME's will, August 17, 1967. Photocopy provided by Charles Young, Martha's Vineyard; Suzanne Sekey, Journal, May 17 to July 22, 1969, entry for May 19, EMIIA2.

88. Andrew Dasburg, Ida Rauh's former partner, quoted in Gardner, *"Friend or Lover": The Life of Louise Bryant* (New York: Horizon, 1982), 352n6.

89. Jeffrey Fuller to Richard Green, May 11, 1969, EMIIA2. Personal communication, Rebecca Agnes Young to Charles Young, April 6, 2015. Even the exact date of Dan's death is not clear. YE received the news on September 30, 1969; likely he had died the day before (journal fragment, EIIA2). Requests for a death certificate were unsuccessful since no immediate family members have survived.

90. Personal communication, Rebecca Agnes Young to Charles Young, April 6, 2015.

91. Sekey, Journal, May 17 to July 22, 1969, entry for August 3, EMIIA2.

92. William Buckley to YE, May 20, 1969, EMII.

93. Ken Ringle, "Popular Nude Beach Sold," *Victoria Advocate*, September 6, 1972; Jonathan Miller, "A House Built on Sand," *New Republic*, September 3, 1972.

94. ME to Charles Neider, December 16, 1964, cc, EMII2A.

95. Stan Hart, as quoted in Mike Seccombe, "Going Au Naturel: Is There a Future for Nude Beaches on the Island?" *Martha's Vineyard Magazine*, August 2008.

96. Interview with Daniel Aaron, Cambridge, Massachusetts, February 5, 2013.

ACKNOWLEDGMENTS

I would not have written this biography without the encouragement and inspirational support of Max Eastman's literary executor, the extraordinary Breon Mitchell, who gave me unrestricted access to Eastman's archives and offered excellent counsel along the way as well as when I was finished. This book owes its final shape to his guidance and wisdom. Crystal Eastman's grandson and Max Eastman's grandnephew, Charles Young, kindly read a draft of this manuscript and helped in many other ways, great and small. George Hutchinson and Susan Gubar enthusiastically supported the idea of a biography of Max Eastman. Of course, my preoccupation with another man's life would not have been possible without the understanding and patience of my friends and family. Much love and thanks to my wife, Lauren Bernofsky, for keeping me reasonably sane, and to Eckart Weiher, for all he has done for my mother when I haven't been able to. Thanks also to Arthur Fagen, for his music and occasional lunches, to Raphael Falco, for reminding me that there is a world beyond my desk, and to Jeremy, for twenty years of love and companionship. And although my father, Hans Dietrich Irmscher, is gone, I feel his presence in everything I do and write.

Several friends and colleagues commented on my evolving manuscript, answered questions, and tolerated me when I could not stop talking about Max. For advice, assistance, and encouragement I thank Jonathan Aaron, Paul Aaron, John Bethell, Steven Brown, Ava Dickerson, Danny Heitman, Archie Henderson, Brooke Kroeger, Katherine Powers, Kathy Smith, Maura Smyth, Jack Trumpbour, Alan Wald, and Waldemar Zacharasiewicz. At a time when I really needed it, Dave Frasier read an early version of this book and cheered me on; I won't forget the many kindnesses he showed me during the often painful process of revision. I am also grateful to my friends James Nakagawa and Jeff Wolin for helpful conversations about photography. Daniel Aaron was my first reader and constant interlocutor and, as he had been so many times before, my best and most important critic. The world is empty without him. I miss him tremendously.

An earlier, longer version of this book benefited greatly from the recommendations of two reviewers, Nicholas Delbanco and Werner Sollors. My research assistant, Anna Arays, was part of the project from the beginning, made many helpful suggestions, and translated Russian sources. Paul Gutjahr, chair of the English Department at Indiana University Bloomington, awarded me use of the Susan Gubar Endowment for one year, which helped with travel and other expenses. In addition, the Office of the Vice Provost for Research at Indiana University supported my work with a New Frontiers grant, and Provost Lauren Robel graciously allowed me a teaching-free semester. My outstanding students at Indiana University have contributed to this book in many ways. Their questions and suggestions kept me going.

Several libraries and librarians have made my work possible, and my debts to them are acknowledged in the notes. Here I want to thank my friend Joel Silver, Director of the Lilly Library, and Cherry Williams, the Lilly Library's former Curator of Manuscripts, as well as Erika Dowell, the current Curator of Manuscripts, and the librarians Rebecca Baumann, Jim Canary, David Frasier, Erika Jenns, Kristin Leaman, and Isabel Planton for their generosity and help. With a few exceptions, all the photographic reproductions were made by the Lilly's amazing photographer, Zach Downey. Unless otherwise mentioned, the photographs are from the Eastman family collections and appear by permission of Breon Mitchell. Diana Carey at the Schlesinger Library facilitated access to the Crystal Eastman papers. For invaluable help in understanding Florence Deshon I am deeply indebted to Mike Mashon at the Library of Congress and Nicola Mazzanti at the Cinémathèque Royale de Belgique. Robert Reed at the National Archives kindly assisted me during my FOIA request regarding Max Eastman. John Wilhite of the Indiana University Foundation has done exemplary work preserving Max's legacy on the Vineyard.

Special thanks go to all those involved in the book's publication: my agent Andrew Stuart and my editor Jaya Chatterjee, as well as William Frucht, executive editor at Yale University Press. Jaya and Bill championed this book at an early stage and did what they could to make it happen—I hope they like the result. My copy editor, Lawrence Kenney, was the most exacting reader I could have hoped for; thanks to him this is an infinitely better book. No praise can be high enough for my production editor, Dan Heaton. His wit and professionalism helped me get through that agonizing home stretch when a book seems done but really isn't. No end of kudos to the intrepid proofreader, Nancy Moore Hulnick.

Last but not least, I want to express my gratitude to Max Eastman's friends, family members, and their friends and descendants for answering my questions: Daniel Aaron, Ted Daniel, Philip Danks, Nick Delbanco, Susan Neider, Catherine Stern, Chris Stern Hyman, Charles Young, and Rebecca Young. Charles graciously welcomed me to Max's house on the Vineyard, and James Tuman, the current owner of Max's former home in Croton, opened his doors to me on a sweltering summer afternoon, even though I was none too presentable after the unexpectedly steep walk up Mount Airy Road.

Max Eastman struggled mightily with fatherhood. I hope I have done a little better in my life, but as an immediate attempt to alleviate my guilt over the hours I didn't spend with them when I was writing this book and as a token of my boundless love, I offer this book to Julia and Nick.

INDEX

Page numbers in **bold** indicate illustrations.

Eastman, Max Forrester (*Continued*)
261; with *Reader's Digest* (see *Reader's
Digest*); rejects right-wing label, 327,
346; relationship with father, 13, 61,
106, 108; relationship with mother,
15, 16, 21–22, 24–25, 42, 43, 44–45,
57, 64–65, 74, 80–81, 288–89;
religious upbringing of, 18, 69, 308,
354–55; return to U.S., 210–12; right-
wing conversion of, 5, 6, 288–89,
294, 296–97, 322–24, 326–27, 346–
48; in Rome, 317–18; in Russia (*see
Russia, Max's visit to*); as Russian
affairs expert, 198, 203; Russian
language proficiency of, 170, 175–76,
177–78, 188, 312; and seize-the-day
philosophy, 224, 387n12; self-analysis
of, 106–8, 207, 223, 303; and sense
of failure, 296–97, 360; serial
philandering of, 146–47; and sex
drive decline, 303–4, 342–43; sex
drive of, 264; sexual liberation of,
138–39, 308–9, 340; sexual
repression during adolescence, 44,
57, 74, 85, 122, 308, 310, 378n6;
social equilibrium advocated by, 278,
326–27; socialism renounced by, 6,
276–79; suffering from Parkinson's,
317, 410n84; in suffrage movement,
70–78; sun worship of, 4, 23, 135, 152,
177, 178, 188, 200, 202, 209, 268,
316, 323, 364; in Tangier, **86**, 86–87;
as teaching assistant at Columbia
University, 54, 55, 56, 63, 65, 73, 74,
312; in theatrical performances, 46,
66, 109; in treatment for back pain,
49–50, 51; and Trotsky's biography of
young Lenin, 358–59, 390n88;
Trotsky's quarrel with, 232–36;
Trotsky's works translated by, 225–
27, 234–36, 358–59; and *Tsar to Lenin*

documentary film, 3, 245–47; and
violence, 190; on voting, 321;
Western travels of, 38–40; and
Whitman's poetry, 49, 61–63, 135;
at Williams College, 26, 30–38, **38**,
42–43, 44, 46–47; women's
attraction to, 3, 224, 261, 264–65,
274–75, 301, 315; Woodrow Wilson's
meetings with, 111–12; and zest for
life, 34, 135, 346
Eastman, Max Forrester, writings of, 3,
4, 6; "Am I a Conservative?" 347,
408n50; "Animal" (poem), 267;
Anthology for Enjoyment of Poetry,
269, 270; *Art and the Life of Action*,
250–51; *Artists in Uniform*, 236–40,
240; "At Santa Marguerita" (poem),
387n12, 410n86; "At the Aquarium"
(poem), 89–90, 102, 116, 363,
373n55; "Bull in the Afternoon,"
249–50, 251; *Child of the Amazons*,
101–3, 104, 105; "Child of the
Amazons" (poem), 101–2; "The City"
(poem), 111; *Colors of Life*, 103, 133–35,
148, 346; "Diogenes" (poem), 323;
"Egrets" (poem), 227; "Eliena"
(poem), 31; *The End of Socialism in
Russia*, 255; *Enjoyment of Laughter*,
65, 247–49, 259, 290, 313; *Enjoyment
of Living* (autobiography), 7, 38, 72,
169, 171, 299, 308–15, 331, 335;
Enjoyment of Poetry, 98–99, 104,
196, 328; "Epitaph" (poem), 361, 363,
410n86; *Everybody's Magazine*
articles on psychoanalysis, 105–6;
Great Companions, 234, 343; *Heroes I
Have Known*, 145; "Is Woman
Suffrage Important?" 76; *Journalism
Versus Art*, 95; *Kinds of Love*, 170,
227–28, 262; *The Last Stand of
Dialectic Materialism*, 232, 395n79;